Hawthorne Centenary Essays

Edited by

Roy Harvey Pearce

Ohio State University Press

Introductory Note

W HEN plans were being made for the Centenary Edition of the Works of Nathaniel Hawthorne, the general editors decided that for such an edition only textual and historical introductions were appropriate. However firmly rooted in historical understanding, critical studies, we decided, would not in their very nature have the staying power of the texts we should establish. Accordingly, the introductions to volumes to the Centenary Edition are meant to supply information relevant primarily to Hawthorne's texts and their history. Still, we wanted to commemorate the centenary of Hawthorne's death with a volume of studies which would show him and his work as they presently confront us. We trust that the texts of the Centenary Edition will make it all the surer that Hawthorne will not change. But surely his readers will. If there continues to be a Hawthorne problem, it is, as it always has been, a problem which he sets for his readers. The essays which follow offer so many solutions to that problem as it now stands, so many interpretations of "our" Hawthorne.

R. H. P.

Contents

Hawthorne Centenary Essays

Robert Lowell

Hawthorne

Follow its lazy main street lounging
from the almshouse to Gallows Hill
along a flat, unvaried surface
covered with wooden houses
aged by yellow drain
like the unhealthy hair of an old dog.
You'll walk to no purpose
in Hawthorne's Salem.

I cannot resilver the smudged plate.

I drop to Hawthorne, the customs officer,
measuring coal and mostly trying to keep warm—
to the stunted black schooner,
the dismal South-end dock,
the wharf piles with their fungus of ice.
On State Street
a steeple with a glowing dial clock
measures the weary hours,
the merciless march of professional feet.

Even this shy, distrustful ego
sometimes walked on top of the blazing roof,
and felt those flashes
that char the discharged cells of the brain.

Look at the faces—
Longfellow, Lowell, Holmes and Whittier!
Study the grizzled silver of their beards.
Hawthorne's picture,
however, has a blond mustache
and golden General Custer scalp.
He looks like a Civil War officer.
He shines in the firelight. His hard
survivor's smile is touched with fire.

Leave him alone for a moment or two,
and you'll see him with his head
bent down, brooding, brooding,
eyes fixed on some chip,
some stone, some common plant,
the commonest thing,
as if it were the clew.
The disturbed eyes rise,
furtive, foiled, dissatisfied
from meditation on the true
and insignificant.

The Tales and Romances

Terence Martin

The

Method

of

Hawthorne's Tales

H AWTHORNE'S primary concern as a writer was to gain access to what he once called "the kingdom of possibilities." Repeatedly, he speaks of his need to attenuate the American insistence on actuality. The burden of the prefaces to his major romances is that he requires a latitude for his imagination, a "neutral ground" set metaphorically between the real world and the imaginary. His romances take form—he would have us believe—in the context of poetic precincts and fairy lands, part of the geography of the "neutral ground." Hawthorne's effort to dilate reality for the purposes of his art ends only with the significant admission in his introductory letter to *Our Old Home* in 1863 that "the Present, the Immediate, the Actual, has proved too potent for me."

What all such statements signify is that Hawthorne needed a fiction to create fiction. And long before he turned his energies to the romance, he had confronted the problem of how to bring his fiction into being in the form of the tale. The method of Hawthorne's tales reveals the achievement of a writer who had to establish the *conditions* of his fiction in the very act of creating that fiction itself. As he himself acknowledged, Hawthorne did not improve steadily as a writer of tales. Some of his best work came surprisingly early: "My Kinsman, Major Molineux," "Young Goodman Brown," and "The May-Pole of Merry Mount" were first published in 1832, 1835, and 1836, respectively. Slight tales appeared in the same year with major tales. *Twice-Told Tales* (1837) was considered superior as a collection to *Mosses from an Old Manse* (1846) by Poe, Melville, and most later critics. Yet "Rappaccini's Daughter" (1844) and "Ethan Brand" (1851) clearly attempt and achieve more than do, say, "The White Old Maid" (1835) and "Mrs. Bullfrog" (1837). The movement of Hawthorne's tales, indirect and often unsure, is toward *The Scarlet Letter*. But it took twenty years of striving before Hawthorne's triumph in *The Scarlet Letter* exhausted the tale for him as a working form even as it transformed the tale into the romance. During those years Hawthorne tried continually to set the proper conditions for his fiction as a way of resolving his most fundamental problem as a writer.

THE CONDITIONS OF FICTION

Hawthorne opens "The Hollow of the Three Hills" (1830) with an abrupt evocation of a mysterious past: "In those strange old times, when fantastic dreams and madmen's reveries were realized among the actual circumstances of life, two persons met together at an appointed time and place." He begins, that is, by equating the real and the fantastic. If there were such a time, we see immediately, when dreams and reveries existed as a part of actual life, then surely there could be no more congenial setting for his tale. As the condition of his fiction, Hawthorne postulates the existence of "strange old times," then uses the immense latitude he thereby acquires to relate a tale of domestic tragedy from a thoroughly non-domestic point of view.

By means of the crone's powers, with their suggestion of Satanic darkness, the lady of the tale can look back into her life to see the tragic consequences of her actions. She has wrung the hearts of her parents, betrayed her husband, and "sinned against natural affection" by leaving her child to die. Amid a setting redolent of witchcraft and evil, she experiences her visions of society. After each vision, Hawthorne makes a studied transition back to the hollow, thereby reinforcing the reality principle of the tale. For this is where the lady's sins have led her. She must consort with witchcraft and deviltry if she is to have even a glimpse of society. To measure the distance of her fall, she must make use of powers antithetical to heart and home. Taking advantage of the latitude assumed in (and achieved by) his abrupt opening sentence, Hawthorne has turned the world as we ordinarily know it inside out—we see society only in momentary visions from the standpoint of the marvelous. He has managed the form of his tale so that it embodies in a unique way a theme characteristic of his work.

The opening sentence of "The Hollow of the Three Hills" constitutes a Hawthornesque variation of the time-honored opening of the fairy tale. It was a method of getting his fiction immediately under way which Hawthorne would use repeatedly. "The Great Carbuncle" (1837), for example, begins, "At night-

9

fall, once in the olden time. . . ." In "The Lily's Quest"
(1839), this has become "Two lovers, once upon a time. . . ."
And in "Earth's Holocaust" (1844), "Once upon a time—but
whether in the time past or the time to come is a matter of little
or no moment. . . ." By adopting the convention of the fairy
tale, Hawthorne achieves at a stroke the imaginative freedom
he requires. And most often he shapes the ensuing tale into a
modern fable complete with a moral regarding human wisdom
or folly. The lesson of "Earth's Holocaust" is that reform will
fail if the human heart is not first purified. "The Great Carbuncle" points up the wisdom of rejecting a jewel which would
dim "all earthly things" in favor of the "cheerful glow" of the
hearth. "The Lily's Quest" spells out laboriously the idea that
happiness is predicated on eternity. Wrought with greater discipline, "The Hollow of the Three Hills" does not offer a moral
refrain. What it says about human guilt and woe is implicit
in the achieved drama of the tale, which stands as the best
evidence of what Hawthorne could realize in fiction by adopting
the method of the fairy tale to the uses of the imagination.

Emerson complained that Hawthorne "invites his readers too
much into his study, opens the process before them. As if the
confectioner should say to his customers, 'Now, let us make a
cake.'" With his usual shrewdness, Emerson was right; though
one need not endorse his criticism, there can be no doubt that
Hawthorne frequently assembles the materials of a tale and
prescribes the proper recipe before the reader's eye. Both "David
Swan" (1837) and "Fancy's Show Box" (1837), for example,
move explicitly from the statement of an idea to its illustration.
Of numerous events that might have had a momentous influence on our lives we are totally unaware, says Hawthorne in
"David Swan": "This idea may be illustrated by a page from
the secret history of David Swan." Are we guilty in thought as

well as in act?, Hawthorne asks in "Fancy's Show Box": "Let us illustrate the subject by an imaginary example." In "The Threefold Destiny" (1838), Hawthorne's workshop method is even more clearly exemplified. "I have sometimes produced a singular and not unpleasing effect," he begins,

> so far as my own mind was concerned, by imagining a train of incidents in which the spirit and the mechanism of the fairy legend should be combined with the characters and manners of familiar life. In the little tale which follows, a subdued tinge of the wild and wonderful is thrown over a sketch of New England personages and scenery, yet, it is hoped, without entirely obliterating the sober hues of nature. Rather than a story of events claiming to be real, it may be considered as an allegory, such as the writers of the last century would have expressed in the shape of an Eastern tale, but to which I have endeavored to give a more life-like warmth than could be infused into those fanciful productions.

Such a paragraph obviously serves as an unannounced preface. (The first paragraph of "Roger Malvin's Burial" [1832] has a similar function.) Indeed, Hawthorne's later prefaces are extensions of his workshop method, which typically defines the mode of fictional creation at the outset as a way of making what I have called the conditions of his fiction understood.

Any writer who faces the necessity of establishing the conditions of his fiction will feel a concomitant need to explain processes and intentions to his reader. And such a writer will pay a price for doing so much by himself; he will necessarily expend much creative energy experimenting to gain "effects"; he will, perhaps, endeavor to blend the old with the new, the strange with the familiar, sometimes (as in "The Threefold Destiny") to little purpose. To succeed as an artist, he will have to do the work of generations in a single lifetime and incorporate the mistakes, false starts, and indirections that ordinarily dwarf careers into the broad investment of his genius. Hawthorne would probably have written fewer slight tales had he worked with the legacy of an older literature. Alternatively, he might well have achieved less; for there would simply have been less to do.

In keeping with Hawthorne's stated intention, "The Three-fold Destiny" is subtitled "A Fairy Legend." And it is among a number of Hawthorne's tales having this kind of subtitle. "Fancy's Show Box" is "A Morality"; "David Swan" is "A Fantasy." Such subtitles are neither elaborations of the main title itself nor do they function as alternative titles in the manner of subtitles in many eighteenth- and early nineteenth-century novels. In "Night Sketches: Beneath an Umbrella" (1838) and in "Egotism; or, the Bosom Serpent" (1843), to take but two examples, Hawthorne did use subtitles in these conventional ways. But "A Morality" and "A Fantasy," as well as "A Parable" (for "The Minister's Black Veil" [1836]), "An Imaginary Retrospect" (for "The Village Uncle" [1835]), "An Apologue" (for both "The Man of Adamant" [1837] and "The Lily's Quest"), and "A Moralized Legend" (for "Feathertop" [1852])—such subtitles are attempts to describe the *form* of the tales. They tell not what the tale is about, but what the tale is. They are explicit indications of the *kind* of fiction Hawthorne is endeavoring to write. And it is always a kind which will allow him latitude.

Characteristically, Hawthorne uses twilight as an analogue of the "neutral ground" to achieve his imaginative effects. "The white sunshine of actual life," he says in "The Hall of Fantasy" (1843), is antagonistic to the imagination, which requires access to a region of shadow if it is to function creatively. Young Goodman Brown begins his shattering journey into the forest at sunset. "The Great Carbuncle" begins at nightfall. After the prefatory paragraph in "The Threefold Destiny," Hawthorne begins the tale proper with "the twilight of a summer eve." And the settings of "The White Old Maid," "The May-Pole of Merry Mount," and many other tales depend heavily on twilight, shadow, and Gothic effects.

Twilight is the middle time, between the noon of actuality and the midnight of dream. It corresponds to the point between yesterday and tomorrow that constitutes the setting of "The Haunted Mind" (1835), that profoundly metaphorical sketch in which Hawthorne presents a musing dramatization of the creative process. On the borders of sleep and wakefulness, dream and reality meet and merge. The actual and the imaginary each partake of the nature of the other; the conditions of fiction are displayed in paradigm. But just as it is difficult to remain on the borders of sleep and wakefulness, so the twilight atmosphere can be difficult to sustain. Before the legends themselves are told, the narrator of "Legends of the Province House" (1838-39) draws "strenuously" on his imagination in an effort to invest a contemporary tavern with an aura of the past. While concerns of historical grandeur and plebeian actuality remain with Hawthorne's narrator in the framework, the inner tales move expansively in a twilight of legend. At the end of a tale, the narrator strives to maintain the illusion it has created; but a spoon rattling in a tumbler of whiskey punch, a schedule for the Brookline stage, and the *Boston Times*—couriers of "the Present, the Immediate, the Actual"—quickly defeat his efforts. "It is desperately hard work," he concludes, "to throw the spell of hoar antiquity over localities with which the living world, and the day that is passing over us, have aught to do."

In his legends of the province house, and in other tales as well, Hawthorne equates revolutionary tendencies with the democratic aspirations of the people; colonial history comes to prefigure the spirit of the American Revolution. Wearing old Puritan dress, the Gray Champion (1835) answers the cry of an oppressed people. Typically, as a figure evoked onto a historical neutral ground by the imagination, he stands between the colonists and the British soldiers in an "intervening space," with "almost a twilight shadow over it"; when he disappears, some think he has melted "slowly into the hues of twilight." But he will be at Lexington in the next century, says Hawthorne, "in the twilight of an April morning." For the Gray Champion "is the type of New England's hereditary spirit," opposed equally to domestic tyranny and to the step of the invader.

Endicott's defiance of English authority in "Endicott and the Red Cross" (1837) is presented explicitly as a rehearsal for the American Revolution. "We look back through the mist of ages," writes Hawthorne, "and recognize in the rending of the Red Cross from New England's banner the first omen of that deliverance which our fathers consummated after the bones of the stern Puritan had lain more than a century in the dust." Brooding over the meaning of American colonial history, Hawthorne's imagination came to see and to formulate a continuity in the American Revolutionary spirit. At a time when American writers labored under the constraints of a lack of tradition, Hawthorne employed the colonial past as one effective way of achieving the imaginative latitude he required. His sense of the past is not at all simplistic. If the Puritans embody a spirit that was to find fullest expression in the American Revolution, they are also, in Hawthorne's presentation, harsh, cruel, blind to all liberties but their own. Endicott can resist oppression in one breath and show himself a raging zealot in the next. "Let us thank God," Hawthorne writes of the Puritans in "Main Street" (1849), "for having given us such ancestors; and let each successive generation thank Him, not less fervently, for being one step further from them in the march of ages." In his tales of colonial times, Hawthorne makes

Americans see what they had been as a way of showing them more fully what they are.

During the years immediately following his marriage in 1842, Hawthorne wrote a number of tales distinct in form from his previous work. In these tales—which include "The Procession of Life," "The Celestial Railroad," "The Christmas Banquet," "A Select Party," and "The Hall of Fantasy"—he examines subjects such as reform, social organization, human folly, and modern religiosity. "The Procession of Life" supplies a term to describe the group as a whole. They are, in one way or another, processionals. They are set perhaps in a vague banquet hall, on an undefined prairie, or in a castle in the air; they deal with assemblages of people who are characterized and moved about collectively. In his processionals, Hawthorne assumes such largeness of treatment that he necessarily confronts general human problems in a general way. No personal drama of guilt or suffering could be portrayed effectively by means of such a form, which explores subjects in themselves and achieves latitude by the expedient of perspective. Surely not among his best tales, the processionals do show Hawthorne striving for the kind of effect that only experimentation with the form of the tale would yield.

Among the subjects considered in the processionals is the role of the imagination in human life. "A Select Party," for example, describes an "entertainment" given by a man of fancy at "one of his castles in the air." Many on earth lack "imaginative faith" and are unworthy to attend. But among the admired guests are the Master Genius of the age, who will fulfil the literary destiny of his country, and Posterity, who advises all to live for their own age if they would gain lasting recognition. During the festivities, a sudden thunderstorm extinguishes the lights and reduces the party to confusion. "How, in the darkness that ensued," writes Hawthorne, the guests got back to earth, or whether they got "back at all, or are still wandering among clouds, mists, and puffs of tempestuous wind, bruised by the beams and rafters of the overthrown castle in the air, and deluded by all sorts of unrealities, are points that concern themselves much more than the writer or the public." He concludes with the admonition that "people should think of these matters before they thrust themselves on a pleasure party into the realm of Nowhere."

Innocuous as it might seem, "A Select Party" teaches a complex lesson about the imagination. "Imaginative faith," as defined by Hawthorne, would seem to be a highly desirable trait; those who lack it are bound heavily to the earth. The presence of the Master Genius and of Posterity seems to add ballast to the more fanciful "creatures of imagination"—such as a cadaverous figure who is in the habit of dining with Duke Humphrey (that is, not eating at all). The tone of the piece is at once serious and sportive. Yet there is the final doubt that the party-goers can get back to earth. In a context of frivolity, Hawthorne's admonition comes as a joke. And it is indeed a joke—on the reader as well as the party-goers. We begin to laugh, then realize that the guests, bruised and misled, may be trapped in the realm of the imagination. But there is more to our realization; for in reading the tale, we, too, have been trapped, artistically sandbagged (for it is, after all, Hawthorne's party), forced to enact the foolishness of the party-goers and to share, in some surprise, their fate.

In "The Hall of Fantasy," Hawthorne ponders the "mystic region, which lies above, below, or beyond the actual." The Hall has its obvious dangers: some mistake it for "actual brick and mortar"; others live there permanently "and contract habits which unfit them for all the real employments of life." Still, for "all its dangerous influences, we have reason to thank God that there is such a place of refuge from the gloom and chillness of actual life." Those who never find their way into the Hall possess "but half a life—the meaner and earthlier half." But the imagination has a final value, crucial and unambiguous. In "The New Adam and Eve" (1843), Hawthorne's thesis is that we have lost the means of distinguishing between the workings of nature and those of art. "It is only through the medium of the imagination," he goes on to say, "that we can lessen those iron fetters, which we call truth and reality, and make ourselves even partially sensible what prisoners we are." Implicit here, in its largest and most general manifestation, is the motif of withdrawal and return basic to Hawthorne's fiction. One withdraws into the realm of imagination, views the rigorous confinement of life, then returns to the world with a fuller understanding of the human condition. The ultimate function of the imagination is thus to serve as a unique and judicious critic of reality.

The role of fiction is the product of the role of the imagination. At their best, Hawthorne's tales—public proof that the author has returned from a private journey into the imagination— lessen the fetters of reality so that we may see "what prisoners we are." At their best, the tales invite us to consider the difficulties man faces because he cannot face his humanity. The tales tell us that man must acknowledge his dependence on (even as he should rejoice to participate in) "the magnetic chain of humanity." The alternative is abstraction, a preference for idea, which breeds pride, isolation, and ultimate self-destruction.

The cancer of obsession threatens any Hawthorne character— scientist, man of religion, artist—who prefers an idea to a human being. Aylmer and Rappaccini; Richard Digby (Hawthorne's "man of adamant"), the Shakers, and the Puritans and Quakers in "The Gentle Boy" (1832); the painter in "The Prophetic Pictures" (1837)—all seek to exist on the high, desolate plane of idea beyond the slopes of compassion and love. In historical tales, too, Hawthorne's concern for humanity is evident. The terms of his presentation change: tyranny and oppression represent abstraction, the insistence on idea; the will of the people—democracy—represents humanity. The Gray Champion, a people's hero, resists oppression, which Hawthorne defines as "the deformity of any government that does not grow out of the nature of things and the character of the people." For all his irritability and iron nature, Hawthorne's Endicott stands likewise for the people; thus, he can legitimately oppose any force which seeks to abrogate the rights of the colonists as human beings. And in "Edward Randolph's Portrait" (1838), Lieutenant Governor Hutchinson risks the terror of a "people's curse" by allowing British soldiers to occupy the fort.

If the oppressor seeks to abuse man in history, the reformer seeks to disabuse man of history; both dehumanize. To make mankind conform to the good as he sees it, the reformer wields his one idea like a flail. He repudiates history as the record of man's imperfection and seeks to destroy human foibles by the purity of his idea. The spirit of reform that spreads wildly in "Earth's Holocaust" seeks to burn away the follies and fripperies of the past. But all reformers overlook the nature of the heart (which is to say, the nature of man). Unless the heart is purified, says the dark stranger in the tale, "forth from it will reissue all the shapes of wrong and misery" which the reformers have burned to ashes.

In "Ethan Brand," Hawthorne articulates most explicitly the theme of a man of idea that had run through his fiction for almost twenty years. The definition and focus of the tale are precise; an obsession with one idea has completely vanquished the heart, turning it to marble. "Ethan Brand" bears the subtitle

"A Chapter from an Abortive Romance," and there are several references in the narrative to episodes that have supposedly taken place at an earlier time. Hawthorne presents us with a conclusion, a final chapter. And incomplete as it may be with reference to his original conception, it has a ring of finality, the authority of a literary work that embodies a theme simply and precisely.

Ethan Brand commits a mighty sin of presumption which prefigures his final despair. The quest to commit a sin so vast that God cannot forgive it becomes itself the Unpardonable Sin. In the hour of his greatest despair, Ethan Brand stands revealed as a success; his quest becomes a parable of how to succeed at spiritual self-destruction. And his triumphant suicide is a final gesture for many a Hawthorne character who has destroyed his humanity over a period of years. The unlettered and earthy, however, are given an anti-climactic dividend in the tale. When Bartram finds the bones of Ethan Brand in the lime kiln, he decides that "it is burnt into what looks like special good lime; and, taking all the bones together, my kiln is half a bushel the richer for him." By half a bushel, the bones of Ethan Brand contribute to Bartram's well-being. By half a bushel, Ethan Brand serves the mundane purposes of a humanity he has scorned.

To repudiate humanity, in Hawthorne's fiction, is to fail spectacularly; to accept humanity is to succeed domestically. Throughout the tales, heart and hearth are intimately related. The bantering praise of the open hearth in "Fire Worship" (1843) has its serious counterpart in "The Vision of the Fountain" (1837), in which the fireside domesticates the vision. Ralph Cranston in "The Threefold Destiny" discovers that home is where one's destiny awaits. Dorothy Pearson, the bringer of love to the gentle boy, is like "a verse of fireside poetry." Both "The Great Carbuncle" and "The Great Stone

Face" (1850) draw morals concerning the futility of searching abroad for values inherent in domesticity. In "John Inglefield's Thanksgiving" (1840), home is a stable institution of the heart which beckons even to the errant daughter, whose fall is measured in terms of her moral distance from home. Wakefield (1835) is an apostate from home; whimsy, stubbornness, and a creeping paralysis of will transform him into the "outcast of the Universe." The characters in "The Ambitious Guest" (1835), unsettled by the young man's contagious thirst for fame, are killed by a rockslide when they rush out of their house in search of shelter; their home stands untouched. Home, clearly, is of the heart. To be heartless is to be homeless.

The great importance of Sophia and a home in Hawthorne's personal life suggests the value he attached to domestic resolution in his tales. Yet it proved difficult to counter a profound vision of evil with a peaceful portrait of the fireside—especially in the tale, by definition a relatively short fictional form which promoted intensity rather than scope. In his romances, Hawthorne would strive more explicitly for a redemptive vision (though his blonde maidens, with their indestructible frailty, might seem to promise captivity rather than redemption). In the tales, however, he could do little more than assert the value of domesticity. His greatest achievement would come from his treatment of those who—for one reason or another—have become homeless.

Such, as the world knows, is the case of young Goodman Brown, who is exposed to the mightiest vision of evil Hawthorne ever imagined. Goodman Brown's journey into the forest is best defined as a kind of general, indeterminate allegory, representing man's irrational drive to leave faith, home, and security temporarily behind, for whatever reason, and take a chance with one (more) errand onto the wilder shores of experience. Our protagonist is an Everyman named Brown, a "young" man who will be aged by knowledge in one night. In the forest he goes through a dreamlike experience marked by a series of abrupt transitions and sudden apparitions. From the devil he learns that virtue is a dream, evil the only reality. And once Goodman Brown sees that idea in all its magnitude, he can never see anything else. He has withdrawn into the dream world of the forest, there to find a reality steeped in guilt that makes his return to the village a pilgrimage into untruth and hypocrisy, into what he now sees as a flimsy community dream. From his vision in the forest, Goodman Brown receives a paralyzing sense of the brotherhood of man under the father-hood of the devil. The thrust of the narrative is toward a climactic vision of universal evil, which leaves in its aftermath a stern legacy of distrust.

Robin Molineux also leaves home—for a different reason and with a different conclusion, of course, though he, too, encounters the fantastic and confronts a shocking vision. In "My Kinsman, Major Molineux," Hawthorne blends a personal theme of in-itiation with the historical movement of the colonists against royal authority. To begin the tale, he invites the reader briefly into his workshop; his opening remarks serve quite frankly "as a preface to the following adventures, which chanced upon a summer night, not far from a hundred years ago." The reader is asked to dispense with details and assume a historical situation "that had caused much temporary inflammation of the popular mind." In the context of such a situation, Robin Molineux, a country-bred youth of eighteen, makes his first visit to town, looking for his kinsman, who, childless himself, has indicated a willingness to help Robin make a start in life. As the story unfolds, however, Hawthorne employs a double context; for it also becomes true that the popular fervor which culminates in the Major's disgrace swells to its climactic point in the context of Robin's consciousness. The strategy of the narrative employs Robin-in-history as a way of making us see history-in-Robin. Thus introjected, history affords the latitude of dream.

For Robin, the town takes on the aspects of a nightmare, a world of senseless laughter, temptation, and caricature in which no one seems willing or able to answer his straightforward question about where his uncle lives. Robin's unrelenting "shrewdness," however—emphasized throughout with benign irony —repeatedly offsets the fantastic quality of appearances around him; he blindly makes sense out of what, to him, ought to be senseless. The bizarre appearance of the man with the red and black face intensifies the quality of general and mounting incoherence in the tale. And Robin's ability to account "shrewdly, rationally, and satisfactorily" for this wild and grinning figure disposes even the most sympathetic reader to join the town in laughing at him, to participate, that is, in the drama of his initiation. For how Robin explains "rationally" to himself a man running around with his face painted a grotesque black and red we are not told; that he does so, however, evidences a depth of faith in the dimensions of his own (in-)experience which it would have been difficult otherwise to suspect.

In "My Kinsman, Major Molineux," as in "Young Goodman Brown," Hawthorne sets the conditions of his fiction so that they serve the purposes of his tale with maximum effectiveness. Robin's mind vibrates between "fancy and reality." A feeling of homelessness accentuates his confusion. Locked out of the house of his memory, he has not yet been admitted to the house of his expectations. Thus, he occupies a middle ground, to which (as he sits in front of the church) "the moon, creating, like the imaginative power, a beautiful strangeness in familiar objects, gave something of romance to a scene that might not have possessed it in the light of day." The procession that passes in front of him has "a visionary air, as if a dream had broken loose from some feverish brain, and were sweeping visibly through the midnight streets." The nightmare has indeed broken loose; Robin can no longer avoid seeing it for what it is. At the center of the wild procession, enshrined in "tar-and-feather dignity," sits the Major. The two look at each other in silence, "and Robin's knees shook, and his hair bristled, with a mixture of pity and terror."

The identity Robin had hoped to establish by claiming kin has been swept away beyond recall. His laugh, cathartic and sanative, signifies that the passage from dream to nightmare to waking reality has been accomplished. Significantly, he does not repudiate the Major; to do so would be to succumb to the nightmare through which he has lived. But perhaps, as his new friend suggests, he may wish to remain in town and try to "rise in the world" without the Major's help. To succeed, Robin must put away the cudgel he has brought with him from the forest, dispense with the anticipated patronage of his kinsman, and establish his own identity in a society restively intent on doing the same.

A sense of homelessness likewise underlies the issues confronted in "The May-Pole of Merry Mount." "Jollity and gloom were contending for an empire," says Hawthorne in introducing the opposing forces in the tale. Most immediately at stake is the empire of two young hearts, which is, at the moment the Puritans rush forth, in a state of sadness and doubt. For the love of Edith and Edgar has wrought their moral and emotional estrangement from the community. The former Lord and Lady of the May have "no more a home at Merry Mount"; they have become subject to "doom, . . . sorrow, and troubled joy." It is as if their graduation from folly has evoked a stern adult world; the clash of Puritans and Merry Mounters becomes an imperial context for their emotional initiation into life. Again, the conditions of fiction are made functional to the tale: at twilight, from concealment, emerge the Puritans, whose "darksome figures were intermixed with the wild shapes of their foes," making the scene "a picture of the moment, when waking thoughts start up amid the scattered fantasies of a dream." The dream of Merry Mount—the period of youth and play—is over; Edith and Edgar must now confront the waking—and adult—world. And again, as in "My Kinsman, Major Molineux," a double context: Hawthorne has played out a private drama of maturation in the context of tensions inherent in New England history—just as he has played out a drama of New England history in the more intimate yet more expansive context of awakening love.

A MODE OF CREATION

"Young Goodman Brown," "My Kinsman, Major Molineux," and "The May-Pole of Merry Mount" demonstrate that Hawthorne's need to establish the conditions of fiction could be made to serve the fiction itself. But if the requirements of Hawthorne's imagination called for a neutral ground as a way of conceiving the tale (which traditionally allowed for a heightened presentation of reality), they called also for a mode of creation that would impregnate his work with relevance for the moral condition of mankind. What Hawthorne had to say about sin, isolation, and the desiccating effects of idea came from his conception of a blemished human nature. To articulate his vision of "what prisoners we are," he frequently made use of an allegorical mode, shaping his materials so that they would suggest the contours of an outer and moral reality.

Although his tales reflect an allegorical tendency, Hawthorne was not a master allegorist. In later years he looked with disfavor on his "blasted allegories" (among which he probably included his processionals), the thinness of which caused Melville to say that Hawthorne needed to frequent the butcher, that he ought to have "roast beef done rare." He made use of conventional devices, giving his characters such names as Gathergold and Dryasdust, conceiving them generically as the Cynic and the Seeker, and envisioning his material so that it would illuminate a general truth of the moral world. Typically, he makes apparent his allegorical intent. He asks specifically, we recall, that "The Threefold Destiny" be read as an allegory; he notes that "Egotism; or, the Bosom Serpent" and "The Christmas Banquet" come "from the unpublished 'Allegories of the Heart'"; and he constructs "The Celestial Rail-Road" on the classic allegorical foundation bequeathed by Bunyan in *Pilgrim's Progress*. An allegorical tradition afforded Hawthorne a means of access to the moral world. Because the moral world was essential to his vision of humanity, he brought features of that tradition to bear on the form of the tale.

Hawthorne's most significant adaptation of an allegorical mode can be seen in his habit of presenting bifurcated or fragmented characters who complement each other in the totality of an individual tale. Such characters require, even as they contribute to, the kind of latitude which Hawthorne constantly strove to attain. More than this: by means of the configuration of such characters, Hawthorne confronts themes that define the specific nature of his work. He suggests in a number of tales, for example (and in a manner distinct from that of his processionals), the uncertain relationship between the man of imagination and the man of practicality. In "The Artist of the Beautiful" (1844), the scorn, practical strength, and shallow sensibility of the world (represented respectively by Peter Hovenden, Robert Danforth, and Annie) victimize the artist who must work, if he is to work, out of a determined *mésalliance* to society. As an artist Owen Warland succeeds; he succeeds even more significantly by being able to transcend the destruction of his creation. But he is forced into, even as he willingly adopts, a position of asociality or even anti-sociality if he is to create at all. In "Peter Goldthwaite's Treasure" (1838), the man of business saves the man of fancy from utter ruin. At one (ideal?) time, Peter Goldthwaite and John Brown have been in partnership; after the partnership dissolves, Peter goes through years of foolish hopes and financial disasters, finally tearing down his house in a vain effort to find legendary wealth. John Brown, meanwhile, prospers unspectacularly. No doubt John Brown is dull, unexciting, and basically unimaginative; but he rescues Peter Goldthwaite, arrests a career of sterility and self-destruction, and promises to protect the man of deluded imagination from his own fantasies. When John Brown plays the role of Mr. Lindsey in "The Snow-Image" (1850), however, he is blind to all but common sense. In caustic language, Hawthorne tells us how Mr. Lindsey completely overrides the high imaginative faith of his wife. Unable to withstand his bleak, unknowing, factual stare, the marvelous melts away before his eyes without his realizing that he has played the role of antagonist in a diminutive tragedy of the imagination. In each of these tales, and in others—such as "The Birthmark" (1843)—as well, a configuration of fragmented characters defines the theme and constitutes a wholeness of effect.

Hawthorne found aspects of an allegorical mode useful in articulating his sense of the complexities of the human condition. But the symbolic mode could also involve moral considerations and at the same time offer great flexibility and economy to the writer of tales. Inheriting a penchant for symbolism from the Puritans, disposed, too, toward symbolic expression by the exigencies of the creative situation in his society, Hawthorne came to place dramatic emphasis on the symbol as a way of achieving effective form in the tale. By means of the symbol he could portray the ambivalence of motive and the ambiguity of experience that defined for him the texture of the human condition. Mr. Hooper's black veil, for example, isolates the minister, who sees, simply and profoundly, that all men wear such veils. Feared by his parishioners, shunned by children, Mr. Hooper nonetheless preaches with power and efficacy. The veil is Mr. Hooper's "parable"; it proclaims the truth that all men hide the truth. But Hawthorne's parable suggests the divisive nature of such a truth and the ultimate failure of an eloquence that can illuminate everything but its source.

The symbol for Hawthorne promoted narrative focus and intensity even as it allowed for economy of presentation. Moreover, and with significant formal consequences, it proved possible to organize a tale effectively in terms of one central symbol. One symbol dominates "The Minister's Black Veil." The Maypole commands the focus of "The May-Pole of Merry Mount." And other well-known tales (written between 1836 and 1850) are structured in a similar way, among them "The Great Carbuncle," "Lady Eleanore's Mantle," "The Birthmark," "The Artist of the Beautiful," and "The Great Stone Face." Finally, of course, there is *The Scarlet Letter,* the culmination of Hawthorne's efforts to adapt the form of the tale to the special purposes of his imagination.

According to his publisher, James T. Fields, Hawthorne's original plan was to include "The Scarlet Letter" together with several other tales in a volume entitled "Old-Time Legends: Together with Sketches, Experimental and Ideal." After reading the first chapters of the story, Fields persuaded Hawthorne to "elaborate it, and publish it as a separate work." How much Hawthorne "elaborated" his tale of the scarlet letter we do not know; if a central symbol was to give meaning and coherence to the whole, however, he could hardly give it the expansiveness of his later romances. He wrote to Fields wondering if a book consisting entirely of "The Scarlet Letter" might not be too somber; the *tale,* as he called it, keeps close to its point and simply turns "different sides of the same dark idea to the reader's eye."

With its sustained tone and rigid economy of presentation; its use of the past and concern for the "great warm heart of the people"; its ambivalence, mode of characterization, and exploration of the protean nature of pride; and, above all, its use of a central symbol to generate narrative coherence, *The Scarlet Letter* is the master product of the method of Hawthorne's tales. In *The Scarlet Letter,* he extended the form of the tale until the suppressed imaginative energy of the narrative threatened to make it into something different. *The Scarlet Letter* marks Hawthorne's final accomplishment in the tale even as it signals the beginning of his achievement in the romance; it marks the point at which Hawthorne transformed the tale into the romance in his effort to adapt that form once again to the purposes of his imagination.

The presence of "The Custom-House" in *The Scarlet Letter* is of crucial importance. Afraid that his tale of the scarlet letter would prove too somber by itself, Hawthorne included "The Custom-House" as a way of lightening the tone of his volume. As a form, the sketch had been extremely useful to Hawthorne; it had long given him a way to deal with the present, the immediate, the actual—the very things he had to evade or attenuate for the purposes of his fiction. Hawthorne tended to sketch what was recalcitrant to his imagination. In turn, the sketch became an avenue to the world around him. This we can see in (among other sketches) "Sights from a Steeple" (1831), in "Night Sketches: Beneath an Umbrella" (1838), and in his extremely effective "The Old Manse" (1846). The narrator of "Night Sketches," having given a day to fancy, finds "a gloomy sense of unreality" depressing his spirits and impelling him to venture out in order to satisfy himself "that the world is not entirely made up of such shadowy materials as have busied me throughout the day." Through the medium of the sketch, he re-establishes contact with the world.

The world of the Salem Custom House, Hawthorne tells us, was stultifying to his imagination. He could neither write fiction while he worked there nor treat fictionally of the Custom House afterwards. But he could and did *sketch* the life of the Custom House in a memorable way. And he wedded the sketch and the tale, the present and the past, by his claim of having found the scarlet letter in the attic of the Custom House. In "The Old Manse," Hawthorne had told of exploring the garret of the Manse, which was "but a twilight at the best," and finding manuscripts and other records of former generations. In "The Custom-House," he develops the fullest possibilities of the idea of finding a document and becoming an editor. And his sketch now served the purposes of his fiction; it provided a way to reflect prefatorily on the past, to define the neutral ground as the basis of imaginative creation, and to introduce the fiction by claiming to have found it shunted aside into a corner of the present world. Uniquely and memorably, the sketch established the conditions of fiction in *The Scarlet Letter*.

In later years, Hawthorne's method of integrating past and present in *The Scarlet Letter* must have appealed strongly to him. He planned, for example, to preface *The Ancestral Footstep* with a sketch of his consular experiences at Liverpool in which he would hear from a visitor the legendary story that would constitute his romance. *Septimius Felton* was to be prefaced with a sketch of Hawthorne's residence at the Wayside (similar to "The Old Manse") which would introduce the legend Hawthorne had heard from Thoreau of the man who would not die: "I may fable that a manuscript was found," wrote Hawthorne in a preliminary study of *Septimius*, "containing records of this man, and allusions to his purposes to live forever." Finally, Hawthorne intended that *The Dolliver Romance* would begin with a prefatory sketch of Thoreau, during the course of which Hawthorne would mention the legend that was to be the theme of the romance.

During these years, when he was writing with difficulty and indecision, Hawthorne thus attempted to blend past and present as he had done so brilliantly in *The Scarlet Letter*. The form of the sketch, he hoped, would again contain and yield his fiction, as "The Custom-House" had contained and yielded the scarlet letter. But Hawthorne in the 1860's was working at cross purposes: in the late romances, potentially symbolic objects remained devoid of meaning or else labored under a significance arbitrarily assigned to them; bursts of inventiveness lacked direction and were followed by periods of acute dissatisfaction; "the Present, the Immediate, the Actual" could not be made to accommodate the past, the remote, and the imaginary—and no sketch could of itself bear the full burden of creation. *The Scarlet Letter,* in which after more than two decades as an author Hawthorne made his greatest sketch serve the purposes of his greatest tale, remained a unique achievement, one not to be duplicated.

Charles Feidelson, Jr.

The

Scarlet

Letter

T HE SCARLET LETTER is a moral tale in a Christian setting, but the imaginative method of the book is not distinctively moral or religious. It is distinctively historical, and historical in a rather complex way. The issues of the story and the experiences of individual characters are projected in the peculiar terms of a specific epoch; Hester Prynne, the people of Boston, Dimmesdale, Chillingworth, and Pearl are shaped by and give shape to the meaning of their time. Yet the epoch is not simply "Puritan." It is also more generally "modern," despite the provincial locale and the idiosyncratic culture through which it is rendered. In many respects, Puritan manners and morals here become a modern instance, a test case of life in the "new" (that is, post-medieval) world. And this modern life was Hawthorne's as well as the life of his characters. The author of *The Scarlet Letter* looks back through time, but he exists in historical continuity with the world he describes. The book is most profoundly historical because it is not only *about* but also *written out of* a felt historical situation.

We need not suppose that Hawthorne had any theoretical idea of "modernity" (he had few theories of any kind, and none of much interest). What he had was the nineteenth- and twentieth-century experience of radical solitude, which he sought to encompass by externalizing it, taking it as his imaginative subject. Possibly his twelve years in the lonely chamber at Salem, for which he could "assign no reasonable why and wherefore," were motivated less by a desire for privacy than by an impulse to dramatize his spiritual isolation. He could escape it only by publicly acknowledging and expressing it. In any case, this was a characteristic maneuver of his literary imagination—as he put it, to render in "the style of a man of society" what would otherwise be "the talk of a secluded man with his own mind and heart." Yet "to open an intercourse with the world" in this way was not enough if the world was really a non-world, a society of isolatoes, as his experience drove him to depict it. Nor could he simply assert in the face of his experience that a "magnetic chain of humanity" was always open to the loving heart. The only adequate ground he had for communication and for faith in human community was paradoxical: alienation as a historical datum. Hawthorne turned to American history, the history of alienation, as the basis of his communion. What isolatoes had in common, their magnetic chain, was precisely the spiritual history of their isolation.

Hawthorne became the historian of the historically disinherited.

The Puritans conceived alienation as the cause and consequence of sin, and up to a point it is so represented in *The Scarlet Letter*. Hester's pride of self is the essential crime within her crime and the essential aberration within her later secret heterodoxy. Much the same might be said of Dimmesdale and Chillingworth. But if alienation is equivalent to sin in the perspective of Hawthorne's seventeenth-century Boston, and if Hawthorne himself never wholly abandons that perspective, he also pictures a Puritan society that positively fosters an alienated individualism. Hester Prynne, her lover, and her husband are as much sinned against as sinning in their social isolation; they have been thrown back upon themselves by an inorganic community, a culture that substitutes external law for immediate relations. And if this is so, if the Puritan mind itself is in one sense guilty of the crime it abhors, in a further sense the book does not deal with crime as such but with a moral predicament, a style of thought. Though Hawthorne often echoes the Puritan language of moral reprobation, and though he often turns round and condemns the Puritans themselves for lack of humanitarian sympathy, he is always fully aware of a historical context for these moral stances—a world view that molds the Puritan consciousness as well as his own.

These people have experienced a disintegration of God's world into God-and-nature, a collapse of the secular world into nature-and-man, a fragmentation of the human world into community-and-individual, and a division of the private world into body-and-mind. Obviously there is nothing novel about such disjunctions in the long history of Christian theology and morals; but in the universe of *The Scarlet Letter* they have taken on a primacy that is striking and new. This disjunctive structure has become a metaphysical presupposition, a reality to be assumed rather than an actuality to be deplored. Moral existence is no longer a pursuit of the Good; it is experience in the goods and evils of a dichotomous world. The official creed of Massachusetts Congregationalism is one configuration of that world—an attempt to find coherence by making the most of disjunction. Hester, Dimmesdale, and Chillingworth devise and suffer other versions of the modern consciousness, worlds of profounder terror and hope. The imagination of Hawthorne, partaking of the condition it projects in the book, moves through the pages in a speculative, inquisitive, experimental mood. Like his characters—but on a much larger scale, since his vision is more inclusive—Hawthorne seeks the center of a world where centers do not hold.

His symbolic method, though he himself was among the first to complain of it, is thoroughly in keeping with his historical premise. If the stuff of actuality is thin in his fiction, it is because he renders an actuality consumed from within, attenuated by a problematic reality that feeds upon it. In *The Scarlet Letter,* people know themselves by means of revelatory "images" that inform mind and body, and they apprehend other human beings as powerful "shapes" impinging upon them. Nature is portentous, the everyday scene is starkly structured, and a dream-figure like Mistress Hibbens walks the streets. While this atmospheric "significance" recalls the medieval allegorical universe, it disintegrates instead of supporting the substance of things. The voices of God and Devil are heard in human discourse, and "Providence" presides over the action; but the supernatural voices are the riddles of natural man, and the providential design is something to be discovered, not assumed. The immanent Word has become completely immanent; the only sacramental form is the empty vessel of the letter *A,* whose content alters and grows with time. Correspondingly, the images inherent in the social scene and private experience are fugitive and multivalent. The author collects

34

alternative interpretations; his tone shifts; his opinions are contradictory; his knowledge of fact is often uncertain. Beneath the measured speech and ceremonial behavior of the Boston theocracy is a vast realm of the publicly unsaid and even unsayable—the esoteric community of Hester, Dimmesdale, and Chillingworth. The demands for utterance that punctuate *The Scarlet Letter* ("Speak out the name!"—"What does this . . . letter mean?") are unanswerable theoretically as well as practically; for outside the official consensus no one knows exactly what to call himself or how to construe the significance of the central symbol.

Yet Hester Prynne, who is officially cast down into the underground world of "secrets," comes closest to positive vision and speech, as she comes closest to the substance of fictional character. Deprived of a public voice and reduced to a gray shadow, Hester lives out the problematic situation that everyone in the book knowingly or unknowingly experiences. Deliberately living it out, she emerges on the other side of it. She converts disinheritance into freedom, isolation into individuality, excommunication into a personal presence that is actual and communicable. To do this without denying the negative burden of history—her own and that of her time—is her moral achievement. It is analogous to Hawthorne's aesthetic achievement in the book as a whole. He must undergo his story if he is to tell it at all; *The Scarlet Letter* is imposed upon him, much as the letter itself is imposed upon Hester. But his narration is active; and out of the negative world that he inherits he constructs an image of positive human enterprise.

II

In "The Custom-House: Introductory to 'The Scarlet Letter,'" Hawthorne has nothing explicit to say about such matters as the modern consciousness; indeed, the essay at first seems

35

designed to have as little as possible to do with the story it introduces. But Hawthorne's stance here is wholly consonant with his method in *The Scarlet Letter;* his preface functions as a modest suggestion of the nature of his art.

Reality in "The Custom-House" is history—history in various forms that play upon one another, deny and reinforce each other, until a dense historical world surrounds us. It is a history that moves in chronological sequence from past to present to future, but it also endures. It is unchanging and changing, active and decadent, predetermined and indeterminate, vacuous and full of meaning. Above all, it is both private and public—a reality experienced individually and socially. Though the scarlet letter is discovered at the climax of a personal narrative, it is a public emblem apparently signifying some "rank, honor, and dignity, in by-past times" (appropriately, the letter and its attendant documents are found amid the archives of the Customs, "materials of local history"). Conversely, the symbol communicates its social meaning only to the inner sense of the lonely Hawthorne, not to his analytic and rational public mind, and the documents are "not official, but of a private nature," written by an eighteenth-century predecessor "in his private capacity." When Hawthorne places the letter against his breast, two dimensions of history come into contact. This is a moment of social revelation on the one hand and self-discovery on the other:

> . . . It strangely interested me. My eyes fastened themselves upon the old scarlet letter, and would not be turned aside. Certainly, there was some deep meaning in it, most worthy of interpretation, and which, as it were, streamed forth from the mystic symbol, subtly communicating itself to my sensibilities, but evading the analysis of my mind.
> While thus perplexed, ... I happened to place it on my breast. It seemed to me . . . that I experienced a sensation

36

not altogether physical, yet almost so, as of burning heat; and as if the letter were not of red cloth, but red-hot iron.

It is not primarily a moment of conscience, for Hawthorne carefully avoids any explicit reference to the theme of adultery or even to the idea of sin. As a single letter, the most indeterminate of all symbols, and first letter of the alphabet, the beginning of all communication, Hester's emblem represents a potential point of coherence within a manifold historical experience.

There is another Hawthorne in "The Custom-House," one who is not inclined to take such apocalyptic moments very seriously. He is an image largely projected by style—frank, good-humored, a man of feeling, but urbane, sharp-eyed, something of an ironist. This cultivated and self-assured gentleman is somewhat complacent; and he belongs to a stable, secure public world of ready categories and easy communication. We might call him the Cosmopolitan. As readers, we quickly identify ourselves with him; we are all gentlemen together. Salem, the Custom House and its denizens, the Surveyor himself with his literary ambitions, are the objects of our sophisticated interest. We are capable of reflecting that Hester Prynne, though she may have been an angel on earth for some of her contemporaries, was probably a mere "intruder and . . . nuisance" for others. We accede to the game while our whimsical author spins his tale of mysterious documents and grandly offers to show them to us. This is the social situation that Hawthorne invokes at the very beginning of his essay, when he assures us that he will speak as a man in company addressing "a kind and apprehensive, though not the closest friend." He is a strong exponent of propriety, ensconced in a conventional but comfortable mid-world where the private man and the social forms may come into easy relation. He neither would give unseemly publicity to intimate matters nor (since he will be only the "editor, or very little more," of *The Scarlet Letter*) would he give intimacy to public matters. He would speak in such a way as not to violate "either the reader's rights or his own."

In the part of his mind that always greatly distrusted whatever he had written, Hawthorne obviously wanted to relieve the "gloom" of his book by a jaunty preface. As the Cosmopolitan, he is untouched by the experiences through which he has passed. He views his "autobiographical impulse" as a kind of harmless seizure, and at the end of his discourse he still speaks as from a secure position outside of time. He tells the story of a "well balanced" man in an essentially secure comic world; though he is thrown out of office, no real harm can come to him. But this self-projection is essentially dramatic; and in the essay as a whole, the Cosmopolitan turns out to be the least important of Hawthorne's roles. He is relatively naïve and imperceptive; he maintains his balance by excluding some unpleasant truths.

Throughout the opening paragraphs we feel the presence of an uneasy person within the suave personage who confronts us. Though he arrives at a reassuring formula, we can see him casting about for "the truth" of the matter—his "true relation with his audience," his "true reason for assuming a personal relation with the public," his "true position as editor." Within the gentlemanly consensus that he presupposes, there are factors that pull apart. He reveals them with startling clarity, if only to deny them. On the one hand, there is "the inmost Me behind its veil," the state of alienation when "thoughts are frozen and utterance benumbed." On the other hand, there is a dream of total interrelation, "the one heart and mind of perfect sympathy; as if the printed book . . . were certain to find out the divided segment of the writer's own nature, and complete his circle of existence by bringing him into communion with it." The secure Hawthorne who is content with a social self and a conventional society, who is so much at home in history that he can ignore its tensions, is haunted by an alter ego whose "circle of existence" is painfully incomplete, for whom history is the vain pursuit of total communion by an isolated self.

This malaise is mainly represented through another self-projection, the Surveyor of the Customs, who mediates between the Cosmopolitan and the historical visionary brooding over the scarlet letter. True to his title, the Surveyor makes it his business to "watch and study," to measure his colleagues, himself, and the house they inhabit. He is at once a solitary man, a self-appointed surveyor whose public office is hardly more than a title, and a social man, very much a creature of the "customs" he surveys. Inquisitive but tentative, he wanders through the building or stands aside and observes his fellow officers. He enters into the narrative voice in much the same spirit of inquiry: careless of contradiction, he adopts various perspectives with equal feeling, as though to make an inventory of the possibilities of life. Like the Cosmopolitan, the Surveyor never disappears from view or lapses into silence; at the end of the essay, he is still addressing us. But only in the climactic moment of communion with the letter, when he is transformed, do we see a potential author of *The Scarlet Letter* or a ground on which he can take his stand.

The ground of the Custom House is shaky—not only because Salem has outlived its time, but also because time still moves on. There are two aspects of social history here, to which we are introduced by the long sentence that leads us up the wharf to a "spacious edifice of brick" and down "the track of . . . years" from the old days of bustling commerce to the present era of decay. The house, a stage for mere mock-activity, the "formalities of office" zealously pursued by the custom officials, is also Uncle Sam's going concern. Though Salem, in com-

39

parison with other ports, is fast asleep, there are still merchants here, "men of traffic" whose names Hawthorne tells over. There are days when "affairs move onward" and a bustle disturbs the torpid old retainers. There is even a "man of business" among them. The house itself, as opposed to its functionaries, often represents a commercial and political life full of action and change. The past counts for nothing in Uncle Sam's work. His old records are thrown aside as "rubbish," and the labor that went into them is wholly lost. What counts is the future. Uncle Sam changes his garments, from Whig to Democrat and back again, striking terror into the hearts of those who look for passivity and permanence. His emblem, the national eagle displayed over the entrance to the Custom House, signifies destruction as well as protection. It is the emblem of a "struggling world" that is wholly unstable and immediate, always building the future out of its own dissolution.

On the other hand, there is old and forever unfinished business in the Custom House, work that will never begin again. The building was "originally projected . . . with an idea of subsequent prosperity destined never to be realized," and a large room on the second floor, still unpaneled and unplastered, testifies to an arrest of time. The occasional activities of the customs are always "for the time being": they are present moments without a future, hollow re-enactments of the past. This quality of fixation characterizes the "permanent" officials as they sit in their row of old-fashioned chairs tilted against the wall. They live in a changeless present, keeping their "accustomed" places and ritualistically repeating their old yarns. The Collector, the most experienced of them all, is the most static; he stands on his past as on a pedestal. His life, like theirs, was once full of changes and chances; it was futuristic, like the world of affairs that now surrounds them. But it became a *past* life precisely by stopping short in a permanent present, a "new lease of existence" that negates the movement of existence and even death. The past, as embodied in these old men, is time that has ceased to act and to evolve new content—time denatured. Therefore they retain none of the substance of their earlier lives and seem to have learned nothing at all from their long experience. The Inspector, who has spent all his adult years in the Custom House, is an utterly mindless animal, for without time man ceases to be; his memory is a parody of memory, a long vista of dinner tables ranged behind the dinner of the day.

Just as the futurism of Uncle Sam has nothing behind it and emerges from a dissolving present, so the past of the Custom House officers is history that has come to nothing in a static present. A problematic duality of traditionalism and futurism lies beneath the positive surface of the Custom House world, and there is a certain emptiness within the apparent substance of that world, whether it be backward-looking or forward-looking. This is a very different social milieu from the one projected through the style of the Cosmopolitan. The world of the Surveyor is not a sustaining medium, a rich present; it is vitiated by chronological time, which either comes to a dead halt or abdicates before the putative future.

The Surveyor is very much aware of his own chronology: once a writer at the Old Manse, he is now Surveyor of the Revenue whose "prophetic instinct" tells him that another "change of custom" is in store for him. Back of his sojourn in the Old Manse lie the temporal depths of Salem, his "native place"; beyond his eventual discharge from office lies the time at which he will be a writer again, six months later, and beyond that a further future when he will be "a citizen of somewhere else." His sympathies point in both directions; the intrinsic duality of the Custom House world reappears in him. He is an activist and a decadent, a futurist and a traditionalist.

As an exponent of healthy change, he delights in the Custom

House as a place of new experience for himself. Though his return to Salem has brought him back to his own earliest past and to the past of his race, his position there is a decided change from his more recent life. He has been wholly converted from a writer to "a man of affairs," and his name emblazoned on boxes of merchandise will go where no title page would ever carry it. In this perspective, his previous literary career becomes unreal—becomes, indeed, a traffic in "unrealities." For the futurist Surveyor, literature is not only an archaic activity, out of date in Uncle Sam's new world, but doubly insubstantial, since it is associated with his own outmoded self. It also pertains to the side of him that continues to dabble in the social past, foolishly trying, amid "the materiality of . . . daily life," to go back into another age and create "the semblance of a world out of airy matter." Literature ceases to be suspect only when it ceases to be past-centered and embraces "the reality of the flitting hour." When the Surveyor bids us farewell, he speaks as the realistic author of "A Rill from the Town-Pump," and the flitting hour is carrying him on to other realities. The Custom House "lies like a dream behind me"; Salem is now "no portion of the real earth, but an overgrown village in cloud-land"; and he foresees the time when "the great-grandchildren of the present race" will conceive of him (quite properly) as a "scribbler of bygone days" known only to the village antiquary.

What had brought him to the Custom House, however, was not a quest for new experience but a "strange, indolent, unjoyous attachment" to his birthplace and to the old Salem behind the new one. He has a "home-feeling with the past," a sense of more reality in it than in "the present phase of the town" or his own actual existence. The "earnest and energetic men" who founded his family and helped establish Salem have greater moral validity, "both good and evil," than the activists of the dissolving present. If his relation to them is profitless, it is because their reality annihilates his present life, just as the old active life of the custom officers has terminated in a rigid posture, an empty form. The traditionalist decays because he is fixed; with "oyster-like tenacity" he "clings to the spot where his successive generations have been imbedded." He feels his past as a doom. And if he is a writer, his role is as much diminished in his own eyes by his ancestors' contempt as by the condescension of his readers' great-grandchildren. The old Puritans looking over his shoulder see the future (any change from their pattern) as necessarily decadent; and for them literature, which is wholly a thing of the future, is mere idleness. The backward-oriented mind of the Surveyor can only share their view of himself. As a degenerate "writer of story-books," he takes a feeble vengeance upon them for their tyranny over him: his triviality is their punishment, and he even undertakes, "as their representative," to enter a jocular apology for their sins.

In sum, the chronological world is a trap. If the Surveyor welcomes the Custom House as a "change of diet," he knows all the while that it is a stagnant place, thoroughly detrimental to manly character and to his literary powers. It will change him into permanence ("make me permanently other than I had been"). And if he chooses, with equal paradox, to regard the stagnation as a "transitory life" and look toward "a new change of custom," what can he have in view? Merely an opportunity to "recall whatever was valuable in the past"—in the aesthetic life that his futurism always belittles. Not surprisingly, a literary and intellectual torpor overcomes him. Though he mainly blames it on the inactive, dependent, static life of the customs, which destroys his sense of actuality, his impotence is equally a result of the surrounding practical activity, "actual circumstance," in which his traditionalism can see nothing of value. The two aspects of his world meet only to negate each other; the personal existence of the Surveyor is canceled out by the negative world he surveys.

Superficially at home in the Custom House, the Surveyor

is truly in the alienated condition that the Cosmopolitan mentions and blithely passes over: his "thoughts are frozen and utterance benumbed." In his moonlit room late at night—between darkness and daylight, past and future—he longs for a more productive meeting of "the Imaginary" and "the Actual," personal vision and the public world. In utter solitude, he can conceive of perfect communion between a private imagination oriented toward the past and a public actuality oriented toward the future. But he can go no further in his role of Surveyor. Each factor refuses to "imbue itself with the nature of the other," and his midnight sessions come to nothing. He is finally content with a *modus vivendi* that simplifies his problem without solving it. He finds himself completely caught up in a futurist society; Providence, in the guise of a change of administration, saves him from his impasse. In a sudden flurry of activity, he is defined as the active man despite his apparent passivity. With his head cut off and his sensibility thereby simplified, he sits down to prepare the "Posthumous Papers of a Decapitated Surveyor." He looks back only with tolerant amusement; parodies the backward-looking documents of Surveyor Pue, whose own "mental part" had survived the centuries; and deplores the "stern and sombre aspect" of the *The Scarlet Letter,* in which there are unfortunate traces of his personal "turmoil" in the past.

Yet he notes the odd fact that he was very happy while writing *The Scarlet Letter.* The author of that book, who is quite another person, lurks within the Surveyor of the Customs, just as the latter haunts the Cosmopolitan. Indeed, the moment of revelation when Hawthorne confronts the letter is what the Surveyor is vainly trying to recapture in his moonlit room. This revelation is not a "transcendence." Hawthorne, the potential Author, is as partial to the past as the Surveyor (in the end) is to the future. He returns not only to the "sunless fantasies"

44

of New England legend but also to his literary "habits of bygone days." And he is as solitary as the Surveyor, finally, is sociable. It is in a "deserted chamber of the Custom-House" that his mind returns to its "old track" and he receives his charge from the ghost of Mr. Pue. Traditionalist and solitary, he is thoroughly immersed in the chronological condition. But he does not succumb to chronological determinism, the past that always threatens to come upon him as a doom and fixate him in an empty present. He turns it about, conceives it as an enduring past contained in and latently possessed by the present, as the scarlet letter is "present" beneath the dead records and illusory contemporary world of the Custom House. Nor does he accept the barren role of alienated imagination, reduced to a sluggish "fancy" by the senseless archives of the customs. He converts his solitude into self-pursuit, an active state, which is identical with pursuit of the "deep meaning" of the scarlet letter.

He had earlier felt a similar sense of duration in contemplating the statuesque Collector. Viewed with "affection," the old general seemed to lose his fixity and become the living vessel of a still-living past. Yet in this case, the would-be Author could only arrive at loose generalizations; he could not find his way through the ruins of time to the "real life" that he supposed to exist within the old man's memory. The scarlet letter is a different case because it not only gives Hawthorne a token of duration but also includes him, alienated as he is, in the enduring reality it radiates. Coming to him in solitude, it is relevant to the meaning of his solitude; and he, poring over it, is saved from solitude. He is in communion; he belongs in the succession of Hester Prynne, who first wore the letter, and of Surveyor Pue, on whose mind it was so deeply branded. In a roundabout way, he has found "the divided segment of . . . [his] own nature," completed his "circle of existence."

45

If he is redeemed, he is also invested with a mission. Leaving behind his colleagues "seated . . . at the receipt of custom," he has been summoned "like Matthew . . . for apostolic errands." His mission is not to preach but to act—to appropriate the universe of discourse now open to him and thereby to "interpret" the reality of consciousness that "stream[s] forth from the mystic symbol." In *The Scarlet Letter*, the *A* will hang over the entire story, as in its greatest scene a portentous *A* hangs over and illuminates the persons of the drama: Hester, Pearl, and Dimmesdale on the scaffold, Chillingworth below them, and the surrounding town of Boston. Each of these five figures— for the Puritan town is an agent, not a mere setting—will acquire meaning from the universal center but reconstruct the meaning in a particular way. Thus the sphere of the book (which is full of references to "spheres" and "circles") will be progressively redefined as the emblematic letter is approached and shines out from one side or another. In this large sense, *The Scarlet Letter* will be the icon of a creative mind at work, not merely suffering or resting in its inheritance but actively seizing upon the history that made it. And something analogous to this, translated into moral terms, will be the dominant theme of the book—the major meaning derived from and projected upon the central symbol.

III

The book begins with a vignette of the people of Boston—a single sentence set off in a paragraph by itself: "A throng of bearded men, in sad-colored garments and gray, steeple-crowned hats, intermixed with women, some wearing hoods, and others bareheaded, was assembled in front of a wooden edifice, the door of which was heavily timbered with oak, and studded with iron spikes." Just as Hawthorne gazes at the symbolic letter, seeking the meaning in it, they stand "with their eyes intently fastened on the iron-clamped oaken door," out of which Hester

Prynne will come with the letter on her bosom. In effect, the prison door is their avenue to the meaning of the symbol; and these colorless men and women, though they stand outside the prison, have all the demeanor of prisoners. Any Utopian colony, Hawthorne declares, will soon find it necessary "to allot a portion of the virgin soil as a cemetery, and another portion as the site of a prison"; but these people embrace the necessity. Though they are "founders of a new colony," they have based it upon the oldest facts of human experience—crime and death. Though they would cultivate "human virtue and happiness," they have no faith in any direct approach to this end. The jail and its companion-place, the burial ground, are their proper meeting houses; the scaffold, situated "nearly beneath the eaves of Boston's earliest church," is the center of the society. Not once in the book is a church physically described or a scene actually staged within it. Their true religious exercise is the contemplation of Hester, their scapegoat and counterpart, set up before them on the scaffold. Even as they denounce her, they are fascinated by her as an emblem of the world they inhabit.

The ceremony in the market place is genuinely religious, not merely perverse, but it is oblique. The ministers do not urge Hester to seek divine support but only to suffer her punishment, repent her transgression, and name another sinner. If there were some "Papist among the crowd of Puritans," this woman taken in adultery might recall to his mind the contrasting "image of Divine Maternity." But the Puritans invoke no such image to relieve the horror before them; on the contrary, their faith positively depends on discovering a "taint of deepest sin in the most sacred quality of human life." They would honor a transcendent God who enters this world mainly as law-giver and executioner. His mercy appears through his justice, his love through his power. His incarnation is the impress of his abstract supernatural code, which primarily reveals the evils of flesh

47

and the universality of sin. As administrators of the code, the ministers and magistrates on the balcony have no concrete human existence for themselves or others, and they have no perception of the concrete reality of Hester on the scaffold. "Sages of rigid aspect," standing in God's holy fire, they are blind to the "mesh of good and evil" before them. They see only the abstract Adulteress. As when Hester later views her image in Governor Bellingham's breastplate, she is "absolutely hidden behind" the "exaggerated and gigantic" abstraction that engrosses her accusers.

If they were merely self-righteous and sadistic, these Bostonians would be much less formidable. They are impressive because their doctrinaire moralism has a metaphysical basis: they purge their town in token of a universe where only God is really pure and only purity is of any account. Hawthorne does full justice to the moral seriousness, the strength of character, and the practical ability that their way of thinking could foster. He affirms that the Puritan society "accomplish[ed] so much, precisely because it imagined and hoped so little." And in various ways his Puritans, though eccentric, are old-fashioned folk, not radical innovators. In comparison with the "heartlessness" of a later era of sophisticated moral tolerance, the punishment inflected on Hester, however cruel, is dignified by moral principle. In comparison with later democratic irreverence, the respectfulness and loyalty of the Massachusetts citizens to their leaders are still close to the feudal virtues. In comparison with their genteel descendants, the merciless harpies of the market place still have a moral as well as physical substance, "a boldness and rotundity," that derives from the old England they have put behind them.

But in all fundamental respects Hawthorne's Puritans are both problematic and unprecedented. They are men responding to an extreme intellectual predicament by extreme measures, and

48

their predicament is one with their disseverance from the old world. The pompous forms and dress of their great public occasions, like the aristocratic menage of Governor Bellingham, are nostalgic and imitative, not characteristic. The old order vaguely survives in their consciousness because they stand at the beginning of a new epoch, but it survives much as memories of King James' court flit through the mind of the Reverend Mr. Wilson. It is true that Europe sometimes figures in the book as "newer" than the Puritan colony: the "other side of the Atlantic" is a place of intellectual and social emancipation, to which Dimmesdale and Hester might flee and to which Pearl betakes herself at the end. But Europe is a refuge because, whether old or new, feudal or modern, it signifies no struggle of consciousness, no necessity to reckon with the foundations of the new era. New England is the place where men must confront the founding questions of their time, which are set forth in the topography, the intellectual landscape, of *The Scarlet Letter*.

Above them stretches the heaven of supernatural revelation, where "any marked event, for good or evil," is prefigured in "awful hieroglyphics." The physical heavens are also spiritual, a medium of the divine word. But no civilized society was ever so directly in contact with brute nature. The settlement is encircled by the teeming "Western wilderness" on one side and the open sea on the other. Though the townsmen studiously abjure this "wild, heathen Nature . . . , never subjugated by human law, nor illumined by higher truth," it invades their prison-fortress. Savage Indians and even more savage sailors are a familiar sight in their streets. And physical nature is equivocal in relation to man. While it reduces him to "animal ferocity," it also sanctions "human nature," the life of feeling, and the virtues of the heart. The possibility of a humanistic naturalism lurks in the wild rosebush growing out of "the deep heart of Nature" beside the prison door. The possibility becomes actual in the person of Hester Prynne on the scaffold and later in her cottage on the outskirts of the town between the sea and the forest. What is more, Hester represents a positive individualism, alien to Puritan society but capable of creating a human community of its own. By her refusal to play out her appointed role on the scaffold, she becomes doubly an outcast from Boston; and yet, standing there in all her concrete individuality, she seems to claim a general truth, a concrete universality. She tacitly challenges the abstract city of their abstract God.

The challenge is momentous because she activates problems that their rationale is designed to anticipate and lay to rest. And similar questions rise to the surface, make themselves manifest, in ironic turns of the Puritan mind and behavior. Hawthorne persistently describes the spiritual abstraction of these people in terms of inanimate physical nature. The "rigid aspect" of the sages on the balcony corresponds to "the grim rigidity that petrifie[s] the bearded physiognomies" of the congregation in the market place. These are "iron men," as Hester later says; their creed is an "iron framework," aptly reflected in the "iron-clamped oaken door" on which their eyes are fixed and in the "contrivance of wood and iron," the pillory, that stands on the scaffold. It is as though their aspiration toward abstract supernatural truth has ironically brought them around to an abstract natural automatism, a world of law that is closer to the inorganic forms of stone, metal, and dead timber than to the mind of God. On the other hand, the ferocity of the women in the market place is as lawless and as natural as the lust they denounce, and it complements the rigid natural law that dominates their men. For all of them, "civilized life" consists of putting nature into prison; but the prison itself, the "black flower" of their town, partakes of the subhuman nature they contemn and obsessively scrutinize. The black flower blossoms apace, as Chillingworth observes. Meanwhile, natural affection, the red flower, lives on,

50

unwanted and disclaimed, in the heart of Mr. Wilson and in the potential "heart of the multitude." Two voices of that heart, one of personal sympathy and one of faith in natural virtue, arise unaccountably amidst the chorus of reprobation. They are barely individualized, simply a young wife with a child and "a man in the crowd," but they testify to a community of individuals within this authoritarian society. The official "community" depends on a consensus of power and submission, a free election of individuals chosen to suppress individuality. But the scene in the market place, with elevated individual dignitaries opposed to a shapeless "throng" below, intimates a latent failure within the Puritan social system. The way is open for the "multitude" to gain shape through respect for its own multiple individuality. Puritanism contains and secretly invites its opposite, as it contained Anne Hutchinson from whose footsteps the wild rose bush may have sprung.

In this sense, the Puritans of *The Scarlet Letter* are deeply involved in the dialectic of modern freedom. They themselves are creatures of the early modern era with which Hawthorne explicitly associates Hester—that moment when "the human intellect, newly emancipated, . . . [took] a more active and a wider range than for many centuries before." In Europe, "men of the sword [have] overthrown nobles and kings," and "men bolder than these [have] overthrown and rearranged . . . the whole system of ancient prejudice, wherewith was linked much of ancient principle." The mind of Hawthorne's Puritans is a negative version of this same libertarianism, which has cut loose the secular world from God, mankind from nature, and individual men from universal Man. In them, freedom appears as *deprivation*: a world removed from God and definable only in terms of that distance—a mankind at war with nature and able to create value out of it only by denying its intrinsic value, as God denies the value of man—and an individual alienated from

51

humanity, who can rehabilitate himself only by self-annihilation before an external public law. In their prison-worship, the Puritans define modern liberty as a fearful freedom, and they make the most of fear, the terror of deprivation, in order to regain an idea of universal law, however abstract, unnatural, and inhuman. What dogs them, and confronts them in the person of Hester, is the other face of freedom—an affirmative individualism, humanism, and naturalism. The proscribed individual regenerates their society; they unwittingly are moved, for good and evil, by the nature they vilify; and a multiform, emergent divinity speaks in the forest or shows his features in Hester's elf-child.

By and large, in the course of the book, the Puritan version of the modern consciousness gives way to this positive version. Hester comes to dominate the landscape not only as a character in the eyes of the reader but also as an agent of transvaluation for her contemporaries. The natural affections of the "multitude," oriented toward her, escape from the abstract law of the ministers and magistrates. The final scene in the market place is very different in tonality from that of the first three chapters. There is variety, color, and movement in the picture; the darting figure of the antinomian Pearl weaves through the crowd. And yet we are reminded that "the blackest shade of Puritanism" still lies in the future and that its effect will linger on for two centuries. The populace gathered for this New England holiday are intent on the sign of sin and once more condemn Hester to "moral solitude." The climactic death of Dimmesdale in utter self-negation recalls the basic negativity of the Puritan vision which underlies the solemn procession of dignitaries and his own eloquent sermon on God's work in Massachusetts. For, given Hawthorne's historical method, he can have no intellectual right, and indeed no desire, to represent a complete and irreversible transformation of Puritan orthodoxy. It is the Puritan mind that proposes his subject, postulates the scarlet letter; he can move beyond this negative frame of reference only by keeping it in view. If the letter were not potentially more than a doom and a sign of doom, he could not turn back upon it and repossess it; but if it did not continue to have power to burn, he would not be trying to discover its meaning.

IV

Emerging from the prison, Hester forthwith rejects the "Puritanic code of law" that has put her there. The town beadle, with sword and staff, officially draws her toward the door; but "on the threshold," we are told, "she repelled him, by an action marked with natural dignity and force of character, and stepped into the open air, as if by her own free-will." There is more than bravado in her action, though she is full of shame and uncertain of her ground. She walks out of the prison as representative of an ideal pointedly opposed to "the righteous Colony of the Massachusetts, where iniquity is dragged out into the sunshine." She is converting the isolation of a criminal into the free self-determination of an individual, and she is pitting her "natural" dignity and force against the abstract dignity and force by which the Puritans attempt to annihilate nature. Similarly, the scarlet letter that she wears has been deliberately transformed into a "fitting decoration" for the natural individual. The "fertility and gorgeous luxuriance of fancy" manifested in her gold-embroidered letter, together with the "wild and picturesque peculiarity" of her gown, express both a "desperate recklessness"—what the Puritans condemn in her—and also a creative spirit—the other side of her "impulsive and passionate nature." Thus reinterpreted, the unholy flesh emphasized and stigmatized by the letter becomes a unique physical presence, a "lady-like . . . state and dignity." The spell of the letter, "taking her out of the ordinary relations with humanity, and

53

inclosing her in a sphere by herself," is not cast by Puritan law but by her own sense of its positive meaning; it "transfigure[s]" her into an individual because she has transfigured it into an emblem of individuality.

The naturalism and individualism dramatized by Hester in this scene point toward the "freedom of speculation" that Hawthorne later attributes to her—and beyond that to the scene with Dimmesdale in the forest, for which her "whole seven years of outlaw and ignominy . . . [are] little other than a preparation." When she appears at Bellingham's mansion, she is "so conscious of her own right, that it seem[s] scarcely an unequal match between the public . . . and a lonely woman, backed by the sympathies of nature." The effect of her estrangement, intended to mark her bondage to evil, has been "to set her free." Her liberated "intellect and heart" move through the world of her consciousness like "the wild Indian in his woods." Her appeal to Dimmesdale is calculatedly couched in the language of natural and personal "possibility." The forest-track leads to a point where all tracks disappear: "There thou art free!" The "broad pathway of the sea" opens out into a cosmopolitan civilization where freedom is taken for granted. Both betoken the individual's capacity for endless self-invention —the power to "begin all anew," to give up an old name and "make . . . another."

Hawthorne remarks that Hester's judges, had they known of her free-thinking, "would have held [it] to be a deadlier crime than that stigmatized by the scarlet letter." But in fact Hester's sexual crime hardly exists for the reader as something distinct from her posture on the scaffold and her later philosophic libertarianism. Not that we are led to suppose she committed adultery for theoretical reasons; but we are interested in her deed mainly for thematic reasons. It contains the same sort of ambivalence as she imports into the idea of nature and

54

the idea of the individual. The adultery of Hester and Dimmesdale, subverting the communal law, produces the only real
community in the book. This is presumably her meaning when
she says to Dimmesdale that "what [they] did had a consecration of its own." The proof of the consecration is precisely in
the communion they attained by ignoring the sacrosanct community: "We felt it so! We said so to each other!" Pearl,
dressed to personify the scarlet letter, stands between her parents
to form "an electric chain" binding them together. She is the
immanent word they have freely created. A similar dream of
personal immediacy, according to Chillingworth, was what led
him to marry Hester. The wrong against her that he confesses
is his sin against this dream, the "false and unnatural relation"
of a merely external marriage. The wrong that he feels was
done to him, as he hints, is not so much possible exposure to
public dishonor as a personal affront for which he will seek a
personal revenge. Ironically, then, these three members of an
adulterous triangle commune more profoundly in their dissociation and even in their antagonism than do any of the spokesmen
of society. The monolithic state surrounding them is not only
ignorant of their secret but also unacquainted with the kind of
relation, the intimate good and evil, that they experience. In
this sense, it is the official society, much more than Hester, that
is excluded from the "common nature" of men.

Yet Hester's "freedom"—the creative nature, the individuality,
and the antinomian community she represents—is inherently
dialectical. In order that the letter may be "transformed into
something that should speak a different purport," she must feel
it as "too deeply branded" for anyone to remove. A prevailing
image for her situation throughout the book is that of a lonely
being encircled by "a thousand unrelenting eyes . . . concen-
tred at her bosom." Though she is separated from these observers
as by a great void—whether a "magic circle of ignominy" or a

self-generated circle of freedom—her meaning depends on her "intense consciousness" of what she means to them. The values associated with her have no existence except as transformations of Puritan values. And her self-effacing role after she is released from her prison term, her apparent humility and public conformity, indicates that her business is not an external battle against the established order but an internal struggle to assimilate that order by translating it into her own language. Her consciousness becomes the stage of a lifelong dialogue between the voice of Puritan negation and the voice of that positive freedom which is evinced by the very fact of her lively consciousness.

The process begins while she is still on the scaffold. When she summons up "phantasmagoric forms" from the past in order to escape from the "cruel weight and hardness of . . . reality," the past leads her back to the crushing present, the inescapeable product of all she has been; but her identity is being dramatized all the while in the energy of her thought and the vividness with which she conceives the entire present moment, including herself. This dialectical vocation is what keeps her in Boston, despite the fact that she might easily follow the path she later offers to Dimmesdale, into the forest or over the sea. Her self-respect is bound up with her shame, her freedom with her bondage: "her sin, her ignominy, [are] the roots which she [has] struck into the soil." Her perennial gray costume, resembling a prison uniform, expresses the annihilation of self that the scarlet letter is intended to inflict; it has "the effect of making her fade personally out of sight and outline." Yet simultaneously she is "brought . . . back from this twilight indistinctness" by the embroidered letter, her handiwork, which "reveal[s] her under the moral aspect of its own illumination."

Therefore the movement of her experience—the freedom she enacts, as distinguished from the absolute, ideal freedom she sometimes proposes—is tormented, difficult, full of doubt.

Hester's agony of consciousness is greater than the particular agony of her shame, the "penance" imposed by Puritan law (just as the exercise of her consciousness, the enactment of her freedom, is the only redemption she will ever know). She moves back and forth between aberrant extremes; and in her very effort to conceive a *via media*, she falls into traps of thought.

Almost immediately after her release from prison, Hawthorne notes a kind of tergiversation—"something doubtful, something that might be deeply wrong"—in her attitude toward her sufferings. She cannot adopt the Puritan rationale of sin, penance, and repentance without an oblique assertion of her own self-determining and passionate nature. She imagines herself as proceeding through humiliation and ostracism to a triumphant state of saint-like purity; and the persistence of her "rich, voluptuous, Oriental . . . taste for the gorgeously beautiful" is revealed by the very severity with which she chastens it. On the other hand, her latent idea that what makes for "sin" can also make for good is confused and perverted by a Puritanical concept of evil. From the beginning she has had some notion of a communion of sinners. The passionate nature that in one sense alienates criminals from the community of law can serve in another sense to unite them in sympathy: " . . . Would that I might endure his agony, as well as mine!" At a later stage, she acts on her belief that the "link of mutual crime" establishes mutual responsibility between persons who have "cast off all duty towards other human beings." But the communion of sinners, seen in a Puritan perspective, becomes a communion of sin. When a sympathetic eye (perhaps Dimmesdale's) falls upon the scarlet letter and makes her feel "as if half of her agony were shared," she conceives the moment as a renewal of evil affection, not a transmutation of evil into good. Unable to surrender her faith in final union with her lover, but preoccupied with the Puritan view of their love as wholly evil, she is driven to picture a communion of the damned, "a joint futurity of endless retribution." She struggles against the "sympathetic knowledge of . . . hidden sin" that the letter gives her, for it seems to imply a world of common sin rather than a community of sympathy. Her only recourse is to repress her vision of reunion with Dimmesdale—"bar it in its dungeon"— and try to "believe that no fellow-mortal [is] guilty like herself."

The terrible phenomenon of Chillingworth objectifies and confirms Hester's vision of an evil communion. He foresees and tells her of the perverse "sympathy," the sudden shudder of recognition, by which he will know her lover through the affinity of sin for sin. Doubtless he is present in her mind when the "electric thrill" of the scarlet letter seems to reveal to her a multitude of companions in evil. When she seeks him out again to reaffirm her loyalty to Dimmesdale, the letter burns ironically in token of her relation to Chillingworth, who has become a devil in a world that he envisages as wholly devilish. The bond that she swore with Chillingworth, as she now perceives, was the devil's bond: her sympathetic assumption of Dimmesdale's agony has brought about a perverse intimacy of fiend and victim that mocks her idea of passion self-redeemed in love. Chillingworth destroys her faith in the potential good of the letter she wears, leaving only the mark of universal sin, "the truth of red-hot iron," and a natural world "quickened to . . . evil purpose." The question whether Dimmesdale should be exposed becomes unimportant, for in any case "there is no good" for him or anyone concerned. The path of her speculation is now a "dismal maze." As Chillingworth turns away from her, she revels in her hate of him, accepting the inverted reality that he represents. Seven years of penance not only have "wrought out no repentance" but also have destroyed the new sense that she was trying to lend to the word.

In the wake of her interview with Chillingworth, Hester for

the first time denies that the scarlet letter has any meaning at all. If informing Pearl of the Puritan meaning of the symbol is "the price of the child's sympathy," it is more than she is willing to pay. For she has good reason to distrust any purported meeting ground between the sign of evil and human good; and she is turning toward a conception of unmitigated freedom, which she sets forth in the forest scene that immediately follows. She asks Dimmesdale to believe that he has left his sin far behind him, superseded by a "penitence . . . sealed and witnessed by good works." Going further, she conjures away the very idea of penitence, tossing the scarlet letter aside: "The past is gone! . . . See! With this symbol, I undo it all, and make it as it had never been!" The wilderness around them responds with favorable auguries; the "mystery" of nature, the ambivalent joy-and-sorrow in which her whole history once seemed to center, has been resolved into a single "mystery of joy." Hester is still thinking in these terms as she comes into the market place for the final scene. She contemplates wearing the letter "freely and voluntarily" but with secret disdain and the intention of discarding it forever—"in order to convert what had so long been agony into a kind of triumph." Her attitude is strikingly opposed to her dialectical self-conversion and triumph in her first appearance in the market place; she has solved her problem by cutting the knot.

Yet her dialectical stance persists insofar as she is still trying to find a morality in freedom, not merely to enjoy the sensation of being free. And along her way there have been indications that nature and the individual, fully liberated, become impoverished and disoriented; liberation is ultimately as nihilistic as the presumption of guilt. Taken in either sense, "the scarlet letter [has] not done its office." Thus Hester's "freedom of speculation," though theoretically sanctioned by natural freedom, is in practice contrary to nature. Her personality and appearance are reduced to a "bare and harsh outline," and she is deprived of "passion and feeling" by her independence of mind. The cold abstractness of her free thinking isolates her as much as the public proscription that set her free. Nature, the only ground for her thought, suffers a reversal of meaning and becomes a "wild and ghastly scenery" that "image[s] . . . the moral wilderness" of her speculations. This is the way she pictures herself while waiting for Dimmesdale in the forest. The "dark labyrinth" of liberty is hard to distinguish from the "dismal maze" of deviltry in which Chillingworth left her. Having discarded the letter, seeing only evil in its "stern and severe, but yet . . . guardian spirit," she has entered upon another realm where values dissolve into nothingness. Her dream of an open future with Dimmesdale is ominously preceded and shadowed by the image of their first encounter in the dim wood. They meet as ghosts, awe-stricken at each other and at themselves. It is a true communion of individuals: " . . . the crisis flung back to them their consciousness, and revealed to each heart its history and experience. . . . The soul beheld its features in the mirror of the passing moment." But the hands they extend to one another are "chill as death" and barely convince them of their "actual and bodily existence."

If the world exemplified in Chillingworth, though it has the substance of evil, is ultimately without good, the world of absolute freedom is finally without substance, without "truth." It is the example of Dimmesdale that brings this home to Hester and thereby helps to restore her intellectual balance. For in her conversation with him she is fighting against this realization as much as she is combatting the claims of the scarlet letter. She denies that his private life, cut off from public truth, is "falsehood . . . emptiness . . . death." His public reputation, according to her, is a function of his private substance, and both demonstrate his real holiness. The private communion with friend or enemy that he desperately imagines as a last resort is for her the solution of his problem. Re-established in his benign relation with her and cognizant of his malign relation with Chillingworth, he will be part of a world of personal good and evil that is more substantial than the external Puritan forms for which he yearns. But Dimmesdale, though he agrees to strike out for freedom with her, never accepts her contention that private freedom is more real than public order. The Election Sermon is on his mind as he returns from the forest; and when he passes Hester in the procession, he is "unattainable in his worldly position," far removed from the personal communion of "their mutual world." His voice from the church, telling unmistakably of a personal anguish, nevertheless speaks in the language of impersonal authority. As she stands at the foot of the scaffold listening to him, she is recalled from her dissolving private dream to the solid coherence of social reality: "There was a sense within her . . . that her whole orb of life, both before and after, was connected with this spot [the scaffold], as with the one point that gave it unity."

Still, the coercive social reality that rushes back in the final chapter is not Hester's proper home. It is one dimension of her personal universe, and it exists for her only in relation to her own naturalistic freedom. The scaffold is the center of her orb of life because the letter which society once imposed and she voluntarily assumed on that spot is the center of her dialectical consciousness. Through all her gradations of attitude this problematic center is implied as a reference point; it is the potential focus of her experience. It is also a very actual idea for her—one that she contemplates through the ever-present figure of Pearl. Hester is everywhere accompanied by the thought of her daughter, that "lovely and immortal flower" growing out of the "rank luxuriance of a guilty passion." By dressing Pearl as a personification of the scarlet letter, identifying "the object of her affection" with "the emblem of her guilt," she images the convertibility of terms like guilt and love, affection and passion. This concept of metamorphosis, though it is her own, at first puzzles her almost as much as it does the Puritan elders to whom she later propounds it. How can the "badge of shame" be "capable of being loved"? And how can such love fail to be merely a disguise for unrepentant lust? Her affection will quicken her torment, she tells them; she will be chastened by her sense of the distance between her feeling for Pearl and the shameful deed that brought Pearl into being. What is more apparent, however, is that she has introduced the positive idea of a quickening power into the negative Puritan concept of passionate human nature. The elders have reason to be startled. A direct consequence of this bold intellectual step is her confident "power to do, and power to sympathize," which lead the Puritan populace to reinterpret the "A" as "Able." The "unearthly ray" of the embroidered letter in the sick-chamber is cast by a "warm and rich" earthliness that she does not seek to hide.

As Hester embraces Dimmesdale at his death on the scaffold, she speaks in this dialectical mode. The other side of their common suffering for earthly love, the suffering that is all Dimmesdale now wants to feel or remember, is an "immortal life together." They have "ransomed one another"; if their "woe" implies the evil of passion, their passion reappears as redeeming affection. By a similar logic, Hester is drawn back to Boston at the end and lives out her days with the scarlet letter on her bosom. Here is "real life," for here is the locus of sin, sorrow, and penitence. But the letter is taken up—in a phrase recalling her first appearance in the book—"of her own free will." And her penitence is "yet to be"—for her it will always be unfinished. It can only be conceived and made manifest as a perennial conversion of the stuff of sin and sorrow into positive freedom—the creativity, individuality, and sympathetic community of natural men.

v

In response to Hester's plea, the dying Dimmesdale delivers the most eloquent Puritan statement in the entire book. Though he is lying in her arms, he rejects her faith in their eternal union and maintains that in their love, far from redeeming one another, they "violated [their] reverence each for the other's soul." Sin alone should be in their thoughts, and salvation lies in the torture inflicted by an angry God. Dimmesdale displays his stigmatic letter to the multitude as a token of complete self-abnegation, or rather of a self finally rediscovered in "triumphant ignominy." How did such a man ever come to wander "beyond the scope of generally received laws"?—and why, having wandered, was he not for the rest of his life "safer within the line of virtue, than if he had never sinned at all"? On the one hand, as we are told, his was "a sin of passion, not of principle"; and, on the other hand, as he himself declares and as Hawthorne often repeats, he lacks the courage of his convictions. But in this book passion itself is a principle, and moral cowardice is a symptom of moral embarrassment. In effect, Dimmesdale is as much a creature of his age as Hester and his fellow Puritans: he is a victim (until his final moments) of the divided universe in which they find opposite ways to live. His existence has been contorted into an "inextricable knot"—his simultaneous desire to repent and incapacity to do so—because he entertains conflicting interpretations of his deed. If his final sense of the letter he wears is unequivocal, for most of his career he has worn it as the very mark of equivocation, the sign of two voices warring within him.

His conflicts are more completely internal than Hester's: in him, the disjunctive world is registered as alienation from self.

63

We first encounter him as "a being who [feels] himself quite astray and at a loss in the pathway of human existence, and . . . only . . . at ease in some seclusion of his own." Moreover, his manner suggests a profound uneasiness even in his solitude—a combination of "nervous sensibility and a vast power of self-restraint." His devotees associate his isolation with intellectual elevation, a "purity of thought" that gives him "the speech of an angel." But in this first scene he is dramatically isolated as much by his sensibility as by his intellectual purity. He responds to the voice of feeling in Hester's silence: "Wondrous strength and generosity of a woman's heart!" Under the scrutiny of Chillingworth, his inner division appears as an alienation of mind and body, of his "spiritual" being and his "strong animal nature," of his "soul" and "the hot passion of his heart." Unlike Hester, who even in despair preserves some of her individual integrity, her concrete presence at once mental and physical, Dimmesdale falls apart. He is of all men the one "whose body is the closest conjoined, and imbued, and identified . . . with the spirit," but only to express the body's demand for dominion over the spirit and simultaneously the spirit's utter rejection of that claim. This is the condition signified by his psychosomatic letter and deliberately fostered by Chillingworth.

In one aspect he knows himself as "a true priest, a true religionist," whose inner peace depends on the "iron framework" of his creed. His subjective correlative to the prison-world of Boston is a "constant introspection" by which he seeks to keep his sin in sight and thereby to rise above it. In accordance with the Puritan paradox, he would convert his flesh to spirit by dwelling upon the total disparity of his "sinful" natural body and his intelligent mind. As he marches in the procession, he almost seems to have achieved his goal of "purity." The entire world of sight and sound has ceased to exist for him; he is pure thought. But, all the while, his very striving for selfhood implies a different valuation of himself from any that his Puritan creed would allow. By subjectifying his punishment, making himself at once prisoner and judge, he demonstrates an esteem for his own individuality even while denouncing the natural man within him. And he is fully aware, in certain moods, that the idea of the unique individual counts for as much to him as the ideal of purification. He perplexes Mr. Wilson by declaring it a wrong to "the very nature of woman to force her to lay open her heart's secrets in such broad daylight, and in presence of so great a multitude." In discussion with Chillingworth, he holds that forced confession is not only wrong but impossible in principle; there is no public language for private secrets; and even voluntary confession may be impossible to some "by the very constitution of their nature" or by reason of a desire to redeem evil through good works. These arguments for individual value are not merely self-justification but evidence of a sense of self that brings him close to Hester's naturalism. When Hester at the Governor's mansion explains the meaning she attaches to Pearl, Dimmesdale thoroughly understands and seconds her revision of the idea of evil.

His own sermons illustrate the "truth in what Hester says," for his burden of sin and sorrow gives vitality and efficacy to his words. Like the embroidered letter and the letter doubly "endowed with life" by Pearl, Dimmesdale's "Tongue of Flame" is energized by the earthly passion that his Puritanical self despises. He speaks the language of doctrine, but there is an emotional language of "tone and cadence" interwoven with "the direct purport of the words." Coming back from the midnight vigil in which he renews his sin, he preaches more powerfully than ever before; and he writes his masterpiece, the Election Sermon, with strength acquired from Hester in the diabolic wilderness. The extraordinary communicative power of these sermons must be weighed against his retreat from public confession and his consequent self-contempt. The kind of truth he achieves as the greatest preacher of his time is precisely what makes him an "untrue man" in his own Puritan eyes. His heart speaks immediately to "the great heart of mankind"; he establishes a "sinful brotherhood." In this sense, he has already made confession, and from this standpoint mere self-humiliation would be a perverted "repentance." The very anguish he suffers because of his moral failure by orthodox standards contributes to his moral success as "the voice . . . of suffering humanity."

But he always comes round to "the contrast between what I seem and what I am." Not being the pure spirit that his congregation think they see and hear, and not having shown himself in the guise of a worthless sinner, he conceives himself to be nothing at all. And he is right, according to Hawthorne, to the extent that he claims the identity of a Puritan minister; the only reality in him is his awareness of his unreality. To the extent that he claims identity as Hester's lover, he is equally insubstantial. This is Pearl's reproach: "Thou wast not bold!—thou wast not true!" Though "false to God and man" in his professional role, he has enjoyed a momentary truth of another sort on the scaffold at midnight and in the depths of the forest. He has known the reality of "sympathy" that he expresses in the poignant undersong of his sermons. Unable to go further and declare for personal freedom as the ground of sympathy—unwilling to stand in the market place at noon as he stood at midnight—he is "false" once more. Whether as minister or as lover, he can only look forward to the truth of Judgment Day, when "the dark problem of this life [will be] made plain."

If he does not actually wait until Judgment Day, but finally conceives and displays himself unambigously as "the vilest . . .

of sinners," it is because he has undergone the experience of spiritual isolation to a far greater degree than Hester. As he tells her, "open ignominy" is what makes possible her "open triumph over . . . evil." Since her shame is public, her transmutation of the shame is public, though she arrives at it by private processes. Her life, whatever phases of nihilism and despair she may pass through, is anchored in the society she would transform into sympathetic community. Therefore she is scarcely aware of Dimmesdale's basic problem. She does not perceive that by sparing him the isolation inflicted on her, by trying to preserve intact his individual dignity and freedom, she has actually isolated him completely. Even without the cruelties of Chillingworth, for which she feels responsible, Dimmesdale would have been tortured by a rootless subjectivism, a self-negating freedom. He comes to live in a solipsistic world of visions; in contrast to her train of images on the scaffold, his "spectral thoughts" have no termination in reality. We see him as a creature of the night, always "walking in the shadow of a dream." And this radically subjective world veers toward the deeper psyche; he makes acquaintance with perversities and blasphemies that never trouble Hester Prynne. The "dark transfiguration" that overcomes him for a moment in the forest is a symptom of what he knows to be potential in himself.

By the time Hester goes to meet Dimmesdale, determined to offer him the only truth she knows, he is no longer capable of assimilating individual freedom in the spirit in which she conceives it. She herself goes beyond the proper boundaries of her world by rejecting the letter entirely; but this access of freedom transforms her into an earth goddess, however dream-like and illusory. In him it works as a poison. The "profounder self" that she awakens in him desires "to do some strange, wild, wicked thing or other"; and the world about him, rendered wholly mutable, drifts toward the demon-ridden forest of

Mistress Hibbens. He can only experience his liberation as a pact with the devil, a yielding "with deliberate choice . . . to . . . deadly sin." He has reached the nadir of freedom, a sense of "eternal alienation from the Good and True." At the same time, however, he has stepped over into another universe. By his conviction of mortal sin, he takes his place in the orthodox world where the reality of evil, the fact of alienation, is the very ground of civil and cosmic order. When Dimmesdale in the final scene moves toward the scaffold, he translates a personal existence that has become wholly insubstantial and subhuman into terms of a public world that can make sense of private devils. He is not only confessing a sin but also professing a truth that fulfils his consciousness of himself. He turns to Hester with a very pointed question: "Is not this better . . . than what we dreamed of in the forest?"

Chillingworth can hardly believe that his victim has escaped him; and indeed there is only a difference in emphasis between the experience of evil that leads Dimmesdale to a vision of God and the vision of evil that leads Chillingworth to adopt the role of Satan. The minds of both these cultivated gentlemen, so long resident together, come to rest in the conviction of sin. The letter with which Dimmesdale involuntarily marks himself, and which he eventually displays in token of a reality founded on it, is the same that Chillingworth obsessively imagines and finally unveils with the wonder of a philosopher discovering the key to the universe. This is why the scaffold is the one place in the world where Dimmesdale could elude his pursuer: it is the locus of their similarity, where their difference must be established. Chillingworth once laid claim to it at midnight when his diabolic smile or scowl lingered on a darkness wherein "all things else were . . . annihilated." Now, though defeated, he appropriately claims his place on the platform beside the man who has escaped him by passing through nothingness to the reality of God.

His former power over Dimmesdale also depended on other premises—ones that he shared with Hester (in a sense, Dimmesdale has escaped them both). Like Hester, though obviously in a parodic way, he appears from the beginning as a naturalist, individualist, and humanist. He arrives in Boston out of the wilderness, dressed in a mixture of "civilized and savage costume" and accompanied by an Indian. Usually solitary, this "individual, of singular aspect," wanders the borders of the settlement in search of natural medicines. Even after his hideous transformation, he can admire the "great elements" of personality and of natural good in Hester. These two are the secret free thinkers of Boston, a subversive pair at work within the rigid structure of Puritan ideology. Their secret community is intuitive, subrational—confirmed by the verbal bond they swear in Hester's prison cell, but initiated in a silent exchange of glances in the market place, where "all . . . objects in the visible world [seem] to vanish, leaving only him and her." Their silent interview, while it is intensified by Hester's fear, anticipates the non-verbal, "sympathetic" mode of communication that is characteristic of Chillingworth throughout the book. As he tells Hester, he will abandon his public name not only out of pride but also "for other reasons"; actuated by the "strange secrecy in his nature" that Hester later counts upon, he is bent on "new interests" and a "new purpose" in a personal universe. Similarly, though less deliberately, he abandons abstract, "geometrical" truth in order to "know" in a much more intimate way. He is not an inductive scientist; he proceeds by intuitive affinity. And though his first intent is to mock friendship by keeping Dimmesdale in ignorance, he is even more pleased by Dimmesdale's instinctive awareness of his hostile presence. For he dwells by choice in an underground world of immediate knowledge, an almost sexual "knowing." It is a perverse form of the world of Hester, who alone knows and seeks to know as much as he.

The perversity of Chillingworth lies in the peculiar way in which he combines Hester's sense of natural freedom and community with Dimmesdale's sense of the fact of evil. He envisages a communion of sinners like the one Young Goodman Brown beholds in the forest—united "by the sympathy of . . . human hearts for sin." He himself is cast in the role of grand master of the secret order. The love he once sought with Hester is realized in the hate of his new relationships. His "human heart," no longer lonely, is expressed in the deeds of a "fiend." Shocked as he is when he sees this "frightful shape . . . usurping the place of his own image," there is a fantastic logic in his transformation. To have "violated, in cold blood, the sanctity of a human heart" is not a gratuitous act if all hearts are wicked and all communion is anti-communion. It is the coherence of Chillingworth's vision that reduces Hester to despair, and the logic of Chillingworth is what gives him his power over Dimmesdale. For he sees that if good is impossible, a communion of "evil" is really a communion beyond good and evil. He intimates this to Hester when he first projects his plan: ". . . Elsewhere a wanderer, and isolated from human interests, I find here a woman, a man, a child, amongst whom and myself there exist the closest ligaments. No matter whether of love or hate; no matter whether of right or wrong!" Chillingworth imagines and takes his place in an amoral world of sheer power. He passes beyond the role of the perverse friend, "the Pitiless, . . . the Unforgiving," to that of a supreme mechanist controlling the "engine" of Dimmesdale's life. As a black magician, he achieves his greatest feat not merely in promoting the wickedness of the enemy he embraces but in reducing Dimmesdale to the level of an inhuman natural phenomenon, a force overcome by a greater force. This is the union that Chillingworth finally accepts in lieu of his lost hope of love.

When he declares, "Thou and thine, Hester Prynne, belong to me," he is Satan as the deity of mechanical power.

As such, he remains the villain of the piece, but he is also a kind of victim. His heterodox thought, as he himself comes to see, is dominated by Puritan concepts. When Hester tells him that he might yet re-establish good among them by forgiving the sin against himself, Chillingworth counters her appeal by falling back on the Puritan language of original sin and abstract wickedness. His world, where a "dark necessity" compels every "germ of evil" to grow into a "black flower," is the orthodox Puritan world but without the God against whom the Puritans measured it and by whose power they believed it might be saved as well as damned. His "old faith," in this truncated form, has been with him all along; it is, after all, the practical faith of a people whose town center is "the black flower of . . . a prison" and who have surely "let the black flower blossom" in the case of Hester Prynne. Moreover, the amorality of Chillingworth, his world beyond right and wrong, derives from the negatively liberated, disjunctive world of Puritan theology. The rule of dark necessity, as he points out, would imply that human beings are "evil" only in a manner of speaking: "Ye that have wronged me are not sinful, save in a kind of typical illusion; neither am I fiend-like, who have snatched a fiend's office from his hands. It is our fate." What can one do but act? And in this perspective he cannot and does not claim any special power of action. His own force, his apparent freedom, is no less illusory than good and evil; for in a community of sheer power even the most powerful are determined by the blind forces of the universe, the purposeless workings of natural energy.

VI

The Puritan mind in *The Scarlet Letter* follows a logic of

negative freedom. The antithetical good and evil of Puritan morality reflect a universe that is polarized into external relations on every level, so that good can be conceived only as an external order imposed by God on a fallen world, by man on a fallen nature, and by society on a fallen individual. Hester Prynne does not abandon that framework of thought but conceives and enacts a dialectical relation between evil and good based on a dialectical conversion of negative into positive freedom. She is creative in the face of destruction, and she is constantly making an idea of creativity—of individual value, organic community, and natural divinity—out of the tough negations of Puritan doctrine. Dimmesdale is torn apart, rendered insubstantial, by this dialectic, which gives substance to Hester even while it torments her. Unlike her, he experiences the ambiguity of freedom in a primarily negative form; and at the end of his life he commits himself to the negative Puritan rationale. Chillingworth, perverting both the Puritan vision and Hester's, takes evil as his good and thereby ultimately destroys the meaning of such terms as well as the meaning of 'liberation itself. His amoral world beyond good and evil is also beyond freedom, whether negative or positive.

In one way or another all these persons lay claim to the child that Hester clutches to her when she first appears on the scene. The Puritan elders would instruct Pearl "as to her soul, its present depravity, and future destiny." As the child of sin, she is their human archetype. Dimmesdale, pathetically treasuring the memory of her moments of affection for him, sees her as his hope of life, but infected with the doubtfulness of his hope. Looking at her with eyes accustomed to staring at himself, he cannot say whether one whose only "discoverable principle of being" is "the freedom of a broken law" may yet be "capable of good." Chillingworth, pursuing his amoral drive for power, is struck by Pearl's indifference to "human ordinances or opinions, right or wrong"; and he would use her, the embodiment of an amoral letter, as material for another such exercise of experimental power as he practices upon Dimmesdale. But the child evades them all, literally by skipping away and figuratively by eluding their conceptions of her. She partly evades even Hester, for whom she is identical with the moral dialectic within the embroidered letter. Pearl is not completely seized by any of the claims made on her—and from the reader's standpoint, she can never be fully grasped as a fictional "character" —because she represents something latent in all who observe her but incapable of being completely objectified in a single human form.

✓ Pearl is the very principle of freedom, the essence of her time. She dances among the graves "like a creature that [has] nothing in common with a bygone and buried generation, nor own[s] herself akin to it." Since she seems to have been "made afresh, out of new elements," she "must perforce be permitted to live her own life, and be a law unto herself, without her eccentricities being reckoned to her for a crime." In this sense, Pearl's freedom is not a moral principle; she is prior to moral categories (though not, like Chillingworth, "beyond" them). The only good she affirms is the "boldness" of her "truth." And her truth consists wholly in her multiplicity, the "infinite variety" of her possibilities, the "many children" she intrinsically is. Hester looks in vain for "the master-word that should control this new and incomprehensible intelligence," for all the major terms of the book are applicable to it to some extent. Pearl is sheer energy, as Chillingworth perceives, and aware of her power; but her passionate, impulsive, capricious emotions are not primarily aggressive. She is by turns malicious and affectionate, as Hester and Dimmesdale discover, but never fully intimate in either way. Often she seems an entirely negative principle of "disorder," whose "freedom" is synonymous with the "broken

73

law" that gave her birth. In her attitude toward other children, she accepts the role of "a born outcast." But more often she shrugs off all such Puritan concepts. Though she disclaims a heavenly father, she can deny that the Black Man will ever catch her, for her home is in the benign "wildness" of the "mother-forest." Yet even her naturalism is problematic: if she resembles a pagan nymph or dryad, her beauty and grace also suggest a prelapsarian child of Adam, a throwback to Eden before the fall.

For lack of a focus, a single "point of variety and arrangement," Pearl sometimes seems to disappear into a fluid, insubstantial ideality. She is attracted by the "visionary" counterpart that she finds in a pool on the shore, "beckoning the phantom forth, and—as it decline[s] to venture—seeking a passage for herself into its sphere of impalpable earth and unattainable sky." But she soon concludes that "either she or the image [is] unreal," and she craves reality as much as freedom. If her multiplicity tends to make her vague and indistinct, the "truth" in her tends away from the "remoteness and intangibility" of an "airy sprite" toward the substance of "a human child." Pearl's truth can become substantial, her freedom can become moral, only through a sacrifice of multiplicity—specifically, through the discipline of "grief." Her incarnation as "a noble woman," foreseen by Hester, will be a conversion of her "infinite variety" into human freedom by means of the suffering that is the sign of human limits. While this gives her definition, it will also open possibilities of a new kind, personal rather than impersonal, concrete rather than abstract. The "grief that [will] deeply touch her, and thus humanize," will "make her capable of sympathy." It will bring her into the sphere of free individuals in personal relationship.

So extreme is Pearl's sense of absolute freedom that all the drama of Dimmesdale's final agony is needed to complete her transformation. In some sense, of course, she must already have entered the human world, the world of sorrow, in order to feel his loss at all. Her earlier affection for him, the man with his hand over his heart, like her obsession with Hester's letter, indicates her nascent awareness of suffering and her correlative "humanization." But in the final episode she flits about the market place in utter independence and joy as though to affirm her infinitude for the last time. She must be drawn down to earth by a principle as strong as her own. Dimmesdale's "great scene of grief . . . develop[s] all her sympathies," commits her to "human joy and sorrow," because he has reached an extreme of negation that counterbalances her libertarian extreme. Just as the kiss he asks from her is his last concession to the world of human relations that he rejects in his dying speech, so her bestowal of the kiss is her first act within the human world to which he has drawn her.

Since she becomes fully incarnate only in the final moments of the book, Pearl remains almost as abstract and schematic in her moral meaning as in her premoral multiplicity. We can seldom say with any confidence that she is actually experiencing either the limits or the possibilities of the concrete human life she represents. But Pearl "humanized," however abstractly, comes close to being what her mother sees in her—a symbol of Hester's own moral dialectic. She descends from a realm of total creativity into the middle world that Hester painfully reaches from below, from total self-negation and enslavement. This would seem to be the rationale of her behavior in the forest when Hester herself denies all limits and arrives at a project of absolute liberty. Like the pool on the shore, the forest brook that figures in this scene is a "boundary between two worlds"—between a visionary and a substantial (or human) existence. But it is also the spring of natural human life, where visionary freedom and actual bondage, joy and sorrow, are interdependent. Initially, Pearl can hear only the sad murmur of the little stream of natural life, and she dances off into ideal freedom and joy. When she returns to the boundary, however, she finds herself decisively relegated to the "shadowy and intangible" role of a watery "image." Having been exiled from the concrete world of human sympathy, she becomes poignantly aware of it. Even more, she becomes aware of the mixed world of man because of Hester's attempt to transcend it. By throwing away the scarlet letter, Hester has leveled the distinction between ideal and human freedom; there is no human world for Pearl to return to. Like a little prophetess, she summons her mother back to the reality of joy-and-sorrow that is guaranteed by sorrow: "Come thou and take it up!" She demands her place in a human group—"hand in hand, we three together." And once Hester has resumed the sign of suffering, Pearl kisses it in token of truth re-established.

Pearl has already expressed the positive side of Hester's truth by tracing a letter of grass upon herself, "freshly green instead of scarlet," in virtual answer to her own question as to what the letter means. As a "human child," she is a growing point of human experience, and she betokens a "oneness of . . . being" in the parents who created her. This is her role, apparently assumed with some self-awareness, when she, Hester, and Dimmesdale form "an electric chain." It is validated when the celestial "A" shines down upon this archetypal trio: Pearl, "herself a symbol," is the human counterpart of the divine signature in the sky. Though the noonday light that suffuses the scene is like that of Judgment Day, it is not a visitation by an angry God; if it gives a new "moral interpretation to the things of this world," it does so by consecrating the emergent meaning of temporal life—in Dimmesdale, "with his hand over his heart"; in Hester, "with the embroidered letter glimmering on her bosom"; but especially in Pearl, "the connecting link between those two." And in this role Pearl is an aesthetic, as well as a moral, exemplar. She represents not only a secular morality but also a secularized symbolism. She recalls us once more to the distinctive imaginative medium of her author—the liberated modern consciousness that often dissolves, like Pearl, into a "vast variety of forms," but of which, again like Pearl, the imaginative structure of *The Scarlet Letter* is a "living hieroglyphic."

Marcus Cunliffe

The

House

of the

Seven Gables

H AWTHORNE is said to have preferred *The House of the Seven Gables* to its immediate predecessor, *The Scarlet Letter*. Though not many would agree with him, his satisfaction is understandable. *The Scarlet Letter* was a "hell-fired" story with a crushing sense of fatality; it was, as Hawthorne said in the novel's final words, a somber legend, relieved like the escutcheon on Hester Prynne's tomb "only by one everglowing point of light gloomier than the shadow." *The Seven Gables* has a similar initial effect of grimness. Yet Hawthorne was able to bring the book to "a prosperous close"—to cross the gap he had established in his writing, and yet was always seeking to bridge, between the imaginary and the actual, the haunted gray New England past and "our own broad daylight."

He was entitled to feel that he had accomplished this and more in *The Seven Gables*. While the detail and the implications of the plot are complex, the essential outline is simple. It is a "powerful" story, originating in the wrong done to Matthew Maule by Colonel Pyncheon, somewhere near the end of the seventeenth century, in having him hanged for witchcraft. The consequences reverberate down through the decades. The Pyncheon family, persisting in pride and greed, is persistently punished. Moral and physical heredity march together. The Pyncheons whose conduct and appearance resemble those of Colonel Pyncheon die in the same hideous manner, as if under the same curse as that pronounced on the Colonel by the condemned "wizard"—"God will give him blood to drink!" The scheme likewise enables Hawthorne to trace the decline of the Pyncheons; for those members of the family who are not hard and covetous become increasingly ineffectual and impoverished. The curse is dissipated when Holgrave and Phoebe, the youngest representatives of the Maule and Pyncheon families, fall in love and marry. One other subsidiary problem is solved: Holgrave reveals to the Pyncheons the secret hiding-place of title deeds to an immense tract of land secured long ago by Colonel Pyncheon—papers missing ever since his death. They are quite worthless, and have been for at least a century. But it is important for the symmetry of the story that the family —as represented by the dreamy Clifford Pyncheon and his crabbed but harmless sister Hepzibah—should face this fact. All is now reconciled. Evil plans, vain illusions are dispelled; the past is past.

The drama of the Maules and Pyncheons allows Hawthorne to develop three wider ideas about family and heredity, which can be summarized as follows:

1. An evil deed may have far-reaching consequences.
2. Family pride and acquisitiveness are deplorable, whether or not they involve wrongdoing.
3. Family pride, even where not actively harmful, is absurdly out of place in the American context of rapid social change.

These notions, which for convenience may be labeled Evil, Lineage, and Impermanence, matter a good deal to Hawthorne. In *The Seven Gables* each is stated more than once, as for instance in the following quotations (taken respectively from the Preface, from comments by Holgrave, and from an interpolated observation by the author):

1. Evil: ". . . The wrongdoing of one generation lives into the successive ones, and . . . becomes a pure and uncontrollable mischief. . . ." *pp. 14*
2. Lineage: "To plant a family! The idea is at the bottom of most of the wrong and mischief which men do."
3. Impermanence: "In this republican country, amid the fluctuating waves of our social life, somebody is always at the drowning point. The tragedy is enacted with as continual a repetition as that of a popular drama on a holiday."

It is not surprising that such *dicta* should figure in Hawthorne's work since they were aspects of the history of his own family. "The Fall of the House of Pyncheon," says Austin Warren, "was the Hawthornes' fall."[1] The first of Hawthorne's Salem ancestors, William Hathorne, and his son, John Hathorne, were dynasts of dubious renown. As magistrates, they had handed out harsh justice against the Quakers. A fellow judge of John

Hathorne, indeed, had sentenced a Quaker named Thomas Maule to imprisonment in 1695.[2] Three years earlier, Judge Hathorne had played an active part in the Salem witch trials. According to tradition, he had been cursed by one of the victims, though in fact the curse had been aimed at his colleague Nicholas Noyes, to whom the accused woman said, "I am no more a witch, than you are a wizard;—and if you take away my life, God will give you blood to drink."[3] In the introductory section of *The Scarlet Letter,* Hawthorne wrote of John Hathorne:

> [He] made himself so conspicuous in the martyrdom of the witches, that their blood may fairly be said to have left a stain upon him. . . . I know not whether these ancestors of mine bethought themselves to repent, and ask pardon of Heaven for their cruelties; or whether they are now groaning under the heavy consequences of them, in another state of being. At all events, I, the present writer, as their representative, hereby take shame upon myself for their sakes, and pray that any curse incurred by them—as I have heard, and as the dreary and unprosperous condition of the race, for many a long year back, would argue to exist—may be now and henceforth removed.

During the trials of 1692, John Hathorne and another judge had arrested John English and his wife on charges of witchcraft. The bad feeling that resulted between the two families was patched over many years later through the marriage of a grandson of Judge Hathorne with a great-granddaughter of John English. The English house, one of several substantial old homes in Salem that may have served as a model for the House of the Seven Gables, passed into the possession of a Hathorne. Grand but decaying, it stood empty in Hawthorne's youth, and was finally pulled down in 1833.[4]

Other elements in the novel lie close to Hawthorne's heritage. The Pyncheon claim to the huge Indian tract in Waldo County,

Maine, had its counterpart in Hawthorne family legend. From his great-uncle Ebenezer Hathorne, the novelist heard a curiously mixed stock of anecdotes and theories: a combination of pride in family genealogy and of "the most arrant democracy." Like the reformer Thomas Skidmore, Ebenezer believed that "nobody ought to possess wealth longer than his own lifetime, and that it should return to the people."[5] Hawthorne himself, though skeptical of radical proposals, was equivocally involved in them. "Brook Farmer," brother-in-law of the transcendentalist bluestocking Elizabeth Peabody, contributor to the *Democratic Review,* avowed Democrat who owed his appointment as "loco-foco Surveyor" of the Port of Salem to party favor—Hawthorne was well versed in all the current arguments about privilege and egalitarianism. Great-uncle Hathorne's "arrant" views, and to some extent those of Nathaniel himself, appear in Holgrave's outburst to Phoebe Pyncheon:

> "Shall we never, never get rid of this Past? . . . It lies upon the Present like a giant's dead body! In fact, the case is just as if a young giant were compelled to waste all his strength in carrying about the corpse of the old giant, his grandfather, who died a long while ago, and only needs to be decently buried. . . .
>
> "The truth is, that, once in every half century, at longest, a family should be merged into the great, obscure mass of humanity, and forget all about its ancestors. . . ."

Events in family history probably account for some of the details in "Peter Goldthwaite's Treasure" (1838), the short story in which Hawthorne lightly anticipates *The Seven Gables* and, in particular, the novel's third theme, Impermanence, i.e., the absurdity of delusions of grandeur. As for Phoebe, she is a version of the purity, femininity, and cheerfulness that Hawthorne found in his own bride, Sophia Peabody, whom he had nicknamed "Phoebe" in the early years of their marriage.

The Seven Gables, then, was an exercise in the arrangement of a cluster of conceptions which had an intimate significance for Hawthorne. Some critics have found it—in comparison with *The Scarlet Letter*—a rather straggling, episodic novel. Hawthorne himself might properly have shared the view of more enthusiastic students that the book is economical, ingenious, and structurally sound.[6] Though a far longer span of time is covered than in *The Scarlet Letter,* the historical preliminaries are swiftly despatched. True, the tale of Alice Pyncheon, which is supposed to have been written by Holgrave, takes the narrative back again into the past. But unlike many of the plots within plots casually inserted in the novels of Hawthorne's day, this one can be defended as a deliberate device: it reveals the intensity of Holgrave's interest in the Maule-Pyncheon history and points the contrast between Holgrave's magnanimity and the wickedness, under a similar temptation, of his necromantic ancestor, Maule the carpenter. If it is hard to say who is the main character of the novel, at any rate Hawthorne makes do with a very small cast. Each character, except perhaps for Holgrave, "stands" for something distinct. Apart from the brief railroad excursion of Clifford and Hepzibah, the whole action is confined to the central setting: the House of the Seven Gables built by Colonel Pyncheon on the land he has wrested from the Maules. Here the Colonel dies, seated in his high-backed chair in the parlor, under his own portrait. The scene is re-enacted near the end of the novel, in the almost identical death of Judge Jaffrey Pyncheon. Battered, fading, increasingly irrelevant to and estranged from the life of the street outside, the House symbolizes the fate of its owners. It nicely accommodates various subordinate symbols: Alice Pyncheon's harpsichord, unused and out of tune; Alice's exotic flowers, surviving in a neglected crevice; the ruined garden; the ludicrous inbred fowls that wander there; the brackish well that was once pure.)

Yet though the House is a witness of terrible events, Hawthorne does not avail himself of the opportunity to endow it with sinister properties. There are no ghosts, or none whose presence is intrusive. Despite the wild words of Holgrave and Clifford—on the need to tear down, to cleanse by fire, and so on—Hawthorne avoids the melodramatic and lurid finale he could have contrived. There is no collapse, no conflagration. The House remains. It matters to the story, as the Mississippi matters in Twain's *Huckleberry Finn*. But like the Mississippi, it is ultimately no more than a witness, a physical fact. Human beings are the determinant. Holgrave and Phoebe can bring brightness to the House; Alice Pyncheon's flowers can still come to bloom. In the logic of the story, we must assume that the House will no longer be lived in. It can be left to disintegrate, slowly and naturally, like the actual Salem house of the English family.

This is Hawthorne's "prosperous close." Some critics think the last chapter of *The Seven Gables* as inappropriately jolly as the closing section of *Huckleberry Finn*. The denouement reminds one exasperated commentator of Artemus Ward's account of the "Osowatomie Brown" show:

> Tabloo—Old Brown on a platform, pintin upards, the staige lited up with red fire. Goddiss of Liberty also on platform, pintin upards. A dutchman in the orkestry warbles on a base drum. Curtin falls. Moosic by the band.[7]

Hawthorne's final chapter may indeed be considered too "stagey." But whatever one's reservations about his last few pages, we may agree that the general effect was intended. Twain—to continue with the comparison, now that it has been introduced—interrupted the composition of *Huckleberry Finn* for a period of several years: Hawthorne wrote *The Seven*

Gables in a single undistracted five-month spell. Twain often improvised from one sequence to the next: Hawthorne traced the ramifications of his germinal idea with scrupulous care. We never feel that he has taken himself by surprise, any more than he expects or attempts to surprise the reader. Where everything is so contrived, so fore-known, we do not even ask that the characters should express astonishment. Nor do they: when Holgrave discloses to Phoebe, his betrothed, that he is really named Maule, she reacts as though she has known this all along. In Henry James's phrase, "Hawthorne always knew perfectly what he was about."[8]

True, there is the famous Hawthorne ambiguity, or what Yvor Winters has called his "formula of alternative possibilities."[9] This may lead him into, or help to conceal, certain dilemmas; I will deal with these later. But in intent and in effect, the formula does not lead to mystification. On the contrary, it codifies and clarifies. Broadly speaking, Hawthorne's method is to provide two main sets of explanations, a natural and a supernatural. Thus, in *The House of the Seven Gables,* the supernatural explanation is that Maule's curse accounts for the death of no less than four Pyncheons, from the Colonel down to the Judge, and brings about subsidiary phenomena such as the tainting of Maule's well. The alternative, "natural" possibility is that the Pyncheons have a hereditary tendency to death by apoplexy, heightened, perhaps, by fits of guilty conscience: a belief in the validity of the legendary curse may reinforce their congenital weakness. Affairs *seem* to be shrouded in mystery; statements are qualified by a host of "perhapses" and "possiblys." Yet the main alternatives are clear. Hawthorne is at pains to supply each set with adequate supporting evidence, so that each is self-contained and self-consistent. The reader may, of course, complain that the result is irritating if not bewildering. Each alternative is alluded to often enough to acquire status. If one must be discarded, is this not a wasteful technique? The answer, I think, is that Hawthorne wishes us to entertain both sets of explanations, so far as we can. They are meant to support rather than clash with one another. They are not so much alternative as complementary possibilities.

In Hawthorne's eyes, *The House of the Seven Gables* would meet such a test: indeed, would be admirably suited to his characteristic formula. Fact and fancy overlap. As Holgrave tells Phoebe, he shares Hepzibah's conviction that all the calamities of the Pyncheons began with the quarrel with the "wizard" Matthew Maule. He believes it "not as a superstition, however, but as proved by unquestionable facts." Holgrave and Phoebe represent modernity. They are almost free from the operations of the curse. Perhaps Phoebe is entirely free; she asks Holgrave how he can believe "what is so very absurd." But though he lives in a more rational and optimistic moral climate than his forebears, Holgrave is linked to them by possessing a mesmeric gift akin to their talent for necromancy. Mesmerism is both a new discovery (described by Clifford, in his hectic conversation with the old gentleman in the train, as one of the "harbingers of a better era") and an ancient potency. A neat double explanation, then, for Hawthorne; and with the additional advantage of enabling him to introduce one of his favorite parallels—that of the artist and the necromancer. Art, Hawthorne likes to hint, frequently has a tinge of the black art; there is something wicked, or at the very least something deficient, in the cold scrutinizing detachment of the artist-intellectual. It is a quality which mars Holgrave: a quality for which Hawthorne supplies a genealogy, so to speak, in Holgrave's Maule ancestry. In becoming a normal, happy, married man, thanks to Phoebe, he can leave behind a heritage of chilly separateness.

The framework of *The Seven Gables* allows Hawthorne to

explore two human types that held a particular fascination for him. They might be called the impotent and the overweening. For the one, typified by Clifford and Hepzibah Pyncheon, he expresses a remarkably sensitive sympathy. For the other, typified by Jaffrey Pyncheon, he conveys an almost ferocious scorn. In these character-studies, Hawthorne ranges far beyond the mechanisms of the plot. He is a connoisseur of the broken spirit, the vain regret, the self-indulgence, and all the other subterfuges of failure. It has often been pointed out that he is more interested in adversity than in prosperity. The metaphor he employs to describe social change is of *drowning*. Its effect is to exclude those who are rising in the social scale; for in water, the best one can hope for is merely to stay afloat. A robuster sense of the beneficent features of change invades his argument. He is whimsical, even jocular, in depicting Hepzibah's transformation from patrician lady to plebeian woman. The situation is, he suggests, somewhat ludicrous. Nevertheless it is a "tragedy" of the everyday. We are much more sorry for Hepzibah than amused by her; and there is a genuine pathos in poor, bemused, ineffectual Clifford. The shock of their exposure to the outside world is beautifully conveyed in their railroad excursion—half flight, half liberation, and hopeless in either case.

Jaffrey Pyncheon is a more solid, more memorable portrait, belonging firmly to the province of the novelist, where Clifford and Hepzibah suggest the essayist side of Hawthorne. Pyncheon is a classic type. He is the kind of man we are warned against in the Bible (Luke 20:46):

> Beware of the scribes, which desire to walk in long robes, and love greetings in the markets, and the highest seats in the synagogues, and chief rooms at feasts.

Hawthorne may feel uncertain whether to lament or to welcome the American social flux: he is quite certain that the busy, pompous, carnal, office-seeking Pyncheons are detestable, like all such persons, whether or not they have been actively wicked. Note the animus in Hawthorne's assessments of the Judge:

> He had built himself a country seat within a few miles of his native town, and there spent such portions of his time as could be spared from public service in the display of every grace and virtue—as a newspaper phrased it, on the eve of an election—befitting the Christian, the good citizen, the horticulturist, and the gentleman.
>
> As is customary with the rich, when they aim at the honors of a republic, he apologized, as it were, to the people, for his wealth, prosperity, and elevated station, by a free and hearty manner towards those who knew him; putting off the more of his dignity in due proportion with the humbleness of the man whom he saluted, and thereby proving a haughty consciousness of his advantages as irrefragably as if he had marched forth preceded by a troop of lackeys to clear the way.
>
> The sudden death of so prominent a member of the social world as the Honorable Judge Jaffrey Pyncheon created a sensation (at least, in the circles more immediately connected with the deceased), which had hardly quite subsided in a fortnight.

These comments reveal a passion of distaste and a choleric mocking precision which are unusual in Hawthorne. No doubt they owe something to his own painful experience in being ousted from the surveyorship of Salem through the unsavory maneuvers of the Whig politician Charles Upham; and perhaps they throw light upon Hawthorne's complicated private defenses against worldly success. Whatever the origins of his feeling, he establishes and then destroys Judge Pyncheon with an expert relish. Villainous, vainglorious, and ultimately unimportant, Jaffrey Pyncheon embodies Hawthorne's three principal themes —Evil, Lineage, Impermanence—associated with family and heredity. There is a glittering, sardonic eloquence in the justly celebrated chapter which enumerates the various engagements that are being missed by Jaffrey, struck dead in the parlor of the old House. It is the revenge of the impotent against the overweening.

The House of the Seven Gables is remarkable, too, for a group of insights relating to the ideas of time and reality. Hawthorne endeavors to bring his story out into the daylight of the present day—or "an epoch not very remote from the present day": the era of railroads, daguerreotypes, "temperance lecturers," and "community men." Ned Higgins, the child with the passion for gingerbread, and Old Uncle Venner are firmly located in the *now* of Hawthorne's narrative, at the most commonplace level. The contemporariness of Holgrave and Phoebe is insisted upon (though it is a little hard to imagine this unaffected country girl obeying "the impulse of Nature," as Hawthorne drily says she does, "by attending a metaphysical or philosophical lecture"; here she sounds more like Sophia Peabody). Yet the character whose responses to *now* are most acutely analyzed is Clifford; and Clifford, like Rip Van Winkle or some victim of a time machine, is a person from another generation. Unjustly imprisoned for a crime he did not commit, Clifford has been in jail so long that he has missed half a lifetime. Returned to living after thirty years, he sees the world with the eyes of a boy: "his life seemed to be standing still at a period little in advance of childhood"; and in his dreams "he invariably played the part of a child, or a very young man." When he gazes from the arched window of the House of the Seven Gables, everything that has changed in the thirty-year interval startles him. Each time he hears the train approach and catches a glimpse of it, "flashing a brief transit across the extremity of the street," he is taken by surprise. The "terrible energy" it implies—so novel, and in such contrast to his own passivity—alarms and defeats him. Clifford cannot cope with the present. For Hawthorne, too, in this novel, despite the jolly emphasis upon nowness, the present is either rather gross and cruel—witness the callous gossip of the street—or else, and above all, unreal. Hawthorne is wonderfully perceptive in his handling of Clifford, and brilliant in suggesting what the railroad signifies, not merely to Clifford. It symbolizes velocity, disturbance, dislocation. Other contemporaries were struck by the oddity of the new mode of travel: they could hardly fail to be. Emerson noted in his journal:

> Dreamlike travelling on the railroad. The towns through which I pass . . . make no distinct impression. They are like pictures on a wall. The more, that you can read all the way in the car a French novel.[10]

Hawthorne makes a train journey serve as a more astonishing confrontation with the present; for Clifford and Hepzibah:

> Everything was unfixed from its agelong rest, and moving at whirlwind speed in a direction opposite to their own.

The journey stimulates Clifford to a wild flight of fancy: a glimpse of a future in which life has become completely nomadic. This is an extreme revulsion from the past-haunted torpor of the House of the Seven Gables. It is only a momentary vision. The future is blank to him. But the present is equally unreal. To Clifford—and to the rest of us, Hawthorne seems to say—"this visionary and impalpable Now, . . . if you look closely at it, is nothing."

In other words, *The House of the Seven Gables* is a rich and closely textured epitome of themes that preoccupied Hawthorne. Even if one does not care for the general texture of Hawthorne's prose, or for some of the elaborate figures and set-piece passages, one should add that there are many incidental remarks which remind us how acute his novelist's intelligence could be. Here is an example:

> A recluse, like Hepzibah, usually displays remarkable frankness, and at least temporary affability, on being absolutely cornered, and brought to the point of personal intercourse; like the angel whom Jacob wrestled with, she is ready to bless you when once overcome.

The Seven Gables, then, is a work of high interest, of which Hawthorne might justifiably have been proud.

But it raises questions that deserve a closer investigation. The qualities that have been listed are formidable. The crucial question is this: do they form a satisfactory whole? Or do they weaken one another? Does Hawthorne's formula provide an essential structure, or does it lead him into absurdities? Do we, in the final analysis, admire him for partial or oblique perceptions which, though no doubt envisaged in his structural scheme, remain somewhat extraneous, or which could better have been stated by other means? In his interweaving of natural and supernatural, environment and heredity, present and past, does he display a wise refusal to commit himself, or a rather sluggish reluctance to think clearly?

Let us consider the interior logic of Maule's curse. Colonel Pyncheon's motives are certainly mixed: he covets the property of the alleged wizard. But there is no indication that he feels he has sent an innocent man to his death. At the moment of being cursed, Pyncheon's countenance is "undismayed." A recent critic contends that Matthew Maule was entirely innocent of the charge of witchcraft: it is his *ghost* and his posterity who become witches.[11] This is a way round an awkwardness in the plot. But even if conceivable, the theory accepts the existence of sinister forces: forces quite as evil as those typified by the covetous Colonel Pyncheon. If so, the Pyncheon descendants are as much victims as aggressors; and their sins begin to seem correspondingly less black. Is it not plausible to assume, though, that the first Maule did have temperamental oddities which, in the fevered atmosphere of the time, laid him open to the accusation of wizardry? And that Pyncheon, not the only one to suspect him, may have believed the accusation? Or that, indeed, Maule *was* a witch, who reveals his diabolical gift by encompassing Pyncheon's death in the manner prophesied? Hawthorne mentions the remote possibility that Pyncheon might have been strangled. If so, presumably by Matthew Maule's son? But whether by family vengeance or by necromancy, was Colonel Pyncheon's death not enough to end the curse, which as spoken by Matthew Maule seems directed only at the Colonel—God will give *him* blood to drink—on the principle of a life for a life? No: we learn later from the tale of Alice Pyncheon, which Holgrave has written, that the curse will not be lifted until the claim to the House of the Seven Gables has been surrendered by the Pyncheons, even if the malediction has to last a thousand years. We learn also from Holgrave that the Maules have developed quite unmistakable necromantic powers. The grandson and namesake of the "wizard" casts a spell of "sinister or evil potency" upon the blameless Alice Pyncheon and brings about her death through his own malevolence. The wizard's carpenter son, whom Colonel Pyncheon has engaged to build the new House of the Seven Gables upon Maule's plot of ground, exacts another revenge. He manages to get hold of and conceal within the House the parchment deed entitling the Pyncheons to their huge tract of Indian land. Whether or not the title was honestly secured, they are deprived of it by the Maules. Old Matthew's vengeance would seem dreadfully complete—indeed, excessively so.

What of the complementary, "natural" set of explanations? Suppose that Hawthorne claims nothing more than the hereditary transmission of certain characteristics, notably a hypnotic talent among the Maules and an apoplectic tendency among the Pyncheons (possibly intensified, as we have said, by accumulated superstitious anxieties). This view is offered near the end of the novel by Holgrave in reassuring Phoebe that Jaffrey Pyncheon has died a "natural" death:

> "This mode of death has been an idiosyncrasy with his family, for generations past; not often occurring, indeed, but, when it does occur, usually attacking individuals about the Judge's time of life, and generally in the tension of some mental crisis, or, perhaps, in an access of wrath. Old Maule's prophecy was probably founded on a knowledge of this physical predisposition in the Pyncheon race."

It represents an ingenious interpretative modulation. And, as Daniel Hoffman points out, we may fall back upon the theory that the Maules have ceased to count: the curse has turned inward, so that the Pyncheons destroy themselves.[12] Even so, some doubts linger, at any rate for me. It does not matter much whether aptitudes such as those of the Maules and disabilities such as those of the Pyncheons are in fact transmissible, or whether hypnotists can actually exercise so formidable an influence over their subjects. In Hawthorne's day these were plausible suppositions; and some years later, the "medicated" novels of Oliver Wendell Holmes were to place quite as great a strain upon the reader's credulity. But Holmes's aim is to raise an issue that Hawthorne passes over: namely, whether people ought to be held responsible for traits they have inherited.[13] In what "natural" sense can the repeated deaths of the Pyncheons be regarded as a proof of their iniquity? And if Holgrave's final explanation is acceptable to him as well as to us, ought he and Phoebe not to consider the chance that their children may inherit the Pyncheon weakness?

One may answer that such conjectures make heavy going of Hawthorne's romance, with its deprecating, half-sober, half-magical mood; and that it was against just this sort of quibbling that he claimed immunity in designating his story as a romance, not a novel. But then, his alternatives are so carefully documented that he positively invites inspection, with something of the candor of a stage magician anxious that there be no deception. His elaborate scheme seems to raise as many difficulties as it solves, and to raise them unavoidably even if one would like to dismiss them. To me, the alternatives weaken instead of reinforcing one another.

This is partly a consequence of the interfusion of the three themes—Evil, Lineage, and Impermanence. The trouble is that the first two conflict with the third. Nor do the first two, Evil and Lineage, co-exist altogether comfortably. Evil, for Hawthorne, is an abstract force, working "inevitably," wreaking "uncontrollable" mischief. It is stylized, impersonal: something asserted, to be received without demonstration as a "truth." Abstractness is not necessarily an inappropriate mode for a certain kind of fiction; and indeed Hawthorne's story seeks to demonstrate its operation circumstantially. But he proceeds as if not wholly sure what to do with it. One clue is provided by Holgrave's statement, halfway through the story, that in the House of the Seven Gables, "through a portion of three centuries, there has been perpetual remorse of conscience, a constantly defeated hope, strife amongst kindred, various misery, a strange form of death, dark suspicion, unspeakable disgrace. . . ." *A portion of three centuries.* What this means, strictly, is that the woes of the Pyncheons embrace a few years of the seventeenth century, the whole of the eighteenth, and about half of the nineteenth. If Holgrave spoke of this span as "a century and a half," it would have a less awesome effect. Hawthorne is anxious to dwell upon the enormity of the

Pyncheons' iniquities and misfortunes: they must entail prolonged duration—more prolonged, ideally, than the evidence of
his own plot allows, and much more prolonged and catastrophic
than the actual family history upon which he draws. The
notion of Evil is meant to confer solemnity upon the less abstract
notion of Lineage. To some extent it does, as when Hepzibah
implores Jaffrey Pyncheon not to torment her enfeebled brother:

> "Then, why, should you do this cruel, cruel thing? So mad a
> thing, that I know not whether to call it wicked! Alas, Cousin
> Jaffrey, this hard and grasping spirit has run in our blood these
> two hundred years [*note again the slight stretching of duration*].
> You are but doing over again, in another shape, what your
> ancestor before you did, and sending down to your posterity
> the curse inherited from him!"

Here we are ready to believe that Hepzibah, at any rate, believes
in the curse; just as we see nothing odd in Clifford's allusion,
when he and his sister are running away from their hateful
kinsman, to Christian and Hopeful escaping from Giant Despair. Such attributions grow out of the fiber of the story. Too
often, however, Evil operates as a didactic distortion. Hawthorne
then is in danger of lapsing into copybook morality.

He is also in danger of bringing in too much solemnity, too
much direness. Lineage itself tends to become an abstract
notion, a subject for sermonizing language. We are assured in
the Preface, for example, of "the folly of tumbling down an
avalanche of ill-gotten gold, or real estate, on the heads of an
unfortunate posterity, thereby to maim and crush them, until
the accumulated mass shall be scattered abroad in its original
atoms." Pulpit talk of this kind denies us the understanding we
need of *why* men strive to plant a family, and of the mixture
of good with bad in their motives. In harping upon the past,
posterity is left out of the picture. The future may be blank:

men nevertheless try to chart it, if only in narrow and self-regarding ways by ensuring the perpetuation of their own name through the prosperity of their family. In emphasizing the harm done by Lineage, Hawthorne fails to make any distinction between reasonable and inordinate family pride. He writes lyrically of the redeeming power of love; and though there is no mention of a marriage ceremony between Holgrave and Phoebe, we must presume that they do marry and are likely to produce children.

This brings us again to the problem of the conclusion of *The House of the Seven Gables,* which critics have fastened upon as the book's chief weakness. Holgrave, the despiser of Lineage, becomes wealthy along with the surviving Pyncheons. The Judge's handsome fortune passes to Clifford, Hepzibah, and Phoebe (and thence to Holgrave) through the sudden death, at almost the same moment as his father, of the Judge's son, who has been traveling abroad. None of the heirs expresses dismay at the tainted inheritance. Even before it comes their way, Holgrave, in declaring his love for Phoebe, tells her:

> "I have a presentiment that, hereafter, it will be my lot to set out trees, to make fences—perhaps, even, in due time, to build a house for another generation. . . ."

Shortly afterward, when the inhabitants of the House of the Seven Gables are discussing their new-found happiness and wealth and are about to remove to the Judge's "elegant country seat," Holgrave speaks so much like a propertied conservative that Phoebe teases him for so sudden a change of face.

In defense of Hawthorne, it can be said that he too is teasing Holgrave. He has already indicated that Holgrave's radical opinions, though generous in impulse, are unsound. Holgrave now makes the discovery for himself. Moreover, he does so not because his bride has come into money but simply because he has fallen in love. Love laughs at doctrinaires no less than locksmiths. The situation has a wry quality reminiscent of the ending of Henry James's *The Bostonians*. Holgrave's explanation for his presentiment that he will build a house for another generation is: "The world owes all its onward impulses to men ill at ease. The happy man inevitably confines himself within ancient limits."

The defense is inadequate. It forces us to reconsider the total picture of Holgrave and to see that he is a mere Identi-Kit of Hawthornian types. Their disparate aspects—artist-necromancer, transcendentalist come-outer, resilient Yankee—are shrewdly observed but do not merge into a recognizable human being. His retreat into conservatism follows the dictates of a particular Hawthorne theorem (and perhaps corresponds to Hawthorne's own experience in love), but at the expense of the whole movement of the book, which should run successively through Evil to Lineage to Impermanence, like the movement of American history itself. Instead, Impermanence is discarded in favor of a revised, sunny version of Lineage for which we have not been prepared.

Much of the damage could have been avoided if Hawthorne had made the daylight of the final chapter less broad and bland. He provides prizes for everybody, including "the prettiest little yellowish-brown cottage you ever saw" for Uncle Venner and a lavish tip for little Ned Higgins. One senses the author's desire to polish the story off. The pace quickens to a trot. Previous indications that Hawthorne might have been toying with the idea of exposing poor Clifford to further indignities—because of his fugitive dash at the time of his cousin's death—come to nothing. There are signs of carelessness. Thus, in this chapter, the son of Judge Pyncheon who dies so conveniently is described as his only child. In Chapter XV, however, there is a brief reference to "an expensive and dissipated son," disinherited by the Judge, who has died some years before. Hawthorne may have meant "only *surviving* child." The suspicion though is that he had forgotten the previous reference in his haste to finish; and that it would not have lodged in his memory because he was not interested in the Judge's lineal posterity, except to arrange that there would be none. Lineage for Hawthorne is confined to the past until, abruptly, he has to say what will happen to those who are still alive. His answer is not bizarrely at variance with certain ingredients of the story; but it evades rather than resolves. The irony of Holgrave's reversal, unlike James's climax in *The Bostonians,* is fatigued and inconclusive.

As for the third theme, Impermanence, this might seem to be perfectly expressed in the closing scene of *The Seven Gables.* Clifford and Hepzibah have suffered much; the past can never be entirely obliterated for them. Yet when a coach arrives to take them away from the House of the Seven Gables, "as often proves to be the case, at moments when we ought to palpitate with sensibility—Clifford and Hepzibah bade a final farewell to the abode of their forefathers with hardly more emotion than if they had made it their arrangement to return thither at tea-time." If the theme were handled with such subtlety throughout, the result would be beyond criticism. One facet, the vanity of human wishes, has a genuine solemnity. Death mocks ambition: the Judge is remembered by his associates for only a couple of weeks.

But the main feature of Impermanence in Hawthorne's scheme of things is less bleak. What strikes him, and us, is the past-denying briskness of American life. Old wrongs fade into oblivion. Old pretensions turn into absurdity. The travelers on the train symbolize a social order in which nothing stays put. Like Peter Goldthwaite's treasure, the Pyncheon land-claim is a comical anachronism and has long been so. The actual settlers "would have laughed at the idea of any man's asserting a right

. . . to the lands which they or their fathers had wrested from the wild hand of nature by their own sturdy toil." Morality becomes blurred. In some actual situations of Hawthorne's era, such as the Anti-Rent War of the 1840's in New York, each side can believe it is in the right and passionately says so. But one feels that landlord and tenant alike also have a slightly bad conscience. Indignation and buffoonery are curiously commingled in the controversy.[14]

Hawthorne knows this, and has as much difficulty as other Americans in making sense of the national development. He knows that, however fascinating the old legend of the Hawthorne curse, it is a picturesque and rather thrilling *excuse* for the seediness which has overtaken one family among others in a declining town. Why, then, all the bother about Evil and Lineage? Why alternate between the portentous and the playful —for this, surely, is what baffles the reader of *The Seven Gables,* not the alternation between supernatural and natural details of the plot? Why pretend to a seriousness that has to be imposed? Perhaps because otherwise Hawthorne would have no way of reducing the social flux to coherent order: because, like William Faulkner, he sought meaning in a tenuous heritage he could neither wholly admire nor wholly deplore. Each added a letter to his name (Hathorne : Hawthorne; Falkner : Faulkner) to differentiate himself from his ancestry. Each liked to think of himself as an ordinary citizen; each suspected his own introspective activity. Each grappled nobly with the problem of relating an unsatisfactory past to an unsatisfactory, yet fantastically altered, present. Each denied discontinuity in a search for significance. Each resorted to a wide and sometimes incompatible range of literary modes, Hawthorne with more diffidence but with an equal and almost staggering ambition.

To me, *The Seven Gables* is a flawed book, whose strengths are somewhat incidental to its plot. They lie in Hawthorne's acute response to the victims of social change—Hepzibah and Clifford—and to the complacent bullies—Jaffrey Pyncheon and his kind—who come close to committing the Unpardonable Sin but who do not know there is such a thing. Pyncheon is perhaps the most fully realized of all Hawthorne's characters. He is more substantial, for instance, than Chillingworth in *The 'Scarlet Letter.* He would have regarded the legend of Maule's curse as a piece of nonsense, to be left to more miscellaneous and divided characters such as Holgrave. And that, indeed, is what Hawthorne has done. Holgrave is left with the necromancy, and with sundry other components of the author's heroic, hesitant effort to make literature out of the proposition that happy families, in common with happy countries, have no history, backward or forward.

Robert C. Elliott

The
Blithedale
Romance

M ILES COVERDALE projects the romance of Blithedale
into the future one summer day, as he and Hollingsworth lift
stones into place to repair a wall. In a century or two, he says to
his silent companion, Zenobia, Priscilla, Hollingsworth, and he
will be mythic characters; legends will have grown up about
them, and they will figure heroically in an epic poem. But to
Hollingsworth, feckless speculations like these are infuriating;
the utopian project at Blithedale is, in his view, a wretched,

insubstantial scheme, impossible of realization and worthless if possible. "It has given you a theme for poetry," he growls at Coverdale. "Let that content you."

It is a question whether Hawthorne's experience at Brook Farm brought him more, although he boasted, according to Emerson, of having lived in the utopian community during its heroic age. He was there, on his own explanation, to find a way of supporting a wife, but he was there against the grain. A shy, solitary man, Hawthorne was always cool to reform movements, always skeptical of the possibility of progress. Still, impelled by whatever unaccountable enthusiasm, he left Boston for Brook Farm in April, 1841, arriving (like his fictional counterpart at Blithedale) in a snowstorm: "Here I am in a polar Paradise!", he wrote to his fiancée Sophia Peabody. He labored manfully, though with rapidly diminishing enthusiasm, in the "gold-mine" and in the fields; and, predictably, he became disaffected. The proposed union between intellectual and manual labor turned out to be less natural than had been hoped. Brook Farm proved, said Elizabeth Peabody, Sophia's bluestocking sister, that "gentlemen, if they will work as many hours as boors, will succeed even better in cultivating a farm." Hawthorne was more interested in the harsher lesson on the other side of the coin: "a man's soul may be buried and perish under a dungheap, or in a furrow of the field, just as well as in a pile of money." Hawthorne left Brook Farm before the end of the year; what it was he sought there he had not found. But he had been given a theme for poetry.

Hawthorne, it is true, denied it, claiming that he had from Brook Farm not a theme but a theater where the creatures of his imagination could play out their "phantasmagorical antics." It was no part of his purpose, he said, to deal in his fiction with his former associates of the socialist community or to make any judgment with respect to socialism itself. Brook Farm offered itself as the setting for his romance because it was the closest analogue he could find to the poetic and fairy precincts, shadowed and obscure, so abundantly available to Old World romancers, so lamentably lacking in the sunshine of America. He chose Brook Farm because, in a special sense, it was unreal. His own experience there had been unreal even at the time he was living it. "It already looks like a dream behind me," he writes to Sophia Peabody during a fortnight's vacation from the rigors of farm work. His life at Brook Farm is an "unnatural . . . and therefore an unreal one." Ten years later, the experience has been transmuted into the most romantic episode of his career: "essentially a day-dream, and yet a fact,—and thus offering an available foothold between fiction and reality." In short, an American setting for romance.

It is doubtless true, as the late Richard Chase and others have argued, that the American genius for fiction has expressed itself most characteristically and most brilliantly in the romance with its infusion of the mysterious, rather than in the novel proper with its sturdy grounding in the actual, the solid, the real. Given *Moby-Dick* and *The Scarlet Letter*, we would be churlish to complain. But many a reader of *The Blithedale Romance* has wished that in this instance the allurements of the mysterious had given way in Hawthorne's mind to a concern for the actual; we would gladly trade veiled ladies and handsome villains with false teeth and snake-headed canes for a Flemish portrait of Brook Farm. Admittedly, there has been a good deal of speculation about whether the book is in fact a *roman à clef,* and some members of Brook Farm felt that Hawthorne's portrayal had done them injustice; but in truth so little of the actuality of Brook Farm appears in the book that, as Henry James said, the complaining brethren had more reason to feel slighted than misrepresented.

Hawthorne's refusal as an artist to confront the issues posed by Brook Farm is one of a series of evasions that make this work tantalizing, slippery, finally unsatisfactory. His choice of Brook Farm as a setting necessarily entailed legitimate expectations from readers. This is a matter of history and fact, not of literary device. Brook Farm was famous even in its failure; interest was high in the social theory by which it had operated and in the great personalities who had been attracted to it. When the book appeared (five years after the final break-up of the Association), many people concluded immediately that Zenobia's character was modeled upon that of Margaret Fuller, whose close association with Brook Farm (although she was not a member) was widely known. Miss Fuller's tragic death by drowning two years before *Blithedale's* publication was a significant link in the identification and revived interest in Brook Farm itself. Most important, Hawthorne had been there—a witness and a participant in an episode that was real in American history, if not in his own imagination. Given these special circumstances, the setting of his book created its own demands; it cried out for detailed, novelistic treatment: for description and solidity of specification and judgment as the novelist appropriately renders these. But Hawthorne evaded such claims by his choice of form, which precluded, he said, "the actual events of real lives," as well as a moral or political judgment of socialism. He wanted it both ways at once—the romance of Brook Farm without making the commitment that evaluation would have entailed. The evasion provoked some readers to indignation. Would he have refused judgment similarly if his setting had been a picturesque slave plantation?, demanded George Eliot.[1]

To be sure, despite Hawthorne's disclaimers, judgment of Blithedale does emanate from the book. It is not, however, the product of a hard look at the workings of the community—its hopes, tensions, follies, achievements, failures; we see almost nothing of this. It comes instead from scattered comments, mostly unfavorable, of two or three of the principal characters and from the pervading tone of the work. The tone is imparted, of course, by the narrator, by Miles Coverdale, minor poet, *voyeur extraordinaire*, assiduous parrot of Hawthorne's Journals, dubious spokesman for his creator. Coverdale's relations with Blithedale are most complex. One is never sure, for example, why he made the initial plunge: why he puffed out the final whiff of cigar smoke and left his bachelor rooms in Boston—the fire burning in the grate, the closet stocked with champagne and claret—to sally out "into the heart of the pitiless snowstorm, in quest of a better life." The gesture is generous, idealistic, self-revealing, and Coverdale hastens to clothe himself in irony. He speaks with mock grandiloquence of his own "heroism," of "the mighty hearts" of his companions and himself, which barely had throbbing room in the narrow streets of Boston, of their task: "the reformation of the world." The mannered hyperbole belittles both the speaker and the enterprise on which he is launched. It is a consistent tone.

From the beginning, Coverdale has doubts about the legitimacy of the Blithedale venture. His first meeting with Zenobia, that magnificent woman, throws everything else out of focus: her mere presence at Blithedale "caused our heroic enterprise to show like an illusion, a masquerade, a pastoral, a counterfeit Arcadia." Occasionally he takes a positive stance, as in his fine climactic scene with Hollingsworth where he speaks fervently of "this fair system of our new life, which has been planned so deeply, and is now beginning to flourish so hopefully around us. How beautiful it is, and, as far as we can yet see, how practicable!" But more characteristically he laughs aloud in mocking recognition of the ridiculousness of their scheme. Like Hawthorne with Brook Farm, Coverdale can doubt the reality of the whole experience. A few days away from the farm and it all comes to seem "dream work and enchantment" to him. The lofty aims and fine assurances of the first few days have evaporated; what remains in his mind is the deadening reality of hard work.

In his most ambitious moments of assessment, years after the experience, Coverdale makes explicit the duality of his feeling toward Blithedale. The enterprise was folly, he muses, but admirable folly. It was a vision, impossible of achievement but worthy to be followed. It was generous, but fully as absurd as generous. Coverdale had toyed with utopia and seen it fail; and like a middle-aged American today looking back on a rash plunge into political experience in the 30's, he is proud that he once had the idealism to be misled.

Coverdale's ambivalence toward Blithedale is a favorable judgment compared to other evaluations. Hollingsworth is contemptuous of the project from the beginning, seeing it as a miserably frivolous thing compared to his own scheme for reforming criminals. Zenobia at first takes something of Coverdale's tone as she plays with self-conscious irony on the notion that they are reconstituting Paradise. But at the end, after her fortune is presumed gone and Hollingsworth has thrust her aside for Priscilla, her condemnation is bitter: "I am weary of this place, and sick to death of playing at philanthropy and progress. Of all varieties of mock-life, we have surely blundered into the very emptiest mockery, in our effort to establish the one true system." Even Westervelt adds his variation on the theme as he ridicules the inhabitants of this latter-day Forest of Arden.

Thus every major character in the book (except Priscilla) rings changes on the notion that life at Blithedale is mock-life, artificial, insubstantial. As in the masquerade scene, everything is "put on" for the pastoral occasion; and the pastoral is the most studiedly artificial of genres. Miles Coverdale, who confesses to having a "decided tendency toward the actual," finds himself getting so far out of reckoning with the real that he has to leave Blithedale to get his moorings once more. For reality Coverdale goes to Boston.

An odd twist shows here. The very quality of life which made Brook Farm available to Hawthorne as the setting for his book constitutes, in the mouths of his characters, a criticism of the socialist experiment at Blithedale. This critique may be summed up by citing Coverdale's harsh comment on the manner Zenobia chose for her death: her drowning had "some tint of the Arcadian affectation that had been visible enough in all our lives, for a few months past."

Here, singly and in sum, is judgment in plenty; and no voice is raised in opposition. Is it Hawthorne's judgment? Given the operative conventions of fiction, of course it is not. Furthermore, many of the negative criticisms have the most dubious bearing on Blithedale. Any remark of Westervelt, for example, can be immediately dismissed because he is the devil, or a very near relative. Hollingsworth is a monomaniac, incapable of seeing beyond his own incredible scheme; his opinions of Blithedale lack cogency in proportion as he lacks balance. Zenobia's denunciation of the "mock-life" of Blithedale tells heavily against the community, but as criticism it is not earned by the experience depicted in the book. Zenobia is sick to death, not of the socialist experiment, but of the perverseness of a New England blacksmith who could choose the debile and childlike Priscilla over her own opulent self. Psychologically plausible as it is, Zenobia's outburst reveals far more of her own sickness than any of Blithedale's. "Take the moral of Zenobia's history," writes George Eliot, "and you will find that Socialism is apparently made responsible for consequences which it utterly condemned." George Eliot overstates, but it is an overstatement that the economy of the book abets.

Miles Coverdale is the only character in the romance whose judgment of Blithedale bears directly and with relevance on the kind of experience Hawthorne had lived at Brook Farm. Coverdale is ambivalent, as we have seen, proud at one moment to be on the point of progress as it thrusts out into chaos, shrewdly skeptical the next as he reflects on the anomalous position of a utopian community forced to compete for livelihood with the world it has rejected. But this is practical criticism, not moral judgment. A condition of moral judgment— if it is to carry weight—is that we have full confidence in the judge; in his character, his sensitivity, his human sympathy. Coverdale is not a man to inspire such confidence. True, in his frank characterization of himself, his charm and intelligence come through; and his very frankness in revealing his own failures of character predisposes us to sympathy toward him. This is one of a number of seductive consequences following upon our being exposed to a sustained "inside view" narrative. But sympathy falters when Coverdale tells us of the "cold tendency" which makes him pry into other people's passions—a tendency that has helped, he says, unhumanize his heart. He shows us himself in a series of scenes as a compulsive Peeping Tom (he even dreams of peeping); we see him being sadistically cruel to Priscilla, malevolent to Zenobia, bitterly revengeful toward Hollingsworth. What are we to make of a man who, looking back over the avowed emptiness of his life, searches his mind for a cause worth dying for and finds one, in these terms: "If Kossuth . . . would pitch the battle-field of Hungarian rights within an easy ride of my abode, and choose a mild, sunny morning, after breakfast, for the conflict, Miles Coverdale would gladly be his man, for one brave rush upon the levelled bayonets. Further than that, I should be loath to pledge myself." Somewhere Coverdale refers to the "customary levity" of his speech; the phrase characterizes precisely the tone of his moral life. He is not one—Hawthorne will not let him be one—whose judgment of the Blithedale experiment can command assent.

Thus, although there are many judgments of Blithedale in the book, none of them—singly or in combination—can be said to represent Hawthorne's own final and reliable judgment; in this sense his disclaimer in the Preface is justified. One must feel that this is a major weakness of the book—the weakness that Henry James was touching upon, I think, when, with his eye upon opportunities lost, he complained that Hawthorne was not a satirist. "There is no satire whatever in the *Romance,*" he lamented; "the quality is almost conspicuous by its absence." This is not entirely accurate. Zenobia sometimes functions as a satirist; she spins a fine satirical fantasy on Coverdale turned country bumpkin, for example—the fantasy a sharp critique of the sentimentality of Blithedale values. Westervelt, that implausible villain, draws a deft satirical portrait of Hollingsworth and is so overcome with delight at his accomplishment that he bursts into metallic laughter, thereby disclosing the brilliant sham of his dental arrangements. Even Miles Coverdale demonstrates an occasional feeling for the tone of satire, as when he decides (mistakenly) that Hollingsworth is, after all, a philanthropic man—"not that steel engine of the devil's contrivance, a philanthropist!" But all this is quite incidental and does not affect the validity of James's point. What is wanted at the heart of the book is the stringency of the satiric view.

The difficulty is bound up in the conception of Miles Coverdale, a narrator whose self-protecting irony enables him to avoid taking a rigorous stand on anything. The most common rhetorical pattern in Coverdale's musings throughout the book is for him to make a statement of judgment or conclusion—this followed immediately by a new sentence beginning with "But . . . ," which retracts or qualifies or blurs what has just been stated. Coverdale is the classically uncommitted man; he could hardly have been a satirist any more than he could have been a single-minded utopian.

The most tantalizing puzzle in the *Blithedale Romance* is that involved in the relation between Hawthorne and the man he created to tell his story. If we look at the work with a post-Jamesian eye, it is possible to think of Coverdale as an "unreliable narrator," in Wayne Booth's terms, with Hawthorne standing in a critically ironic relation to him. Hawthorne, after all, is the one who makes Coverdale display himself as a deplorably inadequate human being. "I have made but a poor and dim figure in my own narrative," Coverdale writes at the end. At times, Hawthorne seems to be laughing at his alter ego. In the grotesque voyeur scene in Boston, for example, Coverdale has been caught out by Westervelt and Zenobia as he peeps into their window across the street. Zenobia, hurling a glance of scorn "directed full at my sensibilities as a gentleman," drops a window curtain between them. The speed with which Coverdale rationalizes his outrageous behavior can be nothing short of comic: "I had a keen, revengeful sense of the insult inflicted by Zenobia's scornful recognition, and more particularly by her letting down the curtain; as if such were the proper barrier to be interposed between a character like hers and a perceptive faculty like mine." The play on words here is amusing and pointed (Coverdale is consistently proud of his delicate intuitions but relies overmuch on his excellent eyesight); it reinforces our momentary sense that Hawthorne may be mocking his narrator.

But when we look for further evidence of this kind, evidence developed at all systematically, we do not find it. So little ironic remove is there between Hawthorne and Coverdale that we are forced to think of the play on "perceptive faculty" as either unintentional or an isolated, and therefore incoherent, flash of wit. If Hawthorne deliberately created Coverdale as an unreliable narrator (and in some sense he unquestionably did so create him), he provided almost no clues by which the reader could redress the unreliability.[2] He is no more a satirist with respect to Coverdale than Coverdale is a satirist with respect to the utopia he left. Neither Blithedale nor the man who tells of Blithedale is finally placed in the moral (which is to say, the fictive) structure of the book. This is a limitation sanctioned only superficially by the form Hawthorne chose; the true limitation, we must feel, is in the romancer, not the romance.

Despite some interesting efforts by recent critics, it has seemed to most readers that *The Blithedale Romance* suffers from a radical incoherence. Even the greatest ingenuity cannot bring into meaningful relation the Veiled Lady–Fauntleroy–Westervelt business with the thematic interests of the work, nor do these interests reveal themselves in notable harmony. It occurs to me that the harmony was available, implicit in the experience described, but that Hawthorne failed finally to achieve it because, like Coverdale, he remained a witness and refused the role of judge. Or, if this is overstated, at least he refused to push his judgment to that point which would have enabled him to unify the ideological materials with which he worked.

Of course certain morals are drawn in the clearest terms. Zenobia is a figure straight out of homiletic literature, out of Juvenal, say, or *The Vanity of Human Wishes*. All that makes her the superb woman she is—her vitality, her intelligence, her radiant sexuality—all that sets her apart as a figure of heroic drama, conspires to her ruin. She is what she is because she lives "out of the beaten track"; and it is this, she says, drawing her own bitter moral, that pulls the universe down upon her.

Hollingsworth's career is even more clearly an exemplum; the analysis of his character is relentless as we are made to see into what makes this gifted man move, as we watch him, impelled by noble motives, become dehumanized under the pressure of the *idée fixe* that rules him. Evidence in the manuscript indicates that one tentative title of *The Blithedale Romance* was *Hollingsworth*—some measure of the importance Hawthorne placed on the character and the theme he embodies. Men like Hollingsworth, remarks Coverdale, are not motivated so much as *incorporated* by their single principle. "And the higher and purer the original object, and the more unselfishly it may have been taken up, the slighter is the probability that they can be led to recognize the process by which godlike benevolence has been debased into all-devouring egotism." As self-consecrated high priests, they will sacrifice whatever is most precious before their idol, in whose features they see only benignity and love. Hollingsworth's own soul is doomed to be corrupted, Coverdale sees, by the "too powerful purpose which had grown out of what was noblest in him." The shape of the corruption is etched in by Zenobia as at the end she sees the man she has loved for what he is. "Are you a man? No; but a monster! A cold, heartless, self-beginning and self-ending piece of mechanism!" Hawthorne's theme is as old as Aristotle, and it could not be more clear: *corruptio optimi pessima.*

Blithedale itself might have been encompassed by the same moral referents had Hawthorne chosen to show us, in concrete terms, the community recapitulating in large the progress of its most powerful member. The theme is broached, as a matter of fact, although in fairly abstract terms. We know that the community of Blithedale originates out of the most generous motives, that it is dedicated to the loftiest aims, and that it falls victim to corruption generated out of its own virtues. Blithedale failed, and deserved to fail, says Coverdale in retrospect, because it lapsed into Fourierism. (Three years after Hawthorne left Brook Farm, the members announced officially that they gave unqualified assent to the principles of Fourier and proposed to organize themselves into a "perfect Phalanx," with, presumably, the total systematization of life that implied.) Coverdale's remark recalls an earlier scene. During his convalescence at Blithedale, he read widely in Fourier, ploughing through the tedious volumes because he recognized an analogy between Fourier's system and their own, opposed as their respective principles might be. Coverdale explains parts of Fourier's system to Hollingsworth and translates some of the more egregious passages for his benefit. They take particular delight in Fourier's famous prophecy that in the fullness of progress the ocean shall be transformed into lemonade. Both men are contemptuous of Fourier's principles and his grandiose plans. Fourier "promulgates his system, so far as I can perceive," says Coverdale, "entirely on his own responsibility. He has searched out and discovered the whole counsel of the Almighty, in respect to mankind, past, present, and for exactly seventy thousand years to come by the mere force of his individual intellect!" Hollingsworth is outraged that Fourier should choose man's selfishness as the motive force for his system. "To seize upon and foster whatever vile, petty, sordid, filthy, bestial and abominable corruptions have cankered into our nature, to be the efficient instruments of his infernal regeneration!" The devil himself could contrive no worse. "And his consummated Paradise, as he pictures it, would be worthy of the agency which he counts upon for establishing it."

How remarkable Hawthorne's prescience is!—his sensitivity to the signals that issues of the future send out before them. Here we have two men, members of a utopian community, discussing the corruption of the utopian principle, seeing that in the absolutism of Fourier's vision lies the making of a utopian hell. Coverdale's reference to the awful truth in *Pilgrim's Progress*— "from the very gate of heaven there is a by-way to the pit" —is made with Hollingsworth in mind; but its application in this context is exact. Hawthorne is on the verge of one of the twentieth century's most compulsive themes: the fear of utopia. There are adumbrations here of the ideology behind Ivan Karamazov's vision of the Grand Inquisitor (that great vision of utopia turned in on itself), behind Eugene Zamiatin's extraordinary novel *We*, behind *Brave New World*—adumbrations of a good deal that is most significant in twentieth-century thought. *Corruptio optimi pessima* sums it up well enough.

Remarkable as Hawthorne's insight is, however, we must not claim for him too much. The discussion of utopianism is brief and abstract. In only the most casual way is it made to bear on Blithedale: the community fell into Fourierism, says Coverdale years after the event, and deservedly failed. We are not allowed to see that failure: how it was and what it meant. Coverdale's remark has a factual bearing only; it is not the statement of a novelist.[3]

In his fine essay on *The Blithedale Romance*, Irving Howe speaks of the temptation to write about the book it might have been rather than the book it is.[4] I am conscious of having succumbed to that temptation—an arrogant procedure perhaps, but not entirely gratuitous. Hawthorne chose to write a romance, which in this instance entailed "phantasmagoric antics," "Sybilline attributes," satanic stigmata. Such materials, with their vague intimations of allegorical significance, could not have been of great interest even to a receptive nineteenth-century audience; they are of no possible interest today. Hawthorne also chose his setting which for historical reasons was inevitably interesting; perhaps inadvertently he found himself in the dilemma of the historical novelist, where "background" takes on independent life and moves to the fore, disrupting the normal relation of figure to ground. In any event, his setting could be successfully rendered only in proportion as he was willing to introduce "reality" into its presentation—the kind of reality that

Miles Coverdale discovers in a picture in a Boston saloon, and rejects.

Coverdale, we recall, once toyed with the fancy that he might figure as a hero in the future epic poem celebrating Blithedale. It would never have occurred to him that he might write that poem. Zenobia, who sees the whole affair as a tragedy, accuses him of trivializing it, of turning it into a ballad. When she suggests a moral for his poem, he wants to soften it. The ballad, one fears, will be sentimental.

Hawthorne's situation once again runs parallel to that of the poet he created. He was by no means the man by conviction or temperament to write the epic of Brook Farm. Nor was he prepared to write a novel (to say nothing of a satirical novel) grounded in range and depth in his own experience; to do this would have required that he commit himself, that he *judge* what he had lived in a way that he was unwilling to undertake. His choice of romance as the form to incorporate his material gave him at least superficial justification for evading these issues. The aesthetic choice was at the same time a moral choice. It is impossible not to wish that he had chosen differently.

Harry Levin

Statues

from Italy:

The Marble Faun

I**T IS A** salient fact of American fiction that so much of it
has been set in foreign parts and that every important novelist
has managed to write at least one expatriate novel. Since Na-.
thaniel Hawthorne was so congenitally house-bound, so thoroughly identified with his region in almost everything else he
wrote, he seems to provide the *a fortiori* case. Certainly *The
Marble Faun* stands at some remove from his three other major
novels, which came so close together some years before and

constitute a kind of New England trilogy. Hawthorne's last completed work is by far his longest one, and he seems to have exercised an author's privilege in considering it his best. Henry James called that judgment into question, in his life of Hawthorne, while conceding that *The Marble Faun* was then probably the most popular of the four novels. James's revaluation may have had some effect on its declining status in the canon, as well as on the gradual heightening of critical interest in *The Scarlet Letter* and *The House of the Seven Gables,* if not in *The Blithedale Romance.* But *The Marble Faun* was destined from the first to date more than the others, because it was more dependent on changing tastes and literary conventions. Always a self-conscious writer, Hawthorne was never more so than here; yet the result is uncharacteristic because, so far from home and unsure of his ground, he had to reinforce the delicate outlines of an ambitious plan by drawing heavily on bookish precedent and unassimilated tradition.

In the typical odyssey of the man of letters, Italy is cast in the role of siren, whose dalliances have been celebrated by Goethe's elegies, Byron's declamations, and countless other poetic tributes. The special attractions that beckoned American writers and artists seeking to fulfil their "dream of Arcadia"—especially that form of nostalgia which could be diagnosed as "Rome-sickness" —have been chronicled by Van Wyck Brooks.[1] Historic and aesthetic factors combined to make "the Pictorial Land"[2] a brilliantly ominous backdrop for the intrigues of Gothic romance, and Hawthorne had made an earlier entry into this storybook realm through the poisonous garden of "Rappaccini's Daughter." For a novel with a Roman setting, his most influential exemplar was Madame de Staël's *Corinne, ou l'Italie,* with its gifted and ill-fated heroine, its cosmopolitan passions, its philosophic discourses, rhapsodic improvisations, and educational tours of the principal monuments. Margaret Fuller, during the

Roman phase of her career, came to be regarded as a New England Corinne; and Hawthorne himself explicitly imitates a gesture from Madame de Staël when the lovers look for reflections in the Fountain of Trevi. He justified his choice of terrain in a preface, which—like his other prefaces—is also a plea for imaginative license and, more specifically, an apologia for his chosen genre, the romance, as opposed to the usual novel of manners or social observation. The crucial paragraph has been frequently quoted; but, since Hawthorne is never more elusive or ironic than when he claims to be stating his intentions, perhaps it may be quoted once again:

> Italy, as the site of his Romance, was chiefly valuable to him as affording a sort of poetic or fairy precinct, where actualities would not be so terribly insisted upon as they are, and must needs be, in America. No author, without a trial, can conceive of the difficulty of writing a romance about a country where there is no shadow, no antiquity, no mystery, no picturesque and gloomy wrong, nor anything but a commonplace prosperity, in broad and simple daylight, as is happily the case with my dear native land. It will be very long, I trust, before romance-writers may find congenial and easily handled themes, either in the annals of our stalwart republic, or in any characteristic and probable events of our individual lives. Romance and poetry, ivy, lichens, and wall-flowers, need ruin to make them grow.[3]

Our reading of this passage is retrospectively slanted by the underlined and amplified paraphrase in James's critical biography, the famous litany of cultural landmarks whose conspicuous absence made the American scene such unpromising territory for the artist. This may have been a justification for James's decision in favor of what the ivied ruins seemed to promise, the direction pointed by the later Hawthorne and pursued by the early James in "The Last of the Valerii" and

Roderick Hudson. But if we reread Hawthorne's statement in his own context, the key phrase seems to be "without a trial." He had prodigiously tried to overcome the difficulties of which he is complaining; and, though he was never the man to relinquish his qualms, surely it may be said—and James would agree —that Hawthorne succeeded. Elsewhere he would have been the first to admit that he had been preoccupied most of his life with the delineation of shadows. Was there "no picturesque and gloomy wrong" to be discerned in the United States on the very eve of the Civil War? Writing from England where he composed his romance during 1859, basing it upon impressions noted during his previous year in Italy, and caught in the ambiguous position of an American between two worlds, he could only view them both with irony. It was dubious homage to the Old World to repair there in search of the sinister. As for the prosperous actualities of the New World, he had come to terms with them in his Custom House sketch before turning back again into that twilight America whither his European admirers preferred to be led.

He had been at his best in casting a romantic light on the commonplace, or in investing familiar objects with symbolic meanings. Noting down his visit to Arezzo, and to a certain well described by Boccaccio, he expressed the modest hope that he might be remembered for his description of the town pump at Salem.[4] He had tried and would try again, without success, to work out one or another of the related ancestral themes that had been haunting him during his English sojourn. In America the limitations of his material had stimulated him in the techniques of enhancement; in England there was so much paraphernalia, already so enhanced and overfraught with the trappings of association, that he found little or nothing to add. The traditional richness of the symbols seemed to keep him from making effective use of them. He was not near enough to his subject matter, as he had been in America, or far enough from it, as he might be in Italy. There he was too far away, Henry James would feel, and that feeling was doubly significant: "Hawthorne forfeited a precious advantage in ceasing to tread his native soil."[5] Many years afterward, generalizing on *William Wetmore Story and His Friends,* James faced the problem more squarely with a sort of retraction: "the 'picturesque' subject, for literary art, has by no means all its advantage in the picturesque country."[6] Hawthorne really could not be expected to improve upon the coloring of his Italianate scenery. Rather, he exploited it as a richly contrasting background for those somber characterizations which he was better qualified to portray.

Mrs. Hawthorne, in editing *Passages from the French and Italian Note-Books,* parenthetically affirmed that her late husband's insight "was only equalled by his outsight."[7] Such wifely praise is well merited by the *American Notebooks;* and the two capacities are still commensurate, if somewhat bedimmed, in the *English Notebooks.* As for the continental notebooks, we must await Norman Pearson's complete edition in order to judge them fairly. Yet it might be observed that the *Passages* highlight the hard-headed Yankee facets of Hawthorne's character, whereas his native journal disclosed more of the dreamy Transcendentalist. Travel abroad brings out common traits in dissimilar compatriots, and Hawthorne as a tourist stood closer to Mark Twain than to a cultivated European who might have crossed the Alps for his *Italienische Reise.* Though Hawthorne was more the shy puritan than the bumptious philistine, he remained painfully conscious of his provinciality. He did not guy the guides with Mark Twain's stock question, "Is he dead?" But Rome, as a city of tombs and vaults, the graveyard of past cultures, ministered congenially to his lifelong preoccupation with death. *The Innocents Abroad* could even find laughing matter in the grisly cemetery of the Capuchin Convent, elaborately decorated with human bones. Touring the adjacent church a decade before, Hawthorne had happened on one of those physical details which he cherished for their emblematic potentialities: a monk, laid out for burial, suddenly bleeding. Hawthorne had been in Rome less than a month, and here was a whole chapter for his new book: "The Dead Capuchin." Here was the body, then, but where was the mystery?

It seems to have been one of Sophia Hawthorne's editorial principles to omit the main passages that had been worked into *The Marble Faun,* so that her published text does not allow us much opportunity to watch Hawthorne at work. However, we can see him noting down such locations as the Virgin's Shrine, storing up such encounters as the buffalo calf on the Appian Way, and entertaining such fancies as the possibility of lodging in one of the papal tombs at Saint Peter's. We can even learn that his hero's tower room, presided over by the skull in the adjoining oratory, was actually the bedchamber of his fragile daughter, Una. The place that lends its landscape to the sub-title of *The Marble Faun, or The Romance of Monte Beni* is closely modeled on the antique Villa Montauto rented by the Hawthornes for two summer months at Bellosguardo, not far above Florence, where Fenimore Cooper had been—and Henry James was to be—among the various American sojourners. Now habitations are not merely backgrounds but often the very matrix of Hawthorne's fictions, which sustain a cloistered indoor atmosphere occasionally relieved by a breath of fresh air. *The Marble Faun,* though refreshed by a series of sylvan interludes in Tuscany and the Campagna, is set for the most part in the macabre and malarial capital. Hawthorne's strongly ambivalent attitude toward "the sad embrace"[8] of Rome is tensely poised in the remarkable two-page sentence at the beginning of Chapter XXXVI. Spending two successive carnival seasons there, he reacted to the first with all his inherent austerity and participated rather more in the frolic spirit of the second one, as another strategic chapter attests.

Good American husband that he was, he had conscientiously accompanied his "artistic" wife around the monuments and through the galleries, and he had not neglected to do his sight-seeing homework in Murray's guidebooks. This was scarcely an adequate preparation, as he must in his modesty have realized, for acting as *cicerone* to a wide circle of Anglo-American readers eager to wander vicariously among the masterpieces. For all his antiquarian sympathies, he was very easily put off by the faded or encrusted state of so many primitive paintings—a response which, in his wife's estimation, simply asserted his own perfectionism. Actually, philistinism can seldom have ventured farther than the suggestion, in *The Marble Faun,* that it would be charitable to cover the frescoes of Giotto and Cimabue with whitewash.[9] Yet fascination was not always overmastered by inhibition when Hawthorne confronted the female nude, in spite of Sophia's retroactive blue pencil. He lingered nervously over the sensual impenitence of Titian's Magdalen before he concluded, on a note of virtual self-reproof, "Titian must have been a very good-for-nothing old man."[10] Most of the living artists he knew were Americans, and he knew them better as fellow New Englanders than as artists. Hiram Powers, the ingenious Vermonter in Florence, delighted him because he did not "put his life wholly into marble."[11] William Story, the affable dean of the American colony in Rome, had originally turned from law to sculpture in order to execute a statue of his eminent father, Mr. Justice Story of Massachusetts. And when Hawthorne sat for his own bust, the sculptress was Miss Maria Louisa Lander of where else but Salem?

Under the circumstances, it was extremely bold of him to attempt anything in the nature of a *Künstlerroman,* and altogether unlikely that such an attempt would be highly seasoned by

Scènes de la Vie de Bohême. Though his artists have their
studios which reflect their respective imaginations, their initial
meeting place is a museum, the Campidoglio; and their further
walks and talks together have somewhat the aspect of guided
tours. Between the travelogue and the story, however, a neutral
distance is kept; otherwise the characters would be dwarfed by
the age and scope of their environment. The pathos of their
individual strivings, as contrasted with the impersonal chill of
the museum-world through which they stray, is emphasized in
such chapters as "The Emptiness of Picture Galleries." Except
for the beggars, the street urchins, and the omnipresent and
invisible clergy, we meet few Roman citizens. Nothing beyond
the occasional glimpse of a French uniform tells us—and Hawthorne himself seems totally unconcerned—that we are standing
on the threshold of the Risorgimento. For nineteenth-century
Americans, a trip to Europe was bound to become a return to
the past—classical, medieval, or Renaissance in Rome, but never
quite modern. The visual analogue for Hawthorne's art was
that which Washington Irving had cultivated: the sketchbook
of the traveling amateur draftsman, whose water colors owe
much of their gentle charm to the unfamiliar scenes they catch
in so artlessly personal a fashion. Fortunately the vistas now
opening up before Hawthorne had been familiarized through
many a reproduction or set piece, so that he could more or less
take their literal contours for granted and concentrate upon his
psychological evocations.

In his preface he apologizes for having made fictional use of
certain actual sculptures by his artist-friends. Such an acknowl-
edgment failed to allay the wrath of Arnold Schönberg when
Thomas Mann ascribed the twelve-tone system of musical composition to the demonic hero of *Doctor Faustus.* But Hawthorne's American sculptor, Kenyon, seems a mild and marginal
figure by comparison, an observer-spokesman who is clearly

related to the artist-inventors of Hawthorne's tales, endowed with similar powers of cold penetration, but not so obsessive and more urbane. His relation to the title character is that of counselor if not confidant, and there are moments between them that remind us of the all but psychoanalytic interchange between Chillingworth and Dimmesdale in *The Scarlet Letter*. In speaking of a title role, we are stretching a point, since the marble faun itself can be no other than that of Praxiteles, from which the narrative takes its Capitoline departure. The faun-like human being, Donatello, linked by the Florentine sculptor's name with his boyish David, is unquestionably a creature of flesh and blood. What comes into question—what gives the book its more didactic English title, *Transformation*—would seem to be his hard-won acquisition of a soul. The author of *A Wonder-Book* and *Tanglewood Tales* looked upon "this race of fauns" as "the most delightful of all that antiquity imagined."[12] A story "with all sorts of fun and pathos in it" might be contrived about their intermingling with humanity. Hawthorne could be trusted to moderate the fun; and it remains a striking thought that he chose, in the very year of Darwin's *Origin of Species*, to celebrate "a natural . . . link betwixt human and brute life, with something of a divine character intermingled."[13]

From the cerebral Hawthorne, attracted by the very paganism of the theme, Italy seems to have compelled a belated respect for the animal side of human nature—not in its uneasy coexistence with the spiritual side, but in a pristine purity of its own. Donatello, to the woman who loves him, seems "a creature in a state of development less than what mankind has attained, yet the more perfect within itself for that very deficiency."[14] Strange, sweet, playful, friendly, rustic, wild, charming—Hawthorne's epithets make quite a pet of him. He may be a throwback to the childhood of the race, an atavism from the Golden Age, when all men were spontaneously happy because they lived in uncorrupted harmony with nature. Hence he has the gift, or has had it before his Roman exposure, of conversing with the animals. His lineage, both natural and supernatural, can be traced back to the Greek migrations, and also can be linked with a local Tuscan myth sadly involving a tutelary naiad. The ambiguity of his whole situation is invisibly symbolized by a train of speculation to which Hawthorne keeps coyly returning until the last sentence: whether or not Donatello's curly hair conceals the hirsute and pointed ears of a faun, not to mention whether he possesses "a certain caudal appendage."[15] This tricksy sprite coalesces with the image of a contemporary who is hardly less vague, the Count of Monte Beni, a young Italian aristocrat who does not know his own age and has never read Dante. The romance about him was inspired, so the narrator informs us, not so much by the Marble Faun of Praxiteles as by Kenyon's unfinished clay model of Donatello's head, with its groping hints of his perplexity, struggle, and change.

For his pair of heroines, Hawthorne chose to reincarnate an old antithesis: blond for innocence and brunette for experience, as in *The Blithedale Romance*. Hilda, like the fair Priscilla, would have been called a White Lily by D. H. Lawrence; but where Priscilla's feelings were externalized, Hilda's are projected from within. "Her womanhood is of the ethereal type, and incompatible with any shadow of darkness or evil," says her fellow American admirer Kenyon, who has modeled a replica of her hand—even as Hiram Powers had of his little daughter's— and has put her into plaster as maidenhood gathering a snowdrop.[16] Hilda is an orphan whose transparent virginity seems to have won her the unmolested freedom of the menacing city. She has not ceased to be, as Hawthorne does not tire of reminding us, a daughter of the Puritans. It is paradoxical and yet not inappropriate that she practices her own cult of the Virgin,

tending the lamp at a shrine which adjoins her studio amid
the doves on the roof top. Her pursuit of the arts, as Hawthorne
intimates that a woman's should be, is sensitively appreciative
rather than strikingly original; in short, her skill is that of a
professional copyist. In vivid contradistinction to her, the other
heroine, who comes as close as any character to being the real
protagonist of the drama, is not only an ambitious painter but
seems to specialize in forceful depictions of "the idea of woman,
acting the part of a revengeful mischief towards man."[17] Over
and over again the subjects of her sketches compulsively re-enact
the battle of the sexes, which invariably culminates in the grim
triumph of aggressive feminism: Jael assassinating Sisera, Judith
exulting over Holofernes, Salome with the head of John the
Baptist.

Miriam Schaefer's family name accords her a doubtful advantage over the other characters, since it proves to be an assumed
one. She proves to be indeed the darkest of Hawthorne's dark
ladies. Though her fate is not so blankly tragic as Zenobia's at
Blithedale, her origin is considerably more mysterious and her
allure is appreciably more magnetic. Her appearance seems to
have been suggested to Hawthorne by the sight of a raven-
haired Jewess at a Lord Mayor's banquet in London some years
before. Though the precise details of Miriam's identity continue to be shrouded in secrecy, she is evidently the hyphenated
child of an Anglo-Jewish mother married into a decadent line
of Italian nobility. Whenever the veil is lifted a little, the
breath of a scandal is felt; but it is wafted to us so delicately
that we can never be sure how far she has been compromised
by it. She has experienced sorrow and suffering, obviously; but
to what extent has she experienced sin? Can she be innocently
involved and not be contaminated? Hawthorne exhibits his
usual compunctions in equivocating between fatality and the
responsible will. Artistic allusion conspires with historical innu-

endo to associate Miriam with the favorite Reniassance heroine
of the Romantics, Beatrice Cenci, and with the dark doom of incest and parricide related by Stendhal and dramatized by Shelley.
Historically speaking, it would now seem that the veritable
Beatrice was less victimized by her father and more compliant
in his murder than the notorious tale would have had it. Yet
her tearful visage, as Henry Murray points out, "had been
assimilated to the most moving theme of the current mythology
of the heart, that of *abused female innocence.*"[18]

Her portrait by Guido Reni in the Palazzo Barberini, which
was rumored to have been painted shortly before her execution,
was the most widely admired and the most commonly repro-
duced picture of the day. Pilgrims sought it out with a curiosity
which could only be compared to the subsequent and slightly
more sophisticated vogue of that *femme fatale,* the "Mona Lisa."
"The History is written in the Painting," Charles Dickens had
responded to it in his *Pictures from Italy,* "written, in the dying
girl's face, by Nature's own hand."[19] Miriam and Kenyon
might well debate the merits of Guido's "Battle between Saint
Michael and Satan," but his Beatrice seemed beyond the reach
of mere art. She had dominated a recognition scene in Herman
Melville's *Pierre,* and Melville eagerly procured a copy for himself at Rome in 1857. Even Henry James, though cognizant of
the disillusioning afterthoughts, could meditate on "our prolonged sentimental consumption of the tenderest morsel, as we
have mostly felt it, in all pictorial portraiture."[20] It is not surprising, then, that Reni's Beatrice become a talisman for Hawthorne, or that his recurrent adjective for her was "magical."
Her influence was present already in the pathetic and poisoned
decoy, Beatrice Rappaccini. In the notebooks, the expected
tribute is duly paid: "It is the most profoundly wrought picture
in the world."[21] Yet Hawthorne, who repeatedly came back to
see it, was shrewd enough to wonder whether the canvas itself

would exert the same appeal if the beholder were unaware of the extraneous associations. Nevertheless, it is Hilda's supreme accomplishment, in *The Marble Faun*, to be able to copy the original and to capture all its nuances. More than artistry, her accomplishment presupposes affinity.

"She is a fallen angel," Hilda comments on Beatrice, "—fallen, and yet sinless." Miriam cannot let so naïve a contradiction pass by her unchallenged; and when she reminds Hilda of Beatrice's tragedy, Hilda becomes implacably severe in her condemnation: "Yes, yes; it was terrible guilt, an inexpiable crime, and she feels it to be so."[22] Thus the conversation leads us back, as all occasions do, to Miriam's secret. This has its malign personification in her model, the villain of the piece, whose speeches are well-night inaudible and whose misdeeds are never quite pinned down. Visually, he is picturesqueness itself, "dark, bushy-bearded, wild of aspect and attire," ready to pose as saint or sinner without revealing his own personality.[23] Hawthorne presents him enveloped in "Subterranean Reminiscences" and heralded by a legend of the catacombs not unlike the motif of the Wandering Jew: a man-demon restlessly seeking a companion in misery.[24] Miriam is shadowed by her specter, is presumably blackmailed by his obscure claim upon her, and is threatened with an ostracism from which the ardent Donatello suddenly acts to deliver her. In the one decisive action of the plot, prompted by her glance of mute entreaty, Donatello seizes upon an opportune moment to plunge her evil genius down to his death—and afterward to his startling final emergence as the dead Capuchin, whose corpse turns out to be the accusing symbol of their crime. The height from which he has been thrown is the Tarpeian Rock above the Forum, whence the ancient criminals were dispatched. As for the timeless depth it overhangs, Miriam has just declared to Hilda: "The chasm was merely one of the orifices of that pit of blackness that lies beneath us, everywhere."[25]

The deed, from which the doers recoil in spontaneous horror, has had an unseen and half-unseeing witness; and that is where Hawthorne, whose habitual stance is the aloofness of the detached onlooker, comes forward to score a Dostoevskian point. "While there is a single guilty person in the universe," so Hilda reproaches Miriam, "each innocent one must feel his innocence tortured by that guilt."[26] Miriam, though she has not raised a hand, is implicated as Donatello's accomplice. Hilda, who unwittingly found herself looking on and registering the shock, feels caught up in a chain of complicity which runs around the world. Consequently it is her own self-portrait that she beholds in the pictured and copied lineaments of Beatrice Cenci, and the resemblance is generally remarked and variously interpreted when Signor Panini depicts her as "Innocence, dying of a blood-stain."[27] In virginal discovery of evil, as a lone sufferer for the sin of another, she wanders through the labyrinth distraught until she finds herself at the ultimate center, "The World's Cathedral," Saint Peter's, where she paradoxically endeavors to ease her Puritan conscience within the confessional.[28] This episode would be even more extraordinary if it had not been anticipated by a novel which Hawthorne may well have read, Charlotte Brontë's Villette. There the issue is more centrally the romance between a Protestant heroine and a Catholic hero. Here it is more tangential, since Hilda cannot claim the Church's solace without embracing its doctrines, and her Kenyon will be shocked by the halfway lengths to which she seems willing to go. Yet it serves to discharge the mounting tensions between respect and suspicion which drew Hawthorne to, and repelled him from, the "Altars and Incense" of Roman Catholicism.[29]

The two accomplices seem the less likely couple to have been drawn together. But Donatello has acted to share the burden of Miriam's moral estrangement, and Miriam is more than willing to share the moral responsibility for Donatello's act. Momentarily, during an interlude in the Borghese Gardens, he had shown her his bucolic world; he had set everyone dancing, whereupon her nemesis had interrupted the dance. What seemed to be Arcadia was Eden, after all, whose denizens were foreordained to fall and be expelled. Miriam and Donatello would seem to be bound forever by the serpentine coils of their guilty collusion, and we might expect them to take their further way like Adam and Eve—or like the young groom and bride at the end of "The May-Pole of Merry Mount." Yet Donatello's immediate reaction is to flinch from Miriam's tender advances; when she tests him by laying her hand next to his, he refrains from taking it; thereupon he must leave her and make a penitential retreat to his tower in the Appenines. There his sympathetic visitor and traveling companion is Kenyon, who in turn receives a clandestine visit from Miriam. His reserve has prevented her from confiding in him before, albeit she might have provided more inspiration than Hilda for the smouldering voluptuousness of that tigress-like Cleopatra which he has somehow been sculpting. Now, when Miriam pours out her heart to him, he is able to reassure her of Donatello's love. It is as if the crime had to take place and be fully assimilated before the passion could manifest itself and be consummated. The two experiences are so intertwined that Kenyon arrives at this severe, if tentative, verdict: "Worthy of Death, but not unworthy of Love."[30]

Love, in a Hawthornesque efflorescence, blossoms among the ruins. The lovers are reunited under the blessing of the bronze pontiff who oversees the market place at Perugia; and though they subsequently disappear and reappear in altered guises, Hawthorne leaves their wanderings uncharted to give them privacy for sexual fulfilment. This, too, is marked by its symbolic statue—a fallen goddess, if not an angel, recovered from underground, pieced together, and hailed as the long lost and vastly more beautiful original of the Venus di Medici. Hawthorne's notebooks again contain an account of the excavations that gave him the notion, as well as an account of his prolonged flirtation with the Venus di Medici herself, standing "in chaste and naked grace" at the Uffizi in Florence: "I felt a kind of tenderness for her; an affection, not as if she were one woman, but all womanhood in one."[31] So bemused was he by his morning communion with her that, after spending his evening with the Brownings, he could not help concluding his daily notation: "The Venus di Medici has a dimple on her chin."[32] Melville, paying his respects in a lecture on "Statuary in Rome," had reminiscently likened her modest pose to that of the native maidens he had seen in the Typee Valley.[33] In conferring an extra dimension upon his characters by associating them with counterparts in the sphere of art, Hawthorne resembles Proust. To be sure, his range is much more limited; his taste is insecure, to say the least. His preference for sculpture, rather than painting, lends his creations a tangible quality which they might otherwise lack. It also favors a marble whiteness over the colors on the painter's palette. He was emphatic in his objections to the flesh-tinted statues of John Gibson.

Hawthorne may or may not have read Lessing's *Laokoon*, albeit the snake-entangled group at the Vatican could not but appeal to his allegorical instincts. Kenyon's aesthetics are not unlike Lessing's, however, when he criticizes the "Dying Gladiator" and remarks that "in any sculptural subject, there should be a moral stand-still, since there must of necessity be a physical one."[34] The approach of *The Marble Faun* is sculptural; the stasis of the ages is upon it; and its movement is reducible to a sequence of standstills or *tableaux vivants*. For a longish novel, it has a small cast: mainly the four characters introduced in the first chapter, plus the model whose protean disguises are not enough to enlarge the *dramatis personae*. Three of the four are artists in some degree and, therefore, primarily spectators: the sculptor, the painter, the copyist. The fourth, idly posing for them, would seem to be the most passive of all; yet his quick shove is the single burst of activity; and his psychic transformation could be rendered as a metamorphosis in stone. All of them strike attitudes and engage in colloquies: duets, trios, and quartets in varying combinations. The ambulatory pace and unwieldy pageantry put us in the mood for opera—let us say *La Vestale*. The construction of the book displays Hawthorne's neatly symmetrical workmanship. There are fifty chapters, each with its essayistic heading and its topographical shift. The fatal climax occurs betimes in Chapter XVIII, followed by a remorseful withdrawal extending through Chapter XXXV, and completed by an accelerating countermovement toward the center and toward an equilibrium. The total pattern may be roughly divided into three equal sections: the first is melodrama; the second, pastoral; and the third, carnival.

The style is more formal in conversation than in the author's narration, which does not differ much from the whimsical tone and speculative habit of the notebooks. In operatic or Shakespearean fashion, characters apostrophize situations or address themselves in streams of self-consciousness:

> "Be quiet," said Miriam to her own heart, pressing her hand hard upon it. "Why shouldst thou throb now? Hast thou not endured more terrible things than this?"[35]

The second person singular is warranted, here and elsewhere, by the assumption that some speeches have been translated from the Italian. Yet, though she professes to have thrown decorum to the winds, Miriam's heart-to-heart talk with Kenyon about Hilda—presumably in English—leaves something to be desired in the way of untrammeled expressiveness:

"Oh, you are right!" said Miriam; "I never questioned it; though, as I told you, when she cast me off, it severed some few remaining bonds between me and decorous womanhood. But were there anything to forgive, I do forgive her. May you win her virgin heart; for methinks there can be few men in this evil world who are not more unworthy of her than yourself."[36]

It could not be argued that the spoken language sounds much more colloquial in Hawthorne's other writings, and it may be relevant to recall that he himself was noted for taciturnity. Yet, in his own person, he maintained an open and amiable relationship with his reader, whom he was fond of taking by the hand while discursively pointing out the sights, illustrating with anecdotes, and moralizing with symbols. Thus the first page of *The Marble Faun,* among better known statuary, calls attention to a sculptured child between a dove and a snake—an allegory of "the Human Soul, with its choice of Innocence or Evil."[37] A casual fig tree at the side of the road, twisted by the grasp of a clambering grapevine, becomes an object lesson inviting a temperance lecture. Kenyon, who makes this observation on Hawthorne's behalf, is constantly being challenged by Donatello to supply a pat moral for each passing instance. Hence Kenyon plays the moralist at the conclusion: looking back at Donatello's involvement and retribution, he proposes a pair of alternative morals; but they are mutually incompatible, and Hilda is both too hopeful and too reverent to accept either of them.

The second, the theological alternative, has been more commonly accepted by critics. This invokes the Augustinian doctrine of *felix culpa,* the fault that bears a fortunate consequence. In the long run, it may be all for the best that the Faun blundered into his mortal trespass; for it has taught him the ethical basis for distinguishing between good and evil; and, by struggling through that grim education, he has achieved a higher state. Such is the opinion that Miriam naturally holds. Accordingly the book becomes in essence a *psychomachia*, a conflict within the soul; there the Archangel and the Devil pursue their unending fight; and it is fitting that the bust of John Milton can be viewed in Kenyon's studio. "Did Adam fall, that we might ultimately rise to a far loftier paradise than his?"[38] If we retain any doubt, if we follow Lawrence's advice for dealing with Hawthorne and "listen to the diabolic undertone," we should reconsider the prior alternative, which is based on naturalistic premises and opposes a pessimistic heresy to an optimistic orthodoxy, pagan degeneration to Christian regeneration.[39] This entails belief in man as potentially a happy and healthy animal, whose "genial nature" could not but be warped by the serious pressures and complex demands of latter-day living.[40] Such a conception looks forward to the hard primitivism of Nietzsche, rather than backward to the soft primitivism of Rousseau. Though Hawthorne's treatment of sex is ostensibly tepid—as we might expect from a son of the Puritans lately accredited to Queen Victoria—there are Lawrentian implications in the love story he does not tell but insinuates between chapters and behind scenes, which has its subterranean archetype in the buried and rediscovered fragments of Venus.

Conceivably those alternatives might be reconciled by being transposed into modes of twentieth-century thinking. That the Fall should give rise to self-improvement is a hypothesis which parallels Toynbee's theory of Challenge and Response in the growth of cultures. That civilization should be attained at the cost of a certain anguish fits in with the Freudian progression of consciousness from the id to the superego. Hawthorne's hero pays the price for evolving by literally undergoing imprisonment, while Miriam concludes by kneeling in prayer—significantly at the Pantheon, inasmuch as the frame of reference has broadened from the Catholic to the pantheistic. Her honeymoon with Donatello has ended, in the masquerade of a Contadina and Peasant, amid the "polluted flowers" and grotesque confusions of the carnival—a kaleidoscope which Hawthorne cleverly shakes, instead of carefully tracing his patterns to a detailed culmination.[41] His ambiguous ending so mystified readers that he was forced to add an explanatory post-script to the second edition wherein he refrained from explaining his ambiguous postulate. Understandably, he did not feel obliged to unravel everything like Mrs. Radcliffe, and he had gone further than ever before in moving "between the Real and the Fantastic."[42] Yet it had been harder this time to stay on middle ground; he had oscillated between an archaeological reality and an allegorical fantasy; his vision of evil had become so generalized that even James would complain of vagueness. Hawthorne's defense would be Hilda's attack upon "this inclination, which most people have, to explain away the wonder and mystery of everything."[43] And it is through Hilda's eyes, through her sense of wonder, that the final prospect is relayed to us.

Hilda is the precursor, not merely of James's international heroines, but of his private ambassador who discovers that Europe is more entangling than could be foreseen. She has not only shared the guilty knowledge of her two friends' transgression; she has been lured, through her duty of delivering Miriam's packet, into the Palazzo Cenci itself; for even Hilda must go underground, as it were; and during her incarceration, the Virgin's Lamp is extinguished. Hawthorne is loth to account for her temporary disappearance, except by opaque allusions to those clerical auspices which she had once besought and which seem to have the situation well in hand. Inevitably, she and Kenyon are brought together in their mutual loneliness. Homeward bound, she is still linked to the sphere they are leaving through Miriam's bridal gift, the Etruscan bracelet with its seven sepulchral gems. Hawthorne is never more himself than in the nostalgic paragraph where, mingling his sensibilities with hers, he contrasts the "crumbly magnificence" of Rome with the "native homeliness" of her New England village.[44] Easing "the exile's pain," he loses no opportunity to bring the parable home by transatlantic cross-reference: the weather, the vegetation, the sanitation, the housing, the sociability, the wine versus the cider. It is an American who refuses to join in Donatello's improvised bacchanal; it is a less dignified member of our "Gothic race" whose confetti damages the dignity of a Roman Senator's coachman.[45] And it is "An Aesthetic Company," a moonlight ramble of young American artists, which makes the Via Sacra reverberate to the choral strains of "Hail, Columbia!"[46] When Kenyon goes back, the sculpturesque clouds will be his sole art gallery; yet he has seen no spectacle as gorgeous as a sunset in America.[47]

Half a generation later, Roderick Hudson would opt for Europe, where his talent would fizzle out at Rome. His fellow sculptor, the Franco-Italo-American Gloriani, who is a cynic and seems at times a charlatan, would reappear at Paris in *The Ambassadors,* where he would personify the wise maturity of the artist who has intensely lived. If an innocent New World met a corrupting Old World to frame a beginner's formula for James, he could develop the corollaries and vary the complications: a refined example is the adjustment of the Italian prince in *The Golden Bowl,* who is so propitiously named Amerigo. From *Daisy Miller* (1878) to Tennessee Williams' novella, *The Roman Spring of Mrs. Stone* (1950), we could trace the decline in American innocence. In William Styron's recent and powerful novel, *Set This House on Fire,* the agent of corruption is an American; the Italian peasants are the true innocents; and a Hollywood company has appropriately been producing a film about Beatrice Cenci. Hawthorne, almost exactly a century before, intervened none too soon in repatriating his two expatriates; and his own return journey across the Atlantic took place not long after he had finished his romance. His four remaining years were not truly productive, doubtless for a complication of reasons. One of them may have been that what James suggestively calls the apple of Europe had turned—even more suggestively—into a "Borgia cup."[48] At all events, though *The Marble Faun* may not be as compact or controlled as Hawthorne's former successes, there are moments when it reaches farther or plunges deeper. His horizons opened late in life; but it must have been a great satisfaction, for the contriver of "Drowne's Wooden Image" or "The Snow Image," to reshape his fancies in classic marble.

Edward H. Davidson

The

Unfinished

Romances

B ETWEEN 1858 and 1864, Hawthorne tried to write four novels. Two of these he tentatively called "Romances of England" and in their published form were afterward titled *The Ancestral Footstep* and *Doctor Grimshawe's Secret.* They were intended to trace the narrative of a young American who comes on a trip to England and half-whimsically, half-seriously, seeks to locate the place from which his ancestors had emigrated nearly three hundred years earlier. This youthful traveler has various adventures; he is waylaid and beaten and taken to a charitable home for twelve indigent men; upon recovering his strength, he wanders about the countryside and is particularly drawn to an old castle about which there is a strange legend. Just three hundred years ago, a young man had been expelled from the house and, on leaving, had impressed the indelible print of a bloody footstep at an entrance. The present owner of the estate invites the traveler to pay him a visit. Not long after his arrival, the American is drugged and imprisoned in an underground dungeon where he meets an old and mysteriously concealed man. There Hawthorne ended the narrative; we never know what finally happened.

One of the interests of this Romance of England in its several versions is that it depended almost exclusively on Hawthorne's own experience as consul to Liverpool. Hawthorne had spent many days traveling about the English countryside, inspecting Elizabethan manor houses, peering at gravestones in a half-humorous attempt to find the name of an ancestor buried in English soil, and keeping a voluminous notebook in which these manifold impressions were stored. He was toying with two themes for that romance he hoped to write once he should be free of the consulate: one was the meeting and clash of two cultures, that of the Old with that of the New World. Indeed, he saw himself as a representative American, strong in his resolve to keep his native ideas intact and yet feeling the teasing lure of English costumes, English charm, English history; thus the Romance of England, in whatever dishevelment it remains, has a strong personal and autobiographical tone. The other theme was quite different. During the four years Hawthorne spent by the grimy Liverpool wharves, he found himself continually besieged by indigent and foolish Americans who had such fantastic notions as seeking an interview with Queen Victoria, or discovering long-lost documents attesting to claims to an English barony and wealth, or, as with the pathetic Delia Bacon, opening a grave in Stratford and there finding proof that Shakespeare had not written the plays. The theme might allow Hawthorne to write a wry or savage commentary on Americans who wished to abandon their native land and culture. Despite the numerous experimental studies and three long drafts in which Hawthorne tried to set in order the narrative and the characters for the Romance of England, he never brought the two versions, *The Ancestral Footstep* and *Doctor Grimshawe's Secret*, to a conclusion.

Hawthorne abandoned his projected romance just as the guns of the Civil War were sounding in the spring of 1861. The war brought him back to a tale he had heard nearly ten years before from Henry Thoreau. It seemed that sometime during the years of the American Revolution there had lived in Hawthorne's own house, The Wayside in Concord, a young man who thought he would never die. This had been all that Thoreau had known about the deluded youth, but it was enough to set Hawthorne thinking, especially in 1861 and on into 1862 when men seemed to lose their heads in the sheer joy of battle. The tenuous parallels between the Civil War and the Revolutionary War might allow him to write a fable for his own times. He first considered a young man whose aims would be so noble that he would be set apart from the cruelties and madness of the present but who would, quite without his willing, be forced to take a part in the conflict and slowly, steadily, lose his purpose and become, at the last, even contemptible. This "Romance of Immortality," as Hawthorne called it, went through numerous stages, experimental sketches, and large drafts, and was never finished. The Civil War was too pressing to allow Hawthorne the leisure and quiet he needed; his finances were being drained in the necessary expenses for a growing family, and his health began to worsen. By the opening of 1863, he was showing the effects of a strange illness which baffled Dr. Oliver Wendell Holmes. In the spring of that year, he took a journey to Washington and to the Virginia countryside in order to see for himself the war which he recorded in his essay "Chiefly about War Matters"; and in that same year, he published under the title *Our Old Home* a series of essays on his travels through and his impressions of England—almost the very stuff which had failed him in the Romance of England. Even so, Hawthorne was haunted by his failure to deal with the young man of Concord who thought he might live forever; as he pressed on and tried to bring the narrative to a conclusion, he oscillated between a vague admiration and an outright contempt for the youthful experimenter in elixirs of life. When he finally put aside the large pile of manuscript later to be known as *Septimius Felton*, he had written many thousands of words and had accomplished nothing.

Yet, in the last months of his life, from the autumn of 1863 to the opening of 1864, Hawthorne tried again to write a Romance of Immortality. Instead of a youth who would lose his high aims in mere self-satisfaction, he created a wise old man, named Dr. Dolliver, who wanted to live beyond the normal term of years in order to see a granddaughter grow to young womanhood. Hardly had Hawthorne written three segments of this story than he died in May, 1864. The opening chapter of this last abortive romance lay on his coffin during the funeral in Concord.

II

In *The Marble Faun*, written just at the beginning of this final phase of his career, one can see that Hawthorne was beginning to sacrifice the real for the conceptual world and that, to an increasing extent as the last years showed, he was adrift in his own artistic speculations. *The Marble Faun*, with its dreamy discourses on art, its hazy evocations of history stretching from the earliest myths to the present day, and its misty recollections of crimes buried deep in the accumulated waste of centuries, suggests that Hawthorne was more and more posing a set of speculative abstractions against the facts of daily, commonplace existence. This tendency resulted in a loss of immediate and felt particularization, which one can see played out in the relation of Miriam to her model: the real theme of revenge is made to illustrate a conceptual argument concerning the ever-pervasive character of evil in the world. An incident of dramatic importance when Donatello throws the model from the Tarpeian Rock—an occasion when personal morality is able to cast doubt on the sanctity of human life—serves the cause of an antecedent design; that design is nothing less than a principle regarding human guilt and infamy which Hawthorne had decided long before the incident had actually taken place. In the end, therefore, the incident sacrifices the reality of its action and reduces the pain and suffering the sinners are meant to feel. The curious resolution of that pain and degradation is the moment Miriam and Donatello stand before the body of the model, and "a little stream of blood" oozes "from the dead man's nostrils": the characters live only to serve the conceptual argument which brought them into being.

In these last writings, the major burden is that of posing the real and the conceptual dimensions of life, between, that is, what a character is actually doing and what Hawthorne, the writer, meant to show in the behavior of that character. The meditative asides, the reminders, and the long conjectures which fill so many manuscript pages of these last writings—all deal with the central problem of Romance: it is the attempt to deal generally and conceptually with human experience and to reach conclusions about experience without first being able to particularize the living details which give rise to that experience. In the preceding years of great accomplishment, Hawthorne had already discovered and clearly organized in his mind those elements and sources of experience from which a conceptual argument might be derived: in the long "Custom-House" chapter prefatory to *The Scarlet Letter,* we are given a clear disclosure of the working of Hawthorne's imagination as it moved from the dense world of men, of piles of cargo, of the desultory life of Salem, and of the carved eagle atop the building to the second floor of the custom house, the discovery of Surveyor Pue's papers and the letter itself, and, finally, the moonlit speculations which resolved all disparities and virtually empowered Hawthorne to write the romance as if he were moved by his own imaginative energy.

In quite extraordinary ways, Hawthorne was capable of bringing great theoretical and imaginative force to bear upon his art; but the force had to be mustered and resolved before the workmanship, the actual composition of sentences, had begun. The speed with which he wrote his four major novels testifies to the planning, the power of thought, and the sheer imaginative dexterity which were his when he was at his best. The solidity of each novel's argument, the quite resolute detailing of the ambiguous behavior of men and women, and the clarity of design—all show that Hawthorne's mind, for all its distrust of empty and formal abstractions, moved in a range of speculation which we rightly call moral and philosophical. The true imaginative force Hawthorne brought to his art was in bridging the speculative distance between the real and the abstract, between the commonplace and the conceptualized, and between the trivial and the grand, even the divine; it was a power both of devising an abstract moral idea of experience and of particularizing just those elements and just those human beings which would make that idea vivid and meaningful. In these last romances Hawthorne seems to be, in each of the four fragments, only at the beginning of that inquiry which, in the major writings, had been accomplished before the action got under way.

His growing incapacity to mediate between these disparate qualities of life, between, that is, life as it is daily lived and life as it is truly known in experience, brought Hawthorne sharply against the theory of romance he had set forth in the prefaces to *The House of the Seven Gables* and *The Marble Faun*. It was not so much a systematic theory as it was a program for imaginative movement between the commonplaces of this known world and the intangible, inscrutable activity of human thought. The pivot for these motions was what he called the "central idea" or the "moral center" of a novel which, despite the vagaries of plot and the inconsistent behavior of men and women, would hold the novel as though by "the vertebrae of the back-bone."[1] When he was not able to specify what this central idea ought to be—whether the American traveler in England should be lured into subservience to England's charm or remain stalwartly American; whether the experimenter in elixirs of life should be high- or low-minded—then Hawthorne had to stop, retrace his steps, and try to set down a satisfactory, if provisional, statement of his "moral." In these last romances, the warnings that he must resolve this initial premise become sharper as the pages of manuscript increase. "I have not yet struck the true key-note of this Romance," he remarks in *The Ancestral Footstep*, "and until I do, and unless I do, I shall write nothing but tediousness and nonsense. I do not wish it to be a picture of life, but a Romance, grim, grotesque, quaint. . . . If I could but write one central scene in this vein, all the rest of the Romance would readily arrange itself around that nucleus."[2] In *Doctor Grimshawe's Secret*, he warns himself: "The narrative must be pitched in such a tone, and enveloped in such an atmosphere, that improbable things shall

147

be accepted; and yet there must be a certain quality of homely, common life diffused through it, so that the reader shall feel a warmth in it."[3] And as his troubles deepened in *Septimius Felton,* he noted sadly: "I find myself dealing with problems and awful subjects, which I but partly succeed in putting aside."[4]

These are indications not so much that a writer is having trouble with his daily stint of work as that a lifetime's practice in the craft of fiction is breaking down. A writer like Hawthorne may suffer from too great a moral and imaginative sophistication and thereby come to have contempt for the very workmanship which had brought him his earlier success. The breakdown came, therefore, first, because of a method of composition which had served Hawthorne very well throughout his whole career; secondly, because of a method of characterization; and thirdly, because of this rift between real and conceptualized experience—a rift which widened perilously and then disastrously as these last years moved on. We might take these matters in order.

However effectively Hawthorne had thought about and had resolved in his own mind the action for one of his major romances—he brooded for more than a dozen years on the woman who wore a red letter *A* on the front of her gown— there was, nonetheless, a considerable range of improvisation, of guessing and conjecturing, of trial and supposition in Haw-thorne's craft of writing. On first reading the meditative asides in *Doctor Grimshawe's Secret,* one is struck by the apparently hit-or-miss method of planning and workmanship; yet it is not the improvisation of a man who does not know quite where he is going. It is the craft and practice of an artist who knows that life is touched, not forced, that the meaning of an action may lie in the power of the questing imagination, and that, quite without anyone's knowing how it comes to pass, the "central idea" may release itself by virtue of its own inner necessity. Nowhere is Hawthorne closer to Melville than in his awareness that both the statement and the form of an idea may inhere in the most jumbled and incongruous exposition of life. It is what he called, in a striking phrase in *The Ancestral Footstep,* "imaginative probability": a moral abstraction, a human action, even a fantastic legend such as the bloody footstep may, Hawthorne noted, "bring its own imaginative probability."[5]

Yet what was that "probability"? One cannot say with respect to these unfinished romances simply because the end of a question in probability rests not on its hypothetical or abstract statement but rather on its fulfilment. Dealing as we must with only portions and fragments, we must be wary of supposing that Hawthorne had in mind a formal and coherent artistic presupposition; the very waywardness of his imagination as he worked through these unfinished drafts testifies both to the improvisation and even to the chance of the moment.

We can suppose, nevertheless, that the central subject of these last romances was, as it had been for *The Marble Faun,* the dependence of modern life, of progress, even of human restoration and redemption, on antecedent decay, corruption, and fall. In order to give this subject a modern cast and to have contemporary implications, Hawthorne must have a modern hero—one freed from the stifling controls of tradition and an eager adventurer into the most daring and effective ideas of his time. Thus the hero of the "Romance of England" would face the rigid ethical system of England's durable past and, all the while admiring it, choose to return to the noisy, troubled world of present-day America. The hero of the "Romance of Immortality," at least in Hawthorne's earliest conjectures, would live at the time of great unrest when the ethical order of the past would virtually disappear; thus the young experimenter would be forced to create a moral system which would serve him and his contemporaries until such a time as the re-establishment of enduring codes of ethics. The subject of the romances would be, accordingly, on the theme of the Fall—the fall of a single traveler and then his restoration or, conversely, the fall of a whole society in the upheaval of war.

Yet the Fall is not, in Hawthorne's fiction, an incident in a man's life or a single event in history; it is a continuing, pervasive condition of nature and of the whole of mankind whereby human beings are permitted, if they are privileged to be enlightened, to understand themselves in their degradation and in their truth. The Fall is, therefore, a crisis in individual comprehension: it allows Goodman Brown, Parson Hooper, Hester Prynne, or Miriam the moment which brings sympathy and profound understanding of themselves and their world, and yet it can leave them perilously adrift in the irresolute domain of their own speculations.

The conceptualized idea of the Fall was, for Hawthorne, both a principle and a method of workmanship. When he got into trouble, as he did so frequently in these fragmentary romances, he tended to improvise on the question of the Fall; he sought to work backward in the lives of his characters; he tried to deepen the "imaginative probability" by construing any number of ancillary events as rightly pertaining to the "central effect" and to the main action. The Fall took him ever toward that antecedent corruption and decay by which he sought to invest his characters with the vivid lineaments of Romance. Indeed, the Fall and the idea of Romance joined: one equaled the other in the logic of imaginative probability.

Nowhere is Hawthorne's habit of improvisation more clearly evident than in his reaching backward in time in order to draw a connection between present living and past life. Over and over again he told the legend of the bloody footstep as though, quite on its own, it would bring up the links between past crime and present-day guilt. He longed for some emblem of buried evil which, festering through centuries, might darken the sunlight of the contemporary world: he conjured up a coffin supposedly full of gold which, on being opened, contained only masses of golden hair into which a woman's body had been transformed. Hidden documents, secret nostrums promising eternal life, relics long buried in the earth or a tomb—these might be the embodiments of man's perpetual sharing in the world's core of evil. Hawthorne had a similar way of studying or "deepening," as he called the method, his characters: generally speaking, he devised his protagonists by going backward. He began with a man or woman at the last and dramatic occasion of the romance; then he worked his way through the earlier life of that person until, as in *Doctor Grimshawe's Secret*, he was at the very beginning of his hero's story. When, as they sometimes did, these two modes of improvisation crossed or overlapped, Hawthorne found himself in a double peril: the Fall had its twin versions, in the world and in individual life, and he was unable to extricate himself from the dilemma.

Yet to accuse Hawthorne of merely playing with one of his central themes and of crudely piling up incidents is to falsify a great writer's craft. The difficulty was not that Hawthorne's method of composition was failing him; indeed, it was the very force of his improvisation which gave him so many directions to follow and so many variations to play on his central theme. The difficulty in these last expositions of the Fall was that Hawthorne's imaginative and critical faculty was being brought to bear, with really too great emphasis, on men and women who were somehow outside or freed from the implications of the very Fall in which they were supposedly involved. This issue brings us to the second supposition concerning Hawthorne's breakdown.

Hawthorne's method of characterization was based in large part on his embodying in human form certain abstract moral truths such as Innocence, Hardness of Heart, Sympathy, Ambition, and so on. Hawthorne was, however, intelligent enough to consider these somewhat shadowy human figures ambiguous for the very reason that an abstraction can never be fully informed with human life. Yet he was enough of a moralist, and a Puritan, to confer on these abstract characters a certain causal power: they were part of a vast and mysterious ethical system in existence long before they were created, and their actions through the course of an invented narrative achieved dignity and power by reason of that antecedent system. In the last romances, however, Hawthorne essayed both to invest his characters with the dark lineaments of the past and yet somehow to bring them into the light of a new day which had none of the implications of that age-old system, or of the Fall. Indeed, the movement of human life might come from individual impulse, as if men were finally freed from the tragic imputation of original sin; experience could now be presented as though it were lived now and as though the new privilege of life were that it could be self-sufficient, self-contained, and self-understanding.

Yet Hawthorne's characters who have enjoyed the most experience are ever afterward prevented from further experiencing. As we meet them in the major writings—Goodman Brown, Parson Hooper, Coverdale, Miriam, and Kenyon—they have already done virtually everything they will do in life, and life has put on them that mark which we the readers are required to interpret. Thus, having passed through experience, they are endowed with the power of rendering experience abstract.

In these fragmentary romances, Hawthorne's characters are not yet privileged to have experience; they have not begun to experience anything but are forced by the unwitting and heedless world of conjecture and possibility to assume a simple, temporary guise and thereby to exclude the many-sided values which might lend them interest and importance. Thus these romances pose the good-heartedness, sometimes the whimsical and stubborn recalcitrance, of self-asserting human beings against a proven, a durable ethical system—against, that is, the Fall. Of one of his heroes, Hawthorne wrote: "young America shall show a promising blossom in him—there shall be a freedom of thought, a carelessness of old forms of things, which shall sometimes . . . contrast oddly with his imaginative conservatism in other respects."[6] Throughout the narrative, Hawthorne sought to cast real doubt on "old forms of things" and to present a modern, self-reliant hero, even a radical man, who would disavow any hold of the past on the present. Yet, when we come upon them, these characters have not lived at all nor have they been granted enough experience and leisure to view the many moral possibilities which face them; they live and move as though they were thrown suddenly and loosely upon the world and must make their way until, in good time, their experience will be sufficient to be turned into an abstraction. "Do not stick at any strangeness or preternaturality," Hawthorne advised himself; "it can be softened down to any extent, however wild in its first conception."[7] In the end, Hawthorne's characters in these unfinished novels cast serious doubt on the validity of an ethical system which had remained unchallenged throughout Hawthorne's literary career; these seekers of ancestral wealth and magical nostrums pursue most high-minded aims and yet, at every turn of the action, countermand the moral principles which allow them their only right to exist.

The meditative asides in *Doctor Grimshawe's Secret* are full of Hawthorne's concern for the appropriateness of events to his characters or, conversely, of the characters to the events. When everything was askew, Hawthorne broke out in self-excoriation: "This wretched man, still. . . . A propensity for drink? A tendency to feed on horse-flesh? A love of toads?

A badge of the mud which has clung to him in the depths of social degradation in which he has been plunged? Surely, there is some possible monster who would precisely fit into this vacant niche. . . . Amen. The thing! The thing?"[8] Sometimes Hawthorne tried to cast experience in the form of a dream, as though the hazy intangibility of dream would mediate between the disparate claims of life; the American traveler in England continually feels himself "in a dream." Hawthorne advised himself quite frequently, "Make all dream-like," as though the very mystery of dream would solve the difficulties which a hero, bent on destroying the fixed ethical system, imposed on the narrative. When, as it so often happened, the hero could not be budged farther than the most sedate, or intransigent, flatness of the commonplace, then Hawthorne again had recourse to the strange and the spectacular—to the bloody footstep, the coffin filled with golden hair, the unraveling of a long-buried mystery; and when they refused to yield their secret and thereby limn the dark underside of human consciousness, Hawthorne felt only contempt for his creatures and broke out into such self-condemnatory remarks as "What unimaginable nonsense!"[9] He had events, more than he could ever employ; he had human beings, some copied from men he had known in England and Italy, others, like the old pensioner of the charity in England, modeled directly on his neighbor Alcott. Experience was there to be lived; yet he had no one fit to live it. On the one side was "the reality," the commonplace existence which is the lot of most of mankind—"the point of view where things are seen in their true lights." On the other side was "the true world . . . like dark-colored experience," "the absolute truth . . . all outside of which [is] delusion."[10] The narrative and the characters must join these two visionary possibilities; when they failed, then the romance failed utterly. The pathos and the tragedy of these last romances is that, as his problems deepened and the confusion worsened, Hawthorne's characters were no longer capable of those discriminations, of tenuous or profound moral judgment, or of those dark, ambiguous probings of their own sensitive minds; they were moral incompetents in a morally incompetent world; and their creator's vengeance on them was dire and terrible.

III

Even in their disarray and confusion, the imaginative habits of a lifetime could not be put aside, and thus the workmanship in these last romances conformed to the artistic deployments of more than thirty years' experience. The main habit of a lifetime's writing was to follow the way of Romance, with its marvelous and supernatural elements: the bulging English notebooks demanded some release of their lode. Yet this impulse met head-on a counter tendency—that peculiarly moral cast of Hawthorne's mind and imagination which saw men and women as having already passed through experience and, therefore, as being proper figures in Romance only to the extent that they were capable of looking on and judging their experience. Thus Hawthorne's power of invention, his "Gothicism," which conjured strange and suggestive events, was forced to yield to the form of the action in which the characters should move and have their being: that "form" was a lifetime's habit of conceptualizing, of thinking abstractly about the otherwise common exigencies of life, and then of adding, as though in an afterthought, the elements and particulars out of which concepts are made. The interest of these posthumous fragments is that, while he had tentatively resolved the marvelous and the moral requirements, Hawthorne was trying to make clear to himself just those minute particularities out of which concepts are made. He kept reminding himself that he must "Specify, specify"; it was not the marvelous and the supernatural which were lacking; it was the simplest investment of the common day, those most ordinary details that writers like Dickens and Trollope made the very stuff of their writings.

In attempting to mediate between the marvelous and the commonplace, Hawthorne effected a curious and almost imperceptible transformation in the heroes of these fragmentary novels. They began as creatures in a world of Romance, whether in Salem, in a midland county in England, or in Hawthorne's own Wayside in Concord during the opening months of the Revolutionary War; and they became more and more recognizable as men in the busy world of the present, of Liverpool, of American military and political life. As he went on tirelessly and painfully, Hawthorne abandoned his theory of romance and tried to write a moral fable for his own time.

It was the protagonist of the projected novel who wrought the change. He was not, even in his beginnings in the preliminary studies, quite that Hawthornesque character who, like Parson Hooper or Coverdale, had lived all the life he would ever know and was, therefore, having experience after the event. This young man was, by contrast, a very modern hero, whose unbending desire for self-satisfaction and for worldly success, both in England and in America, is set grotesquely amid the peaceful relics of a long-past time. Middleton, Etherege, Redclyffe, Septimius Felton, or whatever the provisional name this young man bears is the new middle-class hero of Dickens or Trollope—a young man with no parentage, with meager beginnings, with a rude, canny intelligence, and with an overweening passion to get ahead in the world; yet he is for a time inhabiting a special place in which commercial greed, modern industry, and the moral advantages of poverty do not exist.

The Ancestral Footstep and *Doctor Grimshawe's Secret* required that this commercial hero should come upon a long-established ethical system, be quite unaware of his own moral incompetence, and never understand the havoc he may be causing by reason of his researches into his family history. Yet, instead of setting a self-reliant hero against an intractable ethical system and allowing that system to come under harsh surveillance such as would be the hallmark of the bourgeois romance from Defoe through Dickens to Orwell, Hawthorne made the ethical establishment the final moral authority and thereby tried to effect, in his own words, "a bitter commentary" on the presumption of a man to be a claimant for anything in this shifting and fallible world. Melville had already treated the same theme in *Pierre*: there, of course, "the ambiguities" make the difference, for Melville's hero is an introspective, demon-driven man whose reckless adventure is into dark byways of self-understanding and for whom the outside world of commerce and bourgeois advantage is a ring of horror. The misadventure of Hawthorne's counterpart to Pierre is that Middleton, Etherege, or Redclyffe succumbs to the very lure of greed and vanity he was meant to loathe; the shambles his creator makes of him is one of the most frightening in American literary history.

In the "Romance of Immortality," the premise is reversed. Instead of sending a commercial man across the ocean and having him confront or fall victim to an established ethical system, Hawthorne placed a most moral young man in a time of moral disarray, even collapse. Thus human virtue abides only in this young man, Septimius Felton; he seeks not for wealth or a lost patrimony but for some relief from that most dread burden of existence, namely death: life is not lived long enough, so this young man reasons, and each age repeats the insensate follies of the past. If given a chance, mankind might enter a truly perfectible world wherein the lessons learned in one age of history can be carried over into succeeding ones.

The difficulty was not that the youthful experimenter in elixirs of life lifted himself far beyond society's power to control or subdue, but that Hawthorne tried to draw a metaphysical rebel, one who sought to overthrow everything that sustained society, and in doing so fashioned once again the man with the diabolized heart—the cold-blooded villain whose very excellence of mind and motive is his own and others' doom. Hawthorne might have been devising a bitter commentary on nineteenth-century meliorism, Utilitarianism, and the illusion of earthly progress. Perhaps he was: the Blithedale community of an earlier time revealed the corruption which lies just beneath the ruminative surface of man's most exalted intentions. *Septimius Felton* reveals, more suggestively, that when he had not clearly informed himself of the moral theme for his romance —the fragments reveal a distressing improvisation with almost palpably felt ideas—Hawthorne sought refuge in the most errant inventiveness or "romancing," as if the very piling up of incident and detail would magically solve the difficulty. In the last fragment, *The Dolliver Romance,* Hawthorne tried to invest his hero with all goodness and sweetness of temper; the projected narrative would not risk a protagonist who should become a fool. Here, for the last time in his career, Hawthorne would again have that distinctly moral man whose life is all in the past and who has the power to invest experience with those glowing colors which moral insight can give it.

IV

In these unfinished romances, Hawthorne was less interested in the way the story moved and more concerned with what at every turn the narrative might reveal. This is not to say that in his major writings Hawthorne had not been the allegorist; it is to say that, in the earlier writings, he brought greater imaginative and moral force to the action, to the symbolic design, and to the human beings who should exemplify the subject of the romance than to the subject itself. In the posthumous romances, Hawthorne directed his very considerable imaginative power, not toward disclosures of his ideas in the lives of men and women, but toward the themes themselves; he took them with profound seriousness; he felt oppressed by them; and, when he could not effect that "imaginative probability" in the lives of his characters, he turned on them with ruthlessness and contempt. Thus, when they failed him, as they did every time, Hawthorne made them the victims of a critical intelligence which was scrupulous, exacting, and severe. The scorn he poured out seems, in the following instance, to be directed against a villainous English lord, but it is really against himself: "Something monstrous he must be, yet within nature and romantic probability—hard conditions. A murderer—'twon't do at all. A Mahometan?—pish. . . . A monkey? A Frankenstein? A man of straw? A man without a heart, made by machinery. . . . A cannibal? a ghoul? a vampire. . . . Ye Heavens! A man with a mortal disease— a leprosy?—a eunuch?—a cork leg?—a golden touch?—a dead hand?—a false nose?—a glass eye?—A crossing-sweeper?—a boot-black? . . . 'Twon't do."[11]

The failure of these last romances would be only a minor incident in American literary history and of interest only as a coda to Hawthorne's great career if that failure were merely of biographical and personal moment. The failure is, however, an occasion in the continuous history of the American imagination and bears striking relevance to events in the lives of other writers—Melville, Mark Twain, and Emily Dickinson, to name only a few. The issue was fundamentally that of the artist and his subject. In order to function properly, the artist in American letters had three gaps to fill: through knowledge and experience he must discover the past, the evil in the world, and those people who would illustrate for him the ideas he considers imaginatively probable. He must show his men and women as losing their innocence and then becoming purified by their recognition of, and their triumph over, sin and corruption. And the artist, together with his creations, must emerge with the capacity to deal, if not profoundly, at least cogently with the basic issues of his art.

With almost unvarying frequency we find that American writers of the nineteenth century are marvellously competent to deal with the first two of these provisions; it is the question of art itself which so often defeats or frustrates them. Melville, as an example, moved from the sturdy, muscular world of *Typee* to that of *Moby-Dick*, wherein he cast his vision of life in the form of a metaphysical adventure from the known to the unknown; along the way are the increasing signs that the journey is less reasonable and meaningful as it proceeds. In *Billy Budd*, his final testament, he turned to the merest, the virtually absolute simplicity of the past, of evil, of human life, and disavowed all concern for the artist and his art; *Billy Budd* is the art of an artist who has ceased to exist; he has become only a transcriber. In his last years Hawthorne found himself cut off from his central subject, namely, the peril and the wonder of moral man finding his way to, and his place in, a God-ordained and, therefore, ethical universe. When he set this presumably moral man in a time very close to the present—the English romance would be as contemporary as Hawthorne's own life in Liverpool—Hawthorne became painfully aware of his impotence and unworthiness to understand his hero's destiny.

The difficulty was not really with the subject, or with the times, but with art itself—that continuing and pervasive difficulty with which American writers of the nineteenth century struggled. Hawthorne may not be adequately representative of them all; yet, behind his questions concerning his shadowy characters and their futile dreams of wealth and elixirs of life, he does reveal that the imaginative power he had formerly expended on the display of moral ideas in the lives of men and women was now turning inward and being brought directly to bear on the issue of art and the imagination. The question was not so much, What is the writer doing when he writes?, as it was, What must be the writer's ethical warrant and place in the diffuse and indeterminate life of his world and time? Perhaps the only nineteenth-century American writer who found a satisfactory answer to this question was Henry James, one of whose distinctions was that he admitted his debt to Hawthorne.

It has already been supposed that Hawthorne lived and wrote most vitally between the seemingly opposite imaginative poles of the Romance and the Moral and that, in these last years, the separation between the two became so disastrously widened that Hawthorne presents the uncomely picture of a writer tormented by his unwillingness to yield to or to abandon one or the other. This was not an uncommon situation with writers who were troubled by questions of their art: from Dickens to Mark Twain, to speak most generally, writers either yielded to the demands that their art come fully to the front of their age or that their art dispose the trials of the time behind the mask of irony, even deceit. As an example of the one is Dicken's revised and happy ending to *Great Expectations*, in which Pip and Stella are presumably united at last; as an example of the other is the inconclusive ending of *Huckleberry Finn*, wherein the hero starts for some land of Nowhere.

The parallel is not intended to be a bland witticism in the history of fiction; it is meant to suggest that, through the nineteenth century, there was a pervasive discontinuity in the art of fiction of such proportions that Dicken's Pip could inhabit the Gothic world of Mrs. Radcliffe and that Twain's *Huckleberry Finn* could be the moral picaresque of a heedless Everyman. In either case, this lack of any logical congruence in modern life lies at the moral center of much American, and for that matter English, fiction of the nineteenth century: it was that the artist sought to work through his creations in order to deal cogently, perhaps profoundly, with certain quite well-defined moral issues but that, especially with American writers, the larger problem of art itself eventually triumphed over and submerged those men and women who should have been the living representatives of ethical ideas. Hawthorne ended with the inconclusive commentary of his last years; Mark Twain ended with the ethical abstraction lodged in a title and a question, *What Is Man?*

The case of Hawthorne is not, of course, typical of his generation or of the times which followed his own; yet because he was, as James correctly pointed out, America's first truly serious and comprehensive novelist, he can be taken as an example. Human life had to be brought under the controlling force of certain well-defined, sometimes almost tritely phrased, moral ideas such as were scattered from Hawthorne's earliest journals to the last English and Italian notebooks. These statements were the aftermath of experience already lived: thus Hawthorne's expositions of moral ideas came as a result of very considerable and concentrated thought, not on the particular lives his characters might lead, but rather on abstract forms of living which would somehow lift these transitory lives of men and women above the commonplace requirements of daily existence. Human life did not give dignity and vividness to moral ideas, quite the contrary: moral abstractions bestowed distinction on life. "Imaginative probability" was the infinite calculus of possible relevance between the world's timeless law of good and evil and the energetic, haphazard, and oftentimes futile actions of human beings. Thus the effective moral thought of the writer grants to life more than it deserves to have; even in the fragmentary romances of the final years, we can see these people beginning with the most trivial self-deceits and then be almost mysteriously lifted up by the impelling power a moral idea can bestow on them; and when Hawthorne could not decide what this "central effect" or "moral center" ought to be, the characters disintegrate or become the objects of his scorn.

The failure of any writer is a mystery; it does not help to explain another writer's loss of power and decline. Hawthorne's artistic collapse, even if it should offer backward glances to the time of his great accomplishment, is virtually a self-contained narrative. Yet even in these final years of despair, Hawthorne well knew the state of his mind; he did not have the effrontery to blame the troubled times in which he lived. If he did turn on his half-formed characters the venom of his frustration, he knew that he alone was the cause of his trouble. That trouble was too great for contempt, for pathos, even for understanding. It was fortunate that Hawthorne died before he had said his own last word on it; that word might have been the bitterest of all.

Art and Substance

Hyatt H. Waggoner

Art

and

Belief

. . . And the Poet himself comes
out of his millennial rooms.
With the digger wasp and the
occult Guest of his nights . . .

Blur yourself, clear eye, in which
the man of reason placed his
trust. . . .

—St.-John Perse, _Winds_

H AWTHORNE thought of himself as a poet, though he wrote
only prose, and as a Christian, though after a Unitarian up-
bringing he stayed away from all churches, including that one.
He found Bunyan's understanding of life truer than Emerson's,
but preferred not to commit himself, except in the most general
terms, on the degree of historicity in Bunyan's myth. Paradox
lies at the center of both Hawthorne's art and his belief.

His natural inclination, both in print and out, was to skirt matters of aesthetic and religious belief, or, when unable to do so, to treat them lightly, with a touch of whimsy or self-directed irony, not because they meant little to him, but just because they were close to his heart. He had a large emotional investment in them, but he had not thought them through in any systematic way and did not believe it profitable to try to do so. The light tone was defensive. He was no philosopher or theologian, and he knew it; but he had to write and live in terms of an assumed aesthetic and an assumed theology, and he knew that, too. He found any situation calling for clear commitment in these matters a little embarrassing.

The relationship between art and belief in Hawthorne's work is, therefore, a subject harder to come to terms with and reduce to clarity than it is in the work of most artists. With Emerson, for example, one comes to his poetry knowing pretty well what his beliefs are. Despite his dictum about a foolish consistency, there is a consistency *here*. The problem becomes more difficult only when we try to square some of Emerson's beliefs with others, or the moods and insights of the private man with the statements of the public philosopher. Or Thoreau: we find the beliefs clearly enough set forth in the Journals, and we may follow the process by which they are worked up into the mythopoetic form of *Walden*. But Hawthorne's Notebooks record, with very few exceptions, either *experiences* which might later prove useful or bare *subjects* for possible stories—a week in Maine with his friend Bridge, a visit to a ruined castle in England, the diary of a coroner, life seen as a procession. They do not normally provide us with statements of general belief. Both Emerson and Thoreau, in contrast, sought commitment as strongly as Hawthorne avoided it; and the art of both carries over from their journals a large amount of plain statement of the general truths to which they were firmly committed.

As a writer of fiction, Hawthorne was not free to express

his opinions directly, even if he had wanted to. When he spoke out as intrusive author in his concluding morals, in the fashion of the day, he often undercut his generalizations as he was presenting them. When he had one of his characters say he could not separate the symbol from the idea it symbolized, he might have been, and probably was, thinking of himself. As a "thinker," Hawthorne was, from one point of view, indolent, from another, an artist rather than a philosopher: he followed the implications of images, dwelt on paradox, and was content not to resolve certain mysteries. Ambiguity, far from offending him, seemed to him necessary in any fully honest and complete treatment of experience. Irony, the double mood, was the response of both man and artist to most situations.

He went to the heart of the matter once in *Our Old Home,* commenting on his consular duty to advise Americans in trouble:

> For myself, I had never been in the habit of feeling that I could sufficiently comprehend any particular conjunction of circumstances with human character, to justify me in thrusting in my awkward agency among the intricate and unintelligible machinery of Providence. I have always hated to give advice, especially when there is a prospect of its being taken. It is only one-eyed people who love to advise, or have any spontaneous promptitude of action.

Typically, he attributes his failure to understand the "machinery" of Providence to a personal deficiency, at the same time implying that those who think they have a clearer understanding than he are deluded. At this point the lines of his skepticism and those of his romantic heritage cross to produce an almost total lack of confidence in the vision produced by the clear eye of the man of reason.

Since he felt this way about matters of ordinary experience, it is not surprising that he was even more reticent about his

169

religious beliefs than about most matters close to his heart. Untypically, he once recorded the core of his belief in his English Notebooks:

> God himself cannot compensate us for being born for any period short of eternity. All the misery endured here constitutes a claim for another life, and, still more, *all the happiness*; because all true happiness involves something more than the earth owns, and needs something more than a mortal capacity for the enjoyment of it.

But he almost never spoke about religious matters as such even to his family.

Those who knew him best are unanimous in their testimony that he thought of himself, and inspired others to think of him, as a deeply religious man. But on Sunday mornings in England when Sophia and Una went to church, he and Julian would usually go for a walk. When he thought of himself as a Christian, it was in no light or merely honorific sense; and he imbued in his children a lasting religious concern, but they never were able to say later just what he believed. When, after his death, both his daughters became nuns, one Anglican, one Roman Catholic, they were fulfilling what their father might have seen, with no doubt his usual mixed feelings, as a kind of family destiny. Were they, we can imagine his asking himself, the products of their past, fated to move on from where he had left off in his, and New England's, religious history?

He would not have known, for sure, the answer to this question, or at least would not have wanted to say. But the subject might have appealed to him for a romance. If he had written it, we should have had to look in *it* for the evidence of what he thought; and even after we had made due allowance for the dramatic character of the work, interpretation of the evidence would not be simple. For there were several Hawthornes, among them one he tended to be and one he wanted to be. The one he wanted to be often gave assent to the leading ideas of the age, but neither Hawthorne was much interested in—or, as he felt, equipped to deal with—ideas as such, the abstract propositions that engage us as men of reason. This is the burden of his meaning when he defined himself as a writer of "psychological" romance: a probing of the psyche, the secret inner and most real self as it experiences belief in action. Not the idea of man's total depravity as a theological doctrine, but how one might come to believe it and what the existential consequences would be, this is what really interested him. What would it be like to be a young Goodman Brown? Not what is the "psychology" of Brown in any purely naturalistic, reductive, or behavioristic, modern sense, but what would it be like to *live* a theology? Insofar as a lived theology is expressible only in the terms Hawthorne chose, the dilemma of the would-be analyst of the relations of art and belief in Hawthorne is complete.

In the most revealing statement of his conception of his role as artist, Hawthorne spoke of himself as one dedicated to "burrowing" into the "depths"—of the cavern of the heart, we might have expected him to say, in one of his favorite images; but into the depths of "our common nature," he actually said. The paradox of the dual, or multiple, Hawthorne is here revealed: "common" brings the *essences* back into the picture. In general, and for the most part, Hawthorne thought we could not *know* anything about essence: he concentrated on existence, which he did know, in the most compelling way. But his anti-rationalism was not complete or his skepticism absolute. The darkness in which man found himself was almost, but not quite, total. Some beliefs are warranted and necessary, but not many, and the more precise they are, the less certain.

The rationalist aspect of Hawthorne produced the works

closest to traditional allegory, complete with their implied systems
of moral and religious belief. Meanwhile the Hawthorne of
"the deeper mind" was creating an existential art concerned not
with perfectly controlled but with haunted minds, not with
abstract sin but with personal guilt, not with ideas but with
felt thought, not with things as they are, objectively considered,
in themselves, but things as seen with the mind's eye, preferably
from a distance great enough to blur all but the most significant details.

II

It is not really surprising, therefore, that the religious significance of Hawthorne's work and the personally held beliefs of
the man himself have been so variously described. He has been
labeled a transcendentalist, a Puritan, an essentially orthodox
Christian, a skeptical heir of the Enlightenment, and a naturalist.
With the exception perhaps of the last, each of these descriptions
represents a valid response to some part of the evidence, to that
part that seems to the interpreter, with his special interest and
bias, the crucial part. But bias alone is not sufficient to account
for the variety of the descriptions of Hawthorne's religious
position. Emerson's interpreters presumably have their biases,
too, but no one has ever labeled him religiously orthodox or
denied his individualism in spiritual matters or questioned
his Platonism. Surely, there must be something about Hawthorne and his works which permits, or even encourages,
such disagreements.

The description of him as a transcendentalist is ambiguous
and, at best, not very helpful. Does it mean he was a transcendentalist in Plato's sense, or in Kant's, or in Emerson's? If it
is taken to mean that he believed in a transcendent reality, the
description is true but does not distinguish him from most others

of his age; but if it means that he shared the outlook of the Concord transcendentalist group, its truth is so partial that it need not detain us for long. To be sure, he created Hester, but he also disapproved of her views. (He created Ethan Brand, too, that notably self-reliant character.) He thought Emerson saintly, but he almost never agreed with his wife in her enthusiasm for the new philosophy. He was "transcendental" in his aesthetic theory, so far as he had thought it out, as "Drowne's Wooden Image" and "The Artist of the Beautiful" will show us, and thought of nature as a symbolic language capable, when responded to imaginatively, of revealing a truth and reality perceived through, but lying beyond, the senses. But such matters as these did not occupy much of his attention: again, as he knew, he was no philosopher, and he thought he had no questions to ask of Emerson as a philosopher. From this distance, we may discern a number of ideas and attitudes they held in common, some of them potentially very important. But for both of them, they were operationally less important than the ideas they distinctly did not share. Both would have been shocked by having their views equated.

The description in naturalistic terms is even more misleading. True, he thought the ways of Providence "unintelligible," but it has often occurred to believers that God moves in a mysterious way His wonders to perform. The term *Providence* signified a reality to Hawthorne, but a reality man could not hope to understand. "I am that I am": Tillich's and Buber's refusal to specify a propositional content for the concept of God has a long history, not simply among existentialists, and, one may well hold, has good reasons behind it. It is essentially the same position as Hawthorne's on Providence. He could differ with his Puritan forebears here without ceasing to be religious, or even biblical, in his thinking. For Job, too, God's ways remained, even at the end, "unintelligible" in any strictly rational sense.

From Hawthorne's own point of view, he was too much the Christian to be a naturalist, even if he did not look, with Cotton Mather, for the signs of Special Providences. If he constantly naturalized and psychologized leading Christian ideas, especially the Fall, it was not because he was interested in denying Christian dogmas but precisely because he was interested in penetrating to their existential truth and thus re-establishing and preserving them. Father Ficke's conclusions in his careful and thorough study of Hawthorne's religion are too well documented to be questioned. *The Light Beyond: Hawthorne's Theology* leaves many problems unsolved, some of them very important to the literary critic, but not this one: Hawthorne was not, in any significant sense of the word, a naturalist.

Much more plausibly, Hawthorne is often, especially in the older literary histories, called a latter-day Puritan. If one comes to this description fresh from those that take the transcendentalist or naturalist tack, it is likely to seem refreshingly apt. It acknowledges his religious concern and differentiates his religious attitudes from those of his more transcendental neighbors. His strong imaginative identification with his region's past, his constant concern with problems of conscience, his relative conservatism in religious matters in an age and region of Unitarian liberalism, his anti-Utopian tendencies in a time of great confidence in progress, his tendency to stress man's finitude and innate sinfulness—all these traits and others seem to justify the old label.

But the more one learns about the man and his work, the less adequate the description comes to seem. For one thing, it almost entirely overlooks the crucial matter of *belief*. Hawthorne was not a Calvinist, and a strict Calvinist might well have denied his right to be called a Christian. Hawthorne, in turn, thought his Puritan forefathers religiously misguided, morally insensitive to the demands of their faith, and personally unat-

tractive. He exposed their bigotry in "The Man of Adamant"
and their defective theology in "Young Goodman Brown." Their
biblical literalism seemed to him wholly mistaken and the
fine-spun arguments of their theological tracts irrelevant. Thank-
ing God that he had not been born in those "stern and gloomy"
times, he honored the Puritans for their strength of purpose and
moral earnestness and for the seriousness and depth of their
grasp of human nature and destiny. He shared many of their
concerns and characteristic attitudes without sharing many of
their distinguishing beliefs.

His view of the Puritans was essentially that of his age.
Despite his close acquaintance with their writings and his
imaginative sympathy with them, he judged them, a modern
historian would be likely to say, unfairly, betraying a typical
nineteenth-century bias. Finding them bigoted, cruel, continuously gloomy, and far too anti-humanistic for his tastes, he
condemned them in work after work. With his typical insight,
he admitted that "strong traits of their nature have intertwined
themselves with mine," but these were precisely those traits in
himself that he did not like and tried to replace. He would
surely have been greatly displeased to find himself called a
Puritan by the scholars. In answer, he would have pointed to
his sketch of the Puritans in "Main Street," or to his portrayal
of them as among the damned because of their spiritual pride in
"The Man of Adamant," or as sinners casting the first stone
in the opening pages of *The Scarlet Letter*.

Much more to his liking than the American Puritans were
what he called affectionately the "old-time" authors in a more
centrally orthodox and less literalistic Christian tradition. His
feelings on this matter are at least as important a clue to his
religious orientation as is his kinship with his Puritan forefathers. Spenser was his favorite writer—and Spenser was a
Christian humanist. Dante was another, and Bunyan, Milton,

175

and Samuel Johnson were others. In those areas of thought and attitude where the American Puritans agreed with such writers, Hawthorne, too, tended to agree. "The Canterbury Pilgrims" might almost have been written by Spenser, and its theme would certainly have been approved by him—though not, probably, by Dante, because of its anti-ascetic aspect. Dante would have understood "Rappaccini's Daughter," and Bunyan might have thought that everything essential in "The Celestial Railroad" came from him. What Hawthorne shared with the Puritans, on the level of belief, was their "orthodoxy," so far as they kept in touch with the central Christian tradition; what he chiefly disapproved in their outlook was their Calvinism and its after-effects, their "heresies," in short.

True to his time and place, Hawthorne thought religion both a private matter and a matter chiefly "of the heart," but insofar as his theological views were formulated and expressed with any clarity, they must be described in terms that will ally them with the traditional, the historic, and, broadly speaking, the orthodox. To press for clarification of these matters, to demand to know, for instance, precisely what ideas Hawthorne held about the Trinity, would result in no increase of understanding: Hawthorne himself resisted clarification in these areas. He held on as best he could to a faith he honored and, as he hoped, shared in its essentials, despite his doubts, a faith he saw every-where being rejected, fragmented, or diluted—rejected by the transcendentalists, softened and moralized by the Unitarians, transformed into a legalistic code or a simple emotional formula for salvation by the fundamentalistic descendents of the Puri-tans. To hold on at all often meant reinterpretation of the historical in psychological terms.

From such a religious orientation, Hawthorne wrote "The Celestial Railroad," which shows us his reasons for believing that salvation is not easy or automatic or virtue a matter of simple self-trust. A highly effective defense of Bunyan's moral and religious outlook as against that of the Unitarians and Transcendentalists, it makes it unnecessary for us to wonder why Emerson privately thought Hawthorne's works not worth reading. "Earth's Holocaust" arrives at the same point by a different approach. To those who might reply to "The Celestial Rail-Road" by pointing to the reality of progress, Howthorne here declares that nothing outward can save a man, nothing less difficult to produce than a change of heart can be really redemptive. Political, scientific, and technological progress *is* real, he concedes, and important, too; but it does not solve the lasting and fundamental problems. Man's basic existential condition remains what it has always been. A creature aware of his guilt and faced with the nothingness of death, he knows anxiety and despair in any society, no matter how "advanced." And though progress does seem to be real in some areas, man may expect many of the old evils of society to return in new forms unless he has a change of heart. Mere political or institutional reforms are never enough: an evil will can find a way to corrupt the best-arranged society. "The heart, the heart,—there was the little yet boundless sphere wherein existed the original wrong of which the crime and misery of this outward world were merely types."

Such a view of evil and its origin may be called romantic, subjective, psychologically oriented, or Christian. All these terms fit Hawthorne and his works, and each of them points to a characteristic which the others also illuminate. That each of the terms has meanings that do not apply to Hawthorne is true but not to the point. Hawthorne is not romantic in the sense of having confidence in the innate goodness of unfallen man; or subjective in the sense of tracing all reality back to the private consciousness; or psychological in the sense of reducing moral questions to the *merely* psychological, that is, to the conditioned;

or Christian in a sense that would be approved either by funda-
mentalists or by churchmen in a Catholic tradition. But his
concern with inward, subjective experience and with "irrational
man" was the gift to him of the romantic movement; and his
understanding of man's moral and spiritual nature, the gift of
the Puritans and the great Christian writers he loved so well.
Unsatisfactory though they may be, we shall have to be content
with such generalizations as these if we hope to clarify the
relations of art and belief in Hawthorne.

For he deliberately blurred his eye on some matters, did so
as a matter of principle; and for the critic to achieve definitional
clarity in areas of belief where Hawthorne resisted clarity would
not be helpful. Hawthorne thought truth was to be glimpsed,
not grasped, glimpsed under the proper conditions only, not, in
any of its aspects that really interested him, to be deduced by
cold abstract reasoning or arrived at by any amount of experimentation. Humanly significant truth, he thought, was "of the
heart." And it was more given than achieved, given in the
epiphanies and revelations of symbols. To the discovery of the
kind of truth he was interested in, the wide-awake mind and
the clear eye might indeed be obstacles: *his* truth seemed more
likely to come to what he called "the passive sensibility" in a
state halfway between waking and dreaming than to yield to
the purposeful grasp of directed thinking. It was to be found by
the responsible imagination, the intuitions, and the heart, in the
fullness of personal experience. No wonder he believed he
could do his best thinking by following the implications of
images. He was right. There is more to be learned about his
operative beliefs from even minor sketches like "Fancy's Show-
box" or "The Haunted Mind" than from the Notebooks, despite
the occasional revealing statements of the latter. Hawthorne's
art reflects and expresses his belief; and to a degree greater
than with most artists, we can find the belief only in the art.

178

III

"Night Sketches: Beneath an Umbrella" takes us to the center of Hawthorne's religious sensibility and reveals much about the qualitative aspect of his beliefs. Though it is one of his best sketches, it has never, I believe, received any comment. Its subject is nothing less philosophical than the relations of dream and reality, and the light and the dark in the world, including false lights and true; nothing less, finally, than being and nothingness. The vehicle is a brief walk out into a rainy winter night after a day spent in a warmly cheerful and lighted room, and then an implied return to the fireside.

Hawthorne's control of his material is perfect. Raising the deepest metaphysical questions, he manages to commit himself, in the propositional terms of the philosopher and theologian, on none. Exploring the questions Melville confronted in *Moby-Dick*, exploring them by following the implications of images, he followed a different route to a different answer, as befitted a different temperament and a different outlook; but we can see from the sketch why Melville hailed Hawthorne as a kindred spirit. Nothing could be more typically Hawthornesque than the mixture of seriousness and self-mockery, commitment and ambiguity, doubt and faith we find here. "Onward, still onward, I plunge into the night. . . . " Yes, truly, into a very dark night indeed; but the speaker never ceases to be aware that the greatest risk he *really* runs is getting his feet wet. He explores the power of darkness to the very limits of the town (there is more beyond, but he already knows its nature from what he has encountered), but does so without the least suggestion that he shares Melville's self-image as Prometheus. One thinks rather of Coverdale, similarly challenged and similarly enticed by his fire, his cigars, and his wine.

The title states the major theme, which will get all the necessary qualifications in what follows but will never be denied or taken back: it is a dark, cold, and rainy world we live in, a world whose characteristics are in the sharpest kind of contrast with the warmth, comfort, safety, and light—especially the light —of our firesides; a "stormy and dismal" world in which we are truly "night wanderers." The speaker's night walk in the rain and the scenes he notes are emblematic of man's journey through life, as the speaker makes increasingly clear throughout and states at the end. He moves from light into darkness and back into light. But why go into the darkness at all? Why test one's courage?

The first sentence tells us, implicitly, why, as it introduces the long paragraph devoted to stating the counter theme: the world inside the chamber, safe from the storm. There is no immediate necessity to explore the discomforts outside. "Pleasant is a rainy winter's day, within doors!" Shut in on such a day, one travels in imagination, visiting strange and exotic places as unlike the world outside the window as possible. The rain beating on the glass makes the imaginative escape all the more pleasant. Dream and reality are in perfect opposition, and dream is easier and more delightful for being unchecked.

But as the day wears on toward evening, the rain makes itself heard more insistently and the daydreaming becomes less and less satisfactory. The "visions" vanish and cannot be reinvoked. "A gloomy sense of unreality" takes their place: the speaker is impelled to venture out to satisfy himself "that the world is not entirely made up of such shadowy materials." After a day of dreaming, he must explore the night. The dreaming has been enjoyable, the night walk will be unpleasant, and he has no desire to punish himself unnecessarily; but he really has no other choice but to go out, for the dreams "will not appear again" at his bidding. Reality will not be permanently shut off. If the sketch ended here, it would suggest that Hawthorne's stance was considerably more like Melville's than it actually was.

But this is only the beginning. After returning us briefly to the literal in the next paragraph—it was after all just a rainy night, requiring, fortunately, no great courage to explore it—the speaker ventures out and looks up at the night sky. What he sees there is appalling—or would be if he let it be. He is plunged immediately into that reality that is the counterpart of his daydreams:

> I look upward, and discern no sky, not even an unfathomable void, but only a black, impenetrable nothingness, as though heaven and all its lights were blotted from the system of the universe. It is as if Nature were dead, and the world had put on black, and the clouds were weeping for her.

"As if Nature were dead": precisely. The charnel house Melville stared at in fascinated horror, an unfathomable void, an impenetrable nothingness, a world of total darkness. Contact with the literal has restored the speaker's sense of reality, but at what cost! Nature has spoken in its symbolic language and what it seems to say might well test the courage of braver men than the speaker lays any claim to being. The sky, the heavens, Heaven—all gone. Or rather, it looks *as if* they were gone. The last two clauses of the sentence following the awful revelation progressively qualify it: the world, we know, is not really in mourning for a dead nature, and we cannot picture the raindrops as the tears of the weeping clouds except humorously.

The speaker stares briefly into the night and moves on. He will not rest in total negation. Not that Hawthorne is afraid to follow the implications of his symbols all the way, as some would charge, but, as the rest of the sketch makes clear, he does not think the first glimpse of outer darkness has revealed all there is to be known, even of the night outside; and there is always the lighted chamber to return to when he has had enough of the dark. Meanwhile he will search out any lights there may be beyond the Slough of Despond through which he has floundered just beyond his doorstep.

As he had anticipated, even at the time of his initial shock, the darkness turns out not to be total. Many kinds of light pierce the gloom, but some of them would lead the walker astray, and some of them have the effect of exaggerating the darkness. The most dangerous of the false lights, though, are those that create the effect of dispelling the darkness entirely:

> Methinks the scene is an emblem of the deceptive glare which mortals throw around their footsteps in the moral world, thus bedazzling themselves till they forget the impenetrable obscurity that hems them in, and that can be dispelled only by radiance from above.

The speaker moves on, generally letting the images speak for themselves. The darkness is everywhere, the lights intermittent. He passes a lingering snowbank and is reminded that winter is sometimes colder even than this night. He thinks of floods and shipwrecks and decides that only experienced seamen know how to interpret storms: "The blast will . . . be understood by all of them." (No wonder Melville felt a kinship with Hawthorne. *He* would have understood Hawthorne's reference here to the "Marine Insurance Office.") He thinks, too, of water nymphs and river deities, as he sees what appear to be their modern counterparts. Myth and fact, dream and reality blend. Gleams from lighted windows alternate with intervals of total darkness in Manichean opposition, but the speaker is gaining confidence as he proceeds: he will not accept the unresolved patchwork as final. He is not, he says, "altogether a chameleon spirit, with no hue of its own." He will search out light.

But before he finds it, he encounters once more, for the last time, a darkness that seems total, like the nothingness that met his gaze as he first stepped out his door:

> Now I have reached the utmost limits of the town, where the last lamp struggles feebly with the darkness, like the farthest star that stands sentinel on the borders of uncreated space.

Hawthorne might have anticipated Frost in claiming to be one acquainted with the night. But the speaker does not choose, like the one in the poem, to outwalk the farthest city light. He stops at the limits of the town to watch a coach full of passengers move out into the darkness. The passengers will dream, he thinks, as they journey through the night to their destinations. Finally he sees a solitary figure lighting his way with a tin lantern that casts a mottled "circular pattern" of brightness around him. This figure, he notes, "passes fearlessly into the unknown gloom, whither I will not follow him."

It would be easy at this point to miss Hawthorne's meaning, to see him as compromising, drawing back from the final implications of his symbols, playing Starbuck to Melville's Ahab. But it is not only the final darkness he is not ready yet to test, it is the light of the stranger's lantern as well. Only death could provide the decisive test of the opposing powers, could reveal certainly which would prevail, the light or the dark. The speaker has explored the darkness as far as human knowledge can take him. Beyond the limits of the town there is no light but that supplied by faith. Not to follow the stranger, then, is, first, the final example of that constant return to the literal which we have noted throughout as Hawthorne's way of controlling his implications; second, an expression of the speaker's awareness of the limitations of his own faith—he is not ready to walk by faith alone; third, evidence that his search for light has been successful—he does not *need* to make the final test,

for he has found that a true light does shine in the darkness
and that its radiance is from above. The stranger's light is no
stronger than that a candle can shed through the holes in an
antique metal lantern, but it is sufficient: he

> fears not to tread the dreary path before him, because his
> lantern, which was kindled at the fireside of his home, will
> light him back to that same fireside again. And thus we, night
> wanderers through a stormy and dismal world, if we bear the
> lamp of Faith, enkindled at a celestial fire, it will surely lead
> us home to that heaven whence its radiance was borrowed.

The sketch is built on a set of polar oppositions: light, dream,
wish, imagination, true knowledge, love, the fireside, faith;
darkness, fact, the literal, ignorance, isolation, cold, windy
spaces, doubt. Lights may be from below or from above; if
from below, they may be true or false. If true, they are analogous with, and perhaps the vehicle of, the radiance from above.
Dreams may be false, mere escapes from reality into imaginary
travel, or they may be true lights in the darkness. The darkness
is almost complete at the start and really total at the end—
except for the light carried by the stranger.

Like Kierkegaard, Hawthorne believed all the more firmly
because he had explored the depths of doubt. He understood
and valued the light because he knew so well the degree and
extent of the darkness. As he put it earlier in the sketch in
imagistic terms, "the black night hangs overhead like a canopy,
and thus keeps the splendor from diffusing itself away." Here
for once, at what I suppose is the deepest level of meaning of
the sketch, there is no ambiguity, no qualification, no double-
ness of attitude or mood. Hawthorne's religious faith was
inseparable from, and in a sense dependent upon, his tragic
vision. He expressed the same point of view years later in
Our Old Home. Commenting on English poverty, and particu-

larly on the diseased, dirty, crippled and deformed, and starving children he saw in the streets, he continued,

> It might almost make a man doubt the existence of his own soul, to observe how Nature has flung these little wretches into the street and left them there, so evidently regarding them as nothing worth, and how all mankind acquiesce in the great mother's estimate of her offspring. For, if they are to have no immortality, what superior claim can I assert for mine? And how difficult to believe that anything so precious as a germ of immortal growth can have been buried under this dirt-heap, plunged into this cesspool of misery and vice! . . . Ah, what a mystery! Slowly, slowly, as after groping at the bottom of a deep, noisome, stagnant pool, my hope struggles upward to the surface, bearing the half-drowned body of a child along with it, and heaving it aloft for its life, and my own life, and all our lives.

For Hawthorne, in short, faith arises out of doubt and hope out of despair. Emerson, by contrast, just because he minimized, explained away, or would not for long face the dark ("I have never been able to make evil seem real to me"), found less reason to cherish either the radiance from above or the gleams from the hearth. He thought, or at least publicly proclaimed, that he had sufficient light within to make any such aids unnecessary. The mysteries Hawthorne pondered Emerson seemed never seriously to have considered. No wonder Hawthorne felt he had no questions to ask of him.

Though it is both possible and profitable to explore the outlines of Hawthorne's theology in the way in which Father Ficke has done it, noting Hawthorne's implied or stated commitments to historic Christian dogmas, a different approach is suggested by "Night Sketches," and, indeed, by most of the best of Hawthorne's art. His "theology" (the word is too rationalistic to be wholly appropriate) is very much like that of the

185

religious existentialists of his own time and ours. With Kierkegaard, he moves from doubt and despair to faith; with Marcel,
from alienation to reunion. Like Tillich, he "psychologizes"
the faith, not in the sense of explaining it away, but in making
it inward and personal, in refusing to externalize or objectify
it. Like Buber, he thinks religiously by exploring the implications of symbolic images, moving always in the opposite
direction from that in which Bunyan moved, moving from
existential experience to the transcendent. Though they would
deplore the way he "compromised" by suggesting the availability
of a light from above, a revelation from beyond our experience,
even the atheist existentialists could find in Hawthorne a kindred spirit: he explored the depths of existential anxiety, then
countered Kierkegaard's "Dread" and Heidegger's "Nothingness" with "Commitment."

"Night Sketches" begins in a way Sartre ought to approve,
by contrasting bright subjective daydreams with dark external
reality, but it ends by rejecting the dichotomy it began with.
The hearth is as real as the storm, and not all dreams are false.
Implying an equation between human love and divine revelation (the "family circle" is responsible for gleams not unlike
those cast in a "circular pattern" by the lantern of the stranger),
its answer at once to the sense of unreality produced by daydreaming and the feeling of despair produced by the first glimpse
of the outer darkness is the true dream. The man beneath the
umbrella has not discovered the truth of doctrines but experienced a movement of the heart. There is nothing demonstrable
here; unaided reason will never discover this answer. At the
center of Hawthorne's religious belief, there is a recognition of
myth as myth, without any tendency to dismiss it as lie. The
darkness of the world is more and not less "real" to the speaker
at the end of his walk, but it is not unrelieved: he has discovered
some real light, too. If the darkness were not so real, the light

would not be so needed. "How difficult to believe . . . my hope struggles upward."

IV

No wonder Hawthorne wrote allegory, but allegory so fluid and subjective that Bunyan might have recognized it only in those tales and sketches that today we like the least, and would not have recognized it at all in such things as "Roger Malvin's Burial." If Bunyan had read Hawthorne, he might have put him in one of his own allegories and called him Mr. Shaky-faith. We can imagine him recognizing the outlines of historic belief, presented in types and emblems and reinforced by biblical allusions (Bunyan would surely catch more of these than we do, and understand them better), but also noting the hovering "as if" and disapproving of it.

Hawthorne wrote "allegories of the heart," as he himself once called them, but the heart took its cue from the historic faith. Over and over again, he retold the story of the Fall; and now and then he managed to imagine its sequel, the redemption effected by the second Adam. Loss of innocence compelled his imagination. That man lived in darkness and separation seemed too obvious to be questioned. The light, whether from the heart or from above, had to be searched out and affirmed as real, just because it was not immediately "given," like the darkness. Retreat into fantasy would not do, cherishing dreams because while they lasted they had been delightful would not do: the man under the umbrella had to leave the snug comfort of his brightly lighted chamber and brave the discomforts of a dark, cold, and rainy world, to see the world at its worst, before he could affirm that a proper faith could be trusted to lead us home through the encompassing darkness. Mr. Shaky-faith: the doubt is real and the faith genuine. The two together, varying in their

187

proportions but never ceasing to be in some sort of creative conflict, do more than anything else to give Hawthorne's work its distinctive shape and quality.

The faith of Bunyan and Spenser was less "reasonable," but their work was more "rational." There were more elements in their religious belief that modern man would have to label untrue, or not true in the way they took them to be, or even positively false. Hawthorne's faith was pared down, more skeptical: he was indeed, in a sense, the child of the Enlightenment, as all who are aware of history are. Knowing myth to be myth, he could not confuse faith and knowledge. If Genesis was shaky history but his deepest experience made its meaning seem to him in some sense still true, there was nothing he could do but reinterpret the Fall in terms the heart could understand. Man falls whether Adam ever lived or not.

But if his way of presenting the faith was more reasonable, less offensive to modern reason, than Bunyan's and Spenser's, it was also less rationalistic. Their faith may have been "false" in some of its elements, but it was a public, shared faith assumed to be objectively true, not needing to be validated, except in some ultimate and strictly personal sense, by the heart. Unlike Hawthorne, they did not see heart and head as in inevitable and unceasing conflict. (Hawthorne thought redemption, wholeness, would come only when the conflict ceased, when the two co-operated; but this was a wished for, not an experienced, state of affairs.) They could write more objectively because the dream that shaped their works did not seem like a dream; they were quite sure, indeed, that much of it was fact, not dream at all. Their symbols could have the kind of objectivity that is provided by known, public referents. They could be, in their own eyes and those of their contemporaries who shared their beliefs, men of reason without committing treason to the heart.

In Hawthorne's work at its best, on the other hand, the

meanings of the images are partly determined by their analogy with historic myth, mostly Christian, and partly determined, internally, by context. And always, again when he is writing at his best, they are to some degree ambiguous. That is why it remains possible for commentators so inclined to give narrowly, even reductively, psychological interpretations to some of his works, and for other commentators to give strictly theological interpretations to the same works. Often, both types of interpretation are "valid," but neither is complete alone. What the "right" interpretation is cannot be settled for Hawthorne's work in the same way it can for Bunyan's. Symbols that often begin by being ambiguous and end by being almost wholly contextually determined are not "rational" in the sense that Spenser's political allegory is.

Of course Hawthorne's practice varied all the way from the almost perfectly traditional (and "rationalistic") to the almost mythic and archetypal in the modern sense. He wrote "The Great Carbuncle" and also "Roger Malvin's Burial," "Lady Eleanor's Mantle" and also "My Kinsman, Major Molineux." In "Young Goodman Brown," he called Brown's wife Faith, as Bunyan might have done; but he also treated the revelations in the forest more ambiguously than Bunyan would have found aesthetically possible or religiously desirable. In "Rappaccini's Daughter," he exercises his privilege as intrusive author to remind us of the parallels between his story and the story of the expulsion from an earlier garden, but he so manipulates his archetype that in the end it becomes impossible to draw any point-by-point allegorical analogy. Critics are likely to continue to differ on just where to locate the center of Hawthorne's practice; but that his special quality as a writer is a function of his unique relationship to both the form and the content of traditional Christian allegory, on the one hand, and to modern symbolism, on the other, seems hardly open to question.

189

One thing seems certain in this whole difficult area. Where Hawthorne's beliefs are surest, he writes most traditionally. In effect, this means that when his subjects have the strongest theological implications, they are treated the most ambigously, mythically, and subjectively; and when they are moral in the most limited sense, they are clearest, most rational, and most traditional. Of course, the theological is never without moral implication in Hawthorne, or the moral without implied theological sanction and result. The distinction I am using is by no means absolute, or even clear-cut. But it is useful for the purpose at hand, which is to comment on the reason why so many of Hawthorne's most traditionally allegorical tales, like "Lady Eleanore's Mantle," are concerned with relatively simple moral problems—simple in the sense of not necessarily directly involving any ultimate religious beliefs.

Hawthorne thought he knew the moral meaning of pride. It was a sin, in some sense deadly—about this he had no doubt at all. He wrote "Lady Eleanore's Mantle" in a way that Bunyan would have understood and approved. He had clear and firm convictions about materialists and cynics, and produced "The Great Carbuncle." He had no doubt about where bigotry led—though he could see that it might have its origin in mixed motives, some of them good—and he wrote "The Man of Adamant." He disapproved of any monkish withdrawal from the world into ascetic purity: his disapproval is clearly and allegorically recorded in "The Canterbury Pilgrims."

On the other hand, how was he to take the atonement, Unitarian that he was by family tradition if not by any sympathy with what seemed to him its greater follies? That man could not save himself by his own unaided efforts he felt rather sure; but clear orthodox Trinitarian, he was not. "Roger Malvin's Burial" makes a sacrificial death the means of redemption, echoing, as it does so, both the Abraham and Isaac story and the story of Christ; but the rational clarity of allegory is wholly lacking in the tale, and it would be unwise to claim orthodoxy for Hawthorne on the basis of it. A better claim could be based on the much more allegorical episode of the birch cup filled with clear water offered to and refused by the man of adamant. Since the offer is made in terms that echo the liturgy, it seems impossible to rule out a reference to the Holy Communion here, however surprising the allusion may seem in a child of the Puritans who almost never went to church. But if this is a part of the meaning, it is only one part; and another emphasis is possible: nature (the water from the spring) and scripture (the cup) co-operate and agree in offering redemption here as elsewhere in Hawthorne.

Clarity and ambiguity, allegory and myth, clear conviction and tentative belief. *The Scarlet Letter* is not, it seems to me, an allegory in the traditional mode, though it has often been so called and has many allegorical elements. But the deterioration of Chillingworth, his becoming a fiend and creeping along the ground like a snake, is allegorically handled. Hawthorne was perfectly clear in his mind about the moral status of revenge, or, more relevantly to Chillingworth, about the results of treating other people as though they were objects, using them to satisfy our curiosity, performing experiments on them, as Chillingworth did on Dimmesdale. But he was not sure about the mechanism of forgiveness or the machinery of redemption, any more than he was about the "machinery of Providence" into which he hesitated to thrust his awkward agency: the ultimate fate of Hester and Dimmesdale contains a certain ambiguity that is never dispelled, even by Hester's apparent halo or the minister's dying gestures and words, which are so recorded as to remind us of Christ on the cross. Indeed, the ambiguity is reinforced by the closing words of the novel, with their images of black, which counters the hope suggested by the Christ allusions of the last scaffold scene, and red, which is by this time thoroughly ambiguous.

The "ambiguity device," isolated and discussed so well years ago by Matthiessen, is thus no mere "device" but an expression in technical terms of the essential condition of Hawthorne's belief. It is a method of blurring the clear eye, of refusing to specify how literally something should be taken, of believing in Providence while not pretending to understand its machinery. It is a method, we may say, of avoiding clarity—but the kind of clarity that is avoided is the kind Hawthorne thought either specious or irrelevant. Something supernatural seemed to have occurred; a natural explanation, or several natural explanations, could be given. But would the explanation, even if we could be sure it were true, render void the religious significance of the strange event? It is easy to imagine Hawthorne writing—in fact, he *should* have written, though I cannot recall that he ever did—"Whether Adam lived or no. . . . "

If, as I have argued, the shaping force behind Hawthorne's art is the special character of his religious belief, it is not surprising that the so-called ambiguity device should be one of the most characteristic features of his writing and that a more generalized ambiguity should be so typical of it. For Hawthorne's religious belief was existentially oriented, not institutional or traditional. He found in his own *experience* reason for looking at life as the "old time" writers had, reason for believing the Scriptures would never be destroyed by the bonfires of reform. But religious experience—not doctrine or dogma, but experience—is always, and necessarily, ambiguous. Did the god speak or did we merely imagine his voice? If he did really speak, it is clear that only the prepared, the imaginative ear could receive the words. It is possible to argue that only the faithful saw the risen Christ without intending to impugn the reality of the Resurrection.

The decision as to which is the true dream and which the false must be made by the individual in the depths of his inwardness. Hawthorne was not without his commitments; and in some areas of thought he was willing to declare them, preferably in allegorical form. But on matters closest to his heart, he was either unable to attain commitment or reluctant to declare his commitments propositionally. His ambiguity, whether inseparable from the greatness of his finest writing or the mere idiosyncrasy it becomes in his poorest, is a translation of this aspect of his belief into art.

v

Hawthorne was an idealist who wrote in the age of philosophical idealism. He did not seriously question the general philosophical assumptions of his age. When he defined the special area occupied by his writing as lying between the real and the ideal—or, when implicitly apologizing for the furry ears of Donatello, between the real and the fantastic—he was using the words in a sense it is easy to misunderstand today. He did not mean between the real and the unreal, but between external and internal, between thing and idea, between meaningless fact and ungrounded meaning. The perennial battle between realism and idealism as philosophical positions is relevant to his meaning. Idealism locates reality in the nature of the knowing mind, realism in the nature of the thing known. One reason why philosophers today often do not feel required to take a stand for one position or the other is that, even if they do not see such problems as insoluble, mere verbal problems, they are inclined to see the dichotomy as a false one, with both camps right and both wrong. Existentially, we cannot separate knower and known so clearly.

It would certainly be essentially misleading to try to make a case for Hawthorne as a philosopher, and I have no intention of doing so. But one of the implications of his work is that he anticipated contemporary philosophy (without thinking the issues through philosophically, needless to say) in refusing the ideal-real choice. Between Emerson, who in his youth, at least, tended to think the world plastic to mind and recommended the theory of the ideal because it fitted our needs and desires, and later realists, who stressed nature's intractible and even alien aspects, Hawthorne took his stand.[1] Fact, he implied, was of no use until interpreted by mind; but mind must always return to fact to keep in touch with reality. Less the idealist (to drop a strictly philosophical sense and turn to a more popular one) than Emerson, he thought he knew some unpleasant facts we must take account of whether we liked them or not. Any theory which ignored them could not be true. But he did not think we were bound to take the apparent meaninglessness of nature at face value: if some dreams were mere figments, others were true.

He invented an art form about half way, at its center, between pure interpretation, or mind triumphant, and uncreative recording, or mind in abdication—between allegory and the naturalistic record. (Both these extremes are mere whipping horses for critics, of course; neither, if pure, would be art at all; neither is, perhaps, even possible, whether we call the result art or not.) Unlike Bunyan, he would not write simply to teach, to convey meanings: he would render scenes, as James would say later. But he would render them clarified, purified of irrelevant detail. He would use facts, but *meaningful* facts, facts taken into heart and mind and seen humanly.

"Night Sketches" begins with mind triumphant in daydream, moves to the shock of the initial confrontation with the impenetrable void of meaningless nature, and ends with the darkness illuminated with the true light, meaninglessness shaped into sufficient meaning by the true dream. In religious terms,

Hawthorne seemed to find himself faced with a choice between Bunyan's faith and utter meaninglessness, which is what a completely naturalistic outlook would have meant to him. He refused the choice. The true faith, he seems to have thought, would be more like Bunyan's in general outline than like Emerson's, but it would take account of things Bunyan did not know. The faith could, perhaps, be preserved if its form were purified.

For the man, this meant validating the religious vision of his favorite Christian authors by expressing that vision in the language and concepts of a new age, without committing himself to their religious literalism, their confusion of history and myth. For the artist, it meant transforming traditional allegory into a mythopoetic art sometimes close to Bunyan and Spenser, sometimes close to Faulkner, but at its best in an area all its own. For both man and artist, it meant devising a way of distinguishing false lights from true by observing their effects in the night. It meant, ultimately, correcting the dream in order to conserve it. Both as man and as artist, Hawthorne knew how to value the little circle of light in the darkness of human life.

Daniel Hoffman

Myth,

Romance,

and the

Childhood of Man

N O EPOCH OF THE TIME can claim a copyright in these immortal fables. . . . Certainly, so long as man exists, they can never perish; but, by their indestructibility itself, they are legitimate subjects for every age to clothe with its own garniture of manners and sentiment, and to imbue with its own morality." So Hawthorne confidently introduced his *A Wonder-Book for Girls and Boys* in 1851, a redaction of myths so popular that he offered a sequel, *Tanglewood Tales,* two years later. Hawthorne had timed his myth books shrewdly, for the romantic revival of myth reached its height in America in the 1850's.[1] As Douglas Bush has said, speaking of English poetry, "The fundamental impulse of the mythological renascence was contained in the romantic protest against a mechanical world . . . stripped, as it seemed, of imagination and emotion, of beauty and mystery. . . . The old allegorical tradition, which had never quite died, took fresh root in romantic idealism and flowered again in rich mythological symbols."[2] Hawthorne in his own tales combines myth with the allegorical tradition; in his children's books he allegorizes myths and substitutes "a tone in some degree Gothic or romantic" for what seemed to him "the classic coldness . . . as repellant as the touch of marble,"[3] Toward his young readers, Hawthorne professed little condescension, saying that "children possess an unestimated sensibility to whatever is deep or high, in imagination or feeling, so long as it is simple likewise." Yet sometimes he treats them with such ponderous coyness as, "The king's palace attained to the stupendous magnificence of Periwinkle's baby-house." Nonetheless, these tales still have power to hold children from play, if not the old from the chimney corner. The trials, conflicts, and triumphs of myths are indeed indestructible.

Hawthorne's statement on the imperishability of myths may serve as one wedge by which to split apart some of his other works to observe the grain to which their narratives conform. Like his Yankee woodcarver in "Drowne's Wooden Image"—a tale that garnishes the myth of Pygmalion—Hawthorne is likely to try to liberate the form he finds inherent in his materials. The narrative structures provided by myths were a source of strength in his best writings. As his fables of artists alone would show, his is a mythopoetic art: an art precariously poised between the opposing claims of allegory, romance, and realism, between the "morality" and the "manners" of the age. A *Wonder-Book* and *Tanglewood Tales* engaged Hawthorne's fancy rather than his imagination; for in them, he undertook only to garnish, not to remake as his own, the stories he chose from Homer or Ovid or Anthon's *Classical Dictionary*.[4] Yet some of the important themes and sources of the imagery in his fiction are sketched in these books of myths for children.

Take, for instance, his attitude toward childhood and toward the Age of Myth as the childhood of man. The latter notion is, of course, a commonplace made attractive both by Romantic idealization of the child and by progressive theories of cultural evolution. A confusion of myth with childhood seems a boon to the redactor of ancient legends: Kingsley, whose version for children, *The Heroes,* appeared only two years after *Tanglewood Tales,* wrote of the Greeks, "While they were young and simple they loved fairy tales as you do now. All nations do so when they are young."[5] The United States, barely three score and ten, was a young country, too; and, as we shall see, Hawthorne in his early tales was consciously attempting to provide his native land with a moralized mythology. To retell Greek myths to American children would seem a blessing of the youth of one nation with the fruits of the youth of another. Yet Hawthorne, speaking of stories similar to Kingsley's, finds them "brimming with everything that is most abhorrent to our Christianized moral sense." Some are "hideous," others "melancholy" and "miserable"; among these the Greek tragedians "sought their themes, and moulded them into the sternest griefs that ever the world saw; was such materials the stuff that children's playthings should be made of?"

But Hawthorne makes these objections only to refute them. One notes, however, that the objections are made in his own voice, the rebuttals by his auctorial *persona,* Eustace Bright. This fictive narrator of *Tanglewood Tales* answers Hawthorne,

> The objectionable characteristics seem to be a parasitical growth, having no essential connection with the original fable.

They fall away, and are thought of no more, the instant he puts his imagination in sympathy with the innocent little circle, whose wide-open eyes are fixed so eagerly upon him. Thus the stories (not by any strained effort of the narrator's but in harmony with their inherent germ) transform themselves, and reassume the shapes which they might be supposed to possess in the pure childhood of the world.

Even at this level of discourse, however, Hawthorne cannot refrain from a gentle ironic peroration, casting doubt on what had seemed as clear as an article of belief:

When the first poet or romancer told these marvellous legends (such is Eustace Bright's opinion), it was still the Golden Age. Evil had never yet existed; and sorrow, misfortune, crime, were mere shadows which the mind fancifully created for itself, as a shelter against too sunny realities; or, at most, but prophetic dreams, to which the dreamer himself did not yield a waking credence. Children are now the only representatives of the men and women of that happy era; and therefore it is that we must raise the intellect and fancy to the level of childhood, in order to re-create the original myths.

In addition to the sinister suggestion that the mind even then created evil, his praise of childhood must be qualified by the inexperience of the youthful Eustace. A mere college student, he has not yet crossed the threshold of his own life into the realm of responsible action. Whether for better or for worse, this is the progress all of Hawthorne's heroes must make. That Eustace Bright's romantic views of both childhood and pre-history are sentimental illusions, we may infer from the way he himself tells the story of Pandora's Box. Characteristically, in *A Wonder-Book,* Hawthorne has Eustace give his tale of the coming of woes into the world an optimistic title, "The Paradise of Children." We find the infantine Pandora with idle hands and, consequently, about to get into mischief:

But children led so easy a life, before any Troubles came into the world, that they had really a great deal too much leisure. They could not be forever playing at hide-and-seek among the flower-shrubs, or at blind-man's-buff with garlands over their eyes, or at whatever other games had been found out, while Mother Earth was in her babyhood. When life is all sport, toil is the real play. There was absolutely nothing to do. A little sweeping and dusting about the cottage, I suppose, and the gathering of fresh flowers (which were only too abundant everywhere), and arranging them in vases,—and poor little Pandora's day's work was over. And then, for the rest of the day, there was the box!

Hawthorne cannot conceive of the Golden Age without foreboding. In "The May-Pole of Merry Mount," much more powerfully than here, it is a reproach to say, "O, people of the Golden Age, the chief of your husbandry was to raise flowers!" There, too, "the whole colony were playing at blindman's buff, except a single scapegoat, whom the blinded sinners pursued by the tinkling bells at his garments." A paradise of children indeed. In few authors is the longing for paradise as poignant as in Hawthorne. He dramatizes his conviction that the nature of man must have been different before the Fall. Aware that salvation would have been impossible without the commission of sin, he always renders prelapsarian characters as incomplete, wanting in the fatal knowledge whose lack denies them full humanity. This is plain in Hawthorne's treatment of Pearl and of Donatello; both are children of nature and bring into *The Scarlet Letter* and *The Marble Faun* (subtitled *The Romance of Monte Beni*) the equivocal values of Merry Mount. What further makes impossible Hawthorne's unqualified approval of a Golden Age is its very essence, so clearly dramatized in the Maypole story. A Golden Age is, of course, a time outside of time, a living eternity, such as Heaven is and Eden once was, but not a life like ours. In his fiction, Hawthorne's characters must live in our life; and therefore, the maypole is hewn down by iron Puritans, Pearl is received into society at her father's confession of guilt, and Donatello can be transformed from fauna to humanity after his commission of an original sin.

Yet Hawthorne does uphold the purity of childhood in which Eustace Bright believes. This quality is crucial to Bellerophon's pursuit of Pegasus. In "The Chimaera," the hero must bridle the winged horse in order to conquer the monster. Inquiring at the Fountain of Pirene, fortunately "Bellerophon put his faith in the child, who had seen the image of Pegasus in the water, and in the maiden who had heard him neigh so melodiously, rather than in the middle-aged clown, who believed only in cart-horses, or in the old man who had forgotten the beautiful things of his youth."

Again the legend merely imitates what Hawthorne had already expressed with deeper resonance in his own fiction. Yet in his tales the power resides in myths adapted to his needs. In "The Snow Image" (1848), he had offered with sustained charm the fancy of having children named for flowers (as are Eustace Bright's "little auditors") create an imaginary playmate of snow, who lives only as long as her life is believed in. The tale is subtitled "A Childish Miracle," and this indeed it is; for Violet and Peony bring their playmate to life by the power of faith—a faith in the reality of the imagination. Thus far Hawthorne has invented something midway between a Concord fairy tale and a transcendental saint's legend. By placing the imaginative purity and faith of the children against the blundering skepticism of their father, the hardware merchant, he turns his "legend" into a delicate yet dramatic statement of the difficulty of artistic creation in a society ruled by rationalism and materialism.

As was true of the Lindsey children's snow-sister, Owen Warland's butterfly soared or drooped according to the observer's desire to believe in it. But in "The Artist of the Beautiful," it is Baby Danforth who smashes to pieces the artist's supersensual mechanism. There the child is not the possessor of imagination but the inheritor, from his Grandfather Time, of enmity toward the creations that seek to live in eternity. The eternity toward which Owen Warland aspires is indeed as remote from our sufferings as was the Golden Age, but the artist can triumph where the revelers at Merry Mount failed. He does not achieve eternity in life as they thought to do; his transfiguration of time is imaginative and endows his spirit with imperishable blessings. How else could Owen endure such isolation, being left with but a handful of broken spangles?

"The Artist of the Beautiful" well illustrates how Hawthorne made his narrative and its supporting metaphors from mythic prototypes of action and image. As was true in "Drowne's Wooden Image," the origin of artistic creation is the artist's love of beauty. Although Owen Warland does not, like Drowne, try to reproduce the beauty of the woman he loves, the other alternative suggested for Shem Drowne's success is true of Warland: his passion brings to life the image he has made. In Owen's image, however, Hawthorne substitutes for the Pygmalion legend a suggestion from the story of Psyche, that the soul is bodied forth as a butterfly. The life cycle of the insect provides organic imagery in the descriptions of Owen's appearance: his sinking into a stuporous fatness after his setback, and his bursting forth in the glory of his successful achievement. Yet the underlying structure of the story is borrowed from, or rather dramatizes, still another myth, Diotima's account in *The Symposium* of the ladder of love. When we follow the course of Owen's devotion from Annie Hovenden, his chosen muse, to love of all beautiful things, thence to love of the idea of beauty, we are reconciled, as Owen is, to his losing the hand of the girl to a bluff, simple blacksmith. Annie, the daughter of

Father Time, could not have understood what Owen was up to; but by the time he knows this, he no longer needs her. Owen's progress is philosophically consistent, although, like transcendental theory, a little cold on the human side.

Although much of this tale is based upon classical myths, the story is unmistakably localized in New England. This is only partly due to its circumstantial atmosphere, almost local color. Hovenden's is an actual shop with real clocks, Annie a believably flirty village girl, Danforth a stout-hearted blacksmith. Yet these realistic persons are fairly allegorized. Hovenden is called Father Time, and his role surely suggests Hawthorne's aversion to the Newtonian conception of God as the Watchmaker in a mechanistic universe. Annie, the artist's muse, is inescapably Father Time's daughter, while her successful suitor is, like the unsuccessful Owen, an artisan of sorts—a fellow metal-worker at that. These relationships go far toward humanizing and localizing, as well as making allegorical, Hawthorne's fable of the artist's lonely pursuit in opposition to all of society's expectations for him. Imprisoning the artist in a clockshop is one of Hawthorne's happiest inventions, a beautifully complete image of the time-serving, spirit-killing, machine-mastered non-life that is taken as the norm by a materialistic culture. How can the artist escape his servitude to time? Hawthorne's answer, while illustrating Platonic and transcendental aesthetics, also takes advantage of those energies of the local scene that might be pressed into the service of a native myth or an analogue of myth. The industrial revolution of course made fascination with machinery as common an attitude as repulsion by it, and Owen Warland shows both feelings. He is repelled by naked power— his fear of the steam engine perhaps anticipates Henry Adams' recognition of the dynamo as the centrifugal image of the age. Yet Warland is a master mechanician on a scale his feelings and senses can control. He is a sort of Yankee inventor *par excel-*

lence; though to escape from the prison of time he foregoes all Down-East shrewdness and works with no thought of gain other than that spiritual gain for which one must renounce the goods of this world. And that, too, is a strain that runs deep in the native character. Inventing a mechanical butterfly more perfect than any natural creature—a machine, yet alive—Owen completes this image for the spiritualization of matter. His gadget is perfectly adapted to his purpose, and the artist's pride in outvying the hand of nature—so like that of Dr. Rappaccini or Aylmer, in whom heart and head are fatally separated—is hardly perceptible. For Owen has not worked his will at anyone else's expense; and in the end he can accept the destruction of his handiwork because his joy was in the process of creating perfection, not in possessing it.

II

In his prefaces to his longer works Hawthorne is at pains to distinguish between the novel and the romance. He clearly conceives realism to be the domain of the novel, which aims to conform "not merely to the possible, but to the probable and ordinary course of man's experience." But the romance, he remarks in his Preface to *The House of the Seven Gables,* must "as a work of art . . . rigidly subject itself to laws," and it must be faithful to "the truth of the human heart." The author of a romance, unlike the novelist, has the freedom "to present that truth under circumstances, to a great extent of [his] own choosing or creation." When he adds the auctorial privilege of using "the Marvellous," we may infer why Hawthorne found so congenial the mythical elements he used in so many of his tales.

Marius Bewley has noticed that Hawthorne tried to analyze the writer's problems "not in terms of the relation of the artist to his art, but in terms of his relation to society." To this critic, Hawthorne seems ultimately unable "to reconcile the roles of artist and citizen in the context of American society, or to make a workable creative marriage between solitude and society."[6] Yet the dissociation of the ideal from the real in "The Artist of the Beautiful" succeeds in making artistic capital of a cultural situation which many another observer found typified in American life. We soon shall see how Hawthorne could mythologize reality and so use it in his fables, if not make it ideal. But though he protests perhaps too much the difficulties that American life put in the artist's way, it does not follow that these difficulties were illusory. Visiting America during the same years when Hawthorne was writing *Twice-Told Tales,* Tocqueville outlined the radical effects of a broad egalitarian commitment upon the writer's relation to the past and to his public.

> Aristocracy naturally leads the human mind to the contemplation of the past, and fixes it there. Democracy, on the contrary, gives men a sort of instinctive distaste for what is ancient. . . . Among a democratic people poetry will not be fed with legendary lays or the memories of old traditions. The poet will not attempt to people the universe with supernatural beings in whom his readers and his own fancy have ceased to believe; nor will he present virtues and vices under the mask of frigid personifications, which are better received under their own features.

Little comfort to Hawthorne that Tocqueville can add, "But Man remains, and the poet needs no more."[7] This would be Whitman's opportunity, not Hawthorne's. For Hawthorne, egalitarian life seemed remorselessly hostile to the artist, a man innately superior to plebeian mediocrity. In "The Custom-House," he demonstrates the very thinness of texture in American life which Henry James would so eloquently arraign in a study of his work. The sensualists, office politicians, and time-servers in the Custom House had no contact with any past further back than their last dinner; scant material their lives seemed to offer for an art that aimed to reveal the eternal truths of the human heart. Only the unacknowledged artist in their midst could transform a packet of fusty papers into a legend disclosing a truth. And he can do so only when thrown out of office by a new administration; for, he tells us, as long as he remained in the Custom House, his imagination was "a tarnished mirror."

On one side of his imagination Hawthorne was deeply committed to what R. W. B. Lewis has called "the party of Memory," the values held by conservators of tradition in American culture. The effect of the egalitarian temper, as Tocqueville diagnosed it, is not only felt to produce an environment hostile to art, it further specifically denies to literature four of the resources on which Hawthorne most depended: the past, myths, the marvelous, and allegory. These attributes are inherent in the very form of fiction which Hawthorne recognized it was his gift to write. A fuller definition than his own is Northrop Frye's synoptic description of that form:

> The essential difference between novel and romance lies in the conception of characterization. The romancer does not attempt to create "real people" so much as stylized figures which expand into psychological archetypes. It is in the romances that we find Jung's libido, anima, and shadow reflected in the hero, heroine, and villain respectively. That is why the romance so often radiates a glow of subjective intensity that the novel lacks, and why a suggestion of allegory is always creeping in around its fringes. . . . The novelist deals with personality, with characters wearing their *personae* or social masks. He needs the framework of a stable society. . . . The romancer deals with individuality, with characters *in vacuo* idealized by revery, and, however conservative he may be, something nihilistic and untamable is likely to keep breaking out of his pages.[8]

Hawthorne, a divided man on every subject that claimed his deepest energies, equivocates in *his* definition of romance. Advocating introduction of "the Marvellous," he then advises its "very moderate use" as rather "a slight, delicate, evanescent flavor, than as any portion of the actual substance of the dish offered to the public." In other words, he will follow a mixed recipe, combining the realistic observation of detail found in the novel with the traditional patterns of action that present enduring truths, for whose revelation the supernatural may be invoked. Such a mixed form as Hawthorne devised, a romance-novel or novelistic romance, is not a compromise but the successful enactment in art of the conflicts of conviction which divided his mind. The tensions between the artist and his culture, between aristocratic values and egalitarian hopes, are also, for Hawthorne, tensions between two conceptions of destiny held with divided fervor. His dilemma may be epitomized by a quotation from Coleridge used by Bulfinch to introduce *The Age of Fable:*

> The intelligible forms of ancient poets,
> The fair humanities of old religion . . .
> They live no longer in the faith of reason;
> But still the heart doth need a language; still
> Doth the old instinct bring back the old names;
> Spirits or gods that used to share the earth
> With man as with their friend. . . .[9]

For Hawthorne, too, the faith of reason seemed to deny the language of the heart. This is the imbalance of the persons in his stories. Because Hawthorne is so divided, his best tales and romances are both ambiguous and sinewed with contradictions. Because he was a great writer, he could dramatize both sides of his nature and of his quandary. It is in the dramatic ordering of these contrasts that his authority as an artist resides.

III

If conservative values could be served by reiterating mythic actions as old as humanity, what forms of character or action could serve the progressive, rationalistic, and millennial energies of contemporary life which Hawthorne had to represent with equal imaginative force? Such synoptic and eclectic combinations as we have seen in "The Artist of the Beautiful" are typical of Hawthorne's way. He took his types and archetypes not only from Greek myths but from all the other important cultural legacies he lived by. These included Puritanism; the popular antiquities of Old World tradition; the Gothic mode; the materials of colonial history; and the emergent American folklore and popular culture of which Hawthorne was among the earliest major writers to avail himself. These categories at many points overlap, and in his most successful work he draws on several simultaneously. Further, several of these legacies offered the materials of novelistic verisimilitude as well as types of myth, allegory, or the marvelous. Such eclecticism is of course characteristic of any author who uses ancient forms to express contemporary modes and themes. Among Hawthorne's favorite models—Spenser, Shakespeare, Milton—may be found similar combinations of classical myths with Christian themes, of figures drawn from pagan rituals and used to dramatize contemporary political, religious, and psychological conflicts. Hawthorne mythologizes actual history and makes mythic actions appear historical. His repertoire is rich, for he draws on all the strains of legend and fable his culture provided.

We may take first a simple instance of his mythologizing New England's annals. Hawthorne's interest in the Puritan past is intrinsic with his impulse to view history as fabulous. The impulse is plain in such titles as "Legends of the Province House," or "Old-Time Legends," of which he at first conceived *The Scarlet Letter* to be one. He based the opening story in

Twice-Told Tales upon an episode, or anecdote, recorded in Thomas Hutchinson's *History of the Province and Colony of Massachusetts-Bay:* the mysterious appearance at Hadley of "a grave elderly person" who rallied the settlers against an Indian attack.[10] The colonists' savior was said to be Goffe, the regicide, a fugitive in the New World from the vengeance of the Crown. Scott, in *Peveril of the Peak,* greatly expanded the tale, changing the identity of the Angel of Hadley from Goffe to Whalley, another Puritan signatory of King Charles's death warrant. In "The Gray Champion" Hawthorne takes this legendary motif, a local variant of the theme in world folklore of the ancient hero (originally a god) returned to deliver his people,[11] and turns it to a different use from what his sources made of it. In "The Gray Champion" the conflict is not between whites and Indians but between New England's "religious multitude, with their sad visages . . . " and their "despotic rulers, with the high churchman in the midst . . . all magnificently clad, flushed with wine, proud of unjust authority." The scene represents "the condition of New England, and its moral, the deformity of any government that does not grow out of the nature of things and the character of the people." Clearly the miraculous appearance of the Gray Champion is Hawthorne's invocation of a Divine Providence on the side of the oppressed. Faith in the Providence, or wonder, which inspired Hutchinson's original version, not only domesticated to New England an ancient folk belief, but is, for Hawthorne's purposes, a specifically Puritan expression of God's intervention on the side of righteous men in their rebellion against arbitrary power.[12]

The unconditional approval of rebellion in "The Gray Champion"—obviously a "type" or analogue of the Revolution—is greatly qualified in a later tale on a similar theme. "My Kinsman, Major Molineux" is a much more complex dramatization of the conflict between an aristocratic past and a demotic future, and its dependencies in myth are accordingly richer. Inextricably welded to the political conflict (the plot of rebellious colonists against their royal governor) is the psychological conflict of young Robin's coming of age. The action conforms doubly to ancient patterns of ritual: the ceremony of a youth's initiation into knowledge, and the expunging of evil through the sacrifice of a scapegoat king.[13] That the youth is a Yankee bumpkin, callow and unillumined by a full recognition of the tragedy of which he is witness and participant; that the scapegoat is both his uncle (an obvious displacement of the father) and an inoffensive, dignified aristocrat, makes this tale particularly suggestive of the consequences for America of both personal and national independence. Use of the pattern derived from scapegoat ritual gives the tale a further suggestion of the renewal of fertility with the supercession of the old, exhausted ruler by the vigorous revolutionaries. At the same time, Robin learns that he must come to terms with his father's original sin (presented in sexual terms—the prostitute is familiar with his kinsman); his assumption of adult independence means also his assuming responsibility for sin. A further qualification of rebellion is that the conspiracy against the governor is led, not by a divinely ordained ghostly champion, but by a conspiratorial ruffian disguised as a devil with a double mask, the Lord of Misrule in the Saturnalia. Insofar as Hawthorne proffers any consolation, it is in that his misrule is succeeded by the calm wisdom of the stranger who befriends Robin at the end. And he represents the wise, loving, but unpossessive elements in the paternal figure whose other aspects appear, as in a dream, split among Robin's sinful, absurd, and threatening interlocutors—as well as in the victim kinsman.

Another source of "the Marvellous" appears in his "Legends of the Province House," which like the foregoing tales mythologize New England history. "Howe's Masquerade" and

"Edward Randolph's Portrait" are Gothic allegories of the fall of tyrants, and "Lady Eleanore's Mantle" displays the sins of a proud aristocrat. These "legends" are told in a mansion, once resplendent with "vice-regal pomp" but in the present democratic era a dilapidated tavern, which somewhat qualifies the author's endorsement of the allegories. The Province House not only represents the unfortunate leveling effects of democracy, it actually *is* the haunted house of the ensuing legends. Hawthorne takes over the stock machinery of Gothic fiction—besides the haunted house, there are supernally prophetic pictures, allusions to witchcraft, a retributive curse.[14] Such properties, devised to reveal the demonic, libidinous, and anarchic energies of the unconscious of which rationalism took no account, were all too readily used in the service of mere sensation. But Hawthorne presses them into the service of morality, makes them function in allegories expressing serious political ideas and psychological conceptions. In the fourth legend, "Old Esther Dudley," we see again the predicament of his imagination, committed to overthrowing the past whose values he would cherish in an age of change. He has Governor Hancock (in fact a firebrand of the Revolution) treat the slightly demented and pathetic old Loyalist with dignity: "We represent a new race of men—living no longer in the past, scarcely in the present—but projecting ourselves into the future," he says in a passage prophetic of Holgrave's millennial politics. "We will follow her reverently to the tomb of her ancestors; and then, my fellow-citizens, onward—onward! We are no longer children of the Past!"

The Gothic mode proved more resonant still when used to explore the psychology of the Puritan character. Taking superstition as seriously, for imaginative purposes, as he took religion, Hawthorne based "Young Goodman Brown" on a similar ritualistic structure to that of "My Kinsman," the initiation of a youth into the meaning of his life. In Young Goodman Brown's journey through the dark wood toward the culminating orgy of the Witches' Sabbath, Hawthorne brings powerfully together masterful images of witchcraft, a conception at once historical, theological, folkloric, and literary. Hawthorne had read with fascination and, he tells us, guilt in the trial proceedings of 1692, when an ancestor had been an unrepenting judge of those accused. Through the writings of Increase and Cotton Mather, Hawthorne became familiar with theological interpretations of witchcraft from the *Malleus Maleficarum* (1489) down to their day. Further, Hawthorne knew, and used in his tale, folk beliefs common in New England. Witchcraft thus provided a widely accepted, fully developed set of metaphors for a rebellious, parodic inversion of Christianity—a form of forbidden knowledge into which an acolyte seeks initiation. Traditionally, witchcraft meant sexual abandon, demonism, the Devil's Compact.[15] In Goethe's *Faust* and in Cervantes' *El colloquio de los perros* (both of which Hawthorne had read with care), witchcraft is specifically allied both to sexuality and to nightmare. Hawthorne restores to this superstition its mythic grandeur as a religion that rivals the true faith. Young Goodman Brown's unhappy pilgrimage is a compelling study of what seemed to Hawthorne the least admirable aspects of the Puritan mind, its repression of instinct and the consequent risk of the denial of both faith and love. For Faith, Young Goodman's bride, was also at the orgiastic black mass. Unlike her husband, she can accept man in his fallen state and love him still. He who loves perfection only must have a chilly heart. Others of Hawthorne's Puritan characters are ennobled by their knowledge of personal guilt as a part of the general guilt of mankind. Such is the case for Mr. Hooper, for Dimmesdale, for Hester. But Brown is isolated by his fellowship with the fallen.

Clearly, witchcraft provided Hawthorne with the obverse of the unfallen Eden of Merry Mount. Mythic action requires the plausibility of the supernatural. The cosmology of Hawthorne's antique New World includes the unattainable and undepicted Heaven of which the Puritans strove to be worthy in the harsh discipline of their Earthly City; the orgiastic image of the Devil's Font, where the generations of men repeat their original sin and find a fellowship that mocks both the Heavenly and the Earthly City; and the Arcadian alternative, a chimaera of Heaven since salvation is not possible without knowledge of sin.

In writings set in contemporary time, the claims of realism require that the use of such mythic properties be more covert. But, as was true of his tales of artists, Hawthorne found the native analogues of myths in the revolutionary and millennial energies of his time. As Mr. Lewis has noted, in so rudimentary a sketch as "Earth's Holocaust" Hawthorne had "articulated the need he detected in the atmosphere of the day for a purgatorial action," a ritualistic purification making possible a life of unexampled virtue.[16] This is but a modern myth of the Golden Age, the attempt to live as though man could make himself unfallen by an act of will. No doubt the paradigms of "Earth's Holocaust" appeared among the eccentric Millerites, but the energies they so vehemently expressed were as much a part of America's secular, political inheritance as of sectarian zeal. Hawthorne seems instinctively to have embodied this energy in his fiction in a ritualistic structure, associating it with actions that resemble those in myths by their cosmological scope and by their articulation of communally shared emotions.

IV

In the two romances set in contemporary New England the foregoing patterns of mythic action are combined with a careful delineation of actuality. Myths provide thematic structures; the characters are partly romance figures, numinous and abstract, the creatures of myth and allegory, and partly the individualized characters of the novel. In *The House of the Seven Gables,* conflicts between past and present, between a proud aristocracy and an equally proud plebeian class, are drawn from the matter of Puritanism, combined with colonial history, Gothicism, superstition, contemporary folklore, and popular culture. The setting, like the Province House, is the American equivalent of the haunted castle of Gothic romance. The house is haunted by the inherited guilt of both the Pyncheons and the Maules. The conflict is in part political, the oppression of the humble, honest, and unoffending by the rich, privileged, and powerful. Pyncheon prosecutes Maule for witchcraft to defraud him of the land on which to build the house. In their schemes to found a dynastic line of nobles, the Pyncheons reiterate their original sin of prideful alienation from mankind, and merit the curse upon them of the first Maule's dying words. Subsequently, popular belief in the guilt of the Maules encourages the victim's descendants to practice such black arts as the evil eye and hypnotism against the Pyncheons. Because they remain unforgiving, the Maules become witches in fact, and so contribute to the double descent of original sin in the two families. The motifs are thus political, psychological, and theological. The garden of the haunted house is an Eden defiled, and a return to primal innocence is possible only in the present generation, when a country cousin of the Pyncheons, reared in innocence of the family guilt, moves into the house. Phoebe's counterpart among the Maules is Holgrave, an apostle of the latest philosophies of progress who would cast off the dead hand of the past and live as though he were the self-begotten master of his own fate. Holgrave is both a modern Representative Man and the up-to-date version of the Yankee character, delineated in his earlier stages as the resilient peddler in "Mr. Higginbotham's Catastrophe," the naïvely self-reliant bumpkin in "My Kinsman, Major Molineux," and the sententious sage, Uncle Venner. Holgrave seems a more widely experienced cousin of Eustace Bright. Where his proud forebear had driven an earlier Pyncheon lady to madness, Holgrave instead marries Phoebe. As easily as that may ghosts be exorcised in mid-century New England.

The Blithedale Romance takes a much less sanguine view of the possibility of reforming society than even the equivocal ending of Seven Gables suggests. The settlement at Blithedale is an attempt by city dwellers to escape from the corruption of the grimy metropolis and begin life anew, a reconstitution of the unfallen life, as at Merry Mount. Imagery of the Golden Age abounds; arriving in a snowstorm, Coverdale, the ironic narrator, observes, before catching pneumonia, "How cold an Arcadia was this!" The book is his story, an anti-Arcadia chronicling the communitarians' failure to replace pride with "familiar love." The themes explored in The Blithedale Romance are the essentials of life: man's knowledge of himself, of his relationships to others, of his place in time and in nature. None of the communitarians came to Blithedale aware of the truth of any of these. What partial discoveries are made by the principal characters are painful and lead to the abandonment of the communal ideal, the humbling of Hollingsworth's pride, and the suicide of Zenobia. The ironical use of the Golden Age is emphasized by manifold references to seasonal rituals, particularly—as at Merry Mount—May Day, which Zenobia and Priscilla regard as a "movable festival." The voluptuous Zenobia of course is Queen of the May, but what chance of harvest when there is no king? May Day itself is but one of a cluster of images of rebirth; these include Coverdale's recovery from sickness; the illusory rebirth of the topers in the grog shop; Old Moodie's assumption of his present, pauperish personality after the "death" of his former opulent and profligate phase; and of course the very purpose of the Blithedale colony is to bring on the rebirth of society. These psychological, socio-political, and ritual processes support one another. But most of the rebirths in the romance are attempted without the requisite "deaths" or renunciations, and so are doomed to failure. A further current of mythic metaphors appears in the suggestion that Zenobia (the daughter of Old Moodie when he was princely Fauntleroy) and Priscilla (her half-sister, and daughter of Moodie in his poverty) are associated with Aphrodite and Persephone, both the daughters of Zeus. Priscilla is sent to Blithedale, where her arrival unleashes subsequent troubles, by Moodie, the Zeus-like father figure.[17] Old Moodie has a patch over one eye; if he suggests a deity it will be not only Zeus but Odin, also the father god and deity of wisdom and poetry.

Where *The House of the Seven Gables* used mainly Puritan, Gothic, and contemporary materials, *The Blithedale Romance* is built on contemporary experience ironically interpreted against classical parallels and prototypes. Puritanism contributes the iron rigidity of Hollingsworth's character, the repressed skirting of passion in Coverdale's, and the characteristic division of feminine personality into the dark luxuriance of Zenobia and the pale passivity of Priscilla. Gothicism in *Blithedale* is less a matter of setting or of magic than of the manner of telling the tale: Coverdale's story is involuted, complex, mysterious, but the mysteries prove functionally necessary to a romance that demonstrates the difficulties of knowing the primal facts about ourselves.

Although a stylistically distinguished, urbane study of the intelligentsia, *The Blithedale Romance* seems a much less novelistic work than any of Hawthorne's other books. Its complicated structure has been protested by many readers. Yet if we approach it in terms of its own form, *The Blithedale Romance* proves a coherent and effective work. "Myth . . . is one extreme of literary design; naturalism is the other," writes Mr. Frye, "and in between lies the whole area of romance," which tends "to displace myth in a human direction and yet, in contrast to 'realism,' to conventionalize content in an idealized direction."[18] It was by such symbolic architecture, building verisimilitude upon a structure of myth, that Hawthorne dramatized the conflicts in the present between the values of an aristocratic past and an egalitarian future.

Thus Hawthorne could be faithful both to the truth of the human heart and to the laws of art. The ideality of his solution to the problem in "The Artist of the Beautiful" seemed to propose an art so subjective that its only function is the self-realization of its creator. In these other tales and romances, however, Hawthorne achieves an imaginative transfiguration of nature. In such ways as we have seen, he moves us from the domain of necessity to the reality of the understanding. When the materials of this art are not merely the mechanical parts of a toy butterfly but the depiction of a human soul or a society, the artist's perfection of nature leads him and his readers toward that escape from incomprehensible change of which the ancients made their myth of the Golden Age.

At Merry Mount and at Blithedale, those who would transform life into eternity spend their days in pageants, masquerades, and song. The imagery of these mimetic arts in Arcadia allies them to the perfection which their performers vainly seek. Their error is to assume that the escape from time made possible by art is an option allowed in life as well. At Blithedale the society of dreamers had undertaken to create a perfect community. Had they succeeded, this accomplishment would indeed have been their "Romance," in which men had taken the parts of gods in myths and evaded their fates as fallen creatures. Among other things, *The Blithedale Romance* tells us that although man cannot so free himself in action, he can in art discover a fuller understanding of life than life itself provides. It is Coverdale, the ironic and detached narrator, who alone of the communitarians learns, through the wry discipline of his recollections, the true relations of them all to one another, to nature, and to time.

Hawthorne's romances prove more durable than the artist's crushed toy or the melted snow image of the children. These works, intermingling the marvelous with reality, have endured the skepticism or scorn of those who made the author of *Twice-Told Tales* think himself "the obscurest man of letters in America." Like the myths which they clothe with the morality and the manners of their age, these tales seem indestructible. They have become a permanent part of our inheritance.

Roy Harvey Pearce

Romance

and the

Study

of History

For Américo Castro

I N OUR TIME, the image of Hawthorne as symbolic romancer has been marvelously elucidated, verified, and expounded. Yet we may have been too successful in delineating this image. For we have tended to rush on, identifying and collocating his symbols and their forms, and then pursuing them out of space— out of time, too often beyond the consciousnesses of those whose life in art they make possible. I propose here a relatively cautionary enterprise—an inquiry into the style (I dare say the "life-style") of Hawthorne as symbolic romancer. The goal of the inquiry is to comprehend how Hawthorne's art, in its explorations of agonized consciousness, drives him back into the origins of his world, and is thus a means of revealing—symbolically—how it has spawned him and his fellows, his readers.

Confronted with Hawthorne's fictions, puzzled by the fact that they are not novels but romances, fascinated by the complex of symbolic processes which give them their integrity—we have hesitated to place them in this world. For to do so, were we to assent to them, would be also to place ourselves in his world. Instinctively perhaps, we have resisted being drawn out of our world into his. Even ours, we say, is already too much with us. So we have allegorized, mythologized, psychoanalyzed, theologized—all to the end of deriving Hawthorne's symbols from a world which neither he nor we ever could have made. But the burden of Hawthorne's fictions is to teach us that we must learn to live in, to be responsible to and for, a world which we never made . . . or at best did not intend to make. This, I take it, is the burden of the historian—at least when he writes fiction.

Hawthorne, then, is the symbolist as historian. And as such, he derives his symbols not from myth or exotic learning or Swedenborgianism, or post-Kantianism, but from the facts of history itself—the factuality of the American historical experience as he studied and understood it. There are symbolic "correspondences" in his fiction—but, unlike the symbols in the work of his great contemporaries, they are mysterious only for those people in his stories whose culture is at once bound and strengthened by a central commitment to the mysterious. Hawthorne wants always to "explain" such correspondences, not to celebrate them, much less lose himself in them. (Surely, he is the most "rational" of the writers of his period. I suspect that a source of his difficulty for us lies precisely in his insistent rationalism and that his discussions of the qualities of the "romance" are meant to bid us not to confuse the "strange" with the "mysterious." In an altogether American way, he would make the strange familiar without domesticating it.) Explaining such correspondences, Hawthorne is able to reveal a most humane mystery—that of the working of art. For in those of his stories which are studies of history, he repeatedly discovers a larger correspondence—that between past and present. And he demonstrates that this correspondence is a matter of the quite factual continuity of past into present. He is able to take his readers into the past, so to let them discover for themselves that knowing the past as it was is a necessary condition of living in the present as it is.

Like Poe, Emerson, Melville, and Whitman, he was not fond of the America in which he lived—a world in which individualism lacked the institutional constraints whereby it could be contained, shaped, and made part of a true community. In this world, Poe tried to establish the role of literature as a kind of overriding institution which guaranteed the freedom and autonomy of the self; Emerson and Whitman tried to work toward a poetry in which the self, through a renewed sense of its tie to nature and God, would transcend itself and establish a new religion; Melville sought for mythic understanding and ended late in his life, if I read *Billy Budd* correctly, with a Christian orthodoxy which he found second-best but nonetheless inevitable. All, as we know, in effect took from the New England Puritan tradition the emphasis on the symbolic mode of understanding whereby man may know his fate. None of them, of course, could accept Puritan dogma. But all of them, except Hawthorne, looked beyond history, toward something larger than the human situation as given in the past and in the present. Unlike Hawthorne, they looked beyond the temporal and mundane for an authoritative guarantee of the veracity of such symbols as in their art they might discover.

Hawthorne not only took from the Puritan tradition its symbolic mode of understanding but accepted, if not the dogma of Puritanism, at least the conception of human nature, marked by an exacerbated and refined self-consciousness, which that dogma had been taken to confirm and account for. The very power in his rendering of a characteristically American consciousness derives initially from his awareness of its being specifically a form of Puritan consciousness. In one segment of his fiction, he did nothing less than use Puritanism to understand Puritanism, and thus worked toward an understanding—symbolic by virtue of being historical—of the American's Puritan origins. In another segment, he studied later American life, including that of his own time, and showed how it was trying to escape the burden—and was thus missing the rewards—of its heritage. For him, then, Puritanism was, in fact, American history. The factuality of past life had to be transformed into the symbolism of present art and thereby be made part of the factuality of his readers' lives as they might live them. The task he set himself in his art was to make Puritanism "correspond" to American history: through Puritanism and its conception of the nature and destiny of man, to find the means of making the American understand his own nature and destiny in the modern world. Hawthorne set out to make of American history not just a record of events, of successes and failures, much less a working out of a mystique, but a vital, indeed necessary and intrinsic, element in the American's consciousness of himself as American. History, the American's own, was to become a means to knowing and living with the self, the American's own. We are given a variation on Ortega's celebrated dictum, "Man has not a nature but a history."

Hawthorne's variation is: "Man has no nature, except in his history."

Hawthorne was, as historian-romancer, more of a radical than he could bring himself to acknowledge. I use the word *radical* advisedly. For in his work Hawthorne is not only calling for, but forcing his readers—specifically his American readers—toward, a new and radical vision of history. The radical quality derives more from the process whereby the vision is to be achieved than from what is envisioned. But the two—process and substance—are not unrelated. In his fiction—by virtue of his technique as symbolist—Hawthorne would inculcate in his readers not just a sense of what history had been but a sense of what it was to be in history: by virtue of historical understanding to discover oneself once and for all inescapably paying the price for the rewards one reaped from the past. To know the past was not, for him, to view it from the heights of the present. It was to descend into the depths of the past—so to discover quite directly that one could get back to the heights, live in the present, only if he could bring himself to suffer symbolically that painful ascent which constituted the process of history. And the future? Today's heights, it would turn out, were tomorrow's depths.

It is true that Hawthorne wrote in an age obsessively conscious of history: above all, of its own history. But his historical consciousness, the kind he wanted to inculcate, was radically different from that of his contemporaries.

Historical understanding, for Hawthorne's contemporaries, generally entailed what philosophers call a metaphysical philosophy of history: that is, the discovery and elucidation of the laws of historical development whereby one could see how movement from past to present had *necessarily* occurred as in fact it had. There are a number of names for this particular metaphysical philosophy of history: among others, the idea of progress and Manifest Destiny. When, for example, one looks into the plans for the antiquarian societies which burgeoned in the first half of the nineteenth century, one finds stated again and again that the reason men collect historical data is that, when laid end to end, they will comprise a developmental pattern which in itself will guarantee that data-collecting is a meaningful activity. And I am sure that if one looked into the relationship between the sort of data collected and the informing reason for the collecting—the rationale for antiquarian curiosity—one would find operating a kind of preselective factor. The antiquarian found what he was looking for because he had known from the beginning that what he would look for would be "significant." In effect, he was carrying on an operation in deduction in a manner which he was so sure of that he could call it, without the least uneasiness, inductive. Such scientific history, such Baconian history, as it were, was in effect the product of an amateur operation in metaphysics.[1]

The example is perhaps trivial. But when one looks into the establishment of many of the local history societies in the period, one finds that the quantity of such trivial enterprises has great qualitative significance for the period's sense of history. And the example is of a piece with others, surely not trivial. There is, for example, Jared Sparks, whose general statements of his aims as historian read like so many versions of a Fourth of July oration. And at a more sophisticated level, there are Hildreth and Bancroft, whose politics are not exactly alike but whose notions of historical process are essentially the same. There is not yet an adequate history of American history: one which will inquire into the relationship among a given historian's historical commitment, his method as a "researcher," and his style as a writer. If multi-volumed Bancroft is concrete, particular, at times a powerful narrator, it is because he categorizes so well. He renders everything and everyone "typical." And he can do so only because his quite sophisticated metaphysical philosophy of history—charged as it is with the power of post-Kantian ontological concepts—lets him know in the second place exactly what he wanted to know in the first place.

In the context of this essay, it is best to recall the state of the American historical novel in Hawthorne's time. Here is William Gilmore Simms in his Preface to the 1853 edition of *The Yemassee*:

> What is the modern Romance itself? The reply is immediate. The modern Romance is the substitute which the people of the present day offer for the ancient epic. . . .
>
> When I say that our Romance is the substitute of modern times for the epic or the drama, I do not mean to say that they are exactly the same things, and yet, examined thoroughly, and [sic] the differences between them are slight. The Romance is of loftier origin than the novel. It approximates the poem. . . . It does not confine itself to what is known, or even what is probable. It grasps at the possible. . . .

(And later, speaking of *The Yemassee* itself)

> It is needless to add that the historical events are strictly true. . . .

As Simms's words show, the historical romance shares this with historical writing proper: that, like the "ancient epic," it is based on "true" events. I suggest that, as with the "ancient epic," it shares something further: a metaphysical theory of history (in the case of *The Yemassee*, the idea of progress as embodied in the inevitable and necessary victory of civilization over barbarism—or "savagism"). This is the sort of metaphysical philosophy of history that guarantees the significance of the events which, together, constitute the past. The appeal to the pattern of the epic and to the mode of poetry, and also the emphasis on the "possible"—these are justifications for the way Simms makes his version of the idea of progress create rather than derive from the "truth" of the historical events which *The Yemassee* recounts. Thus Simms's style as writer is of the same order as Bancroft's—"better," but of the same order.

It is also of the same order as Cooper's and Parkman's—the romancer as historian and the historian as romancer. There is in them, above all, that quality of "typicality." Their "vividness" is not the vividness of richly particular details, to be known as such, but rather the vividness of the portraitist who composes according to an ideal which has become a necessary idea. The gain is a powerful sense of the meaning of the totality of events with which they deal. The loss is of a sense of complexity and involvement. All in all, Cooper and Parkman operate from the heights. They celebrate the struggle whereby the heights were gained. Because they understand so much, they often cannot see enough. But were they to see enough, they could not understand so much. Behind them, as source and inspiration, lies the work of the great eighteenth-century historiographers, and, most important, the work of Scott. And Scott, too, as recent study of his work has shown, brings to his great historical novels a metaphysical philosophy of history: an idea of progress whereby the past can be conceived, even celebrated, precisely as it has had necessarily to give way to the present.

In the *North American Review* in 1853, Parkman summed up the meaning of Cooper's work and, I think, of much of his own:

> Civilization has a destroying as well as a creating power. It is exterminating the buffalo and the Indian over whose fate too many lamentations, real or affected, have been sounded for us to renew them here. It must . . . eventually sweep from before it a class of men, its own precursors and pioneers, so remarkable both in their virtues and faults, that few will

see their extinction without regret. Of these men Leather-stocking is the representative; and though in him the traits of the individual are quite as prominent as those of the class, yet his character is not on this account less interesting, or less worthy of permanent remembrance. His life conveys in some sort an epitome of American history, during one of its most busy and decisive periods.

One notes the emphasis on Leatherstocking as representative, as "typical"—of his life as an "epitome." It is the inevitability of Leatherstocking's history (civilization "must" destroy if it is to create) which gives Parkman the means of comprehending Cooper's work—as it gave Cooper the means of doing it.

A more recent writer, himself at once master of and mastered by a metaphysical philosophy of history, puts the matter thus:

As an explorer of the forest and prairies of the "New World," [Leatherstocking] blazes new trails in them for people who later condemn him as a criminal because he has infringed their mercenary and, to his sense of freedom, unintelligible laws. All his life he has unconsciously served the great cause of geographical expansion of material culture in a country of uncivilized people and found himself incapable of living in the conditions of this culture for which he had struck the first paths.

The writer I am quoting is Maxim Gorky. And I think it not surprising that a Marxist should clearly comprehend a work like Cooper's. Indeed, the one major book we have on the historical novel is that of a great Marxist critic, Georg Lukacs (his *Das Historische Roman*). Lukacs, from whose study I have taken the quotation from Gorky, is so sure in his own metaphysical philosophy of history (for dialectical materialism is a kind of metaphysics) that he can, in a sort of elective affinity, comprehend and elucidate Cooper, and with him Scott, in a fashion altogether consonant with that of Cooper's Mani-fest Destiny–conscious contemporaries.

229

I cite Gorky and Lukacs to put my topic into a more contemporary perspective. For the metaphysical philosophy of history in Cooper, Parkman, and the others is to Hawthorne's *critical* philosophy of history (so philosophers today would call it) as dialectical materialism is to what is now called existential historicism. (The sentence I have cited from Ortega and what I have called Hawthorne's variation on it are expressions of a central tenet of existential historicism.) The mode of historical understanding characteristic of Hawthorne's work—as a kind of critical philosophy of history—is as radically opposed to that of Parkman's, Cooper's, and the others' as the thought of an Ortega is to that of a Lukacs or a Gorky. This set of oppositions suggests that Hawthorne is "ours" precisely as his sense of history is ours—or, in his art, may become ours. Reading him, we may become more secure in his knowledge that our history has not only produced but includes us. Man has no nature, except in his history.

The problem, then, is to see how Hawthorne, working in the symbolist mode, acting on the assurance that the correspondential method of knowledge was valid at least for art, in effect rejected his age's dominant mode of historical understanding and strove to put in its place a mode altogether consonant with the events of past (particularly the Puritan past) and the present (particularly the New England present) as he knew them, indeed experienced them. For the key word in Emerson's thinking is also the key word in Hawthorne's: "experience." These much-quoted words from Emerson's essay "Experience" are helpful here: "It is an unhappy thing, but too late to be helped, the discovery we have made that we exist. The discovery is called the Fall of Man." Emerson wanted always through experience to transcend experience. Hawthorne resisted that temptation. Indeed, he measured the achievement of many of the characters in his fiction precisely as they did and did not resist that temptation. Existence for him was experience, experience in history. A major burden of Hawthorne's work, I propose to demonstrate, is that human existence is ineluctably historical; and an inevitable aim of his work is to put that burden on us.

Hawthorne's "historical" fiction divides into two types: that in which he treats directly and that in which he treats indirectly of the past—the latter in terms of its bearings on the present or on periods out of the past treated as though they were present.

Of the stories of the first type, the simplest may be represented by "The Gray Champion." Here Hawthorne quite directly memorializes a fabulous, quite obviously symbolic, episode out of American history. The time, it is made quite explicit, is the late seventeenth century, when New England is suffering under the oppression of the Restoration governor Sir Edmund Andros. Hawthorne here creates a kind of folk-tale, with a folk-tale's special symbolic tone. Faced with Andros' tyranny, itself a reflection of the anti-protestantism of James II, the people have need of a defender; and he miraculously appears—an old man, a patriarch, to all appearances a man out of those days earlier in the century when the Puritan way was strongest. He challenges the governor and his entourage, foretells the end of James's Catholic regime, saying: "Back, thou wast a Governor, back! With this night thy power is ended—tomorrow, the prison!—back, lest I foretell the scaffold!" The governor and his entourage turn back; and the next day, the people learn that King James has abdicated, that William has succeeded him and assured the continuity of the protestant, thus New England, the Puritan way of life. The Champion disappears. And Hawthorne will not say whence he came, where he went, who he was. He will say that he is a man who appeared in time of need—as during the Battle of Bunker Hill which began our Revolutionary War. . . . Here, then, *is* a kind of folk-tale; but its teller is not of a folk society, nor even of Puritan society, and so he cannot literally believe in the actual existence of the Gray Champion, nor can his modern sophisticated readers. For those readers, as for himself, he suggests, only suggests, that the old man was a kind of invention of the communal mind in its time of need; a need to have a champion for its rights; a need, that is to say, to have a symbol. The art of the story is to make the reader participate in the invention of the symbol.

This kind of ending characterizes many of the other stories of the first type. And they are artistically all the more credible because Hawthorne makes much of the actual—that is, historically verifiable—existence of the symbolic mode of understanding among the seventeenth-century Puritans of whom he treats in stories of this type. At the end, he always declines, or seems to decline, to believe in the existence in fact of the symbols which his characters discover all about them and in terms of which they order their understanding of themselves and their society. For him—and, thus, in his art, for his readers —historicity lies in an act deriving from the need to invent the symbol, not in the symbol itself. The symbol is thus a product of an act in history. The protagonist of "Young Goodman Brown" leaves his wife (called Faith) to go into the woods a while and keep a rendezvous with Satan. In the woods he learns—or thinks he learns—that all those people in the community whom he had believed good are themselves of Satan's party, even his wife, his Faith. In a moment of fearful revelation, he finds that even his faith in himself is destroyed. And at the end, we are told that he lives out his life thereafter a hollow shell of a man. Hawthorne leaves it a matter of question whether or not Young Goodman Brown literally saw what he is said to have seen; or whether the whole vision, the whole complex of symbols which make up the vision, is a product of Young Goodman Brown's lack of faith and a resulting despair so destructive as to transform the Puritan's usual symbolic understanding of his world into its opposite. Hawthorne's art is such as to make us conclude that, granting the Puritan faith by which Young Goodman Brown lived, granting the Puritan's disposition to see that faith revealed symbolically in his day-to-day life, granting the Puritan obsession with "spectral evidence," it is inevitable that Young Goodman Brown should have envisioned his loss of faith as he did and as a consequence have been destroyed as a person.

Young Goodman Brown enters the underworld of the society depicted in "The Gray Champion." The pattern, of course, is that of Hawthorne's celebrated "ambiguity." What needs particular emphasis here is that the net effect of an ambiguous ending such as this is to insist on the historicity of stories like "The Gray Champion" and "Young Goodman Brown." For hallucination of the sort depicted in them is impossible without the concrete and particular sociocultural situation in which it occurs. Symbol-making on this level is a product of mass hallucination. Hallucination, then, is not per se bad. It must be judged in terms of its results—its products as they do or do not make possible authentic communal existence. When a symbolist operates as a historian, he inevitably operates within the limits of the human.

Many of Hawthorne's great stories are articulated in a pattern such as that in "The Gray Champion" and "Young Goodman Brown." In the pattern, we can make out three modes, or levels, of symbolism: (1) There is the symbolism integral to the life of the seventeenth-century Puritans about whom the stories are told—the sort of symbolism I have been discussing. (2) Deriving from this first level of symbolism, there is the symbolism which Hawthorne chooses to construct by the emphasis and order of his art—that is, those symbols which are made to extend in their implications *beyond* the life of Puritan society: in "Young Goodman Brown," for example, the journey from the town to the woods, the withdrawal of a man from his community, the search for lonely insight into self. (3) In turn deriving from this second level of symbolism, there is the whole Puritan world and its particular sense of the self: our "created" grasp of the Puritan Weltanschauung which, in all its integrity and wholeness, is a symbol, in the American present, of the American past.

We should note that it is symbolism at the second and third levels which show best the power and precision of Hawthorne's art. If it were not for the fact that these modes seldom exist in Hawthorne's work except in reference, implicitly or explicitly, to the first, we might well be justified in considering them only incidentally as symbolic modes. In any case, here the symbols become universal motifs—at least, motifs repeated again and again in Hawthorne's stories. Unlike the symbols of the first level, they are not the products, for good and for bad, of hallucination. We are not asked to believe in these symbols simply because they are symbols and historically definable as such. We are asked to believe in them as Hawthorne's rendering of the lives and minds of his characters leads us to believe in them. The movement from the village to the woods—which is a repeated symbolic motif in Hawthorne's fictions—this we find symbolic because, as we read the stories of people whose movement it is, we find ourselves identifying with them, feeling our way into their very consciousness; and we discover that their symbolic quest is one which may very likely be ours. Such symbolic structures, that is to say, manifest all too human needs, drives, hopes, fears, anxieties, beliefs which we can accept as potentially ours. And so we believe in the symbols as we believe in—understand historically—the people whose lives give meaning to them. It is of the essence of Hawthorne's art that the symbolism of the second and third modes exist to express and achieve perspective and understanding of the first, that symbolism whose authority lies in its historicity.

Thus, as I have said, Hawthorne is, in a way, more of a Puritan than are those Puritans whose lives he treats. For the symbols whereby their lives were lived were fixed, rigid, taken to be not a product of man's power to see what he could but of God's power to let man see what He would. Hawthorne's Puritans—whose symbolism is of the first level as I described it—are confined, restricted, imprisoned by their symbolism. Hawthorne himself, and we as his readers, are liberated by his symbolism—liberated to know, to be, and to act. Yet we are not entirely free; for we are, at the least, obliged to consider the world as in art it may be symbolically understood. And we find ourselves caught up in history—made by it even as we make it.

The greatest of Hawthorne's stories which center on Puritan life directly—the first type of my two—is, of course, *The Scarlet Letter*. And I have meant the remarks I have just made to take me directly into consideration of *The Scarlet Letter*. Let me say briefly how noting the three levels of symbolism as I have described them is a way of beginning to understand Hawthorne's achievement in *The Scarlet Letter*. There is first of all the symbolically ordered world in which Hester Prynne and the others live. All that happens is taken as a "sign" of something; Hester's cloak is adorned with the *A*; and, accepting it and what it signifies to the community, Hester decorates it. She too must accept the symbolically ordered world in which she lives, must accept the symbolic interpretation of her own sin, so that she can accept and acknowledge the fact of its sinfulness. And at the end of the story, when the people in the town see the *A* formed by the clouds and, naturally

235

enough, take it as a sign, Hawthorne tells us how completely—
and in an ironic way, satisfactorily—ordered was this world by
the symbols which its members found everywhere around them.
We should recall, too, that at the end Hawthorne himself
equivocates, as he does at the end of "Young Goodman Brown."
He equivocates so that we may acknowledge how "natural" it
was for the Puritans to find the symbolic *A* in the clouds; so
at the same time, we may grant that we cannot be sure of
anything but what the *A* stood for, what manifestation of all
too human consciousness it might reveal. Still, their hallucination
becomes ours, as their needs become ours.

It is in what I have called the second mode of symbolism—
where we can be convinced that all symbolism is, quite simply,
expressive of the symbol-making capacity of human consciousness
—that we see Hawthorne's art so fully operative as, in the end,
to make the hallucination ours. To note some of the recurrent
symbolic motifs: again the woods versus the village, the human
community versus the natural world; again the motif of isolation
and withdrawal; and more—the contrasts between white and
black, light and dark, the organic and the inorganic, reality and
its mirror images. Much of the most important criticism of
The Scarlet Letter has centered about Hawthorne's way of
working with such motifs. Such criticism has insufficiently
noted, I think, that these motifs represent Hawthorne's selection,
as it were, from symbolic motifs of what I have called the
first mode—those integral with, in historical fact actually part
of, seventeenth-century Puritan life itself. Hawthorne, selecting
such motifs, makes them out to be the products of the working
of the consciousness of his characters. Such symbols represent
the way Hester, Dimmesdale, and Chillingworth *see* the world
and *create* their understanding of it. Seeing their world in this
way, they bring all their consciousness into play—or at least as
much of it as they can will themselves to. And we are to judge

them precisely by their capacity to see their world, understand it, and accept their place in it. Chillingworth is worst; for he will not only understand Dimmesdale but destroy him, will place himself not only outside the community but above it. Dimmesdale finally "saves" himself by confessing in public what, at the central point in the novel, he was willing to confess only in private—in the scheme of the story, a symbolic privacy, that of the mid-town platform in the middle of the night. Hester is best, because from the first she acknowledges her sin, lives with it, suffers toward self-understanding in her isolation from her fellows, and gives love and comfort to the very community which rejects her. And little Pearl, we realize, has virtually no "human" consciousness; she is a living symbol of her parents' sin; but at the end, when all is confessed, we are told she has a name. And is not a name, a symbol—a symbol that one is oneself and that oneself has a place in the world?

Finally, the world of *The Scarlet Letter,* taken all in all, itself constitutes a symbol in what I have called the third mode: a symbol of the American's past, his history. As symbol, what does it "correspond" to? To the fact that the American's history is not something from which he can be cut off, but is rather something which, as in his living in the present he must acknowledge, has for good and for bad had a crucial role in making him what he is. The American in the 1850's, reading *The Scarlet Letter,* seeing his own culture systematically reject-ing the idea that good ends, even those of Manifest Destiny, might be achieved by evil means—this American might well have found his life changed a little as he incorporated *The Scarlet Letter* into his consciousness and into his mode of under-standing his world and of living in it. That all this is so, that Hawthorne meant it to be so, can be discovered by anyone who, if the romance in itself does not convince him, will read and meditate upon its preface. There Hawthorne, with a kind of humor and irony he needed to protect himself from the awful truth, makes himself out to be not a writer of fiction but of history. For him, one is told to conclude at the beginning, fiction was history—symbolic history transformed into symbolist fiction.

I come then to what I take to be the other type of Hawthorne's fiction: that in which he deals with the contemporary world. Here his problem is not to evoke the past as symbol, so to let the reader see how it "corresponds" to something in his own life and the life of his culture; rather, he would show how the past in necessary part becomes the present. Symbolism is thus expressed as process rather than as source or product. The personages in such fictions, and readers as they assent to the existence of such personages, discover that their very lives, in the process of being lived between past and present, are symbolic of the lives of their fellows. Their lives "correspond" to their fellows' lives—and, through the art of fiction, to their readers' lives too. Hawthorne's endeavor here is to show quite directly how the past is in fact, in experience, realized in the present. And he chooses to do so by centering his vision on men who, living intensely or ignorantly (or both) in their own time, have no sense of the past except negatively—so that they would scarcely believe that they have any connection with the past; or if they do have, that at least, they must strive to break that connection and to transcend the past by viewing it from the heights.

Stories of this second type are fewer than those of the first type. Yet they have their own kind of importance. It is interesting to note that very early in his career, in the late 1820's, Hawthorne seems to have set out to write a series of stories of this type and to collect them under the name "Provincial Tales." But the idea of such a collection did not appeal to his publishers; and Hawthorne turned toward writing stories of the first type, perhaps because they could be read as being somehow "safer"—read that way, that is, except by those willing to be adept at Hawthorne's subtleties. In any case, of the stories which were to make up the "Provincial Tales," four distinctly develop the theme characteristic of the second group as I have defined it. These are "My Kinsman, Major Molineux," "Roger Malvin's Burial," "The Gentle Boy" (this in an early version, still extant, different from the later one usually reprinted), and "Alice Doane's Appeal." Not all of these stories deal with contemporary life as such; but all deal with a time when an event out of the past comes suddenly, somehow, to be overbearingly meaningful and so forced on their protagonists an overwhelming sense of contemporaneity—a sense of contemporaneity as necessary condition of a sense of the past. That is to say, an event out of the past comes suddenly to be of enormous importance for the principal characters in the stories; and comprehending its importance, they comprehend its meaning for them and the lives they would live. They discover (often but dimly aware of the fact) that the movement of past into present as they experience it renders their lives and their fates symbolic for their fellows. The burden of their experience is all the heavier precisely by virtue of being symbolic. And it is a burden which the reader is also asked to bear.

The best of such stories is "My Kinsman, Major Molineux." Here, a young man, coming to town in search of his fortune and his paternal uncle, stumbles into a great adventure. The adventure becomes the reader's also, because it is rendered with an overwhelming sense of immediacy. It is the pre-Revolutionary period; and there is a mysterious stir in the town. After a series of Kafka-like failures to find out his uncle's address, the young man discovers that his uncle has found him. The uncle is a royalist; and in the heat of the revolutionary fervor, the townspeople are torturing him and throwing him out of the town.

And, without quite intending to, the young man joins the townspeople, the torturers, and so helps destroy his uncle, his father-figure, a part of his past. But at the end, he is not so sure. He seems to sense (Hawthorne will only let us guess) that the cost of a revolution, however right and necessary, is the useless destruction of human lives and that he will have to live with that cost. Puritan righteousness is again one with Puritan self-consciousness.

Now, why do I call this an essentially contemporary story? Because it opens with a long paragraph, written in the style of historians (with their metaphysical philosophies of history) of Hawthorne's day, in which such revolutionary violence is rationalized out of existence—as the wise saw has it: you can't make an omelet without breaking eggs. And the story in all its presentational immediacy follows hard upon the rationalization—as though Hawthorne were saying that authentic history is not a rationalization of the past but a confronting of it here and now and a living with the knowledge gained in the confrontation. Robin discovers that he is like his fellows, only more so. In this, he is for us clearly symbolic—all the more so because Hawthorne grants him intimations of self-knowledge sharp enough to let him begin to comprehend his symbolic fate.[2]

The greatest example of stories of this second type is *The House of the Seven Gables,* which does deal explicitly with contemporary life. Hawthorne was sufficiently concerned with letting his readers know what he was doing to be quite explicit in his Preface. (He wrote the Preface, I think, because he knew that his readers would need guidance as he shifted from stories of the first type to stories of the second. The "Provincial Tales" were never published as such. "The Gentle Boy," when published, appeared in a version which made it like stories of the first type. And Hawthorne did not choose to republish "My Kinsman, Major Molineux" until late in his life.) He writes: ". . . The author has provided himself with a moral,—the truth, namely that the wrong-doing of one generation lives into the successive ones, and divesting itself of every temporary advantage, becomes a pure and uncontrollable mischief. . . ." This is blunt, certainly—to our tastes perhaps too blunt. But Hawthorne tries to take account of his bluntness and of our being a little put off by saying that if his romance is to teach its moral, to have "any effective operation, it is usually through a far more subtle process than the ostensible one." Only thus may the "high truth" of art be achieved. All this is, I think, Hawthorne's way of telling us (1) that his novel concerns the role of the past in the present, and (2) that a past with such a role must be realized symbolically, as the sum-total of one's sense of the multitudinous traces of the past as they exist in the present. History is a means to moral understanding. As it may be shown to have, or be made to have, an "effective operation," history has "meaning"—symbolic meaning. History is the past in the present about to become the future.

The central character in *The House of the Seven Gables* is Holgrave—symbolically a daguerrotypist: a man who strives to make accurate images of the world, but who is in danger of letting the images he makes in all their exactness be a substitute for the world they depict, who would substitute what he takes to be factual for symbolic understanding. He lives in the House of the Seven Gables, with evidences of its curse all around him: the decline of the Pyncheon fortunes as evidenced in Hepzibah's attempts to open her store and in Clifford's return, now destroyed as a person, from a jail sentence for a crime he didn't commit; and old Judge Pyncheon, the completely successful businessman, who now even wants the decaying House among his possessions. Only Phoebe, raised in the country, away from the House, just partly a Pyncheon, manages to live on, and to make others want to live on with her. It turns out that Holgrave is a descendant of the seventeenth-century Matthew Maule who had been deprived of his rights and his property by a seventeenth-century Pyncheon, and who had cursed the Pyncheons forever. Holgrave wants his revenge. And he is a distinctly "modern" young man, with even some experience of utopian (i.e., anti-historical, future-oriented) living, so that at the same time he feels that he will be getting rid of the past once and for all. But it cannot work out this way. And in the end Judge Pyncheon dies, Clifford's innocence is discovered though his self is never recovered, Hepzibah learns to live a little in the world, and Holgrave and Phoebe are married—he having learned to accept his history, even the partial guilt of his ancestors, rather than reject it.

I suggest that the scope of *The House of the Seven Gables* is larger and more daring than we have realized. There are in its world—as in Hawthorne's own world—only the remnant of authentically Puritan symbols. Both the House itself and its curse are these. This is what I have called his symbolism at the first level, the level at which they have an actual historical existence. And at the second level, there are these symbols as Hawthorne builds upon them, shows how deeply they penetrate into the lives of those who live in their presence. At this level, the structure of symbols out of the past becomes a necessary part of the lives of those in the present. And, at the third level, the level where the past in its totality must be made meaningful—what does this world, understood symbolically, "correspond" to? To the lives of Hawthorne's contemporaries who, in their eagerness to get on with things, would reject the past. And since we are forever the contemporaries of those who write for us, it corresponds to our lives, too, or can be made to do so. Holgrave's fate, as it is central to a romance of this scope, is every American's.

But Hawthorne could in the end not bring it off. Holgrave is

an analogue of Robin Molineux. But he is older, more sophisticated, and wiser than Robin. He consciously wants to cleanse
the present of the past. And so, when he comes to discover
that the present contains the past, when he comes to discover
his own symbolic burden, we expect him to suffer. We expect
his discovery to be experienced with all the immediacy of his
earlier delight of living in the "new" world. Hawthorne, however, lets him off. And the ending is false, the romance not
perfected, the inexorability of its logic aborted. The romancer
does not carry through his role as critical philosopher of history.
Yet he could have. He should have.

Of course, I write here as a man of my time. I am mindful
that a continuing task for our novelists and poets is to write and
comprehend our history symbolically, to deal with it in such a
way as to bring into full play the capacity of consciousness to
construct a symbolic vision of the world and thereby involve
itself in the world—even the world out of the past, above all the
world out of the past. It is a task which persists, since it is the
task of being-in-the-world and so seeing how that world includes
its history. If in our time, as everywhere we are told, we are
increasingly alienated from history, then the example of Hawthorne commends itself to us all the more. Indeed, it might well
be that one of the many things which Americans pioneered as
they first entered the modern world was alienation from history.
If this is so, then it is all the more important that one American
—and I could name others—recognized this modern malaise, this
modern disease of the modern spirit, and prescribed for it: the
transformation of history-as-event to history-as-symbol—to the
end of accepting history as a fact of life, of our lives.

Man has no nature, except in his history. There are, of course,
other ways of achieving understanding of that history besides
Hawthorne's symbolic modes. I would not be understood to say
otherwise. I have only tried to suggest how for a nineteenth-

century American artist, writing so often of the very Puritans whose history is in good part his own, how for such an artist there is a fine inevitability in his having brought history itself, the sense of the past, within the scope of his special kind of symbolist art. And the ultimate meaning of all this? When that great man Max Weber was asked why he went on writing his disillusioning studies in historical sociology, he replied: "I wish to see how much I can bear." So with Hawthorne. In the exercise of his art, he wished to see how much he could bear, how much his readers could bear, how much we could bear. For he knew that what we bear is the weight of our own being, our own consciousness, our own existence, as it is inextricably bound up in our own history.

Larzer Ziff

The

Artist

and

Puritanism

F ROM 1853 to 1860, Nathaniel Hawthorne lived abroad, away from the accelerating controversy that exploded into the Civil War. His residence there was made possible by the political appointment he received from his friend, Democratic President Franklin Pierce, so that added to the detachment from war hysteria that living in Europe gave him was his commitment to an administration which, most Northerners in 1860 agreed, was one of bungling if not betrayal. The town of Concord, to which he returned in 1860, had, in his absence, grown as a center of intellectual abolitionism; and when Northern rhetoric approached the point of ignition, Concord, with its pasture battlefield, stood as the symbol of Yankee independence and intrepidity. Homecoming presented a most difficult process of repatriation for the seven-year exile.

For more than a year after his return, Hawthorne worked in vain to complete the romance he had set aside in his last years in Europe during which he had turned to *The Marble Faun;* but, as the surviving versions show, the tale wound down at one point, or split in two at another, or took a disastrous turn at a third. Accustomed as the young Hawthorne had been to working within his chamber and letting the world go by, the fifty-eight-year-old author, his powers failing, was severely affected by his alienation from a world preparing for war. His country was entering its life trial while he falteringly attempted a romance about an elixir of youth.

Finally, in March and April of 1862, Hawthorne went to the District of Columbia, there to visit his friend Horatio Bridge and there to come to some terms with the civil conflict. He saw President Lincoln, he visited the army camps, and he inspected the hospital facilities, on the whole, finding the experience invigorating. But his detachment remained, reinforced, when he wrote about his trip, by his lifelong habit of authorial irony so that the *Atlantic Monthly* insisted upon revisions and omissions before the piece was published. Wartime was not a time to be qualified in praise of the president, amused at military commanders, or ironic about patriotic efforts.

Visiting army camps, the romancer of the elixir of youth found that preparation for battle was very much like the youth-giving tonic, but that the potion was fit for neither Hawthorne the rapidly aging man nor Hawthorne the author. In "Chiefly about War Matters," he wrote:

The enervating effects of centuries of civilization vanish at once, and leave these young men to enjoy a life of hardship, and the exhilarating sense of danger,—to kill men blamelessly, or to be killed gloriously,—and to be happy in following out their native instincts of destruction, precisely in the spirit of Homer's heroes, only with some considerable change of mode. One touch of Nature makes not only the whole world, but all time, akin. Set men face to face, with weapons in their hands, and they are as ready to slaughter one another now, after playing at peace and good-will for so many years, as in the rudest ages.

Young as America might appear when contrasted with the Europe that had held him fascinated, it was regressing rapidly into an even more primitive state.

In his consideration of the Negro and slavery, Hawthorne saw the accumulated force of history at work; and in his war essay he expressed his perception in an image which was, at the time, more fanciful than effective. Read more than one hundred years later, however, the passage benefits from its cool detachment from wartime hysteria and rings within the ear of a reader of American literature with a clearly modern tone—the tone, say, of William Faulkner. Observing the Negroes south of Washington, Hawthorne says:

There is an historical circumstance known to few that connects the children of the Puritans with these Africans of Virginia in a very singular way. They are our brethren, as being lineal descendants from the Mayflower, the fated womb of which, in her first voyage, sent forth a brood of Pilgrims on Plymouth Rock, and, in a subsequent one, spawned slaves upon the Southern soil,—a monstrous birth, but with which we have an instinctive sense of kindred, and so are stirred by an irresistible impulse to attempt their rescue, even at the cost of blood and ruin. The character of our sacred ship, I fear, may suffer a little by this revelation; but we must let her white progeny offset her dark one,—and two such portents never sprang from an identical source before.

The Christian evangelism of the abolitionist movement had long insisted that white men and black were brethren in the eyes of God, their father, but the force of Hawthorne's passage does not lie in this commonplace. God may be the father, but the mother, the "identical source," he notes, is the most hallowed matron in New England, the "Mayflower," that glorious lady whose descendants are the aristocrats of a democracy merely through connection with her. While her character may suffer from the revelation, she did live another life, and as a result of it brought forth a second and monstrous birth, the African in Virginia; the present conflict is but an inevitable step in what was begun two centuries before.

Though based on fact, the conceit here is extravagant. Hawthorne is having fun with the New England aristocracy, a group with which he had long been at war in his fiction though he himself had the necessary qualifications for membership. Time has lent the passage strength, however, for, as the works of William Faulkner so emphatically illustrate, the relationship of white and black in America has both a strong air of fatality and a profound connection with sexuality. Moreover, the central image of the fated womb awakens echoes of *Moby-Dick*, which, eleven years earlier, had been dedicated to Hawthorne. In that book, men of all races embarked in the fated womb of the "Pequod," and, in the course of their voyage, witnessed a member of one race deliver a member of another from the womb of a whale.

"Echoes of Melville" or "the modern tone of Faulkner" may be vague phrases, but the American reader does find in this passage of Hawthorne dealing with fate, race, and sex an image and an intent which combine to place it in a continuity with which he is intensely familiar, however misty are his formulations of it. The combination which gives the dominant tone to this passage is part of the legacy of Puritanism with

248

its predestinarian doctrine and its suppression of sexuality as the darker side of existence; and although a discussion of Hawthorne and Puritanism must take into account his genealogy and his explicit use of Puritan history for setting and character, the discussion will come to the core of the matter when it questions why reality impinges on the author's consciousness in images such as that of the fated womb.

II

So convincingly has Hawthorne dramatized the force of genealogy in *The House of the Seven Gables,* and so deftly has he played with it in pieces like "The Custom-House," that the reader must exercise some effort before he can place cause and effect in their proper sequence. Nathaniel Hawthorne was, indeed, a direct lineal descendant of Judge William Hathorne, the unapologetic prosecutor of heretics in seventeenth-century Salem and that town's number-two citizen, overshadowed only by militant John Endicott. Many a Quaker or Anabaptist or Familist must have cursed him and his progeny privately, and it is most likely that one or another of them did so publicly. Moreover, Nathaniel Hawthorne lost his father when he was a boy of not quite four, and, growing up with a mother and a sister, the sensitive youth had more than the usual inducements to construct for himself from anecdotes and records a virile ancestry. But his mother was from a family of Maine merchants and farmers and the Salem of his youth was a bustling commercial seaport committed to Whig politics and agreeable to the liberalizing of theology. The twenty-one-year-old Hawthorne who returned from his Bowdoin graduation to take up residence in his mother's house on Herbert Street, Salem, then, needed not to have been deeply concerned about his paternal ancestry. However much he might expostulate about the baleful effects of such a connection and cast over it the air of fateful inevitability, he did, indeed, invite it. The Puritan division between piety and morality—the inward state and the outward show—and the Puritan conviction of the universality of sin and the inescapability of its consequences appeared to young Hawthorne to be needlessly stern and insensitive when formalized in book and institution, but, nevertheless, to be far more accurate explanations of the world around him than were the commercial economic gospel of the Whigs or the transcendental doctrine of evil as misperceived portions of the seamless fabric of good.

More importantly, Nathaniel Hawthorne was a writer, and as he began the practice of his art in the Herbert Street chamber, he had to construct for himself a philosophy, or a religion, or a mythology—some system of orienting the world which would allow him to get on with his task. It needed not to be total, needed not even to be consistent in every last detail, but it had to account for man's relationship to man and to the deity; it had to value and order the prolific world about him and make it accessible to literary exploration. His extended collegiate excursion into fiction had resulted in *Fanshawe,* a Gothic thriller striving manfully to adapt itself to the New England landscape but lacking in an outlook which would place the world of the fiction into meaningful relation—even if but for the sake of a thrill—with the world of the reader. As he worked on in his mother's home, however, Hawthorne came more and more to see the relevance of the Puritan philosophy to the effects he desired from his art. He perceived behind the formidable mass of books and habits which the Puritans had bequeathed to posterity an account of a reality he, too, saw; and if the older books of religion were now meaningless, moldering heaps, at least at one time they had contained some heat, which was more than he could acknowledge about contemporary works of religion—they were frigid from the start. Moreover, he contended in "The Old Manse," "Books of religion . . . cannot be considered a fair test of the enduring and vivacious properties of human thought, because such books so seldom really touch upon their ostensible subject, and have, therefore, so little business to be written at all. So long as an unlettered soul can attain to saving grace, there would seem to be no deadly error in holding theological libraries to be accumulations of, for the most part, stupendous impertinence." Disrespectful as Hawthorne felt the remark might be, it is strikingly in keeping with the thinking of the original American Puritans who held that the saving word was spoken out of the immediate promptings of grace and that the written word was merely for edification. Sermons printed, they claimed, were powerless to convert however much they might instruct, and even the Bible was but an imperfect reflection of the Spirit and could not work a man's salvation. Hawthorne, in his developing outlook, saw the force of the founders' basic principles and distinguished between the founders and their children. For instance, in "Main Street" he writes, "The sons and grandchildren of the first settlers were a race of lower and narrower souls than their progenitors had been. The latter were stern, severe, intolerant, but not superstitious, not even fanatical; and endowed, if any men of that age were, with a far seeing worldly sagacity." A handle to the world was waiting for him to shape it to his grasp.

While such passages indicate the attraction Puritan philosophy held for Hawthorne as a vocabulary for his own view of life, the incomplete tale, "Alice Doane's Appeal," which he in all likelihood began as early as 1830 and which he reworked around 1835, captures very well the surface fascination, at least, which Puritan materials held for his art and dramatizes his shift into this area. In that tale, a young romancer takes a stroll on Gallows Hill in Salem with two female companions and employs his gloomy surroundings in telling them a story of guilt and murder tinged with incest. He wishes it to be moving Gothic romance

251

at its best, but the young man is chagrined to receive a muted response from his companions; they are not touched by the plight of the persecuted heroine. Salvaging the afternoon, he chats with them about the route of their walk and falls into a description of how the procession of innocent witchcraft convicts and guilty accusers must have looked as it mounted the hill to the place of execution, crowning his impromptu sketch with a vivid picture of the hateful Cotton Mather riding in triumph. With amazement, he notes that his companions are crying; he has found an affecting subject matter. In the fragment, the young romancer's conclusion is somewhat disconnected, dealing with the hill rather than with what he learned about his art; but as the story is a reflection of Hawthorne's gathering interests, it has its pertinence: "We build the memorial column on the height which our fathers made sacred with their blood [Bunker Hill], poured out in a holy cause. And here, in dark funereal stone, should rise another monument, sadly commemorative of the errors of an earlier race, and not to be cast down, while the human heart has one infirmity that may result in crime."

"Alice Doane's Appeal" captures a double discovery. First, the would-be American writer learns that his most potent materials are to be drawn from the life once lived on his native landscape and that his most effective settings are those which still exist and carry with them storied associations. Next, he learns that woe or horror, pity or fear, cannot be made to arise so effectively from invented escapades as they can from a view of life which consistently remembers that the root of dread is in man because evil is his inheritance. For every Bunker Hill there is a Gallows Hill, and their meaning comes not from separate sources but both are made significant by the human heart, capable of courage and tainted by sin.

While both discoveries obviously arise from Hawthorne's growing fascination with historical Puritanism, they are also, of course, his particular solutions to the problem faced by all romantic artists. Irving and Cooper before him had realized the difficulty of producing an American fiction in the absence of surroundings rich in associations. The former had, in effect, invented a history for his native city, and, in his better tales, artfully transplanted European legends to the Hudson River Valley soil. The latter had explored a variety of historical themes and was achieving his masterpieces by projecting the struggle of the new nation to be both civilized and natural into the myth of a natural man who could not, nevertheless, dissociate himself from the destructiveness as well as the benefits of civilization. Any ambitious American author in that period would see the need to discover and create the history of his land. But for Hawthorne that discovery was, finally, more than a discovery of political history or of quaint customs; it was the discovery of a way of thinking which deepened his art well beyond the skimmings of Irving and disciplined it to a unity which forever escaped the rambling Cooper.

The Puritanism which Hawthorne first learned by observation in his native town and later broadened by conscious study of records and histories was the way of life of the seventeenth-century settlers of Massachusetts. Holding the Calvinist doctrine of man's relation to God, they had, nevertheless, differed from many of their Calvinist brethren as to the proper ways of institutionalizing this relationship and had migrated to Massachusetts where, they believed, they could establish the proper institutions relatively free from interference by civil or ecclesiastical authorities. In the isolation of the wilderness, both their doctrines and their institutions hardened well beyond the flexibility they would have had to retain for survival in European surroundings, and by the time opposing forces succeeded in wearing down doctrine and institution, a habit of mind had been established.

The doctrine of predestination very strongly influenced Hawthorne's search for a rationalized structure which embodied his perception of reality. The primary principle was that the world was made up of saints and sinners predestined to salvation and damnation since eternity, and totally powerless, therefore, to affect their ultimate status. This is a condition, in its broadest outline, of such appalling absoluteness, presenting the artist, as it does, with a *fait accompli,* that as central as it is for metaphysicians it was not exploited by the writer. While many a sinner turns up in Hawthorne's pages, he is, more often than not, directly related to the devil rather than to a class of men incapable of escaping the evil into which they were born. Roger Chillingworth and Ethan Brand, for example, are acutely conscious of the universality of sin and human frailty, but they have no theological class consciousness. The strong Puritan sense of evil as an active principle was more serviceable when personified than when used to set up two rigid classes of men.

Hawthorne found more serviceable the tenet that followed from the principle of predestination—the belief that man could do nothing to affect his own salvation. All men were born in sin and those who were saved were those who were predestined to have Christ's righteousness attributed to them, not those who behaved well on earth so as to deserve heaven. To be sure, none who was truly saved would behave immorally, since the salvation experience brings with it the power to act in a sanctified fashion. But while piety argued morality, it was not necessarily true that morality demonstrated piety, the gracious state which marked the saint. There were more seeming saints than real ones, and only the Lord could detect the archhypocrite (a persistent theme in Spenser and Milton). Moreover, none could be totally sure on this earth that he was saved, though certain well accepted signs of a gracious state, the steps of the salvation experience, were recognized; and since the eleventh-hour laborer was paid equally with him of the first hour, even the worst man need not despair utterly of detecting the workings of grace within himself.

As Puritan records abundantly show, the great drama of life was transferred from the public world in which man could not act vitally to the inner world in which man saw his impulses and his beliefs at war and which he examined scrupulously, anxious to detect a sign of God's disposition toward him—to confirm a tendency he had seen developing or to check a passion which he believed to be blurring his perception. Even after the theological terminology had been diluted or had disappeared, the struggle within the consciousness was still the great drama for the New Englander, and this consequence of Puritan theology attracted Hawthorne strongly. In his fiction, psychological happenings are central happenings, and the disconnection between man's private condition and his public appearance is a constant burden. Puritanism suited well his habit of mind and supplied it with a rationalized structure.

A writer committed to the vitality of the private drama and the ineffectuality of the public one, however, has little action for his plot so far as the nineteenth century is concerned. But Hawthorne was so committed. Indeed, the commitment became so habitual that in *The Blithedale Romance*, he scoffed openly and long at any who could believe that man's actions affected reality. However ridiculous the reader might find Hollingsworth, the notion of rehabilitating criminals at what is today called a "half-way house" is not far fetched. Yet to Coverdale, the idea presents itself in Chapter XV as "a great black ugliness of sin, which he proposed to collect out of a thousand human hearts . . . that we should spend our lives in an experiment of transmuting it into virtue!" And in *Blithedale*, nothing so clearly shows the villainy of Westervelt as his remark, in Chapter

XXIII, that the alleged powers of the Veiled Lady are the fore-runners of a new era which will "link soul to soul, and the present life to what we call futurity, with a closeness that should finally convert both worlds into one great, mutually conscious brotherhood." In the world of Hawthorne's fiction, such a notion is tommyrot.

Without the primacy of the private drama, a representation of life appeared meaningless to Hawthorne. His forebears pro-duced histories which were either journals of their souls' excursions or allegorical readings of New England history which shaped a voyage across the Atlantic or a raid on the Indians to conform to the central biblical myth as analogues to Abraham's exile or Joshua's battles. Hilda, Hawthorne's sanctimonious nineteenth-century Puritan lass, conveys the same theory into art. What her positive aesthetic is, is rather difficult of discovery and fuzzy when found. But what it is not is made clear in the best passages dealing with her, those in which her chilly confi-dence becomes temporarily upset and she wanders about Rome seeking to unburden herself and, meanwhile, because of her de-rangement, sees things diabolically, which is to say, sees things in an opposite fashion from what she had believed and to which she will, with some slight modification, return at the ending. The demon of weariness who haunts great picture galleries controls her in her upset condition and she becomes bored with the repetitiousness of the old masters, concerned eternally with Christian or mythological themes, "Virgins and infant Christs, repeated over and over again." The same old story everywhere: "Magdalens, Flights into Egypt, Crucifixions, Depositions from the Cross, Pietas," etc., etc. On the other hand, we learn in this same section of Chapter XXXVII, for the first time she comes to admire the earthly realism of the Flemish school: "an earthen pipkin, or a bunch of herrings by Teniers; a brass kettle, in which you can see your face, by Gerard Douw; a furred robe, or the silken texture of a mantle, or a straw hat, by Van Mieris; or a long-stalked wine-glass, transparent and full of shifting reflection, or a bit of bread and cheese, or an over-ripe peach, with a fly upon it, truer than reality itself." For a brief time, Hilda appreciates a world of things unconnected with the Christian myth or with any philosophy of the relation of the material world to the human spirit, an art which appeals because it takes joy in the physical existence of things, be their meaning what it may. But her derangement is temporary.

And for Hawthorne, too, the view is only temporary. "A better book than I shall ever write," he says of the Custom House in "The Custom-House," "was there; leaf after leaf presenting itself to me, just as it was written out by the reality of the flitting hour, and vanishing as fast as written, only because my brain wanted the insight and my hand the cunning to transcribe it." He went instead to the attic of the Custom House, according to the fiction he sets forth, and found there a tale of human frailty more fit for his talents.

If enduring Puritan habits rendered Hawthorne incapable of a serious consideration of any drama other than the private, they also provided him with a means of dramatizing it, with a way around the lack of material for a plot. Spenser and Bunyan vividly illustrate the utmost a Protestant literary art dedicated to the exclusive reality of the inner struggle can achieve—allegory; and, indeed, Hawthorne's first serious literary preoccupations with Puritanism led him in the same channel. Frequently, in his early tales and sketches, he is concerned with one or another allegorical representation, and he composes interesting, but brittle, little wood-cuts illustrative of certain moral tenets, softened, from time to time, and generally weakened also, by the intermixture of nineteenth-century religious sentimentalism. What escapes allegory is often turned into a morality piece, the author unshirkingly chiming in with the explicit moral however adequately the reader may deem it to have been developed already.

But intermixed with these pieces are stories about Puritans set in Puritan times; and here another technique begins to emerge, because the world of the seventeenth-century American Puritan was a world in which, with probability, the private condition could be symbolized in public gesture without dissipating its personal significance. The Puritan occupied a world which was spiritually vocal, in which sunning snakes and falling stars carried their messages about the soul's condition, and in which the spirit of the community could publicize itself by attaching a letter to a bodice or felling a Maypole. These became more than police actions; they dramatized the spiritual struggle and stood as symbols. The ease and probability with which the private became public in the Puritan world offers a particularly rich, if narrow, field to the writer. Arthur Miller, who exploited it in *The Crucible,* said he went to seventeenth-century Salem because: "People then avowed principles, sought to live by them and die by them. Issues of faith, conduct, society, pervaded their private lives in a conscious way. They needed but to disapprove to act. I was drawn to this subject because the historical moment seemed to give me the poetic right to create people of higher self-awareness than the contemporary scene affords."[1] So, in "Endicott and the Red Cross," after reconstructing a colonial Salem street scene, Hawthorne warns: "Let not the reader argue, from any of these evidences of iniquity, that the times of the Puritans were more vicious than our own, when, as we pass along the very street of this sketch, we discern no badge of infamy on man or woman. It was the policy of our ancestors to search out even the most secret sins, and expose them to shame, without fear or favor, in the broadest light of the noonday sun. Were such the custom now, perchance we might find materials for a no less piquant sketch." Working within a Puritan setting, then, Hawthorne could check the icy inward turning of his allegory and pursue his themes of common guilt in a world which would resound to the inner vibration. To be sure, he would never rid himself of the often tedious habit of insisting upon a set symbol and attaching to it a coyness its obviousness did not justify—the hissing bosom serpent and the unmeltable heart of stone recur in the letter on Dimmesdale's breast and the gurgle in the Pyncheon throat. But the Puritan world gave scope to the symbolic habit and led it out of the rigidity of strict allegory. Psychological states could there be dramatized without excessive recourse to personification since there consciousness was forever finding its public counterpart.

The fundamental influence of Puritanism upon Nathaniel Hawthorne, then, is to be seen in his insistence upon the primacy of the psychological drama and in his characterization of happiness or the integrity of the personality in moral and spiritual terms. It is to be seen also in his choice of the Puritan world as the setting for much of his fiction since that world supplied him with an environment in which he could, with probability, make the private public. Together with these, of course, Hawthorne rang a number of variations on basic tenets of the Puritan theology. "Fancy's Show Box," for example, takes up the difference between piety and morality in a modernized setting; "Young Goodman Brown" deals with universal guilt and cautions about keeping it in perspective; "John Inglefield's Thanksgiving" hinges on the irrevocable consequences of overt sin. Other stories deal with the same tenets in other ways, and the romances are built on them.

But this is not to say that Nathaniel Hawthorne was the expounder of a systematic Puritan theology. He was a man of his times as well as of his inheritance, and his moralizing habit was frequently at work about a nineteenth-century commonplace. In "The Great Stone Face," for example, he preaches about the superiority of the simple life; for all his distrust of philanthropy, he offers his redeemable sinners (Hester and Donatello) good works as a road back to righteousness; and his sketches sometimes glorify aspects of life which cannot but appear to be sentimental trivia to any reader removed from the fashions of Hawthorne's day.

Moreover, Hawthorne recognized the difference between Puritanism as a way of life and Puritanism as a scheme for dealing with reality so that it might be shaped into art. Hawthorne's home life was not puritanic, and Hawthorne's fiction builds on the Puritan system but is not used by it; the author was a creative writer, not a theological illustrator. Nothing shows the literary control he exerted over his Puritan themes more clearly than "The May-Pole of Merry Mount," which begins by setting up a contrast between the pagan revelry of the Maypole celebrants and the gloomy grind of life of the Puritan settlement. It is clear that the author endorses neither view of life, but it is equally clear that in the absence of a third alternative—an absence which was not necessarily felt in the world in which Hawthorne ate his breakfast and took walking trips in the Berkshires—the Puritans' way is preferable. The trouble which comes to Merry Mount is inevitable, not because the Puritans will eventually strike, but because the revelers are men and carry their sinfulness with them regardless of whether they are afflicted from without or within. The note of doom is struck in advance of the Puritan raid by the very nature of the Lord and Lady of the May: "Alas, for the young lovers! No sooner had their hearts glowed with real passion than they were sensible of something vague and unsubstantial in their former pleasures, and felt a dreary presentiment of inevitable change. From the moment that they truly loved, they had subjected themselves to earth's doom of care and sorrow, and troubled joy, and had no more a home at Merry Mount." John

Endicott's onrushing band, then, is but a public confirmation of an inner change and seals the lovers' recognition that they were born, like all humans, to an inheritance of sin.

The Puritan community in the works of Hawthorne, as "The May-Pole" shows, serves as a metaphor of the corruption of man. To be sure, man's inherited sinfulness is not the whole of his makeup, but no life can be understood without taking it into account. The Puritan community in Hawthorne's fiction is consistently revealed as an unduly severe and undesirable residence, one which has exaggerated the sinful part until it dominates the whole. But it is a symbolic realization of the inescapable portion of life which those who would live life as if men were perfectible and evil an error in calculation must accept. The realization cannot be escaped, for instance, by Hester Prynne, and so she cannot escape the Puritan dwelling place. Phoebe Pyncheon achieves her maturity only when her residence in the house of the Puritans brings her an awareness of her share in the universal woe. In the romance farthest from explicit Puritan themes, Hollingsworth, too, learns that love and life follow upon his recognition of his fallibility although for him the message has come too late. But while the theme remains consistent, the later novels drift from a Puritan setting, and, in doing so, it may well be argued, become enervated because deprived of strong symbols for the private struggle. Hilda can say, as she does in Chapter XXIII of *The Marble Faun*, "Your deed, Miriam, has darkened the whole sky!", but this is just a way of speaking. The sun over seventeenth-century Boston can behave in a way impossible for the sun over nineteenth-century Rome.

III

To notice the dissipation of force in the later romances is to notice the negative as well as the positive influence which

Puritanism had on Hawthorne. It enabled him to deal with a great psychological drama, but one for which the setting was limited and within which but a restricted play of personality was possible. The Puritan view of reality was narrow as well as deep; and even though Hawthorne, in his later works, attempted modern settings, he compensated for the uncertainty of launching out into the contemporary scene by keeping a tighter grasp on his system than he had in the earlier romances. So the reader is asked to accept the precipitous downfall of Hollingsworth or to sympathize with the priggishness of Hilda although neither setting nor action adequately support them. Hawthorne's view of life stands forth somewhat awkwardly in these romances because he is displaying it in a world which denies him his characteristic vehicles. In *The Scarlet Letter*, he could make the antinomianism of Hester sympathetic, even if it was to be punished eventually, because an intolerant society was holding it in check for him. But Zenobia and Miriam are not afforded this sympathy and are restrained not so much by elements in their environment as by the authorial hand.

The literary ancestor of this Hawthorne heroine is Anne Hutchinson, about whom he had written one of his earliest published pieces. Relatively unconcerned about the particulars of Anne Hutchinson's theology or with the legal niceties of her case, in his essay Hawthorne emphasized three points, all of them startlingly in keeping with the presuppositions of her actual judges. First, he pointed out, Anne Hutchinson was a woman, and, he stated unequivocally, "Woman's intellect should never give the tone to that of man: and even her morality is not exactly the material for masculine virtue." The division line of nature yields absolute psychical as well as physical differences, he argues, and the rules of life are, therefore, naturally in the keeping of men. Second, he makes clear that Mrs. Hutchinson's activity, regardless of the rightness or wrongness of what she said, was destructive of the integrity of the community and therefore imperiled the colony's future. If Massachusetts was to have a significant history, it had to continue along the lines laid down by its male citizens and repress tangents such as hers. And finally, Mrs. Hutchinson committed the sin of separation from her fellows; she claimed for herself extraordinary powers, and, by implication in Hawthorne's version, denied her share in the common guilt of mankind. "She declares herself commissioned to separate the true shepherds from the false," as he paraphrases her, "and denounces present and future judgments on the land, if she be disturbed in her celestial errand." This commission, she claims, comes to her in the form of a purer light than others enjoy.

A feminist, gifted with powers beyond those of her fellows and following them regardless of the consequences to her community and unmindful of history or her share in human fallibility, this is the Anne Hutchinson an unsympathetic young Hawthorne constructed. Years later, his Hester Prynne was to bear a strong resemblance to her. Now, indeed, she was called the "sainted" Anne Hutchinson, and Hester was created with sympathetic understanding, but, as Hester's career showed, what Anne Hutchinson stood for was still untenable.

Hester Prynne perceived that the moral code in which her community formalized the relation of man to God and man to man was as artificially related to the actualities of her nature as the stark dwellings of her fellow townsmen were to the forest on which they bordered. The Puritans were at war with nature, privately viewing its impulses as reminders of their sinful state and, therefore, openings for the devil, loopholes to be firmly shuttered. The nature of the forest about them was chaotic and cruel; it was the dwelling place of the beast and the heathen, the home of the devil. It was, then, the dangerous nature within them writ large and, like it, was to combatted—approached with ax and gun. But the shade of the trees and the sun on the flowers seemed to be beautiful to Hester Prynne and to be organically connected with her existence. Nothing natural was ugly—this was her special perception—and, therefore, when the love in her nature led to her intercourse with Arthur Dimmesdale, it received its own consecration from the harmony it formed with the whole natural world.

The Puritan community found it possible to punish Hester for behavior against its code, but it could not reach to the antisocial doctrine which was at its source. Hawthorne reached to that doctrine and gingerly developed its attractions even as he noted its dangers. Such a doctrine would have to come from a woman because, by nature, she, like the earth, bore life and because she, deprived of the world of affairs, was free to develop a sensibility which was naturally more delicate and idealistic so that the world became organized around her special weaknesses and her special strength. With Hester Prynne, Hawthorne saw beyond the Puritan system and realized its ultimate artificiality, but unlike her, he also believed that as long as human nature is inherently sinful, it must guard against the anarchy which results from placing personal impulse above socially regulated behavior. Perhaps some day a less artificial system of restraints would come about, but it would never arrive as the result of the violation of a law; if it came, it would come as the result of sinful man's learning how to live harmoniously with his failings. In the battle between the community's legalism and Hester's antinomianism, Hawthorne gave the prize to neither. The community failed to break Hester, but Hester was made to accept the fact that what she did had inevitable dire consequences.

As the romances moved from the repressive environment of colonial New England, however, Hawthorne himself provided the legalism that that milieu had once supplied. Zenobia's femininism meets with little sympathy from him, and Miriam's doctrines, when Kenyon agrees to listen to them, are met with mild horror. Kenyon does, nevertheless, at two points essay a watered-down retelling of them to Hilda, only to be told both times to hush, and only to respond, "Forgive me." The system which had been developed as a means of capturing and exploring life, and which, in *The Scarlet Letter* and some of the stories (notably, "My Kinsman, Major Molineux"), had been used not only to explain the mysteries of human behavior but to point to a reality beyond that which it accounted for, had shut down. Whereas Hester made her impression on Boston, Zenobia and Miriam were abandoned to the commonplaces of their culture once they had acknowledged their fallibility and the irrevocable consequences of sin.

IV

With the exception of Anne Hutchinson, an exception which indeed proves the rule, American Puritan history reports no prominent woman. Woman's subjection to man in institutionalized affairs was all but complete, as total, at least, as the community's suppression of sexuality. Unchecked, her particular powers would lead to antinomianism—the substitution of rule by private impulse for rule by public law—even as unchecked sexuality would lead to the overthrow of the family. Meanwhile, the male principle, unchecked, led through legalism to the capitalistic ethic of business being the world's business.

A considerable part of the general Puritan influence on Hawthorne's environment, therefore, was the scorn attached to the profession of belles-lettres. One so engaged appeared to the busy fraternity of Judge Pyncheons to be practicing the trivial and unmasculine occupation of entertaining women, even as the young romancer of "Alice Doane's Appeal" practiced on female companions. The original Puritans, too, would have scorned him as an idler—as he testifies in "The Custom-House"—if they had not punished him as a presumptuous breaker of the second commandment and a heretic who professed to know what the Lord alone knew, the secrets of another's spiritual condition. The young storyteller in "Passages from a Relinquished Work" temporarily abandons his art when he receives a letter from his Puritan guardian. He does not need to open the message from this ministerial counselor to be "affected most painfully," and he equates his guardian with his good fate and his art with his evil fate.

To practice the profession of letters, then, was a very distinct break from a respected ethic which Hawthorne's mind symbolized as Puritanism. But if his inheritance was powerless to stop him, it retained, as has been seen, enough potency to leave its mark on what he wrote. Also, through its influence on his society as well as upon him, it heightened the uneasiness with which he pursued his craft and extended it to the brink of guilt. A majority of the creators in Hawthorne's fiction, be they artists, scientists, or craftsmen, are diabolic figures, meddling with what God alone has the right to touch. Although Hawthorne could lash out against the insensitivity to art of the capitalistic heir of the Puritans, as he did in "The Artist of the Beautiful," he more frequently described the dire consequences of initiating a new nature or tampering with the existing one as Rappaccini and Aylmer (of "The Birthmark") attempted to do. At best, the artist, like the painter of "The Prophetic Pictures," could but foretell a dark fatality. To separate art from morality, from some form of social utility, was to be anti-human.

Hawthorne says of Clifford, in Chapter VII of *The House of the Seven Gables,* "An individual of his temper can always be pricked more acutely through his sense of the beautiful and harmonious than through his heart." The heart was the seat of the moral, not of the beautiful, which, for Hawthorne, was finally related to an intellectually acquired taste. He could be guiltless only so long as he remembered this and remained a moralist. He says further of Clifford that if he "in his foregoing life, had enjoyed the means of cultivating his taste to its utmost perfectibility, that subtle attribute might, before this period, have completely eaten out or filed away his affections." The purgatory of the prison had saved Clifford from the hell his aesthetic appetite would have driven him into. Hawthorne's acceptance of this view is explicit in the banality of his remarks about art and artists in *The Marble Faun* and implicit in the directness with which he carves away much of the profusion of life when creating his fictions. The "heart," not the "taste," must be his guide.

The shadow of Puritan attitudes toward the writer's unlicensed meddling in private affairs lies over the characters who most closely represent the authorial viewpoint in the romances. They are, on the whole, a hesitant, secretive trio, unwilling to engage themselves in the affairs of others, and, in their unwillingness, often denying themselves life itself. They record life, but they dislike the appearance of pretending to affect it. Holgrave is so detached an observer that the first thought Judge Pyncheon's corpse presents to him is that he must photograph it, while Coverdale so scrupulously avoids human entanglements that his view of life is figuratively and, at several points in the book, literally that of a Peeping Tom. Kenyon is more ambitious in his relations with others, although, from one point of view, he sets the catastrophe going by repelling Miriam's confidence on the grounds that friendship should not be required to carry the burden of intimate knowledge of the friend.

In his non-fiction, Hawthorne analogously characterizes himself as an outsider, a peeper. He sits at the window of his house and looks out (and usually down) at the world in his early sketches; he represents the Hawthorne who labored at Brook

Farm as a ghost of the real self who was elsewhere observing the apparition; and he characterizes his consular experiences as those of a "Double Ganger." This, doubtless, is an all but generic characteristic of authors and other basically sedentary people, but the steely passiveness in which the Hawthorne of his self-portraits and his fictional spokesmen hold themselves reflects a cautious view of the artist's role.

In opposition to these chilly figures are the women who are at home as sensitive reactors, who can speak from outside an ethic to which they are confined but to which their natures do not contribute, and whose doctrines tend to the disturbance of the male social system even as the strong sexuality of their presence causes uneasy stirrings within the male physical system. They are never the spokesmen for Hawthorne, in one sense, for they are quick to commit the sin of meddling with the established bases of society, but they are the logically inevitable voices of their creator's alter ego. If the practice of art, according to the ethic of his society, is mere woman's play, then art's function is to shake the complacency of the male world and to restore society to a view that will recognize a fuller life than it pursues.

The final effect of Puritanism to be noted, then, is in the complex way in which Hawthorne regarded his profession. Art was the outlet for the female values of vitality above law, and beauty above business, and, as such, was infinitely dangerous and infinitely worthwhile. The figure of the dark lady fascinated because in her strong sexuality and her antinomian doctrines, she was like the creative impulses which had led him to writing. But in her denial of fallibility and her disregard for history, she was far too destructive. "Woman's intellect should never give the tone to that of man;" and the dark lady became the alter ego while the moral male maintained conscious control. A son of the Puritans, this moral male restrained himself from excessive mingling in the private affairs of others, and he strove to bring a regulation to life that would insure its steady continuity. Never far from his side, however, was his opposite, the beautiful lady whose presence was an insistence that love was above law and art above morality.

The guarded observer and his female companion are metaphors of their creator's mind, characters in the allegory of the Puritan as nineteenth-century romancer. Judge Hathorne might not recognize them in such garb as they wore, but he knew their opposition as well as he knew that there was a minister in the meetinghouse and a serving girl who had run wild with the Indians.

v

The dark lady was not to be given control, and Nathaniel Hawthorne, wearier than his years in 1862, struggled with the fictional possibilities of the elixir of youth even as he noted that the call to arms was rejuvenating his countrymen. Detached now from the potent sources of his art, he cast about in melodrama, as he had done at the outset in *Fanshawe*, searching for the mode which would attach his tale to life. But when he observed the Negroes of Virginia, then his imagination slipped along familiar grooves and called forth his ironic powers. The "Mayflower," that lady as pure and proper as Hilda, had, after all, had escapades worthy of Miriam. She had brought forth the black man as well as the white, destroying the social balance and compelling her first child to come to the aid of the second. It was their fate, for they were children of the same womb. And none should be surprised at the situation, for there is no Bunker Hill without a Gallows Hill, no Hilda without a Miriam, no cargo of freedom without a cargo of slavery. The imagination that held forth such a reality had been marked by the Puritans.

R. W. B. Lewis

The

Tactics

of Sanctity:

Hawthorne and James

T HE BOSTONIANS is Henry James's single major effort at a novel not only set entirely on the American scene but populated exclusively by American characters; and it is hardly surprising that, when he came to write it, James's imagination should be more than usually hospitable to the good influence of his major American predecessor in the art of fiction. The Hawthorne aspect of *The Bostonians* is pervasive: so much so that James's novel seems at times to be composed largely of cunning rearrangements and inversions—on a lower mimetic level (to borrow Northrop Frye's category) and at a later moment in history—of ingredients taken over from Hawthorne. The several similarities between *The Blithedale Romance* and *The Bostonians,* as between novels dealing respectively with the New England reformist temper before and after the Civil War, have been sufficiently pointed out, and we may accept them as among the valid commonplaces of American literary history. But what is striking is that *The Bostonians* carries forward and downward more interestingly yet from *The Scarlet Letter,* and that it significantly perverts elements derived from *The House of the Seven Gables.* I even suspect that James, for the fullness of his artistic effect, may have depended upon our having the novels of Hawthorne in mind: as, for example, Thomas Mann in *The Magic Mountain* depended upon the reader's recollection of the *Odyssey* and the *Divine Comedy,* on each of which he was ringing a number of ironic and terrible changes. If my suspicion of James is correct, it was splendidly continental and un-American of him: the more so because, when the American writings are juxtaposed, they bring into prominence compulsions and strategies that have become generic to American fiction, in good part because Hawthorne made it possible for James to see those phenomena as generic to any imaginative view of that American world which, in *The Bostonians,* James for the first and last time explored in depth.

They bring into view, among other equally absorbing things, what I find no way to avoid calling the American theme; in James's case, we might call it his own local treatment of the intranational theme. One likes to assume that American fiction has displayed a sufficient variety of themes; none of the novels in question is inclined to reduce reality to a single phase or anything as abstract as a theme, still less a theme transfixed and further reduced by a patriotic adjective. But it remains true that one idea more than another has agitated American novelists from Hawthorne's generation to our own, and that this idea is what Hawthorne defined as "the sanctity of a human heart." We should cling to Hawthorne's remarkable and precise wording of the formula, and not shrink the matter to a mere question of "identity" or some polemic for the rights of personality. Understood as Hawthorne and James understood it, wrapped in unmistakable religious connotations, the formula has had an almost explosive power of suggestion for the novel in America (and, from Whitman onward, for poetry too).

It has appeared there, persistently, as a kind of touchstone for human behavior and social organization. True and false human relationships have been identified by appeal to it. It is what is at stake when everything is at stake: what has most aroused novelists when they seek to dramatize the periodic clash between new ideas and old; the real issue in fictionalized moments of historic social crisis and ideological change. It is or has been made to seem the measure of progress and reaction, what threatens the old and is threatened by it. It is or has been made to seem the first of all sacraments in any vital religion, what blasphemes the established order and is blasphemed by it. It is even implicated in the distinction of genres to which American fiction has been prone: allegory, legend, romance, satire, the realistic novel. To these large contentions, a whole range of American writers could testify, though I shall not summon them to do so. I want only to reflect, by means of a few notes and notations, on the extent to which Hawthorne and—following him—James felt the radical force of the heart's sanctity; and on how, making that force palpable in narrative, they showed what the American novel can grapple with and how much it can accomplish. I shall be addressing myself to what Hawthorne's generation called a writer's talent as much as to his genius, his craft as much as his vision; nor do I expect to say anything very new. But the occasion is ceremonial: a time for reaffirmations.

In *The Scarlet Letter,* as in *The Bostonians,* the theme of the heart's sanctity is closely associated with a question about the condition of women, and that question in turn arises out of a supple play of historical perspectives. The patterning becomes evident in the course of the opening scene: though fully so, I shall suggest, rather to the attentive reader than to the actors in the drama. Among the latter, it is Dimmesdale who, for his own mixed private purposes, comes closest to sounding the theme: when, according to John Wilson's report, he argues that "it were wronging the very nature of woman to force her" —as Hester Prynne is being forced—"to lay open her heart's secret in such broad daylight, and in the presence of so great a multitude." Hawthorne has already let us know that he shares Dimmesdale's attitude and goes beyond it, and that in his opinion enforced public exposure wrongs not only the nature of woman but human nature generally, that it violates some urgent, perhaps some sacred, principle of life: "There can be no outrage, methinks, against our common nature . . . more flagrant than to forbid the culprit to hide his face for shame." Unlike Dimmesdale, who is wholly encased within what he believes to be a changeless theocratic structure, Hawthorne is there speaking out of an historical perspective. His voice is that of the humane, nineteenth-century, New England spirit as it broods over the New England of two centuries earlier; and it is the same spirit that had been quick to observe, and from the same historical vantage-point, the awesome dignity as well as the cruelty of Hester's punishment: "On the other hand, a penalty, which, in our day, would infer a degree of mocking infamy and ridicule, might then be invested with almost as stern a dignity as the punishment of death itself." Hawthorne then goes on to enrich the whole matter by some remarks about the female Bostonians of the 1640's that throw a fascinatingly ambiguous light, in advance, over Dimmesdale's appeal.

As he looks at the females pushing and crowding around the scaffold and watches them "wedging their not insubstantial persons . . . into the throng"; as he runs his eyes over their "broad shoulders and well-developed busts," and listens to the startling "boldness and rotundity" of their speech, Hawthorne is led to conclude that: "Morally, as well as materially, there was a coarser fibre in those wives and maidens of old English birth and breeding, than in their fair descendants, separated from them by a series of six or seven generations." For Hawthorne, at least in this novel, the nature of woman is susceptible to historical definition. These seventeenth-century New England women, like everything else in the book, are identified within a long process of physical and moral transformation. Hawthorne traces the process backwards half a century and across the waters to sixteenth-century England and the age of "man-like Elizabeth"—an epoch of "beef and ale . . . [and] a moral diet not a whit more refined"; and forward through the years to Hawthorne's time, noticing how "every successive mother has transmitted to her child a fainter bloom, a more delicate and briefer beauty, and a slighter physical frame, if not a character of less force and solidity."

The passage reveals the characteristic narrative tactic of *The Scarlet Letter,* even though the tactical aim reveals itself more slowly. The temper of the Puritan men during the period of the novel's action is, like the nature of the women, established by the tracing out of an historical process, and one which again stretches back to the Elizabethan age, forward into the later generations of Puritans, and on into the nineteenth century. Hawthorne (in Chapter XXI) pauses in his account of the holiday games to insist that "the great, honest face of the people smiled, grimly, perhaps, but widely too." For they were, he reminds us, "not born to an inheritance of Puritan gloom. They were native Englishmen, whose fathers had lived in the sunny richness of the Elizabethan epoch." They were men, in fact, who, by 1645, were only "in the first stages of joyless deportment"; it was not they but their "immediate posterity, the generation next to the early emigrants, [who] wore the blackest shade of Puritanism, and so darkened the national visage with it, that all the subsequent years have not sufficed to clear it up."

What Hawthorne is doing by means of this recurring dialectic of historical epochs is to create the terms—the very sources of meaning—of the drama he is engaged in describing; and the achievement is a remarkable one. Hawthorne knew, better than any writer of his time, that existence for the Puritan "was completely dramatic, every minute was charged with meaning."[1] In his own words, the Puritans tended to speak of human existence as simply a state of "trial and warfare"—the scene of the great war between God and the devil; a scene overwhelmed by allegory. It was just this quality of Puritan life that made it so attractive a subject for a novelist of Hawthorne's dramatic persuasion. But the crucial point is this: that the meaning with which every minute of the action in *The Scarlet Letter* is charged is never quite the meaning assigned to it by the characters involved; nor could it be. For surrounding the meanings so confidently attributed to events and relationships by the magistrates and the clergymen, the matrons and the maidens, is the creative play of Hawthorne's historical imagination. This is, so to speak, the charging force of the novel; and this it is that invests what I take to be the supreme moment in the story, the swift exchange between Dimmesdale and Hester in the forest, with something like a revolutionary significance.

Between the opening scene and that encounter, much had been happening and much a-building; one of the many things Hawthorne taught James was to let narrative power accumulate at a fairly measured pace, so as to give maximum resonance to those otherwise slender moments when the entire drama is asked to change course and, in doing so, yield up its central meaning. Among the several developments in *The Scarlet Letter*, we may mention the two most obvious ones. There is, on the one hand, the long patient effort of Chillingworth to drag Dimmesdale out of his psychological hiding-place and onto a private scaffold, a place of moral exposure, of Chillingworth's own making. And on the other, there has been the strange career of Hester's interior musings. The exchange in the forest is the created compound of these two developments—and of Hawthorne's handling of them.

In her lonely cottage by the sea, Hester has come into touch with the array of new ideas that, as Hawthorne says, were stirring the minds of Europe and toppling the systems of "ancient prejudice" ("wherewith," Hawthorne characteristically adds, "was linked much of ancient principle"). But she is able to do so because, in her tragic freedom, she is gifted with the mode of imagination that informs the entire narrative: the historical imagination; and she is the only person in the book to be so gifted. Hawthorne permits Hester to share a little in his liberated perspective; she alone envisages the possibility of significant historical change; and she alone is allowed thereby to escape some real distance from the allegorized world of fixed and changeless meanings and conditions and relationships which all other figures in the book inhabit. As Hester reflects upon "the whole race of womanhood," she arrives at the vision of social and sexual revolution to which, Hawthorne implies, women in her position are always liable.

As a first step, the whole system of society is to be torn down, and built up anew. Then, the very nature of the opposite sex, or its long hereditary habit, which has become like nature, is to be essentially modified, before woman can be allowed to assume what seems a fair and suitable position. Finally, all other difficulties being obviated, woman cannot take advantage of these preliminary reforms, until she herself have undergone a still mightier change.

The consequence of all this—as Hester, at the book's end, is still telling the unhappy women to whom she ministers—would be to "establish the whole relation between man and woman on a surer ground of mutual happiness." But until it is revealed to her by Dimmesdale, Hester does not truly perceive the ground of that ground.

Hawthorne reminds us how appalling Hester's speculations would have seemed to the Puritan authorities: "as perilous as demons." He reminds us, too, how genuinely dangerous, how gravely unsettling, such speculations can be for the person who entertains them: They can quite literally, he suggests, draw one on toward madness. But what Hawthorne most deeply distrusts is not Hester's revolutionary dream, but the essentially intellectual source and nature of it. It is too much a product of the head; and "a woman," Hawthorne declares, "never overcame these problems by any exercise of thought." The remark is by no means condescending; for *The Scarlet Letter* is animated by the belief that these problems can be overcome, or at least that the overcoming of them should be among the supreme goals of human effort; and he so far believes that a woman will lead the way, if anyone will, that he grants the woman Hester the unique privilege of entering into his own historical perspective. But his dominant conviction is that the solution must come from the heart; that the problems will themselves vanish when, and only when, the heart "chance to come uppermost." And this, of course, is what does happen during the meeting in the forest.

There, for a brief and perhaps illusory moment, the relationship between Dimmesdale and Hester, between the man and the woman, stands upon that surer ground of mutual happiness that Hester has dreamed of. One even conjectures that for a few seconds the scarlet letter betokens those words—"angel" and "apostle"—with which Hester hoped to associate herself as the destined prophetess of the new revelation. Such religious titles and allusions are, in any event, not out of place. For what comes flickering into view, what the whole course of the novel has been preparing for, and what terrifies Dimmesdale when he catches a glimpse of it, is something much more far-reaching than social reform. It is, indeed, a religious revolution. "May God forgive us both!" Dimmesdale says sadly. And then:

> "We are not, Hester, the worst sinners in the world. There is one worse than even the polluted priest! That old man's revenge has been blacker than my sin. He has violated, in cold blood, the sanctity of a human heart. Thou and I, Hester, never did so!"
>
> "Never, never!" whispered she. "What we did had a consecration of its own. We felt it so! We said so to each other! Hast thou forgotten it?"
>
> "Hush, Hester!" said Arthur Dimmesdale, rising from the ground. "No; I have not forgotten."

In context, the implication is almost breath-taking. It is just because neither of them had violated the sanctity of the other's heart that what they had done—their entire relationship—had had a consecration of its own. Dimmesdale's words release Hester's extraordinary contention and give all her wandering meditations a sudden coherence. It is from the implications of Hester's answer that Dimmesdale shies back in a kind of horror, for he is equipped to appreciate the enormity of them.

He had been trained to pursue his priestly calling among a people for whom "religion and law were almost identical, and in whose character both were . . . thoroughly interfused." But latent in his attribution of sanctity to the human heart, and still more in the suggestion it leads to, that of the sanctification of lawless love, is the seed of a new sacramental order; and one that, from the Puritan standpoint, is altogether blasphemous. No wonder that Dimmesdale rises to his feet, cuts short the exchange, and commands Hester to hush. It is a moment characteristic of Hawthorne: the short glimpse and the speedy covering over of the world-disturbing truth; and Hester hushes. But she does not relinquish her vision, nor will she for the rest of her fictional life.

She takes no steps to bring that new order into being, except for her humane ministrations to the forlorn who come to her door. But Hawthorne tells us that, had matters been otherwise, Hester "might have come down to us in history hand in hand with Anne Hutchinson"—"sainted Anne Hutchinson," as he has called her earlier—"as the foundress of a religious sect." It is the very substance of that projected and unrealized religion that is gradually created by the novel's historical dialectics; and Hester's limited eligibility to lead it can be measured by the limited but real degree of her participation in those dialects. It would be a religion founded on the doctrine of the inviolable sanctity of the individual human heart; and one in which the human relation—above all the relation between man and woman —itself shaped by allegiance to that doctrine (by the mutual reverence of heart for heart), would become the vessel of the sacred, the domain of the consecrated. It would have provided a sacramental basis for a genuine community of the kind envisaged, for example, by Henry James the elder in *Society, the Redeemed Form of Man*. Indeed, it is tempting to look beyond Hawthorne across a dozen decades, to notice how, from the two Henry Jameses onward, writer after writer has reflected the same curious but persistent brand of religious humanism—and usually in an escape from traditional religious institutions and dogmas, and in despite of the world's irreverent practices. But no writer ever succeeded in making this epochal possibility as compelling as did Hawthorne: for no American writer possessed the vision, both historical and transcendent, to set the new possibility amidst and against the stiffening vigor, the hard historical actuality, of the older order. In the clarity of his perception and in his unsentimental compassion, Hawthorne was able, as well, to do honor to both the old and the new, while seeing each as an absolute challenge to the other. If Hester had become the destined prophetess, she "might, and not improbably would, have suffered death from the stern tribunals of the period, for attempting to undermine the foundations of the Puritan establishment." Within the world of *The Scarlet Letter*, the establishment triumphs; but within the novel as a novel, its foundations are constantly and quietly undermined by a play of perspectives to which only Hester is privy; and the fusion of religion and law is giving way to a new conception of sanctity.

II

About *The House of the Seven Gables*, there is for present purposes less that needs to be said; but we can begin by remarking that its narrative method to some extent reverses that of *The Scarlet Letter*, and that the Hawthornian formula emerges here from a different direction. In *The Scarlet Letter*, an action set in the past completes its meaning under the pressure of a shifting later-day perspective; in *The Seven Gables*, events occurring in the present—or anyhow in "an epoch not very remote from the present day"—draw much of their force from the shifting pressure of a long past, through a series of what seem about to be fated re-enactments and turn out to be reversals. *The Scarlet Letter* projects forward, beyond the consciousness of its characters, from the 1640's to Hawthorne's own time; *The Seven Gables* reaches backward from Hawthorne's time almost to the age of *The Scarlet Letter,* touching upon happenings that took place in or around 1670 (Hawthorne's arithmetic is casual), 1707, 1820, and 1850. In *The Scarlet Letter,* Hawthorne, observing the robust physiques of the Puritan matrons, glances ahead to the fainter bloom and briefer beauty of their descendants. In *The Seven Gables,* almost everything is described as diminished or decaying and contrasted with the heartier qualities of earlier times. Even Jaffrey Pyncheon, for all his wicked strength, carries in his face the marks of a physiological decline:

> The Judge's face had lost the ruddy English hue that showed its warmth through all the duskiness of the Colonel's weather-beaten cheek, and had taken a sallow shade, the established complexion of his countrymen.

The brother and sister are dreary relics: Hepzibah is a "far-descended and time-stricken virgin," and Clifford, until the book's climax, is no more than an elderly wreck of what had been a beautiful and brilliant young man. Their habitation, the moldering house with its garden-plot "so unctuous with two hundred years of vegetable decay" and its "ugly luxuriance of gigantic weeds" is dismally appropriate, an objective correlative for their weedy spirits. It is within such an atmosphere that Hawthorne's historical imagination—working with no less agility than before, but, as it were, reversing its direction—once again brings into dramatic play the principle of the heart's sanctity.

The principle, is, no doubt, less central here than in *The Scarlet Letter*: ideas in general are less central in *The Seven Gables* than in its much more dramatic predecessor. But it does make its important appearance, and it is, as formerly (though less tightly), related to a cluster of "new ideas." Given the time-laden atmosphere of the story, we may expect the new ideas in this case to be mainly ideas about newness itself: about getting rid of the past which, as the daguerreotypist Holgrave proclaims oratorically, "lies upon the Present like a giant's dead body," in every conceivable physical, psychological, social, legal, and religious form. Holgrave's rhetoric is, of course, excessive; it warrants the recoiling comment of Phoebe about the ferocity of his hatred for everything old; and it is countered by the very figure of Clifford, by the infinite pathos of a man who really has gotten rid of the past, or been bereft of it. It is Holgrave's personal destiny, in the novel, to come to terms with the past, including his own genealogy. Nonetheless, Holgrave (and Hawthorne goes on to say as much) deserves our attention and that of his fellow characters; for more than anyone else in the novel, Holgrave understands the necessary basis of any new system of life: a quality he himself possesses and which Hawthorne—in the milder and properly more modern but still religious idiom of *The Seven Gables*—describes as "the rare and high quality of reverence for another's individuality."

The phrase occurs (in Chapter XIV) at a moment when Holgrave has very nearly mesmerized Phoebe by his histrionic reading of the story about Alice Pyncheon. The latter, one remembers, was herself completely mesmerized by one Matthew Maule, grandson of that Matthew Maule who had been executed for witchcraft upon the false testimony of Colonel Pyncheon, and who thus takes his family's revenge upon the wicked Colonel's granddaughter. Alice is held in thrall until Matthew's marriage, whereupon she wakes from her "enchanted sleep" and straightway dies—leaving Matthew "gnashing his teeth, as if he would have bitten his own heart in twain," not unlike Chillingworth on the occasion of Dimmesdale's death.

283

This is the supreme instance, in *The Seven Gables,* of the violation of Hawthorne's first principle, a literally murderous invasion
of another person's individuality: Maule "had taken a woman's
delicate soul into his rude gripe, to play with—and she was
dead!" Retelling that story almost a century and a half later,
another Maule (who temporarily calls himself Holgrave) comes
to the verge of re-enacting that earlier sin and of casting a
similarly fatal spell over the susceptible spirit of young Phoebe
Pyncheon. "A veil was beginning to be muffled about her"—one
thinks of the veilings and mesmerizings of *The Blithedale
Romance*—"in which she could behold only him, and live only
in his thoughts and emotions." Holgrave's gesture at this point
not only liberates Phoebe's potentially enslaved self; it is a
victory over his own dangerous and inherited power—and insofar
a reversal and a rejection of the past.

> To a disposition like Holgrave's, at once speculative and
> active, there is no temptation so great as the opportunity of
> acquiring empire over the human spirit; nor any idea more
> seductive to a young man than to become the arbiter of a
> young girl's destiny. Let us, therefore,—whatever his defects
> of nature and education, and in spite of his scorn for creeds
> and institutions,—concede to the daguerreotypist the rare and
> high quality of reverence for another's individuality. Let us
> allow him integrity, also, forever after to be confided in; since he
> forbade himself to twine that one link more which might have
> rendered his spell over Phoebe indissoluble.

And, with a gesture of his hand, he restores Phoebe to herself.
It is because he refuses to repeat his ancestor's blasphemous
act and to make his spell over the girl indissoluble that Holgrave
becomes fitted for that highest kind of human relationship: a
marriage, based not on human empire but on mutual reverence,
a modest example, one supposes, of the right relation between
man and woman prophesied by Hester Prynne. Holding back

284

from the indissoluble spell, Holgrave makes possible the in-dissoluble union, something that will have a consecration of its own. Quite the opposite is the case with Jaffrey Pyncheon.

The Judge is totally bent on acquiring "empire over a human spirit"—a diabolic empire over the spirit of poor Clifford; and he acquires it by repeating the actions of his ancestor, by a combination of murder and false testimony. Those crimes were monstrous enough, but the final sacrilege, the very sin of the crimes as it were, is the utterly debilitating spell the Judge has cast and continues to exercise over Clifford: "That strong and ponderous man had been Clifford's nightmare. There was no free breath to be drawn within the sphere of so malevolent an influence." Clifford is released from his psychic imprison-ment only by Jaffrey's death. Jaffrey, who had believed too much in the past, who believed that the past could endlessly repeat and re-enact itself, and who even believed in the inherited tale of buried treasure: Jaffrey is himself destroyed by the past, by the inherited disease—"the physical predisposition in the Pyncheon race"—and he dies with the legendary blood on his lips. The Judge, as we may say, is defeated by the legend, as he ought to have been; for in the deepest sense, it was a heartless legend, and he is a heartless man. By his defeat and death, Clifford is released from the legend, enough at least to recover something of himself. Holgrave escapes further still from the confines of the legend, as Hester Prynne had—in her thoughts and in her gentle advices to the wretched—moved somewhat outside the confines of allegory. As a work of fiction, The House of the Seven Gables moves similarly away from the legendary and toward the more modern and realistic, and arrives at a form, the romance, in which Hawthorne could present his steadiest belief about human nature and its relation-ships, not as an ideal dimly visible in the far future, but as an immediate possibility among the modern realities.

285

III

"Every one will, in his way—or in her way—plead the cause of the new truths. If you don't care for them, you won't go with us."

"I tell you I haven't the least idea what they are! I have never yet encountered in the world any but old truths—as old as the sun and the moon. How can I know? But do take me; it's such a chance to see Boston."

The new truths to which, in the opening scene of *The Bostonians,* Olive Chancellor so passionately appeals and which her kinsman from Mississippi, Basil Ransom, makes courteous mock of are, like those of *The Scarlet Letter,* ideas bearing chiefly upon the unhappy condition and possible future status of women. There are times, indeed, in *The Bostonians* when Olive Chancellor (though her surname more suitably if very faintly echoes that of Chillingworth) markedly resembles Hester Prynne. Or more accurately, there are times when James is plainly drawing both his rhetoric and his subject matter, not from contemporary historical developments, but—as literary artists tend to do—from existing literature, and especially from *The Scarlet Letter.* "The unhappiness of women! The voice of their silent suffering was always in her ears, the ocean of tears that they had shed from the beginning of time seemed to pour through her own eyes." That is Olive, in James's articulation of her. "Women . . . —in the continually recurring trials of wounded, wasted, wronged, misplaced, or erring and sinful passion,—or with the dreary burden of a heart unyielded, because unvalued and unsought,—came to Hester's cottage, demanding why they were so wretched, and what the remedy." That, of course, is Hawthorne; and if Hester has once "imagined that she herself might be the destined prophetess," so "it seemed to [Olive] at times that she had been born to lead a crusade." It is, like the movement meditated by Hester, to be a religious

286

crusade: "This was the only sacred cause; this was the great, the just revolution." And the nature and scope of it, as they form themselves in Olive's over-heated mind, resemble those of the social upheaval Hester had pondered, with sacrificial death once more the probable and even desirable outcome:

> It must sweep everything before it; it must exact from the other, the brutal, blood-stained, ravening race, the last particle of expiation! It would be the greatest change the world had seen; it would be a new era for the human family, and the names of those who had helped show the way and lead the squadrons would be the brightest in the tables of fame. They would be the names of women weak, insulted, persecuted, but devoted in every pulse of their being to the cause, and asking no better fate than to die for it.

In the near hysteria of tone and the savagery of attitude toward the male race, the passage diverges markedly from the passage quoted earlier from *The Scarlet Letter*. It is, indeed, the meaningful differences between the two novels, the different ways in which Hawthorne and James assemble and, as it were, orient quite similar materials, that I eventually want to stress—and that James himself, as I believe, wanted to stress; for James (to repeat my remark) seems to have counted upon our remembering Hawthorne and to have striven for his ultimate effects by means of a combined echo of, and contrast with, Hawthorne. But we should notice, meanwhile, that if *The Bostonians* shares with *The Scarlet Letter* an interest in revolutionary ideas about the condition of women, those ideas palpitate in *The Bostonians* within a general atmosphere of decline oddly similar to that of *The House of the Seven Gables*. In James's novel, as in Hawthorne's romance, almost every item participates in a pattern of diminution. The historical distance spanned in *The Bostonians* is nothing so vast as that of *The Seven Gables*: it is at most the four-score years of the saintly fool, Miss Birdseye; and James's impressionistic and allusive evocation of even so short a stretch of history illustrates perfectly the remark of T. S. Eliot that Hawthorne's sense of the past "exercised itself in a grip on the past itself," but that "in James it is a sense of the sense." To which we should add, I think, that James had in particular a sense of Hawthorne's sense; and this made it possible for James to include in his own pattern of decay a much larger variety of elements than Hawthorne, and to cover a great deal more of the national landscape.

To begin with, the reformers who gather in Miss Birdseye's rooms appear aimless, bemused, rhetorically corrupted by comparison with "the heroic age of New England life," the age before the Civil War, an age "of plain living and high thinking, of pure ideals and earnest effort, of moral passion and noble experiment." And the social crusade, the marshaling of the feminist squadrons, sounds suddenly almost tawdry when James invokes "the simple emotion of the old fighting-time," the war itself, escorting us, with Basil Ransom and Verena Tarrant, into Harvard's Memorial Hall and remarking upon the "singularly noble and solemn effect" of the "temple" for the fallen soldiers, its symbolism of "duty and honor . . . sacrifice and example." But the conservative temper in *The Bostonians* is in no less sorry a state than the reformist: there is, on the one hand, the virtual medievalism of Ransom and, on the other, the mere muddled snobbishness of Adeline Luna, who, though she liked to think that the word "conservative" was "the motto inscribed upon her own silken banner" (the motto, in short, of her own crusade), limited her conservatism to prattle about the inferiority of republics and the bad manners of servants.

Places share in the general decay and are analogues of it. The entire Boston area is seen as disappearing into the spreading jungle of factories and engine-shops. In James's famous and eloquent description of the western view from Olive's apartment on Charles Street, there is observed "something inexorable in the poverty of the scene," something

> shameful in the meanness of its details, which gave a collective impression of boards and tin and frozen earth, sheds and rotting piles, railway lines striding flat across a thoroughfare of puddles, and tracks of the humbler, the universal horsecar, traversing obliquely this path of danger; loose fences, vacant lots, mounds of refuse, yards bestrewn with iron pipes, telegraph poles, and bare wooden backs of places.

(It is characteristic of Verena that she thinks this view lovely, just as at first she had secretly wished to emulate Adeline Luna rather than her sister Olive.) But if the northern landscape is thus being devoured by an industrial version of those ugly gigantic weeds that smothered the terrain in *The House of The Seven Gables,* the post-war South—"the poor, dear, desolate old South," as Ransom calls it—lies in utter ruin; and swift recollections of its former splendor sometimes flash through Ransom's consciousness, and into ours, as a measure of its present desolation. Within the novel, in fact, and by a pattern of allusion more intricate than I can here suggest, the entire country is represented as having suffered some strange and terrible reversal of fortune (to borrow the phrase used about "the great drawing-room of Europe" in *The Wings of the Dove*). And this aspect is perhaps best summed up in the picture of the Cape Cod town of Marmion (i.e., Marion) which "was a good deal shrunken since the decline in the shipbuilding interest; it turned out a good many vessels every year, in the palmy days, before the war," but now Ransom gathers the impression "that it had had a larger life, seen better days." The larger life, the better days, stand everywhere behind the elements of the novel—persons, places, movements, ideals, interest—and testify to the present unhappy shrinkage.

289

In a much-quoted notebook entry for 1883, James wrote that—as his novel's main concern, and as "the most salient and peculiar point in [American] social life"—he had chosen "the decline in the sentiment of sex." That, certainly, is a major phenomenon in *The Bostonians,* and one which many of the other instances of "decline" explain and illuminate. But it is, I think, as much a symptom as a cause; and what the novel's action as well as its rhetoric more profoundly reveals is the decline of the religious sentiment—that is, of the specific religious sentiment to which, with and following Hawthorne, James was himself most profoundly committed. What is happening in this regard is indicated at a stroke, a single casual remark, almost an aside: when James reports that the Harvard library was "a diminished copy of the chapel at King's College," and that Verena Tarrant introduces Basil Ransom into it "with the air of a person familiar with the sanctified spot." These are lines that, in the theater idiom, James is quite willing to "throw away," and we miss nothing but a momentary pang of aesthetic pleasure and admiration if we fail to notice them. Nonetheless, in context, they fairly bristle with meaning.

We can best formulate that meaning by reference once again to *The Scarlet Letter.* There, Hawthorne set his action among a people—the Bostonians of the 1640's—for whom "religion and law were almost identical, and in whose character both were . . . thoroughly interfused." James set his own American novel among a people—the Bostonians of the 1870's—for whom *religion and ideology* were becoming almost identical, and in whose character both were already dangerously confused.[2] And both pairings are portrayed as the absolute enemy of the fundamental religious sentiment: the sense of the sanctity of the individual human heart. *That* is the sense that characterized "the heroic age of New England life"; that is the sense that has most fatally declined; and that is the sense which the novel, though not the characters in it, seeks in its own subtle and dramatic manner to re-establish.

Olive Chancellor, as we have seen, regards her feminist crusade as a sacred cause. Later in the story, she is made by James very tellingly to reflect that "without Verena's tender notes, her crusade would lack sweetness, what the Catholics call unction"; and with Verena, all during the winter of 187—, she looks forward across "the solemn vista of an effort so religious as never to be wanting in ecstasy." Basil Ransom—who in this regard, as in others, may be thought of as a deliberate inversion of Hawthorne's Holgrave—invests his own reactionary ideas, and especially his passionate anti-feminist speeches, with no less ardent a religious quality; and though with much of what he says James would probably have agreed (in a quieter tone of voice), still Verena responds for James and for us when she is impressed "by the novelty of a man taking that sort of religious tone about such a cause." These are persons, Olive Chancellor and Basil Ransom, who really are violated by ideas, to draw again upon T. S. Eliot's inexhaustibly useful commentary and phrasing; who corrupt their feelings with ideas (the language is still Mr. Eliot's); who "produce the political idea, the emotional idea, evading sensation and thought"—and who make a religion out of the result. They are, in short, ideologues; and worse still, they are ideologues in action. They are not only violated by ideas, they use ideas to violate others; and in particular, of course, they violate, and fight to the death for the privilege of violating, the vulnerable individuality, the susceptible human heart, of Verena Tarrant.

The process need not be spelled out; to do so would be to rehearse most of the book's plot, for the plot turns exactly upon the effort and countereffort of Olive and Basil to possess themselves of Verena, and each in the name of Verena's perfect freedom and the holiness of the conflicting creeds. Two moments may stand for many. When Verena comes to live with Olive, the latter emphasizes the fact that the younger girl "should be as free as air, to go and come." But by that time, James informs us,

> Verena was completely under the charm. The idea of Olive's charm will perhaps make the reader smile; but I use the word not in its derived, but in its literal sense. The fine web of authority, of dependence, that her strenuous companion had woven about her, was now as dense as a suit of golden mail.

The literal sense of "charm" is, of course, a magic spell or incantation; and the suggestion of spells and webs carries us back instantly to the story of enchanted Alice Pyncheon in *The Seven Gables*; while, in a passage that draws attention to its verbal play, the word "mail" cannot but indicate in an ominously punning way the twisted sexual basis of this particular mesmeric process. That masculine suit of mail, anyhow, retains its power, and its nature is reinforced by frequent allusions to actual or metaphoric cloakings and imprisonments: until, on an early spring afternoon in New York's Central Park, Basil Ransom casts his potent counterspell over the impressionable Verena. The sexual element is here all the more notable, since the ideas Basil expounds to her are, from her viewpoint, monstrous. The girl's reflections

> softly battled with each other as she listened, in the warm, still air, touched with the faraway hum of the immense city, to his deep, sweet, distinct voice, expressing monstrous opinions with exotic cadences and mild, familiar laughs, which, as he leaned toward her, almost tickled her cheek and ear. . . . There was a spell upon her as she listened.

As a dramatic construct—combining as it does the oratorical statement of social theory and of attitudes to history with a sort of psychological-cum-sexual hypnosis—the whole scene derives without much doubt from the long scene between Holgrave and Phoebe that extends from Chapter XII through Chapter XIV in *The Seven Gables*. The resemblance is worth emphasizing: because in certain essential aspects, James is carefully reversing Hawthorne, and the force of his accomplishment depends in no small part on our awareness of this. It is not only that all of Basil Ransom's eloquence goes toward getting rid of the present in the name of the past, rather than, as with Holgrave, the other way round. It is also that, Holgrave, for all his temptation to acquire "empire" over Phoebe's spirit, does have the high quality of reverence for her individuality, and releases the girl from her momentary enslavement. Ransom persists in his imperial design to the end of the scene and the end of the novel.

That kind of reversal characterizes the relation consciously aimed at (as I am maintaining) and achieved between *The Bostonians* and the novels of Hawthorne. In the same way, the social revolution proposed by Olive Chancellor would, in its consequences, reverse those of the movement that Hester Prynne might have led. Hester's new sect would bring with it a relationship between man and woman grounded on mutual reverence; Olive apparently would like to see that relationship destroyed once and for all. The relationship Olive does establish in the novel (and even she perhaps comes to realize this) is a sort of paradigm of falsehood: it is sexually wrong, morally wrong, even politically wrong; and from the Hawthornian viewpoint of Henry James, it is religiously wrong. Its radical wrongness is one justification for Basil Ransom's ambiguous victory in the denouement; he is, after all, a man and a manly man. And beyond that—though Basil's crusade to "rescue" Verena from "ruin" is deeply suspect (there are too many examples in James's fiction of the lethally selfish nature of the rescuing impulse)—

there is in Basil some faint occasional glimmer of the distinctive value of another person's individuality, or at least of Verena Tarrant's.

But "value" thus circumscribed is the strongest word we can use. There is no one in *The Bostonians,* like Hester or Dimmesdale (for his moment of insight) or Holgrave, who has and acts upon a clear sense of the heart's sanctity. The person who most nearly does is Miss Birdseye: she, as Verena exclaims, is "our heroine . . . our saint," exactly because she thinks only of others. There is evidence that James adjusted his attitude of Miss Birdseye as the novel progressed: in the early pages, she is the victim of some of James's most brilliant comic writing; but from the second book onward, she grows into truly heroic and saintly proportions, and in her final moments she is affectively larger than the life about her. But she *is* the ancient relic of an older epoch, the old heroic age; and in the book's most portentous scene, she does die. And that, of course, is James's point and the motive of his reversals: the antiquity and the death of the old selflessness, the old sanctity, the old sense of sanctity.

James, in *The Bostonians,* is exploiting Hawthorne to suggest a view opposite to Hawthorne's about the fundamental *course* of human affairs, at least as those affairs were being conducted in America. James saw the American character moving away from, not toward, a belief in the sanctity of the human heart; away from, not toward, relationships consecrated by that belief. Where Hawthorne, in *The Scarlet Letter,* made tragic drama out of the possibility of religious legalism yielding to individual reverence, James, in *The Bostonians,* in an equally impressive display of prophetic power describes individual reverence yielding to a religion of ideology. The world in which that is happening is, as James makes almost appallingly clear, a world without sacrament, without any sort of sacramental sensibility: a world, from the point of view of the literary artist, unavailable to either allegory or legend, and fit primarily for satire and realism.

This, of course, is James in mid-career. During his major phase twenty years later, James for various reasons felt himself liberated in part from the clutch of the contemporary. He was then able to return to something like Hawthorne's tragically hopeful vision, and he would then adopt in consequence something not wholly unlike Hawthorne's artfully contradictory use of allegory and legend—and precisely to suggest that the sacramental consciousness, of a sort unmistakably close to that of *The Scarlet Letter*, could be brought into being even within a world characterized by its lust for violation. But in *The Bostonians,* James made his comment upon the American scene by casting a Hawthornian eye upon a non-Hawthornian world: by reassembling themes and motives and devices and language from Hawthorne and then by twisting and reversing them. It was a comment as well upon American literature, upon what the novel in America had once done and could now do.

Edwin Fussell

Neutral Territory:

Hawthorne

on the

Figurative Frontier[1]

H AWTHORNE was at heart a Western writer. As early as 1820, at the age of fifteen, he wrote his sister in Maine: "How often do I long for my gun and wish that I could again savagize with you. But I shall never again run wild in Raymond, and I shall never be so happy as when I did."[2] As late as 1853, he was still describing in idyllic terms those happy Leather-stocking years: "I ran quite wild, and would, I doubt not, have willingly run wild till this time, fishing all day long, or shooting with an old fowling-piece. . . . That part of the country was wild then, with only scattered clearings, and nine tenths of it primeval woods. . . . I would sometimes take refuge in a log cabin."[3] In 1833 or 1834, Hawthorne apparently made a real Western tour, perhaps as far as Detroit;[4] if so, it was almost certainly for the purpose of refurbishing, consolidating, and confirming the kind of writing that issued from his dismal chamber during his prolonged literary apprenticeship: such tales and sketches as "The Gentle Boy," "Roger Malvin's Burial," "Young Goodman Brown," "Sketches from Memory," "The Great Carbuncle," "The Man of Adamant" (all first published from 1831 to 1836), and so on through "Earth's Holocaust" (1844) and "Main Street" (1849). This line of development culminated in *The Scarlet Letter,* whose thematic setting is the "roughly hewn street of a little town, on the edge of the Western wilderness," and whose main point is that "perennial rebirth" of which Frederick Jackson Turner was somewhat belatedly to speak.[5] Like many another mid–nineteenth century American writer confined to the Atlantic seaboard, Hawthorne made what he could of what he was born with and what he was able to lay hands on. By a judicious use of the Romantic imagination, and sustained by precious little actual experience, he transformed New England into an available prototype of the West.

From the beginning, nationalistic New World writers and readers had "looked to the West" as the source of a new American literature, but what the phrase meant was more often than not obscure. Such men as Daniel Drake and James Hall naturally thought it referred to people like themselves. This was, of course, absurd; the new literature came out of the West only in the sense of emerging from aesthetic contemplations of the West; and the best contemplations occurred in the East, where the contemplative types congregated. Of these, the most notable (after Cooper) were Hawthorne, Poe, Thoreau, Melville, and

Whitman; and among these notables, Hawthorne was the pioneer. In fact, he was much less simple-mindedly concerned with New England than is generally supposed. In *Literary Friends and Acquaintance,* Howells tells us that Hawthorne "was curious about the West, which he seemed to fancy much more purely American, and said he would like to see some part of the country on which the shadow (or, if I must be precise, the damned shadow) of Europe had not fallen." At least on that occasion, our romancer's remarks on New England seem to have been fewer and less pleasant.

Yet in a special way he might have spoken of both sections simultaneously. He was repeatedly drawn to unpopulous pockets of the East—such as the "rocky, woody, watery back settlement of New England" mentioned in "The Seven Vagabonds"—which he could reconceive as Western scenes. Alternatively, he was always following the trail of local history backward until it arrived at the wild West. Neither the literal place nor the literal time was in the final analysis controlling; but conjoined, New England and the past yielded an essential synthesis, the frontier, which, not very paradoxically, was also the American future. As Thoreau desired to be a Western writer without stirring from Concord, and in *Walden* managed to do just that, Hawthorne found it imperative and efficacious to give his writing a contemporary relevance without leaving out, and sometimes without leaving, the past. For Massachusetts, the past was the vanished West; the West was the surviving past. The laterally progressive nature of American historical development made these exchanges ridiculously simple. As James Hall said in a Western story: ". . . It was such as all new towns in the west had once been; such, perhaps, as the hamlets were on the shores of the Atlantic."[6] And Sylvester Judd explained in a local novel: "The house where Margaret lived, of a type common in the early history of New England, and still seen in the regions of the West, was constructed of round logs."[7] Hawthorne was thoroughly knowledgeable about the popular Western literature of his day, as even a cursory glance at his editing of the *American Magazine of Useful and Entertaining Knowledge* (1836) makes clear; and his Notebooks of approximately the same period show him working hard with eye and mind to solidify and complicate his sensuous apprehension of the standard Western images.[8] His best writing results from the confluence of these two streams, though it is not reducible to either.

"All that night," he said, in a travel sketch describing Niagara Falls, "as there has been and will be for ages past and to come, a rushing sound was heard, as if a great tempest were sweeping through the air. It mingled with my dreams, and made them full of storm and whirlwind." This nightmare noise was also the ground bass for "Young Goodman Brown," in which "a confused and doubtful sound of voices" is intermittently heard, blending "the murmur of the old forest" (West) with the "familiar tones" of Salem village (East). Throughout the story, nature howls, roars, creaks, cries, and yells, "in homage to the prince of all," the prince being optionally the Devil and the genius of American history. Visual perceptions are perhaps even more conspicuously implicated in America's Western waywardness. The diabolical baptismal scene simultaneously derives from Hawthorne's eyewitness account of a fire on the banks of Lake Erie, which he thought "might have been transferred, almost unaltered, to a tale of the supernatural" ("A Night Scene," in "Sketches from Memory," Second Series), and from James Hall's account of a Western camp-meeting in "The Backwoodsmen."

"Young Goodman Brown" is about American advance to the West, penetration into the dark forest of the unmapped future, which is also the buried past. As broadly hinted in the opening dialogue, the moral issue is bad faith in every conceivable sense, a failure of integrity sufficiently correlative with the American situation to justify the epithet "national." The hero will journey "'forth and back'" between "'now and sunrise'": Brown's night journey is not merely psychological but is also the temporal duration of the national movement through space to the Pacific Ocean, whose final significance is to be manifest at the end, if at all. With a nightmare mélange of hidden allusions to the American dream, and to the grim work of civilizing a virgin continent, the protagonist plunges darkly into the wilderness. Wherever he goes is a clearing, the trees magically opening and closing around his progress. At one point he sits on a stump, refusing to go farther; plainly, he is not the first pioneer passing this way. The farther he goes, the faster he goes, which was also true of the Westward Movement, "until, quivering among the trees, he saw a red light before him, as when the felled trunks and branches of a clearing have been set on fire." This is not the sunrise of arrival, but a lurid Western landscape— aflame with the conflicting moral passions of actor and author— betokening a previous advance and an intermediate stage.

Brown's failure to keep faith is a failure not only of his own but of several generations. The Devil has helped his grand- father whip a Quaker woman, and encouraged his father to burn an Indian village during King Philip's War; and these are the same behaviors which generated the psychic traumas of "The Gentle Boy" and "Roger Malvin's Burial." Brown's refusal to believe in the sins of the past, or their present consequences, is evidently symptomatic of a representative American shortcom- ing, as evidenced in the disinclination (still widespread) to examine closely the nature of the Westward Movement. "'We are a people of prayer, and good works to boot,'" Brown declares, "'and abide no such wickedness.'" His sudden swing to the op- posite pole, his easy acceptance of the sins of the past, and his use of them to justify a continuing malefaction, may by certain carping critics be thought to hint an equally representative national inadequacy. Through the pages of "Young Goodman Brown," as through the annals of American history, runs the ethical absurdity of it's always being too late to turn back. Brown enters the forest, thinking that Indians may lurk behind every tree; Indians he associates with the Devil; the minute he does so, the Devil is at his elbow. "Whither, then, could these holy men be journeying so deep into the heathen wilderness?" Into the depth of American humanity, which was also the blackness of darkness.

The tradition of cultural understanding within which Hawthorne worked best was a tradition not merely of substance, as in "the matter of the West," but also of metaphor and its correspondent discursive or narrative forms. "The May-Pole of Merry Mount," for example, is both a story about the West and a formal imitation of the Western frontier. In a headnote citing historical authority for this particular "philosophic romance," Hawthorne says that "the facts, recorded on the grave pages of our New England annalists, have wrought themselves, almost spontaneously, into a sort of allegory." Very likely they did, for the poetic space spontaneously occupied by Hawthorne's tale is simply the magnificent but only vaguely geographical ground down the middle of which the American people ran an imaginary metonymous line—"that admixture of civilization, and of the forest," as Cooper called it, or, according to the sardonic Melville, "the region of the everlasting lull, introductory to a positive vacuity"—in order to give their burgeoning sense of national purpose and destiny a perceptible definition and shape.

"Two hundred years ago, and more, the old world and its inhabitants became mutually weary of each other. Men voyaged by thousands to the West," as, in 1835, they were voyaging still. Hawthorne's story concerns the long weary process through which Old World culture was transported to, and modified by, the existentially stricter environments of the New, where two representative and antithetical groups, both oriented toward the American frontier, especially command his interest. "It could not be," says Hawthorne of the Merry Mounters (almost as if he wished it were), "that the fauns and nymphs, when driven from their classic groves and homes of ancient fable, had sought refuge, as all the persecuted did, in the fresh woods of the West." Watching the scenes of revelry, the more solidly established Puritans compare their masqued rivals to "those devils and ruined souls with whom their superstition peopled the black wilderness." Here the Puritans are making themselves at home, in however appalling a fashion—black wildernesses being second nature with them—as the Merry Mounters are not.

It is thus at first glance surprising that Hawthorne declines to award the Puritans a clear-cut victory, as both common sense and his historical sources must have tempted him to do. The anomaly confirms what the headnote hinted: Hawthorne's controlling source is no New England annalist but the typical American conception of the Western frontier, which divided only to unite, and which robbed all unseemly contradictions of their sting. Hawthorne resolves the issue—that "jollity and gloom were contending for an empire," an issue formulated, as usual, only to *be* resolved—by providing as the central focus of his story a pair of young lovers who share the best traits of both sides, as Leatherstocking and Henry Thoreau, to name only two of the age's representative heroes, comprehended the virtues of white civilization and Indian liberty. Hawthorne's allegorical action sets the terms of "life as it is"; but "life as it is" necessarily depends on a sense of American civilization that turns out to be practically equivalent to a definition of the Western frontier. More subtly, the story also reveals the terms of American writing as it is, or as, in Hawthorne's heyday, it was coming to be: neither jollity (imagination) or gloom (realism) wins the New World, but a blend of the two.

This general pattern of thought repeats itself in "The May-Pole of Merry Mount" through a variety of perspectives. The revelers are deliberately located at a point of meeting between the animal and the human; they are "the crew of Comus, some already transformed to brutes, some midway between man and beast, and the others rioting in the flow of tipsy jollity that foreran the change." One youth emblematically wears stag head and antlers, another the "grim visage" of a wolf, a third the beard and horns of a goat. A fourth is disguised as a bear, except that he wears pink silk stockings, and he is mentioned together with a "real bear of the dark forest," who conveniently wanders along, so that his "inferior nature" may ritualistically rise "half way, to meet his companions as they stooped." This mimic metamorphosis also includes a "Salvage man. . . . girdled with green leaves," and "by his side, a noble figure, but still a counterfeit . . . an Indian hunter, with feathery crest and wampum belt." For all the jollity, there is an uneasy air of savagery erupting into civilized conditions, the basic ambiguity of American culture. Civilization in the New World is seen as frail and uncertain, relatively defenseless against raids from either the barbaric wilderness or the befuddled heart of man (in certain of Hawthorne's moods, synonymous). Yet, together with disaster, a saving realism rushes at sunset "from the black surrounding woods," not only in the persons of Puritans but in the actual shadows, which seem to mean, in the following order, death, awareness of death, and a consequent adjustment of wish-fulfillment to fact, as "when waking thoughts start up amid the scattered fantasies of a dream." Even the Anglican priest—"canonically dressed, yet decked with flowers, in heathen fashion"—is figured according to the basic frontier formula, interpenetration of conceptual opposites on some kind of imaginary neutral territory, the same formula found in Turner's classic definition of the frontier as the meeting point between savagery and civilization. Some of the Maypole flowers are "from English seed," while others are "blossoms of the wilderness." Hawthorne's imagination is so colored by the American notion of the Western border that situation after situation, however indirectly relevant, appears to him in that guise.

So it was in the beginning. A quarter-century later, at the effective end of Hawthorne's career, precisely the same animal-human antithesis and reconciliation turns up in *The Marble Faun,* where jollity and gloom contend for an even larger empire:

> A Faun, copied from that of Praxiteles, and another who seems to be dancing, are exceedingly pleasant to look at. I like these strange, sweet, playful, rustic creatures, almost entirely human as they are, yet linked so prettily, without monstrosity, to the lower tribes. . . . Their character has never, that I know of, been brought out in literature; and something very good, funny, and philosophical, as well as poetic, might very likely be educed from them. . . . The faun [is] a natural and delightful link betwixt human and brute life, and with something of a divine character intermingled.[9]

So Hawthorne wrote in his Notebook, after a visit to the Villa Borghese. The ultimate germ of his idea was still the conventional Western frontier and the literary Indian ("lower tribes," "link betwixt human and brute life," and so on) with whom he had identified his youthful literary fortunes in "The Seven Vagabonds." Now these tropes are debased and almost totally disencumbered of geographical, historical, or cultural meaning; yet for all the pretty posturing, and the many peripheral matters into which Hawthorne was eventually led, the diction and rhythm of the novel repeatedly point to the original source: "The characteristics of the brute creation meet and combine with those of humanity in this strange yet true and natural conception of antique poetry and art. . . . Neither man nor animal, and yet no monster, but a being in whom both races meet on friendly ground. The idea grows coarse as we handle it, and hardens in our grasp." This most nebulous of Hawthorne's novels is shot through with allusions to "tribes" and "wilderness," and naturally so, for the Faun's narrative progress is from innocence to civilization, through savagery.

"'He is not supernatural,'" Miriam says of Donatello, "'but just on the verge of nature, and yet within it. What is the nameless charm of this idea, Hilda?'" Hilda does not care to know, and Hawthorne seems to have forgotten—though a creature on the verge of nature and yet within it, like a pioneer happily hovering on the hither edge of free land, would appear to be identified, however confusingly, with the Western frontier. "'There is something very touching and impressive in this statue of the Faun,'" Kenyon replies. "'In some long-past age, he must really have existed. Nature needed, and still needs, this beautiful creature; standing betwixt man and animal, sympathizing with each, comprehending the speech of either race, and interpreting the whole existence of one to the other. What a pity that he has forever vanished from the hard and dusty paths of life.'" The statue sounds suspiciously like an Indian, or like an Indian trader, which perhaps explains Hawthorne's puzzled sense of anachronism, for whether he knew it or not, the frontier disappeared some time between the admission of California as a state and the advent of the Civil War, or, in more literary terms, some time between the writing of *The Scarlet Letter* and *The Marble Faun*. Hawthorne's language is the language of a passing era; in almost the same words, Thoreau argued that mankind needed the Indian, and Brownson argued that mankind needed Christ. (In Brownson's pre-Catholic phase, Christ was a sort of movement-party Natty Bumppo, or reconciler of religious antagonisms.)

306

In the 1840's and 50's, the process of doubling the metaphorical frontier had become almost automatic with American writers, major and minor. Pathfinders like Cooper and Hawthorne had discovered the trick earlier. In "The Haunted Mind" (1835), Hawthorne may already be seen self-consciously attempting to define a pseudo-metaphysical state of being by compelling the Western frontier, which in American writing was almost invariably a figure of speech in the first place, to transfer from one context to another its all too predictable implications. Except for a rhetorical genius like Poe or Thoreau—and Hawthorne was only rarely a rhetorical genius, besides having no talent for metaphysics—this manner of speaking was seldom impressive. At best, the relation between the Western frontier and those ambiguously Romantic mental conditions was only a loose analogy; at worst, the analogy might conceal serious contradiction, or the writer be tempted to say what he would not otherwise care to have said.

"The Haunted Mind" opens with description of that "singular moment" (pun) between waking and sleep; so Edgar Allen Poe declared that his dearest literary wish was to express intuitions arising in the soul "at those mere points of time where the confines of the waking world blend with those of the world of dreams." According to Hawthorne, years earlier, ". . . You find yourself, for a single instant, wide awake in that realm of illusions, whither sleep has been the passport." He is evidently trying to formulate something about arrested time, whatever that might be, and is meanwhile drifting toward a geographical trope. "Passport" suggests going to Europe, but the realm of illusions soon begins to take shape closer to home. "Yesterday has already vanished among the shadows of the past; to-morrow has not yet emerged from the future. You have found an intermediate space, where the business of life does not intrude; where the passing moment lingers, and becomes truly the present." The realm of illusions is the moving Western frontier displaced onto a pure time model: vanished (or vanquished) past to the East of the line, emergent future to the West of the line, and the present (the only reality) *upon* the line—precisely the line Thoreau was determined to toe. But for this occasion the metaphor is wrong, or, more accurately, Hawthorne's motive is inappropriate to the standard metaphor. The frontier fails to specify the intensest cultural reality, the most concentrated meaning, as it was supposed to do; instead, it suggests Hawthorne's irresponsible abdication from them. Along with other self-indulgences which he elsewhere found so contemptible because he was so prone to them, this intermediate space between sleep and waking is welcomed as an amiably lazy withdrawal from reality in favor of "the sluggish ecstasy of inaction." Inaction suggests death, and death calls forth a train of young Hawthorne's ever-ready allegorical creatures. Then he suddenly reverts to a tepid adolescent erotic fantasy, whose initial image reveals the dreamer sinking "in a flowery spot, on the borders of sleep and wakefulness." The flowery spot is evidently a Western prairie, unlocated but presumably in the general neighborhood of the frontier—which could never be located either, but only poetically evoked through the language of grounds and limits, borders and confines, boundaries and verges, intermediate spaces and neutral territories.

"The Haunted Mind" is an invaluable locus for the kind of doubled frontier metaphor with which Hawthorne's writing was embellished from first to last, and which, in his happiest moments, was the informing principle of his fiction (as in *The Scarlet Letter*) and of his theory of fiction (as in "The Custom-House"). In these second-stage metaphors, the original figure of the frontier—civilization, nature, and the neutral territory—was applied to generally comparable situations (such as known, unknown, and the neutral territory) with results sometimes commanding and sometimes calamitous. Especially when too detached from their Western source, these doubled metaphors were often perfunctory and implicit—which in itself is an index to the nature and quality of Hawthorne's literary thought—and it is difficult to estimate what kind or degree of vitality lay behind them, or even whether the author knew they were there. Most of them involve the typically Romantic obsession with boundaries of time, sanity, or existence—situations probably impossible of conception without some sort of spatial language. The more significant fact is that the spatial language regularly chosen by Hawthorne and his American contemporaries was derived from their sense of the Western frontier. In "A Select Party," the Man of Fancy calls a castle in the air "a sort of no man's land, where Posterity may make acquaintance with us on equal terms." Here the frontier is the literary imagination, or point of meeting between present and future, pragma and prophecy. Conversely, in *The House of the Seven Gables,* "there is sad confusion, indeed, when the spirit thus flits away into the past, or into the more awful future, or, in any manner, steps across the spaceless boundary betwixt its own region and the actual world." This metaphor is sadly confused: on the one hand, the neutral territory, or spaceless boundary, is the danger zone between the soul's possession and the impinging world, and, on the other hand, it is the present, defined as the moment of transition between future and past. The boundary is paradoxically "spaceless" because the American frontier was; nobody knew whether it was a line or an area. In such passages as these, the topics and treatments vary; the metaphor remains fundamentally the same. Its explicit Western content is almost always zero; yet its very existence depends upon the prior existence of the American frontier. In "P's Correspondence," it would be comical "if, after missing his object [literary fame] while seeking it by the light of reason, he should prove to have stumbled upon it in his misty excursions beyond the limits of sanity." So Hester Prynne, best of pioneer mothers, and intimately acquainted with every conceivable kind of frontier, recognizes that Dimmesdale stands "on the verge of lunacy, if he had not already stepped across it." The English nobleman in *Doctor Grimshawe's Secret,* according to Hawthorne's plan, "shall walk on the verge of lunacy, and at last step over."

It sounds like the world of Poe, yet Hawthorne was past master of this particular mannerism before Poe began to publish his tales. In "A Gentle Boy," Ilbrahim "led her by the hand, in his quiet progress over the borders of eternity, [and] Dorothy almost imagined that she could discover the near, though dim, delightfulness of the home he was about to reach." Hester's badge of ignominy throws a "gleam, in the sufferer's hard extremity, across the verge of time. It had shown him where to set his foot, while the light of earth was fast becoming dim, and ere the light of futurity could reach him." Hawthorne's metaphorical frontiers are more appealing when more social and realistic. In "Main Street" he judges the Thursday Lecture an institution worth retaining "as bearing relations to both the spiritual and ordinary life, and bringing each acquainted with the other." The Lecture is neutral territory between spiritual and temporal, imbued with the qualities of both, and thereby empowered to reconcile them. In the local newspaper, Hawthorne wrote how American social conditions offered rude and refined "a common ground of courtesy and kindliness to meet upon."[10] More explicitly, in the Palazzo Barbarini, he noted that the servants of cardinal, prince, and duke used a single domestic hall for "a common territory and meeting-ground." Thus closely do we approach the original frontier whence all the fanciful borders arose.

The largest concentration of such metaphors is probably in *The Blithedale Romance,* which also contains a host of unintegrated references to the American West. Zenobia is "on the hither verge of her richest maturity," while Priscilla is "on the outer limit of girlhood." According to Coverdale, "Hollingsworth would have gone with me to the hither verge of life, and have sent his friendly and hopeful accents far over on the other side, while I should be treading the unknown path." The modern mesmerist, "even if he profess to tread a step or two across the boundaries of the spiritual world, yet carries with him the laws of our actual life, and extends them over his preternatural conquests," as if he were administering one of America's Western territories. More reasonably, Coverdale imagines phantoms "that invariably haunt the mind, on the eve of adventurous enterprises, to warn us back within the boundaries of ordinary life," and speaks of "the sense of vast, undefined space, pressing from the outside against the black panes": both of these metaphors accurately and movingly reflect the fundamental American experience, whether of crossing the frontier in the Westward direction or merely of thinking about it at home. Most centrally of all, Coverdale's "hope was, that, between theory and practice, a true and available mode of life might be struck out." Unfortunately, in view of the fact that Blithedale is an obvious paradigm for American civilization, and Coverdale an obvious surrogate for the American writer, "the clods of earth, which we so constantly belabored and turned over and over, were never etherealized into thought. Our thoughts, on the contrary, were fast becoming cloddish. Our labor symbolized nothing." The prosaic world contends with the poetic imagination, not yet entirely at ease in the new environment; the conflict between them was Hawthorne's perpetual problem, as his Notebooks show; or as a character in *Doctor Grimshawe's Secret* puts it, " 'How strangely everything evades me! . . . There is no medium in my life between the most vulgar realities, and the most vaporous fiction, too thin to breath.'" Understandably, Hawthorne's most desperately brilliant appropriations of the major American figure were in the realm of aesthetics.

The innermost chamber of the "The Custom-House" is the passage where Hawthorne fancifully pretends to describe the psychology of his composition. The aesthetic background is the ever portentous dualism of fact and fiction; the solution is through the agency of moonlight, or Romantic imagination. Native refinements are furnished by the metaphorical frontier, since the 1820's moving farther and farther from the Eastern writer and perhaps on that account more and more freeing itself from geographical actualities. "Moonlight, in a familiar room, falling so white upon the carpet, and showing all its figures so distinctly,—making every object so minutely visible, yet so unlike a morning or noontide visibility,—is a medium the most suitable for a romance-writer to get acquainted with his illusive guests." Hawthorne lists some objects in the moonlit room, and proceeds: "All these details, so completely seen, are so spiritualized by the unusual light, that they seem to lose their actual substance, and become things of intellect." Precisely what happens to the Western frontier. "Thus, therefore, the floor of our familiar room has become a neutral territory, somewhere between the real world and fairy-land, where the Actual and the Imaginary may meet, and each imbue itself with the nature of the other." Hawthorne continues to refer to wall, ceiling, furniture, but we are already deep in the magic forest where Hester Prynne from time to time resorts. The neutral territory is the meeting point between the facts of American history and the painfully growing American mind. From that conjunction the metaphor of the Western frontier once more arises to effect a significant restatement of imported European thought. Was it evoked by Hawthorne's awareness that the novel to follow was in essence a novel about the West?

Probably. But perhaps Hawthorne had additional motives for modifying the Wordsworthian formula—"to throw over them [incidents and situations from common life] a certain colouring of imagination, whereby ordinary things should be presented to the mind in an unusual aspect." Wordsworth concentrates on the imagination. Hawthorne's shift to the frontier metaphor, and to the aesthetics of Coleridge, enables him to concentrate on the intractability of experience, an intractability poor Hawthorne had good reason to know about.[11] In the Coleridgean view, if the imagination colors the facts, the facts in their turn color the imagination. And Hawthorne's imagination is the perfect case in point; for the modes of apprehension which he imposed on all the dualistic categories susceptible of the imposition—and these were manifold, since he characteristically thought in dualistic terms—were in the first instance derived from the American sense of the Western frontier as somehow a metaphor resolving the inescapable American dualism, Manifest Destiny *vs.* inferiority complex. Indeed, as we look backward over the tortuous development of our early literature, it seems impossible to determine whether the American mind was primarily formed by the basic facts of American experience or whether these basic facts were primarily formed by the American mind. All we can be sure of is their reciprocity, a reciprocity precisely analogous to the historical situation, as it existed in the imaginations of men, and from which the metaphor of the frontier was born, nature in the neutral territory changing civilization while at the same time being changed by it. "What then is the American, this new man?" Crèvecoeur's troublesome question was answerable only by reference to where the new man lived and what he lived for. Hawthorne's articulation of an aesthetic so closely revealing the literary situation of his country, and embodied in the central metaphor of the national dilemma, marks the moment of final and self-conscious maturity for American literature. What is it but a theory of realism, or imaginative truth, magnificently congruent with the actual conditions of American life?

But this was Hawthorne's high-water mark. His gradual and accelerating decline after *The Scarlet Letter* conceivably reflects the disappearance of the frontier, and with it the American sense of identity and purpose. It is just as easily attributable to the habit of neurotic withdrawal which plagued him from the beginning, and which he finally blamed on his pioneer life in the Maine woods.[12] As he confessed to former President Pierce in the dedicatory Preface to *Our Old Home,* his imagination simply gave up. "The Present, the Immediate, the Actual, has proved too potent for me." In fact, he had come to this pass well before 1863. Except in the earliest years, and then again at the time of *The Scarlet Letter,* the balance he held between private sensibility and public truth was almost unbelievably precarious. In the 1850's, both sides of the equation collapsed. Twenty years earlier, Hawthorne was formed and for a while sustained by his magnificently ironic vision of the horrors and glories being enacted on that ever receding frontier where the newest nation was likewise articulating its uniquely millennial spirit and applying that spirit to the rapid solution of humanity's age-old problems. Then overnight the frontier vanished, the nation began to fall apart, and Hawthorne slowly faded like the Cheshire Cat. The first great phase of American literature was over.

Discovery and Rediscovery

Edwin H. Cady

"The Wizard Hand": Hawthorne, 1864-1900

E MILY DICKINSON wrote, in loyal response to her "preceptor," Thomas Wentworth Higginson's *Short Studies in American Authors* (1879), "Hawthorne appalls, entices—"[1] Rather surprisingly in her, hers was a response standard among the generation of serious American readers first after Hawthorne's death. They saw their great romancer to be precisely that. There was something uncanny, perhaps morbid, perhaps sublime, certainly romantic, piercing, and supremely artistic about him. Obviously, in Hawthorne his native land had produced an authentic genius of literature. The obituary poetry all faithfully said "sorcery." Over Hawthorne's grave, Longfellow lamented,

> The wizard hand lies cold. . . .
> The unfinished window in Aladdin's tower
> Unfinished must remain![2]

Bronson Alcott echoed,

> Painter of sin in its deep scarlet dyes,
> Thy doomsday pencil Justice doth expose,
> Hearing and judging at the dread assize;
> New England's guilt blazoning before all eyes,
> No other chronicler than thee she chose.
> Magician deathless![3]

And so the far less orphic Dr. Holmes recalled, from the Saturday Club, "The Essex wizard's shadowed self. . . ."

> The great ROMANCER, hid beneath his veil
> Like the stern preacher of his sombre tale;
> Virile in strength, yet bashful as a girl,
> Prouder than Hester, sensitive as Pearl.[4]

Finally, E. C. Stedman, aiming at the definitive poem, the characteristic public verdict of his age, summed up in "Hawthorne," 1877:

> Two youths were fostered in the Norseland air;
> One found an eagle's plume, and one the wand
>   Wherewith a seer divines:
> Now but the Minstrel lingers of that pair,—
> The rod has fallen from the Mage's hand.[5]

318

I

In the self-conscious United States, breath-takingly and brutally expanding during the post–Civil War decades, such a national treasure as Hawthorne was bound to achieve popularity and prestige. His works passed through edition after edition. Articles by the dozen of reminiscence and association—memoirs, impressions, the homes and haunts of Hawthorne—clustered into a sort of personality cult. At more serious levels, the great romancer became almost the first true challenge to American criticism. How ought he truly to be elucidated? He stood as an inspiration as well as a mine of suggestion for American aspirants to his art. And his work came to serve as a critical touchstone for the judgment of one's contemporaries. Hawthorne's became the first unquestionably major American fictional reputation.

The tale of Hawthorne's editions between his death in 1864 and the close of the century is superbly told in Volume IV of Jacob Blanck's monumental *Bibliography of American Literature*. James T. Fields, that publishing paragon of the age of steam, pushed hard on Hawthorne dead. "Little Pansie" appeared in three forms, and *Twice-Told Tales* in a "Blue and Gold" edition during 1864-65. Sophia Hawthorne's notoriously edited version of the *American Note-Books* (1868) was followed by the *English Note-Books* (1870) and by Una Hawthorne's edition of *The French and Italian Note-Books* (1871) in a market sequence carefully spaced. Then it was time for James R. Osgood, having succeeded Fields, to continue with family editions of *Septimius Felton* (1872), *The Dolliver Romance* and then *Fanshawe and Other Pieces* in 1876, and, scraping clean the barrel at last, *Dr. Grimshawe's Secret* (1883).

Canny management of manuscript, and of magazine in relation to book publication, thus kept Hawthorne in some sense a current author for two decades after the last publication of his personal lifetime. At length the moment arrived for the ultimate literary monument, the definitive set, edited by George Parsons Lathrop, Hawthorne's son-in-law, and published by Houghton Mifflin, successors in turn to Osgood: *The Complete Works of Nathaniel Hawthorne,* in twelve volumes, 1883.

If all this left no doubt of Hawthorne's prestige, the rest of his publishing history in this period leaves no doubt of his popularity—or his market value.[6] Osgood made the point with sixteen Hawthorne issues in "Little Classic" editions, and Houghton Mifflin drove it home with "Modern Classics" and "American Classics for Schools." Hawthorne was "a classic," and he was to be reprinted again and again. Into the 1880's, as the Textual Introduction to the Centenary Edition makes clear, *The Scarlet Letter* was reprinted "with an impression or more almost every year."[7]

About such a figure, given the traditions of nineteenth-century genius-worship and the exigencies of American cultural nationalism, there quickly clustered a literary personality cult. The wizard mysteries of Hawthorne's life, personality, and art lent themselves to ready exploitation. Some of this was mere gossip, some ordinary self-advertising of the Hawthorne-Knew-Me sort. Much of it consisted of association- and locale-mongering. Inevitably somebody wrote of "The Homes and Haunts of Hawthorne."[8] A certain amount of this flow of recollection and memoir, on the other hand, constituted serious and relevant biography or biographical material. But the best of the genuine reminiscence was quickly concentrated in the major articles and, finally, books which had, within fifteen years after his death, fully certified Hawthorne as an authentic American genius.

The themes for discussion of Hawthorne during this period were largely set by "a nearly forgotten but brilliant Boston critic for whose judgment Hawthorne himself had the greatest respect."[9] E. P. Whipple's "Nathaniel Hawthorne" was first published in 1860 but reappeared in *Character and Character-istic Men* (1866). It was surrounded by a growing set of significant pieces, especially George W. Curtis' "The Works of Nathaniel Hawthorne," *North American Review* (October, 1864); Elizabeth Peabody's "The Genius of Nathaniel Haw-thorne," *Atlantic* (September, 1868); Eugene Benson's "Poe and Hawthorne," *Galaxy* (December, 1868); Dorville Libby's "The Supernatural in Hawthorne," *Overland* (February, 1869); the *Southern Review*'s "Writings of Nathaniel Hawthorne" (April, 1870), and solid chapters in James T. Fields's *Yesterdays with Authors* and the Englishman "H. A. Page's"[10] *Memoir of Nathaniel Hawthorne,* both in 1872. Perhaps the final cachet was that imprinted on Hawthorne's name by a famous English author generously writing for an American magazine: Anthony Trollope, "The Genius of Nathaniel Hawthorne," *North Ameri-can Review* (September, 1879).

In the perspective of these and dozens of slighter or more oblique estimates of Hawthorne, however, it seems clear that it was with the publication of three major works between 1876 and 1879 that Hawthorne became certified as an unchallenge-able American genius. The first of these was the pioneering systematic examination and evaluation of the life and works determinedly entitled *A Study of Hawthorne,* by George Parsons Lathrop, in 1876. The second and most obvious was the almost reluctant concession of a brilliant critic doubly alienated through intellectual development and by self-conscious expatriation: Henry James's *Hawthorne* (1879). The one now least known but possibly, in its proper context, then most significant was E. C. Stedman's public ode, "Hawthorne" (1877).

Invited by the Phi Beta Kappa society of Harvard to deliver a thirty-minute poem, Stedman had devoutly contemplated "The College of the Gods" but felicitously settled upon "Hawthorne." As his authorized biography puts it, Stedman essayed to be "our most popular American Poet of Occasion, the Universal Official Poet, as it were, upon whom a large neighborhood reliance was placed for an illuminating, artistic, sympathetic, even prophetic, expression of the dominant spirit or ideal." The role was one in which Whitman and Lanier failed lamentably. And by invading Harvard for the purpose, Stedman deliberately put himself into competition with the local experts—Lowell and Holmes—in the practice of a wishful, and now little understood, Old American art form: democratic Pindarics, meant bardically to essentialize the highest truths of the national consciousness and so to crystallize them for the guidance and uplift of the nation—in this case, of the national taste.

Hawthorne he placed boldly beside Longfellow as equally a poet, though really the more prophetic of the two: "The one New-Englander!" "—New England's best interpreter, her very own." Nurtured amid wildling beauty but disciplined in solitude, "Two natures in him strove / Like day with night, his sunshine and his gloom." For exercise of "his mysterious gift," the world could well afford that "one" should "meditate aloof" and ignore "the time's heroic quarrel." For "none save he in our own time so laid / His summons on man's spirit. . . ."

> What if he brooded long
> On Time and Fate,—the ominous progression
> Of years that with Man's retributions frown,—
> The destinies which round his footsteps throng,—
> Justice, that heeds not Mercy's intercession,—
> Crime, on its own head calling vengeance down,—
> Deaf Chance and blind, that, like the mountain-slide
> Puts out Youth's heart of fire and all is dark!
> What though the blemish which, in aught of earth,
> The maker's hand defied,
> Was plain to him—the one evasive mark
> Wherewith Death stamps us for his own at birth!

Ah, none the less we know
He felt the imperceptible fine thrill
　　With which the waves of being palpitate,
Whether in ecstasy of joy or woe,
And saw the strong divinity of Will
　　Bringing to halt the stolid tramp of Fate;
Nor from his work was ever absent quite
　　The presence which, o'ercast it as we may,
Things far beyond our reason can suggest:
　　There was a drifting light
In Donatello's cell,—a fitful ray
　　Of sunshine came to hapless Clifford's breast.

Flatulent as Stedman's verse now seems, his diary entry at concluding its composition is pathetic: "I *think* the poem is at my highwater mark—as sustained, analytic, and imaginative, a piece, as I shall ever write." But it was at least analytic. It alluded continuously to Hawthorne's work. It took positions on most of the basic issues of the Hawthorne criticism of the time—standing with Fields and Lathrop against Curtis' attack on Hawthorne's politics; with Whipple, Peabody, and Lathrop on the prophetic power of Hawthorne's imagination, the bardic quality, even, of his prose; with Japp and Lathrop against Whipple on the balance of Hawthorne's mind and character; with Lathrop on the historicity and profundity of Hawthorne's treatment of Puritanism, his evocation of the spiritual essence of New England. Always, in fact, Stedman stood with Lathrop. "Hawthorne" poeticized Lathop's *Study*, accepting it as the definitive word. An epigone of the dying age of romantic idealism, Stedman felt authorized to set Hawthorne up on the plinth of his poesy by the romantic notion that beauty and genius, ideality and art, heroism, misty rhetoric, and windy euphony all went together.

"Hawthorne" foreshadowed the end of an age which faded

into agonizingly extended tenuities. With every allowance for taffy, it is astonishing to hear Dr. Holmes praise its "admirable contribution . . . to our poetical and our critical literature," or Aldrich class it with Arnold's "Thyrsis," or Julian Hawthorne call it "the most true and beautiful tribute yet made to Nathaniel Hawthorne's genius" by one of the two "best poets now living."[11] Ideality, whether as decayed romanticism or as desperate neo-romanticism, was to be long a-dying. And the reputation of Nathaniel Hawthorne during the balance of the nineteenth century was to be continuously involved in the struggles to keep ideality alive.

II

Detailed examination of early Hawthorne criticism would show it engaged from work to work in a good deal of expostulation and reply over relatively minor issues. But the theme of permanent significance was the still current problem of the nature of reality in Hawthorne's work and mind. No question was more central to either the literary or the philosophic battles over ideality; and none was more central to the point of view or achievement of Henry James's *Hawthorne*. Speculation on the question had, of course, begun during the romancer's lifetime. It had become acute after Whipple, only apparently to be resolved by Lathrop. James simply shattered Lathrop's resolution. In doing so, he projected Hawthorne criticism decisively toward the "realism war" of the eighties and nineties.

Whipple, whose work has been called perhaps "the purest example extant of the Victorian development of Romantic organicism,"[12] was a pioneering exponent of what we now think of as a Melvillean insight—that Hawthorne's distinctive vision revealed "the power of blackness." A decayed Christianity, thought Whipple, Puritanic Law with no compensating Grace, provided the key to Hawthorne's "peculiar mind," which "touches the lowest depths of tragic woe and passion—so deep, indeed, that . . . Jonathan Edwards, turned romancer . . . could not have written a more terrific story of guilt and retribution than *The Scarlet Letter*."[13]

Not so, said Elizabeth Peabody and Alexander Japp: Hawthorne's was a valid, if ecclesiastically liberated, Christianity. Lathrop carried the rebuttal to a genuine peak of Hawthorne appreciation—effectively blending his own intuition as to Hawthorne's mind with his own sense of Hawthorne's art. Hawthorne, he said, "had not the realistic tendency, as we usually understand that, but . . . the power to create a new species of fiction." And "the kind of romance that he has left us differs from all compositions previously so called." It is not the "romance" of Scudéry or Fielding, or the German Romantics. "It is not the romance of sentiment; nor that of incident, adventure, and character viewed under a worldly coloring: it has not the mystic and melodramatic bent belonging to Tieck and Fouqué."

There are, Lathrop holds, two things which "radically isolate" Hawthorne's art. These are, first, "its quality of revived belief":

> Hawthorne . . . is a great believer . . . his belief goes out toward what is most beautiful and this he finds only in moral truth. . . . This unsparingly conscientious pursuit of the highest truth, this metaphysical instinct, found in conjunction with a varied and tender appreciation of all forms of human or other life, is what makes him so decidedly the representative of a wholly new order of novelists.

But is Hawthorne not usually thought a skeptic unbeliever? That arises, Lathrop replied, only from a superficial "appearance of doubt" and from "his fondness for illuminating fine but only half-perceptible traces of truth with the touch of superstition. . . . And out of this questioning belief and transmutation of

superstition into truth . . . proceeds also that quality of value
and rarity and awe-enriched significance, with which he irradi-
ates real life until it is sublimed to a delicate cloud-image of
the eternal verities."

Lathrop's Hawthorne thus becomes a genius of vital ideality—
a "fictionist" who "penetrates . . . far into individual con-
sciences" and provides "a profoundly religious aid" for many
readers. And thence, finally, Lathrop is prepared to issue a
transcendent claim for his American genius:

> Hawthorne's repose is the acme of motion; and though
> turning on an axis of conservatism, the radicalism of his mind
> is irresistible; he is one of the most powerful because most
> unsuspected revolutionists of the world. Therefore, not only
> is he an incalculable factor in private character, but in addition
> his unnoticed leverage for the thought of the age is prodigious.
> These great abilities, subsisting with a temper so modest and
> unaffected, and never unhumanized by the abstract enthusi-
> asm for art, place him on a plane between Shakespeare and
> Goethe.[14]

About the decision whether to undertake his *Hawthorne* for
Macmillan's "English Men of Letters Series," Henry James may
or may not actually have said "again and again" to Julian
Hawthorne: "I don't want to do it. I'm not competent: and
yet, if I don't, some Englishman will do it worse. . . . Your
father was the greatest imaginative writer we had, and yet, I
feel that his principle was wrong; there is no more powerfully
and beautifully written book than *The Scarlet Letter;* and yet
I believe the whole conception of it was wrong! Imagination
is out of place; only the strictest realism can be right."[15] But
there can be no doubt that Hawthorne, and still more Lathrop's
Hawthorne, presented the James of the late 1870's with personally painful, as well as intellectually formidable, challenges.

James's only sustained, book-length, and independent literary study, his *Hawthorne* takes on a peculiar significance in the context of its own moment of Hawthorne criticism. If the first two chapters shed but a dim light on Hawthorne, they provide justly famous documentation of the then current state of the mind of Henry James. In one aspect as a work of criticism, James's book is shockingly bad; it is so mincingly self-conscious, so provincially deprecatory in its determination to maintain a "European" point of view, in its implied dismay at Lathrop's intolerable Yankee brag—Hawthorne on a plane between Shakespeare and Goethe, indeed! But in another aspect, James's is a great, free, original critical achievement.

Both the strengths and the weakness of James's *Hawthorne* spring from James's alienations. However necessary to his creative success, even survival, his sorely won expatriation, the need to justify himself to himself made James a blindly supercilious biographical and cultural critic in *Hawthorne*. But it was his intellectual alienation from his father's idealism, in brief, his own agnosticism and his commitment to the wholly this-worldly vision of the secularized continental realism then so bitterly controversial and "modern," which endowed James's view of Hawthorne's mind and art with piercing originality. With mocking ambiguity, James refuses to perceive the existence of Lathrop's unique romancer. Not believing in Puritanism, says James, Hawthorne simply did not believe. Not believing, he treated the matter of Puritanism "from the poetic and aesthetic point of view, the point of view of entertainment and irony." Metaphysically, Hawthorne was "a man of Fancy . . . with a kind of small ingenuity, a taste for conceits and analogies" —a mind easily prey to "allegory . . . one of the lighter exercises of the imagination," and a bore.[16]

"It cannot be too often repeated," James insists, "that Hawthorne was not a realist." His people "are all figures rather than characters—they are all pictures rather than persons."[17] Hawthorne persistently deserted (James almost says "betrayed") his natively high sense of the real, of actuality. As he soars into moonlit tenuity, "we get too much out of reality and cease to feel beneath our feet the firm ground of an appeal to our own vision of the world—our observation."[18] The result is that in the long run Hawthorne becomes to James "a beautiful, natural, original genius" of an almost pure and rather irresponsible artistry. His art is "original and exquisite" and unique: "No one has had just that vision of life, and no one has had a literary form that more successfully expressed his vision."

Yet in the end, James the realist could not take seriously the ideal white magic of the wizard hand. The exasperation of the rebel modernist and secularist shines through the deprecation, even the patronizing, of James's conclusion:

> He was not a moralist, and he was not simply a poet. The moralists are weightier, denser, richer. . . . He combined in a singular degree the spontaneity of the imagination with a haunting care for moral problems. Man's conscience was his theme, but he saw it in the light of a creative fancy which added, out of its own substance, an interest, and, I may almost say, an importance.[19]

Even from the sympathetic Howells, James's book brought the observation that for the Bostonian reaction to some of James's remarks he waited "with the patience and security of a spectator at an *auto da fé,* to see"; and a protest that fairness to Hawthorne demanded a recognition, deliberately withheld by James, of the traditional difference in aesthetic intention between the romance and the novel.[20] To idealists and romanticists, however, attitudes like James's were infuriating. But there was no real point of leverage for their wrath until, quite innocently, Howells provided it in the famous essay, "Henry James, Jr.," of 1882, which initiated the American phase of the "realism war"[21] and plunged Howells, James, and Hawthorne into the semantic middle of a bitter logomachy.

Howells' essay raised such a storm of obloquy, and, as effect led on to effect, delivered him into a warfare so sturdy that it is easy to forget how mild and obvious were the things he said: "It seems to me that an enlightened criticism will recognize in Mr. James's fiction a metaphysical genius working to aesthetic results. . . . The art of fiction has, in fact, become a finer art in our day than it was with Dickens and Thackeray. . . . The new school derives from Hawthorne and George Eliot . . . ; but it studies human nature much more in its wonted aspects, and finds its ethical and dramatic examples in the operation of lighter but not really less vital motives." It responds to "the realism of Daudet rather than . . . Zola": and "this school, which is so largely of the future as well as the present, finds its chief exemplar in Mr. James," to whom "we cannot deny . . . a very great literary genius."[22]

Howells in the same piece wondered if James were not most truly a romancer: ". . . His best types have an ideal development . . . ," but "perhaps the romance is an outworn form, and would not lend itself to the reproduction of even the ideality of modern life." But, to the ultimate chagrin of James, one of the unfairnesses of the succeeding controversy was the fastening of the term "realist" or "modern realist" firmly to "Howells—and—James," as notoriety coupled them. Then there came the sort of confusion of terms inevitable to intellectual warfare. It was recalled that in philosophic tradition "realist" (the opposite of "nominalist") meant "idealist." It was pointed out that the "modern realist" was an agnostic if not a materialist. And it was said with scorn and venom that these "moderns" were prophets of a false, anti-spiritual, anti-ideal, perhaps vicious "reality."

Inevitably the Hawthorne of Lathrop was taken to represent the cause of the "true" realists; Hawthorne the skeptic, Hawthorne the disengaged artist, the Hawthorne of James, became the model of the modernists. Inevitably criticism of Hawthorne as well as the regular passing reference to Hawthorne, of the sort which constitutes the substance of genuine fame, became loaded with this distinction—and with its confusions. And, since the Lathropian Hawthorne was by far the more puissant figure and because such a figure was essential to the idealists, the idealist Hawthorne figured much more frequently. Certainly neither the Hawthorne criticism of the eighties and nineties in either England or the United States nor the general literature of criticism and controversy over fiction in the period can be read accurately without attention to these problems of tactics and terminology.

In general the idealists and agnostics, however customarily unfair to personalities, were correct in their understanding of the intellectual and aesthetic issues: the realist-agnostics were in revolt against the ideal; the romancer-idealists did look toward the substance of things hoped for, things not of this seeable world. The neo-romantics, who wanted romantic (or, as Howells distinguished it, "romanticistic") sensations divorced from romantic faith, constituted a third and mischievous force. "I hold with the poets and the idealists; not the idealizers, but those who have ideals . . . ," said Charles Eliot Norton in 1895.[23] However, "an honest return . . . to the point of view of the early romanticists is now impossible," George Pellew had demonstrated in 1888.[24] "Scott and Hawthorne and Thackeray," urged William Roscoe Thayer, tell us from on high, "The Real includes the Ideal, but the Real without the Ideal is as the body without life, a thing for anatomists to dissect."[25] One neo-romantic commentator was so far carried away as to assert that George Washington Cable was superior to Hawthorne, for the latter is "psychologic rather than moral, an observer and analyzer

of moral problems, and coldly critical, not sympathetic. . . ."[26]
But it was just in that probing intellect that the realist found
Hawthorne's strength. Said Howells:

> . . . None of Hawthorne's fables are without a profound and
> distant reach into the recesses of nature and of being. He
> came back from his researches with no solution of the question
> . . . but the awful warning, 'Be true, be true,' which is the
> burden of *The Scarlet Letter*. . . . It is not his fault that this
> is not intelligence, that it knots the brow in sorer doubt rather
> than shapes the lips to utterance of the things that can never
> be said.[27]

Such remarks represent the spectrum of responsibility toward
the mingled problems of belief and of Hawthorne's mind and
art in this historical period.[28]

III

By the 1890's, these major (as well as a number of minor)
themes were firmly set as background for treatment of Hawthorne in periodical criticism, book- or chapter-length studies,
occasional poems, even the early texts and school-histories of
American literature. Particularly in regard to developments in
the international and historical novels and the literature of local
color, Hawthorne's example served steadily as an authorization
and incitement to writers and, inevitably, as a critical touchstone. Sampling of reviews, to say nothing of critical commentary in every form, suggests that hundreds of testings of the
literature of the age by the Hawthornian touchstone might be
found. Indeed, it suggests that a minor critic might well have
doubted his respectability if he failed to cite Hawthorne whether
in praise of or attack against any writing in question. Howells,
concluding that Hawthorne had left "a legacy which in its
kind is the finest the race has received from any mind," felt
moved to continue wryly, "As I have said, we are always finding
new Hawthorne's, but the illusion soon wears away, and then

we perceive that they were not Hawthornes at all; that he had some peculiar difference from them, which, by-and-by, we shall no doubt consent must be his difference from all men evermore."[29]

A large but profitable study in itself would be that of the influence of Hawthorne on the American fiction writers of this extended generation. Everyone agreed that Hawthorne was a master stylist—an American master of English, or perhaps even a master of American English. Mark Twain, listing in 1879 the national treasures which entitled Americans to be indifferent to the British national contempt, climaxed his list with the comment: "Nobody writes a finer and purer English than Motley, Howells, Hawthorne and Holmes."[30] And, in a characteristic "whoop of joy" at the discovery of a major aesthetic experience, William James wrote to Henry on January 19, 1870, of his delight in reading *The House of the Seven Gables*:

> I little expected so great a work. It's like a great symphony, with no touch alterable without injury to the harmony. It made a deep impression on me and I thank heaven that Hawthorne was an American. It also tickled my national feeling not a little to notice the resemblance of Hawthorne's style to yours and Howells's. . . . That you and Howells with all the models in English literature to follow, should needs involuntarily have imitated (as it were) this American, seems to point to the existence of some real American mental quality.[31]

Though Mark Twain found Hawthorne nevertheless one of the people whom it just tired him to death to try to read,[32] authors so various as Bellamy and Cable, Jewett and Tourgée, James Lane Allen and the followers of F. Marion Crawford devoted themselves to revival of the Hawthornian romance. And, as we have seen, Hawthorne's impact upon the realists was profound. Though a fragmentary literature on the subject exists, no one has yet truly elucidated the ways in which

James and Howells, as features of their very rebellion against "the Mage," repeatedly created—and in psychological, moral, and even mystical, as well as esthetic, developments—significant variations upon themes by Hawthorne.

After the triumph of a foolish neo-romanticism over the realists in their battle for the American public taste during the nineties, the serious idealists and the realists drew closer. Howells pointed out "the difference between the romanticistic and the romance, which is almost as great as that between the romantic and the realistic. Romance, as in Hawthorne, seeks the effect of reality in visionary conditions; romanticism, as in Dickens, tries for a visionary effect in actual conditions."[33] And with the work of the great realistic internationals all turning toward the psychological, even the psychic, the Americans, in the same currents, found it the easier to be reconciled to Hawthorne—though Henry James's latest comment as a formal critic on Hawthorne was only less dry than the conclusions of his book. James now finds Hawthorne to be " . . . an aesthetic solitary. His beautiful, light imagination is the wing that on the autumn evening just brushes the dusky window. It was a faculty that gave him much more a terrible sense of human abysses than a desire rashly to sound them and rise to the surface with his report. On the surface—the surface of the soul and the edge of the tragedy—he preferred to remain. . . . But of all cynics he was the brightest and kindest, and the subtleties he spun are mere silken threads for stringing polished beads. His collection of moral mysteries is the cabinet of a dilettante."[34]

By the turn of the century, however, Hawthorne's mature reader would no longer feel old romantic chills at the touch of the wizard hand. Neither would he, to justify old revolts, feel it necessary to deny the paternity of certain aesthetic impulses. As represented by Lewis E. Gates, for instance, that reader would find nothing in Hawthorne to appal—beside the decadents, Hawthorne's reputed morbidity would seem quaintly wholesome. Only the art and the ideas were enticing to Gates. "Hawthorne is a master spinner of beautiful webs," Gates would write, "and the most rabid devotee of art for art's sake cannot well refuse to enjoy the fineness and consistency of his designs, the continuity and firmness of his texture, and the richness and depth of his tinting. . . . But though Hawthorne dreams in terms of the ten commandments, . . . for some of us who still believe that life is greater than art, his dreams are all the more fascinating artistically because they are deeply, darkly, beautifully true." Not just the date, but the textures of criticism were moving into a new era when Gates would say:

> At present, Hawthorne is at a decided disadvantage, because, while remote enough to seem in trifles here and there archaic, he is yet not remote enough to escape contemporary standards or to be read with imaginative historical allowances and sympathy, as Richardson or Defoe is read. Hawthorne's romances have the human quality and the artistic beauty that ensure survival; and in a generation or two, when the limitations of the Romantic ideal and the scope of Romantic methods have become historically clear in all men's minds, Hawthorne's novels will be read with an even surer sense than exists today of that beauty of form and style and that tender humanity which come from the individuality of their author, and with a more tolerant comprehension of the imperfectness of equipment and occasional faults of manner that were the result of his environment and age.[35]

Soon after the turn of the century, there would come a rich revival of Hawthorne scholarship and criticism with the centenary of his birth in 1904. But by then, figures like George Woodberry, William Peterfield Trent, and Paul Elmer More had come to maturity. Theirs would be a serious, Arnoldian view, heralding the neo-humanism of an imminent era and projecting Hawthorne toward the present century's Age of Criticism.[36]

Seymour L. Gross and Randall Stewart

The

Hawthorne

Revival

D ESPITE his famous assertion in 1851 that he was the obscurest man of letters in America, Hawthorne seems never to have suffered a period of neglect such as that which befell Melville. In his own time there were, of course, those who preferred, as one of them put it, "to ascend to the sunny climes with Nathaniel Parker Willis than to descend to the charnel house with Nathaniel Hawthorne." But Hawthorne had his audience, though it was not quite so large as might be indicated by his remark in a letter to Horatio Bridge that "nobody's scribblings seem to be more acceptable to the public than mine."

335

His popularity during his life never reached the proportions of a Cooper or Irving or of that now all-but-faceless "d——d mob of scribbling women"; but his work was enough in demand for various influential editors, such as Griswold of *Graham's,* O'Sullivan of the *Democratic Review,* Lewis Clark of the *Knickerbocker,* Epes Sargent of *Sargent's,* all to approach him for contributions to their periodicals. Moreover, not only did he spark shocks of recognition in Poe and Melville, but as Bertha Faust's *Hawthorne's Contemporaneous Reputation* (1939) amply documents, his work stimulated a fair amount of what to us would be less significant critical interest as well.

In the second phase of Hawthorne's reputation, the sixty-odd years following his death, interest in Hawthorne was given its most significant boost by the publication of Henry James's excellent monograph in 1879. From the publication of what James called his "critical essay" until 1932, Hawthorne's work (collected in 1883 and again in 1900) evoked enough critical comment to furnish materials adequate for a thesis by William Reid on "A History of Hawthorne Criticism, 1879-1932" (Colorado, 1932).

It is clear, then, that even in the first two phases of Hawthorne criticism and scholarship (taking 1932, the date of the publication of Randall Stewart's edition of the *American Notebooks,* as the inception of the third) Hawthorne's work managed to maintain a "dialogue" with our culture's constant attempt to define its experience to itself; though, to be sure, it was sometimes used by critics such as Brownell ("deficient in passion" [1909]) or Parrington ("alienated from socio-political realities" [1927]) as an instance of the misconstruing of the essential American.

Nevertheless, despite this relatively uninterrupted skein of interest, Hawthorne has become the object of such an astonishing amount of attention in the past three decades that we may justifiably speak of this phase of Hawthorne studies as a "revival." For example, of the 261 items listed under "Hawthorne" in Louis Leary's *Articles on American Literature, 1900-1950* (1954), almost two-thirds of them postdate Professor Stewart's edition of the *American Notebooks;* and in the annual bibliographies published in *PMLA* since the terminal date of Professor Leary's checklist, scarcely another American author has occupied so much total space as has Hawthorne. Since 1932, over seventy doctoral dissertations on Hawthorne have been completed (fourteen in 1961–1962!), and so many others are in progress that Hawthorne may well have become the most "dissertated" of American writers. From Herbert Gorman's *Hawthorne, A Study in Solitude* and Lloyd Morris' *The Rebellious Puritan* in 1927 until Hubert Hoeltje's *Inward Sky: The Mind and Heart of Nathaniel Hawthorne* in 1962, Hawthorne has been the subject of ten biographical studies. In the last two decades, over a dozen book-length studies have devoted themselves to exposing his ideas, sources, traditions; to exploring his methods and development; and to analyzing and evaluating his creative accomplishments. Moreover, more recently, Hawthorne has regularly been taking his place as a crucial, and even pivotal, figure in such special interpretations of American literary culture as R. W. B. Lewis's *The American Adam* (1955), Richard Chase's *The American Novel and Its Tradition* (1957), Harry Levin's *The Power of Blackness* (1958), and Marius Bewley's two studies, *The Complex Fate* (1952) and *The Eccentric Design* (1959), to mention some of the more influential progeny of F. O. Matthiessen's pioneering work, *American Renaissance* (1941).

II

From one point of view, the matter of biography would seem to be the simplest aspect of the Hawthorne revival, since all literate cultures have traditionally been interested in the lives of their great writers. But the history of Hawthorne biography in the past three decades or so cannot be dismissed so easily, for the direction it has taken, especially when viewed against the general trend of Hawthorne criticism, is both interesting and curious. As Hawthorne criticism has increasingly tended toward a speculative enlargement of the issues his work raises in the moral, psychological, cultural, and mythic realms, and has increasingly discerned radical ambiguities, tensions, and paradoxes in his fictive geographies, Hawthorne biography, in what seems an almost conscious effort at counterbalancing, has worked toward creating an image of the man that is, comparatively speaking, solid and clear. Needless to say, a part of this movement toward what Wyndham Lewis calls "the substantiality, the person, the 'this-ness' of an author" is the result of our greater knowledge of Hawthorne. Yet do we know so much more about Hawthorne today than Professor Arvin knew in 1929 that we can account for the change that has taken place solely on the basis of our greater accumulation of data, though that is, of course, a great part of it?

The recent remark by Edward Davidson in his excellent introduction to the Hawthorne section of *Major Writers of America* (1962) that "Hawthorne's life was commonplace, even dull" would have struck Newton Arvin, who published his *Hawthorne* in 1929, as rather strange. Professor Davidson is referring solely to the "other Hawthorne," the one who "lived comfortably and unspectacularly in the world." But for Arvin, Hawthorne was a great American precisely because both his life and his works were two aspects of a single "tragic adventure" that will continue to have "high and durable significance" for the America in which he lived, struggled, and died.

Following the general direction of earlier Hawthorne biography in the twentieth century, though with greater sophisti-

338

cation and critical acumen, Arvin gave final form to the "dismal chamber" view of his subject; that is, he took as his controlling biographical image one which evokes Hawthorne's radical alienation from the "hum and buzz" of his culture. To be sure, in constructing his "myth" (in the good meaning of the word), he frequently psychologized portentously, preferred the darker interpretation of any event (such as the marriage to Sophia), and occasionally gothicized neutralities, as for example when the hotel room in which Hawthorne happened to die becomes "a grave and fitting [symbol] for a life spent in such incorrigible isolation." But in trying to locate the source of the most characteristic works in the life, Arvin was trying to face one of the most important challenges of literary biography: the exploration of that little lower layer where perhaps (only perhaps) some entry can be made into the creative imagination and thence into those works by which the creative imagination tries to make contact with history. The next surge of biographical interest in Hawthorne, however, was to expend tremendous talent and energy in an attempt to overturn this dark view of Hawthorne and present the world with a healthier, more normal, more worldly-wise man.

Although short studies of the "public" Hawthorne had appeared earlier in the century, for example, John Osborn's "Nathaniel Hawthorne as American Consul," in *Bookman*, XVI (1903), 461–64, and Winfield Nevins' "Nathaniel Hawthorne's Removal from the Salem Custom House," in *EIHC*, LIII (1917), 97–132, the counterreformation in the political aspects of Hawthorne's life and works did not gather any real momentum until the 1930's. Aided by the restoration of the notebooks and the discovery of letters and documents, scholars set out to correct the image of a Hawthorne so crucially aloof from the historical issues of his day that his indifference to them was hardened, not modified, by his periodic contacts with such economic, political, and sociological realities as consulate, custom house, and utopian farm.

The titles of articles that began to appear in the 1930's and early 1940's indicate the kind of documentation and emphasis that was going on. Professor Stewart, one of the figures of the movement, using the materials of his research into primary sources, gave us "Hawthorne and Politics" (*NEQ*, V [1932], 237–63), "Hawthorne in England: The Patriotic Motive in the Notebooks" (*NEQ*, VIII [1935], 3–13), "Hawthorne's Speeches at Civic Banquets" (*AL*, VII [1936], 415–23), and "Hawthorne and the Civil War" (*SP*, XXXIV [1937], 91–106). Neal Doubleday read *The Scarlet Letter* as being intimately concerned with the issue of feminism (*PMLA*, LIV [1939], 825–28), sketched out Hawthorne's involvement with the contemporary issue of a national literature (*AL*, XII [1941], 447–53), and, in his "Hawthorne's Criticism of New England Life" (*CE*, II [1941], 639–53) and "Hawthorne's Satirical Allegory" (*CE*, III [1942], 325–37), related Hawthorne's work to various contemporary events and concerns, as did Arlin Turner in "Hawthorne and Reform" (*NEQ*, XV [1942], 700–714), Manning Hawthorne in "Hawthorne and Utopian Socialism" (*NEQ*, XII [1939], 726–30), and William Randel in "Hawthorne, Channing, and Margaret Fuller" (*AL*, X [1939], 472–76). These articles, and many more, came to a kind of culmination in Lawrence Hall's *Hawthorne: Critic of Society* (1944), a thoroughly scholarly work which sets out to place Hawthorne's work against the double background of American society in the nineteenth century and Hawthorne's developing attitude toward it. Whereas before it had "always been easy to regard Hawthorne as anything but the product and spokesman of democratic society," now that all the evidence was in, we could finally see, in Professor Hall's words, that "the portrayal of life in the tales and romances is as democratic as anything which nineteenth-century America produced." How completely we have come to accept the culturally-implicated view of Hawthorne can be seen, for example, in the casualness with which Millicent Bell is able to assert in her recent book on Hawthorne (*Hawthorne's View of the Artist* [1962]) that "he was probably closer to the gritty substance of American history than most of the cause-joiners of Concord." The aroused interest in *The Blithedale Romance* in the 1950's, certainly the most "topical" of Hawthorne's novels, can also be traced, at least partially, to this new image of Hawthorne. Not only has *Blithedale* been discussed in terms of Hawthorne's attitudes toward various facts of social history—feminism, reform, utopianism—as, for example, in Darrel Abel's "Hawthorne's Skepticism about Social Reform" (*UKCR*, XIX [1953], 181-93), Lillian Beatty's *"Typee* and *Blithedale:* Rejected Ideal Communities" (*Personalist*, XXXVII [1956], 367-78), or Alex Gottfried and Sue Davidson's "Utopia's Children" (*Western Political Quarterly*, XV [1962], 17-32), but it has also achieved the status of being viewed as a seminal novel of American politics. Irving Howe, in *Politics and the Novel* (1957), believes that "if ever a novel is written that dives beneath the surface of political life in 20th century America," its author may find a hidden storehouse of fundamental insights in Hawthorne's novel. Marius Bewley has discussed at great length (*Scrutiny*, XVI [1949], 178-95, reprinted in *The Complex Fate*) the influence of *Blithedale* on Henry James's desire to write (in James's words) "a very American tale, a tale characteristic of our social conditions," a desire which became *The Bostonians*. And Richard Chase, in *The American Novel and Its Tradition*, considers *Blithedale* to have "launched," in addition to James's work, such political novels as Howells's *Vacation of the Kelwyns*, Trilling's *The Middle of the Journey*, and Mary McCarthy's *The Oasis*.

As we look back on the commendable and hugely successful

effort of scholarship, especially in its earliest phases, to reverse the image of an historically insular Hawthorne, it is possible to see something besides splendid restorations and discoveries as contributing to the movement. It was not easy in the 1930's, and early 40's as well, to espouse the greatness and relevance of an American writer who did not squarely face up to the issues of the Republic. Had not the influential Parrington, "the father of American Studies," announced accusingly, in 1927, that Hawthorne was the "extreme and finest expression of the refined alienation from reality that palsied the creative mind of New England"? And wasn't *reality* for Parrington, as for many another literary professional of the time, the concrete issues raised by socio-political actualities? In this phase of Hawthorne studies, then, it is perhaps not too fanciful to see scholarship's first duty and responsibility—the discovery of truth —as being subtly supported and moved along by a pleasurable sense of bringing both itself and its subject into a viable relationship with one of the implicit assumptions about the function of literature of the era.

Finally, it should be said that much Hawthorne criticism owes a large debt to these early researchers. In making a place for Hawthorne in his own history, so to speak, this scholarship enlarged our critical field of vision by enabling us to incorporate into it various facets of social history to stand alongside the already established "Burden of Hawthorne's Puritan Heritage." In adding a socio-political dimension to the moral crises in Hawthorne's fiction, it contributed something to Matthiessen's *American Renaissance,* in which Hawthorne's view of tragedy is conceived primarily in terms of social attitudes involved in his tragic vision; it helped prepare the way for such critically complex discussions of the function of historical issues and tensions in Hawthorne's work as Roy Harvey Pearce's "Hawthorne and the Sense of the Past; or, The Immortality of Major

Molineux" (*ELH*, XXI [1954], 327-49) or Marius Bewley's *The Eccentric Design* ("What Hawthorne leaves us with is . . . a set of exploratory symbols which vibrate with a peculiar intensity in a moral ambience that is objectively grounded in Hawthorne's society"); and it gave a factual base for such studies of Hawthorne's concept and treatment of the artist in a democratic society as Rudolphe Von Abele's *The Death of the Artist* (1955), Henry Fairbanks' "Hawthorne amid the Alien Corn" (*CE*, XVII [1956], 263-68), and, most definitively, Professor Bell's *Hawthorne's View of the Artist*.

Running alongside the revision of Hawthorne as cultural disaffiliate—and bolstering it and interrelated with it at many points—was a concerted effort in the 1930's and 40's to normalize the contours of Hawthorne's personality; to replace, that is, the traditional conception of a haunted shadow suffering from some psychic wound with a portrait of the artist as ordinary man. A turning point seemed to come with Professor Stewart's edition in 1932 of the *American Notebooks*, based upon the original manuscripts in the Morgan Library. Mrs. Hawthorne, in her edition of 1868, had, though her intentions were good, so nicenellied and purified her husband's private journal as virtually to misrepresent him. The new *Notebooks* revealed a more earthy, a more manly, man. Here, clearly, was a start.

There is, perhaps, no need to cite each of the bricks that went into paving the road to the "new Hawthorne" who appeared in the three biographical studies which were published in the six months from the fall of 1948 to the spring of 1949. Suffice it to say that Manning Hawthorne, who had access to unexplored family holdings, presented in a spate of articles evidence of his great-grandfather's rather normal early life; and that various scholars, utilizing unpublished letters, showed us Hawthorne as a critic of poetry, a traveler in New England, a husband, and—God save the mark!—a gossip about Salem.

343

Drawing upon all existing materials, published and unpublished, Randall Stewart accomplished in his *Nathaniel Hawthorne: A Biography* (1948) what he had predicted in his edition of the *English Notebooks* (1941): " . . . Out of the restored journals and letters a new Hawthorne will emerge: a more virile and a more human Hawthorne; a more alert and (in a worldly sense) a more intelligent Hawthorne; a Hawthorne less dreamy, and less aloof, than his biographers have represented him as being." In marshaling and distilling the two decades of work upon the "upper layer" of Hawthorne biography, Professor Stewart quietly but firmly split Hawthorne in two. The mind which imaginatively conjured up the perilous moral crises in the fiction (which Stewart treated separately in an appended chapter) was cleanly severed from the husband-father-friend engaged in the everyday routine of practical life—a division which the earlier myth of Hawthorne explicitly repudiated.

Robert Cantwell, in his *Nathaniel Hawthorne: The American Years* (1948), also eschewed the secret space within and presented, instead, Hawthorne's intercourse with the world. In order to give Hawthorne even more substantiality, Cantwell massively documented—often to the point of irrelevancy—his environment, giving to his subject's world the kind of "beef and ale" solidity that Hawthorne wished (or at least said he wished) his fictive world had had. Every figure who entered Hawthorne's orbit, be it ever so fleetingly, was accorded a *DAB*-type sketch of his own; every place Hawthorne lived, be it ever so briefly, was accorded a guidebook description; every fact or occurrence that Hawthorne may have heard of, or thought of, was accorded an essay of its own. Yet, ironically enough in a biography which purported to be an objective account of a man of the world, Cantwell turned the fanciful materials of various sketches into "facts" of Hawthorne's life, and substituted

344

real adventure for the "romance" of the deeper psychology, as when he (on the slightest thread of evidence) implicated Hawthorne in a sensational murder trial in 1830 and turned him into a secret agent for the Treasury Department in 1838.

Mark Van Doren, whose *Hawthorne* (1949) appeared soon after the Stewart and Cantwell biographies, insofar as he incorporated the "normalizing" discoveries of the previous two decades, also depicted the new Hawthorne. But perhaps because he is himself a poet as well as critic-biographer, and surely because he devoted much space to a critical commentary of his subject's works, Van Doren's biography does not give precedence to the Hawthorne who lived the facts. Though he chronicles all the workaday aspects of Hawthorne's involvement with "the world's work," as Hawthorne had himself put it, these tend to be subsumed—not denied—in Van Doren's concentration on "the life within the life." Neither wounded solitary nor healthy citizen dominates the Van Doren portrait. Money was necessary and working to get it even had its rewards. "But the one place [Hawthorne] truly lived and labored in was his imagination." Hawthorne's life, finally, is informed neither by tragic alienation nor its opposite, but rather by the reconciliation that took place in his "utterly serious imagination," which saw both the "horror" and the "honor" in the human condition and "the dignity by which in some eternity our pain is measured."

Two studies which appeared in the early 1950's, Louise Tharp's *The Peabody Sisters of Salem* (1950) and Vernon Loggins' *The Hawthornes: The Story of Seven Generations of an American Family* (1951), as their titles suggest, added information about Hawthorne's family, but neither indicated any particular innovation in the presentation of the new Hawthorne. Edward Wagenknecht's *Nathaniel Hawthorne: Man and Writer* (1961), however, does, in that he *explicitly* sets out to counter the image of Hawthorne that has emerged from recent critical discussions of his work—discussions which, in Professor Wagenknecht's view, are often "as alien to [Hawthorne's] spirit as they are to Cooper or Longfellow or Lowell or any of his other contemporaries whom they neglect." Because we admire Hawthorne's use of symbols and the fiction that can be read on multiple levels, and because Hawthorne "was given to literary ambivalences which suggest the kind of hidden depths into which a psychologically oriented age likes to probe," Professor Wagenknecht feels that we are "making him over in our own image" and missing the "significant things about him." Here, then, we have not only the "two" Hawthornes but a clear suggestion that the man-in-the-world one is the truer one, the one who, presumably, belongs with Longfellow and Lowell rather than, let us say, with Poe or Charles Brockden Brown. Professor Wagenknecht has read almost everything written by and about Hawthorne conscientiously and packs an immense amount of information on Hawthorne's differing attitudes toward various aspects of life into a relatively small book. Yet they are presented not as dualities of some central ambiguity of spirit (which would involve recourse to the deeper psychology which Wagenknecht despises) so much as the normal, un-mysterious contradictions which any man who has lived a long time will fall into. As a result the "tone" of Wagenknecht's life of Hawthorne is lighter, brighter, less portentous, and more self-certain than the mind which modern criticism (and the older biographical myth) induced from the most characteristic, or at least most notable, works. The dark places in Hawthorne are quite theoretical; the real Hawthorne "faced the light."

The new myth of Hawthorne's life toward which the biographical studies of the past three decades have been tending is given final and extreme form in Hubert Hoeltje's *Inward Sky* (1962). Though it is by far the longest twentieth-century biography of Hawthorne, it is notable not so much for the revelation of new facts as for the new concept which informs it. The focus, as in Arvin and Van Doren, is on "the inward life," as the title indicates; the method is "fullest sympathy" ("Here . . . is no book of criticism . . . no surgeon's dissecting knife, nor even the anteroom of the psychoanalyst"); and the myth is "repose" ("In a review of Hawthorne's life and writings nothing is more prominent than a quiet, deeply joyful affirmation"). The healthy sunshine of Hawthorne's *outer* life, which was revealed by Stewart, elaborated by Cantwell, and emphasized as crucial by Wagenknecht, becomes in Hoeltje the warm coloration of Hawthorne's *inner* idyllic landscape: "To recognize the hand of Providence in the affairs of man, to see the unity in the diversity of the world, to perceive in the forms of Nature a majestic and beautiful Idea . . . and to be assured that beyond is still a higher fruition in man's immortality— these were the basic tenets of Hawthorne's belief as a man, a belief, too, permeating all his writings. . . . " The two Hawthornes are once again one. How completely the "white" myth of Hawthorne has supplanted the "black" is wonderfully illustrated in the use made of Emerson's view of the dead Hawthorne in the final paragraphs of the first and last biographies here treated. Arvin: "Emerson, who was among the pallbearers, had a . . . searching insight . . . into the drama just ended. 'I thought,' he wrote in his journal the next day, 'there was a tragic element in the event that might be more fully rendered,—in the painful solitude of the man, which, I suppose, could not longer be endured, and he died of it.'" Hoeltje: "To Ralph Waldo Emerson, in the Concord village church, looking for the last time at the friend who lay in his blossom-covered coffin, it had seemed that Hawthorne's was a powerful head—noble and serene in its aspect." In the contrast between pallbearer and friend, solitude and serenity, are lodged the polar opposites of modern Hawthorne biography.

347

III

In reviewing a critical volume on Hawthorne some years ago, Marius Bewley had occasion to remark that if a literary sociologist undertook to investigate the phenomenon of "revivals," he suspected that the results would be "sinister." By this remark (forgetting for the moment the irony of Professor Bewley's own appreciable contribution to the Hawthorne revival), Professor Bewley seems to have meant that literary band-wagonism, and its beneficial effect on careers, rather than Hawthorne's enduring ability to speak significantly to our present condition, constitutes the essential motive in our renewed interest. Perhaps, perhaps not. No one, not even Professor Bewley's "literary sociologist," could accurately separate out the legitimate from the illegitimate strands in this or any other literary boom. (Nor, as a matter of fact, can it be done in scientific booms; the number of researchers in numerous branches of science who in the last decade or so suddenly altered the line of their investigations and began to zero in on cancer—which is now an iconic rather than a medical term—is suspicious enough to have given rise to the rueful remark that more people live off cancer than die from it.) But it is possible, nevertheless, to discern cultural factors which made the Hawthorne critical revival the result of somewhat less ominous impulses than Professor Bewley implies.

Roughly speaking—which is the only way one can speak of such matters—the critical revival in Hawthorne studies (that is, a new way of reading his works) begins about a decade or so after the biographical. Though, to be sure, Hawthorne's fiction was discussed in print in the 1930's, much of it was directed (as indicated in Part I of this essay) toward the creation of a new "biographical" image. Most of the essays used what might be called a horizontal method: Hawthorne's sketches, tales, and romances were scrutinized for their paraphrasable content in much the same way and for much the same ends that letters and journals were used—so as to present in synoptic form an exposition of Hawthorne's ideas and attitudes. In such essays as Carlos Kiling's "Hawthorne's View of Sin" (*Personalist*, XIII [1932], 119-30) or Neal Doubleday's "Hawthorne's Inferno" (*CE*, I [1940], 658-70), the sketching out of Hawthorne's moral posture is implicitly based on the critical assumption that since literature is the result of putting abstract ideas into concrete form, it can be used as *parallel* evidence along with extrinsic sources of information in order to expose the author's beliefs.

Two comments can be made on such a literary critical method. First, it is essentially optimistic in that it believes that in a relatively short space imaginative complexity can be reduced to synoptic clarity; and second (which is a consequence of the first), it feels no need to read any particular work in depth. This is not to say, let us hasten to add, that such systematic studies of Hawthorne's "mind" are neither valuable nor are not to be found after the 1930's. On the matter of Hawthorne's "Puritanism," for example, or the relationship of that complex of religious-cultural-historical phenomena to his world-view, no serious student of Hawthorne can dispute the value of such horizontally comprehensive studies of the problem as are to be found, for example, in Austin Warren's introduction to *Nathaniel Hawthorne: Representative Selections* (1934), Barriss Mills's "Hawthorne and Puritanism" (*NEQ*, XXI [1948], 78-102), Henry Fairbanks' "Sin, Free Will, and 'Pessimism'" (*PMLA*, LXXI [1956], 975-89), or Joseph Schwartz's "Three Aspects of Hawthorne's Puritanism" (*NEQ* XXXVI [1963], 192-208). It is to say only that a new strategy in Hawthorne criticism did not emerge until the 1940's, until, that is, the formalistic techniques of the so-called New Criticism caught up with Hawthorne and a cultural sense of broken promises in the post–World War II world raised the literary stock of those authors who could be read as having a "tragic vision" of life.

Hawthorne's reputation (along with Melville's and James's) rose immensely in the early 1940's as the reputations of the nineteenth-century optimistic prophets of America declined. In a world in which horror was domesticated in history, and kill or be killed had changed from a metaphor of business to a physical fact, it was difficult to believe, with Emerson, that there was no difference between the slayer and the slain because all men participate in the Oversoul. Cosmic hopefulness was as irrelevant to the world of Buchenwald and St. Lo as phlebotomy and the crossbow. The annihilative powers of blackness of "Young Goodman Brown," the ambiguity of sin or sorrow of "The Minister's Black Veil," the inscrutable moral paradoxes of "Rappaccini's Daughter," or the destructive power of scienticism of "The Birthmark"—these became, for a disillusioned culture, apt predictions of what Richard Chase called the "dark center of the twentieth century."

Moreover, the decay of social hopefulness also affected the Hawthorne critical revival. Whereas Hawthorne's fiction offered nothing positive to the Marxist and semi-Marxist critics of the 1930's—Granville Hicks in *The Great Tradition* (1933; rev. ed. 1935) rejected his work in much the same terms as had Parrington—in the war years and after, the New Liberals found in Hawthorne's awareness of the baffling contradictions of life a deeper insight into the nature of the American experience than that of the purveyors of a socialist-democratic dream. Lionel Trilling, for example, in his Preface to *The Liberal Imagination* (1950), asserted that the "job of criticism [is] to recall liberalism to its first essential imagination of variousness and possibility, which implies the awareness of complexity and difficulty. . . . Because literature is the human activity that takes the fullest and most precise account of variousness, possibility, complexity, and difficulty." And seven years before, Professor Trilling, in his book on E. M. Forster, singled out Hawthorne as having just such a complex vision of life "in his unremitting concern with moral realism," which is not merely "the awareness of morality itself, but of the contradictions, paradoxes, and dangers of living the moral life."

Such a view of the nature of literature implied a shift from a cursory view of a literary work for its abstractable content to a closer scrutiny of the actual concrete embodiments of the text to see what attitudes and insights they bring into being. The critical method for exploring "variousness and complexity" in individual works, however, was to be the contribution of what has come to be called the New Criticism.

Although the formalistic techniques of the New Criticism have their origins in the 1920's, when the first stirrings of discontent with the non-technical modes of moralism and didacticism manifested themselves, as a movement and force New Criticism did not, as Walter Sutton has recently pointed out (*Modern American Criticism* [1963]), rise to prominence until the 1940's. The revolution in the teaching and study of literature which it then effected in English departments all over the country particularly influenced the study of Hawthorne's work because the non-naturalistic fictive mode of much of his writing easily accommodated the New Critical tendency to read fiction as poetry. Such a tendency, according to the notable Hawthorne critic Roy Male, can distort certain kinds of novels, but "Hawthorne's fiction lights up when examined under this kind of intensive scrutiny."

In brief, then, the initial upsurge in the Hawthorne critical revival is the result of a cultural tendency to respond to the

351

more darkly complex visions of life intersecting with the domi-
nance of a critical method which was drawn to fiction that
rendered experience as much by means of image and symbol
as by character and action. The results of this convergence of
forces can be discerned in (1) the kind of Hawthorne story
which has been most frequently singled out for separate analysis; (2) the emergence of studies of Hawthorne's symbolic
patterns; and (3) the new emphasis given to what George
Woodberry in 1902 called "the dark side of the truth" in
Hawthorne.

Perhaps nothing else so clearly demonstrates the nature of
Hawthorne's viability for us as that handful of his stories
which have continued to exercise our critical minds. Of the
over one hundred short pieces he wrote—at least several dozen
of which can be classed as short stories—only a very few have
repeatedly been analyzed individually (not simply discussed
in more broadly focused studies): "Young Goodman Brown"
(seventeen times since 1945); "Ethan Brand" (sixteen times
since 1947); "Rappaccini's Daughter" (fifteen times since
1947); "My Kinsman, Major Molineux" (thirteen times since
1951); "The Minister's Black Veil" (eight times since 1948);
and "The Birthmark," "The Artist of the Beautiful," and "The
May-Pole of Merry Mount," several times each. In contrast to
such prefabricated tales as "The Lily's Quest" or "The Three-
Fold Destiny," these are all stories in which meanings seem to
be felt for rather than imposed, in which implications emerge
complexly and tentatively from densely symbolized textures. It
is to these stories, therefore, rather than to what Hawthorne
called his "tales of evident design" (which far outnumber the
others) that the modern critic has turned to find that variousness
and tragic complexity which constitute for him the essential
Hawthorne.

A critical awareness that Hawthorne's fiction was organized

Brand" in the 1940's (collected in his *Hawthorne's Fiction: The Light and the Dark* [1952]), showed how a close attention to Hawthorne's images and symbols invested the works with a new vitality, suggestiveness, and a whole range of hitherto hidden implications, it was Mrs. Q. D. Leavis who first put the matter unequivocally in a two-part article significantly entitled "Hawthorne as Poet" (*SR*, LIX [1951], 179-205, 426-58). Hawthorne, Mrs. Leavis announced, was a dramatic poet who "can have gone to school with no one but Shakespeare for his inspiration and model"; his language is "poetic," "symbolic," "directly evocative," each story almost "an expanded metaphor," his corpus a poetic saga of American cultural history. Two years later, William Bysshe Stein, in *Hawthorne's Faust* (1953), argued that imagery and action in Hawthorne were mythic, symbolic ritualizations of the archetypal Faustian contract. Hyatt Waggoner's contention that Hawthorne characteristically thought in symbols led him, in *Hawthorne: A Critical Study* (1955), to focus his analyses of the tales and romances on Hawthorne's use of color, symmetry, "intricate tissues of symbolism," and patterns of imagery so as to demonstrate how complexly Hawthorne renders his moral, historical, and psychological ideas. In *Hawthorne's Tragic Vision* (1957), Roy Male asserts that Hawthorne's "accomplished work is a rare combination of poetry and fiction: poetry, in that each image functions as part of a larger design; fiction, in that the narrative . . . preserves some degree of versimilitude." But it is the symbolic "larger design" upon which Male focuses—the "tragic rhythm" which oscillates between the spatial, optimistic, or at least amelioristic, male principle and the timeless, half-dark, half-redemptive female principle. Subsequent articles—such as Sister Hilda Bonham's study of the needlework symbolism in *The Scarlet Letter* ("Hawthorne's Symbols *Sotto Voce*," *CE*, XX [1959], 184-86), Peter Murray's discussion of the season symbolism in *The Blithedale Romance* ("Mythopoesis in *The Blithedale Romance*," *PMLA*, LXXV [1960], 591-6), or Daniel Hoffman's splendid readings of "Young Goodman Brown" and "My Kinsman, Major Molineux" (*Form and Fable in American Fiction* [1961]) as examples of Hawthorne's "most successful fictions," those in which meaning is not separable from the symbol in which it manifests itself—demonstrate the continuing pull in this direction of Hawthorne studies.

There has, of course, always been critical attention paid to Hawthorne's depictions of evil and sin; after all, Melville heavily underscored in religious terms that "great power of blackness" in his friend's work as early as 1850. But the emphasis, before the 1940's, tended to be solely on Hawthorne's "sense of sin" as seen from a theological or religious point of view. That is, the appropriate fictions were scrutinized for revelations of Hawthorne's doctrinal beliefs about the soul's relationship to some supernatural order of reality. (In an author such as Hawthorne, in whose works religious matters often reverberate in the moral-psychological ambiences of his characters, a critical interest in his theological stance will inevitably be aroused. See, for example, such recent studies of the problem as Leonard Fick's *The Light Beyond: A Study of Hawthorne's Theology* [1955]—the most extreme attempt at schematization in terms of such constants as Augustinianism, Thomism, Arminianism, etc.; Joseph Schwartz's "God and Man in New England" in *American Classics Reconsidered* [1958]—which tries, though not too dogmatically, to fit Hawthorne into a Catholic theology of love and hope; or Randall Stewart's discussion of original sin in Hawthorne in *American Literature and Christian Doctrine* [1958].)

In the post–World War II period, however, it is possible to discern a critical dissatisfaction with the interpretation of Hawthorne's dramatizations of sin and evil as being primarily or exclusively concerned with salvational matters. There begins to emerge, about this time, what might be termed a "politicali-zation" of Hawthorne's depictions of moral failure to stand alongside and interact with the more traditional religious evalu-ation. The portrayal of sin in Hawthorne is seen, that is, not only as denoting a spiritual lesion in the soul, but also as a kind of metaphor of the limited possibilities of human accomplish-ment in history. In articles such as Richard Chase's "The Progressive Hawthorne" (PR, XVI [1949], 96-100), Russel Kirk's "The Moral Conservatism of Hawthorne" (Contempo-rary Review, No. 1044 [1952], pp. 361-66), Henry Kariel's "Man Limited: Nathaniel Hawthorne's Classicism" (SAQ, LII [1953], 528-42), Marvin Fisher's "The Pattern of Con-servatism in Johnson's Rasselas and Hawthorne's Tales" (JHI, XIX [1958], 173-96), C. N. Stavrou's "Hawthorne's Quarrel with Man" (Personalist, XLII [1961], 352-60), or Melvin Askew's "Hawthorne, The Fall, and the Psychology of Matu-rity" (AL, XXXIV. [1962], 335-43), the critical view of the origin, nature, and response to sin and evil in Hawthorne's fiction is broadened to include its purely human, existential implications as well. In other words, such a theological concept as original sin, for example, is interpreted not only in terms of man's tendency to defy the precepts of God, but also as a symbol of all those ambiguities, paradoxes, and impenetrable mysteries of experience which circumscribe man's understand-able but doomed desire for infinite achievement in the world in which he lives.

Such an emphasis on the "moral realism" in Hawthorne enabled Philip Rahv, for example, to discuss the "dark ladies" in Hawthorne's fiction, not as "good" or "bad," but as "one heroine" who symbolizes "the contrary values that [Hawthorne] attached to experience" ("The Dark Lady of Salem," PR, VIII [1941], 362-81); Gordon Roper to read The Scarlet Letter as Hawthorne's "examination and acceptance of the darker ambiguities of life" ("The Originality of Hawthorne's *The Scarlet Letter*," *Dalhousie Review*, XXIX [1950], 62-79); Louise Dauner to view "The Gentle Boy" not as an attempt to define a "true" Christian creed but as a grimly tragic reflection of life's moral ambiguities ("The 'Case' of Tobias Pearson: Hawthorne and the Ambiguities," *AL*, XXI [1950], 464-72); and Professors Fogle, Stein, Waggoner, and Male to analyze the Hawthorne canon in terms of its "moral dilemmas," "experiential dualities," "tragic complexities," and "trope[s] representing the dialectic between present and past, rebellion and acceptance, space and time." For good or ill, Hawthorne criticism had moved a long way from the straightforward exposition of beliefs and ideas.

The advent of Freudian psychoanalytic criticism of Hawthorne's fiction is, from one point of view, the result of a general movement that got started in the late 1930's and which would find the fact that Hawthorne grew up in a fatherless household full of females irresistible. But it is also possible to see it as another, more extreme, reaction to moralistic criticism. Simon O. Lesser in his *Fiction and the Unconscious* (1957), which includes his previously published psychological interpretation of "My Kinsman, Major Molineux" (*PR*, XXII [1955], 372-80), explicitly indicates this reaction in his assumption that literature is not "centrally concerned with moral problems." That is, whereas the critics we have been citing expressed their dissatisfaction with moralism by enlarging and complicating their responses to Hawthorne's depictions of "the midnight of the moral world," the psychoanalytic critics (that is, those who read Hawthorne's fiction as the projection of the author's subconscious stresses) simply denied the "public" implications of the symbolizations of sin, guilt, and isolation entirely. By locating their sole reality in the interior of Hawthorne's psyche, these critics removed the fictive crises in Hawthorne's fiction from both history and supra-history.

357

The first to be persuaded of the relevance of such a view were the psychiatrists, of course. Clarence Oberndorf ("Psychoanalytic Insight of Hawthorne," *Psychoanalytic Review*, XXIX [1942], 373-85) and O. L. Zangwill ("A Case of Paramnesia in Nathaniel Hawthorne," *Character and Personality*, XIII [1945], 246-60) read *The Scarlet Letter* as a projection of the author's Oedipal situation, one of his unconscious attempts "to cure himself through repetitive confessional writing." Joseph Levi ("*The Scarlet Letter*: A Psychoanalytical Interpretation," *AI*, X [1953], 291-306) and Lois Adkins ("Psychological Symbolism of Guilt and Isolation in Hawthorne," *AI*, XI [1954], 417-25) also (boringly) follow the formal Freudian theory of the Oedipus complex, though they do not agree about which characters represent Hawthorne's id, ego, and superego. Although Eugene Arden accepts the Oedipal premise of *The Scarlet Letter*, he tentatively suggests (only tentatively since, after all, he is writing in *The American Imago*, "A Psychoanalytic Journal for the Arts and Sciences") that a novel is not solely a case history of its author—Hawthorne could have learned of psychological phenomena from his physician-friend, Oliver Wendell Holmes, amongst other sources of such information. But his amazed "discovery" that Chillingworth follows modern psychoanalytic procedure in 1850 (Hawthorne is a "Freudian before Freud"), because it ignores both Chillingworth's motive and the symbolic meaning of his actions in the total design of the novel, comes to no more than a pointing out of an historical curiosity ("Hawthorne's 'Case of Arthur D.,'" *AI*, XVIII [1961], 45-55).

In each of these "cases," the action of the work is related to the mind of Hawthorne, so that if they have no critical relevance, they may yet be acknowledged as having, *at least theoretically*, biographical relevance. William Bysshe Stein's "'The Artist of the Beautiful': Narcissus and the Thimble" (*AI*,

XVIII [1961], 35-44) is something else again. His reading of
the story as an "almost clinical explanation of the paranoic
symptoms which characterize an individual's struggle to sub-
limate homosexual predispositions," in which the main action
(Warland's attempt to spiritualize machinery) is interpreted as
the "determination of the superego to desexualize the meaning
of copulation," since it is not related to either the mind of the
author or the mind of the audience (which, according to many
theorists of literary psychoanalytic criticism, are the only valid
alternatives, since a fictional character cannot properly be said
to possess a "mind"), is finally nothing more than a summary of
the action by means of a technical vocabulary. Moreover, given
his position, Professor Stein logically concludes that Hawthorne
unequivocally damns his main character, and thus he reduces
Hawthorne's complex vision of the artist in America to a simplicity. Professor Bell's chapter on the story in her *Hawthorne's
Vision of the Artist* can well serve as an indication of how
beside the point Professor Stein's essay is.

Much more sophisticated and far-ranging psychological analyses, because they are not shackled by the restrictive terminology
of psychiatry and are aware of the nature of literary form, are
John E. Hart's "*The Scarlet Letter*: One Hundred Years After"
(*NEQ*, XXIII [1950], 381-95) and Rudolphe Von Abele's
The Death of the Artist (1955). Professor Hart, eschewing the
simplistic triune of id, ego, and superego, interprets the attitudes
and actions of the characters in *The Scarlet Letter* as symbolic
representations of "different sides of [Hawthorne's] own personality," especially as these explore Hawthorne's complex feelings
about the relationship of his art to his guilt feelings about his
implication with the past. Professor Von Abele reads the
romances and two of the tales primarily as projective fables of
Hawthorne's problems with art, sex, and society, and in doing
so tries to account for his artistic disintegration.

Finally, we may look at Professor Lesser's psychonalytic interpretation of "My Kinsman, Major Molineux," in which the action of the story is not interpreted as a revelatory projection of the "mind" of the author but rather as a disguised appeal to the unconscious emotional needs and desires of the audience. In Professor Lesser's view, the career of Robin on its unconscious level is motivated by his desire to be free of adult domination, which he accomplishes in the climax of the story when, in his laugh, he vents his latent hostility for his kinsman and abandons his search. The "meaning" of the story is in its psychological appositeness to the unconscious life of the reader: "What [Robin] is doing, unwittingly but flamboyantly, is something which every young man does and must do, however gradually, prudently, and inconspicuously: he is destroying an image of paternal authority so that, freed from its restraining influence, he can begin life as an adult."

Interestingly enough, Professor Lesser's reading of the tale has been objected to by both a psychiatrist and a literary critic. Louis Paul in "A Psychoanalytic Reading of Hawthorne's 'Major Molineuy' [sic]: The Father Manqué and the Protégé Manqué" (AI, XVIII [1961], 279-88), arguing from a different view of what constitutes normalcy in young men's responses to fathers, asserts that only "neurotic" young men attempt to *destroy* the paternal image. "The healthy son *integrates* selective standards or restraints proposed by the father, as inner constraints, and becomes his own man." As such, Dr. Paul rejects Professor Lesser's reading of the tale as a successful initiation into adulthood, for in his view (shared by no other critic) Robin, at the end of the story, "is about to retreat homeward to resume attachment to mother and the bondage to father." The psychiatrist stands alone; in the dozen or so other interpretations of the story, no matter what emphasis or slant is given to the action by the critics, all agree that some *rite de passage* has been effected. And thereby hangs a tale.

Using Professor Lesser's reading of "Molineux," Roy Harvey Pearce attempts in his "Robin Molineux on the Analyst's Couch: A Note on the Limits of Psychoanalytic Criticism" (*Criticism*, I [1959], 83-90) to demonstrate the "inadequacy and partiality" that results from abstracting a character from his fictive context so as to psychoanalyze him in private. Generously granting Professor Lesser's contribution to our understanding of the character, Robin, he shows that the created world of the whole tale, of which Robin is but one part, opens up dynamic implications which the exclusive concern with Robin short circuits. Robin's "freedom" is achieved at the expense of his and his society's guilt—its cost is the torment and destruction of "a noble, tragic figure, a loyalist caught up in Revolutionary anti-loyalist violence." As such, in the language of "moral realism," Professor Pearce concludes that Robin's attainment of freedom (and his society's) "is dreadful"—for "Molineux" is "a tragic assertion of the inextricable relation of freedom and unfreedom in the world."

The critical interest in the relationships between Hawthorne and Melville and Hawthorne and James, the other two American fiction writers whose work was accorded a revival at about the same time, is a logical by-product of the forces we have been sketching here. These three authors having been singled out as being particularly viable in the culture's attraction to the "complex vision," it was natural that inter-relationships (though not between Melville and James) would emerge.

The Hawthorne-Melville relationship has a longer history. Earlier studies tended to be superficial, such as Hildegard Hawthorne's "Hawthorne and Melville" (*Lit. Rev.*, II [1922], 406), or deflective, such as Lewis Mumford's attempt to make Ethan Brand into a portrait of Melville (*Herman Melville* [1929]), which was refuted by Randall Stewart in "Ethan Brand" (*SRL*, V [1929], 967). Henry Seidel Canby's chapter on "Hawthorne and Melville" in his *Classic Americans* (1931) is, however, an extremely valuable comparative study, and F. I. Carpenter's "Puritans Preferred Blondes: The Heroines of Melville and Hawthorne" (*NEQ*, IX [1936], 253-72) is a brilliant exposition of the way the conservative aspect of the Puritan tradition—"the old morality of purity"—inhibited the imaginative creativity of both authors.

The fullest discussion of the relationship between the two writers is to be found in Harrison Hayford's unpublished dissertation (Yale, 1945), two parts of which have appeared as "The Significance of Melville's 'Agatha' Letters" (*ELH*, XIII [1946], 299-310) and "Hawthorne, Melville, and the Sea" (*NEQ*, XIX [1946], 435-52). Most of the relationship studies are concerned with the two authors as dual reflections of certain cultural, moral, or literary situations rather than with examples of specific influences. For example, Randall Stewart discusses their general similarity of moral vision in "Melville and Hawthorne" (*SAQ*, LI [1952], 436-46); James E. Miller compares their conceptions of the unpardonable sin in "Hawthorne and Melville: The Unpardonable Sin" (*PMLA*, LXX [1955], 91-114); Charles Feidelson, in reaction to what he considered Matthiessen's too emphatic social and political bent, examines the two (along with several other nineteenth-century writers) in terms of their "devotion to the possibilities of symbolism" (*Symbolism and American Literature* [1953]); and Harry Levin chose the two authors (along with Poe) to represent "the symbolic character of our greatest literature and the dark wisdom of our deeper minds" (*The Power of Blackness* [1958]). Of the influence studies, the most convincing are Leon Howard's (*Herman Melville* [1951]) and Nathalia Wright's discussions of the influence of Hawthorne's tales on the conception and execution of Melville's masterwork ("*Mosses from an Old Manse and Moby-Dick*," *MLN*, LXVII [1952], 387-92). Edward G.

Lueders' "The Melville-Hawthorne Relationship in *Pierre* and *The Blithedale Romance*" (*WHR*, IV [1950], 323-34) is an extremely suggestive essay on the effect of the friendship of the two men on their 1852 novels, both of which are more autobiographical than either had written before, both of which criticize transcendentalism, and both of which utilize a contrasting pair of light and dark ladies.

A critical awareness of the influence of Hawthorne on James is almost wholly a product of the 1940's. Before Matthiessen had pointed it out in *American Renaissance* (1941) and in *Henry James: The Major Phase* (1946), only T. S. Eliot seems to have written on the relationship in his "The Hawthorne Aspect" (*Lit. Rev.* V [1918], 44-53). The main work in this area, however, has been done by Marius Bewley, whose 1949 and 1950 articles in *Scrutiny* on "James's Debt to Hawthorne" are reprinted in *The Complex Fate* (1952). The common bond which Bewley discerns between Hawthorne and James is their mutual concern with the relationship of America to Europe, a dichotomy which subsumes the relationship of past to present and solitude to society. Hawthorne's main contribution to James, generally speaking, is, according to Professor Bewley, his pioneering attempt to fashion native materials into art, thereby making them accessible for James's later perfections, and a persistent concern with the reality of moral evil, which may have helped to save James from sharing the hermetically sealed, amoral aestheticism of the expatriates found in some of his fiction. But since Professor Bewley feels that it is better to consider Hawthorne's influence on James as "specifically as possible, for it is extremely elusive of generalizations," he discusses James's use of, and improvement upon, the Zenobia-Priscilla relationship in his depiction of the relationship between Olive and Verena in *The Bostonians;* ascribes the weakness in the portrait of Milly

Theale in *The Wings of the Dove* to James's absorption of the unwarrantedly reverential ideal of New England womanhood as envisioned in Hawthorne's Hilda; and analyzes the strengths and weaknesses of James's handling of the Hawthornian theme of the discrepancy between appearance and reality in *The Golden Bowl, The Turn of the Screw,* and *What Maisie Knew.*

Following Professor Bewley's lead, Edwin Fussell in "Hawthorne, James, and 'The Common Doom'" (*AQ*, X [1958], 438-53) documents his contention that "the very richest aspect of their literary relationship" lies in James's working out in various novels the "Hawthorne theme" of the sin of isolating oneself "from the common life"; Peter Buitenhuis discusses James's various views of Hawthorne to cast light both on "how James was able to learn different things from his predecessor at various stages in his development"—all through the 1880's and 1890's Hawthorne's influence is apparent to some degree—and on how James's responses to Hawthorne indicate his evolving view of America ("Henry James on Hawthorne," *NEQ*, XXXII [1959], 207-25); and Annette Baxter explores a special relationship in "Independence vs. Isolation: Hawthorne and James on the Problem of the Artist" (*NCF*, X [1955], 225-31). A number of articles have a narrower focus. For example, J. R. Lucke's suggestion that a passage in *The Blithedale Romance* is "The Inception of 'The Beast in the Jungle'" (*NEQ*, XXVI [1953], 529-32) is expanded to a discussion of those figures in Hawthorne who can serve as prototypes for James's hero in George Monteiro's "Hawthorne, James, and the Destructive Self" (*TSLL*, IV [1962], 58-71). R. J. Kane's briefly stated surmise in "Hawthorne's 'The Prophetic Pictures' and James's 'The Liar'" (*MLN*, LXV [1950], 257-8) that Hawthorne's tale is the basic source of James's story is convincingly established by Edward Rosenberry in "James's Use of Hawthorne in 'The Liar'" (*MLN*, LXXVI [1961], 234-38). And Robert Gleckner in "James's *Madame de Mauves* and Hawthorne's *The Scarlet Letter*" (*MLN*, LXXIII [1958], 580-86), not only points out parallels in the two novels, but asserts that James's criticism of Hawthorne's method in the forest scene (in his *Hawthorne*) is subtly supported by his own different method of handling a comparable scene in *Madame de Mauves*.

IV

These, then, are the general contours of the Hawthorne revival, though not, of course, all of the facts. The structure of this essay has unfortunately caused much significant scholarship to be passed over without even a nod. No mention has been made of Edward Davidson's definitive study of the unfinished romances, nor of the many valuable source studies by such Hawthornians as G. H. Orians, Jane Lundblad, Frank Davidson, B. Bernard Cohen, and Robert Stanton. Similarly unacknowledged are studies of Hawthorne's revisions by Arlin Turner and Seymour Gross, of his esthetic theories by such scholars as C. H. Foster, Roy Male, Robert Kimbrough, and Harry Clark. Nelson Adkins' brilliant reconstruction of the early unpublished projects and Norman Holmes Pearson's various substantial contributions have also been left out, and others besides.

But one may ask, finally, when confronting this mountain of Hawthorne criticism and scholarship, Is Hawthorne really that good? Does he really mean that much to us, or is our accelerated interest in him primarily the result of various external factors which have relatively little to do with his intrinsic significance? It is true, of course, that he has profited from the dearth of important novelists in American literature before James, from the spill-over of the Melville and James revivals, from a fictive mode that caught the prevailing fashions in

365

Roger Asselineau

Hawthorne Abroad

". . . Everyone in the World is Christ and they are all crucified."

—Sherwood Anderson,
Winesburg, Ohio

A ccording to Pascal, all of man's misfortune comes from one fact, namely, that he is a restless animal who cannot bear to remain shut up in his room and feels an irresistible impulse to roam about the world. Hawthorne apparently was an exception to this rule. Save a sally into Connecticut, an expedition to Niagara and Detroit, and a trip to New Hampshire, for nearly twelve years, between the ages of twenty-one and thirty-three, when men usually are most restless, he spent the greater part

367

of his time in almost total seclusion in the "owl's nest" of his room at Salem, seldom venturing abroad before dark. He probably was the most sedentary of all American writers and as little interested in terrestrial as in celestial railroads. The first forty-eight years of his life (or five-sixths of it) were spent exclusively in New England; and it is worth noting that, before his forty-eighth birthday, he never set foot in New York, that beachhead of the Old World in the New.

This does not mean, however, that he was completely immersed in New England. True, he was deeply read in New England history. He had devoured all the books on the subject which he was able to borrow from the Salem Athenaeum[1] and had reveled in Cotton Mather's *Wonders of the Invisible World* and *Magnalia Christi Americana;*[2] but, contrary to what Van Wyck Brooks claimed and Matthiessen tried to prove in *American Renaissance,* he was never "deeply planted" in New England soil.[3] He only floated over it. According to Matthiessen, the elegance of Hawthorne's diction gives a misleading impression. It has an admirable limpidity, but no tang or raciness. Yet, Matthiessen asserts, Hawthorne had "quite as good an ear for speech-rhythms as Thoreau had, or Melville."[4] He, too, loved the sensuous world and had a keen eye for picturesque details, as his notebooks testify; but he believed in rhetoric and refinement, and he imposed on his occasionally coarse and rustic materials "the style of a man of society," as he called it—which, even so, was not always refined enough for the taste of Sophia Hawthorne. But this interpretation will not do: every writer has the style he deserves, and no style worth the name is a strait jacket. Hawthorne did not deliberately and painstakingly suppress the rank flavor of the New England soil from his style. He simply had no use for it in his tales and romances, which ignored everyday reality. There was a pre-established harmony between his manner and his matter, and the former was per-

368

fectly adapted to the latter. His elegant, non-sensuous language was the medium best suited to his etherealized fiction. So his imagination was not really rooted in New England soil, it actually grew like an orchid, feeding on thin New England air through its aerial roots. When he wandered physically in the forests of Maine or Massachusetts, he was still lingering in fancy about the thick woods haunted by wizards and witches whose description he had read as a child in Spenser's *Fairy Queen,* or in the wilderness through which John Bunyan's Christian had traveled before him.

Thus, from the start, he tried, by reading, to escape "the dryness and meagreness" of New England[5] and to fill that terrible emptiness of America of which he later complained in his preface to *The Marble Faun.* Henry James deplored that in his notebooks there is no mention of his reading, no literary judgments or impressions, "almost no allusion to works or to authors."[6] In fact, it has been proved that Hawthorne was a voracious reader.[7] But, by necessity, his reading was almost exclusively in English literature or New England history. However, he also read some French books—in translation. He was acquainted with Montaigne's and Voltaire's works, had dipped into Corneille, Racine, and Molière; and, when Elizabeth Peabody met him about 1837, she discovered that he had read everything of Balzac that had appeared in America.[8] He must have been attracted in particular by Balzac's interest in mesmerism. But apparently the French book that he liked best of all was Rousseau's *Eloisa* (*La Nouvelle Héloïse*), which he found "admirable" when he was about fifteen.[9] Later, when he visited Clarens on the Lake of Geneva, he noted: "I read Rousseau's romance with great sympathy, when I was hardly more than a boy; ten years ago, or thereabouts, I tried to read it again without success; but I think, from my feeling of yesterday, that it still retains its hold upon my imagination."[10] All this did not amount to much, though, and Hawthorne's knowledge of French literature actually was rather scanty. He knew still less of Italian and German literature. During the first years of his marriage, he tried to master German with the help of his wife, but he never progressed very far. He translated Bürger's "Lenore" and read some of Hoffmann's tales, but that was the sum total of his experience.[11]

So, on the whole, Hawthorne's culture was provincial and even parochial. He had been fed on the skim milk of a theological rather than humanistic tradition. Contrary to Emerson and Thoreau, he was hardly acquainted with ancient classical literature. His works show no trace whatever of the influence of Greek or Latin writers. He was the product of a narrow local culture which corresponded to only one small part of European civilization: Calvinistic protestantism—a "half-civilisation," as Paul Elmer More has called it.[12] One of the results of this limited "education"—in Henry Adams's meaning of the word—was his complete indifference to the plastic arts. At Bowdoin College, as Norman Holmes Pearson points out, he could have visited the very fine Bowdoin collection, but he never took the trouble to do so.[13] His New England training, hardly modified by his personal reading, allowed him only a very partial—though intense—vision of the world. He went through life with blinkers on, a Puritan of the fourth generation with no religious faith worth speaking of, but with an exclusive concern in sin and purity, and an obsession with evil, "that pit of blackness that lies beneath us, everywhere."[14] In short, to take up Henry James's phrase, he was not in the least "Europeanised in advance."[15]

Hawthorne suffered from this state of affairs. He missed something. He felt cramped and stifled, and dreamed of escaping to distant countries. "The time has been," he wrote in an early tale, "when I meant to visit every region of the earth, except the Poles and central Africa. I had a strange longing to see the Pyramids. To Persia and Arabia, and all the gorgeous East, I owed a pilgrimage for the sake of their magic tales. And England, the land of my ancestors!"[16] In July, 1855, he confided to Ticknor: "Well—I am sick of America. . . . I shall need a residence of two or three years on the Continent, to give me a sense of freedom."[17]

However sedentary his mode of life may have been, Hawthorne was thus tormented by the same wanderlust as his father and his grandfather before him, and, by one of time's revenges, so to speak, he eventually returned, in 1853, to that England on which one of his ancestors had turned his back in 1635. "I sometimes feel as if I myself had been absent these two hundred and eighteen years," he noted.[18] It was a very long absence, however, and rather late in the day for such a pilgrimage. Hawthorne was forty-eight when he landed in Europe for the first time as American consul at Liverpool. All his major books were written; and except for *The Marble Faun* and a few undistinguished books of travel, his stay abroad added very little to the list of his works. "The soul needs air; a wide sweep and frequent change of it," he had made Clifford exclaim in *The House of the Seven Gables,* but in his case the change could no longer be beneficial. His arteries were too much hardened by the time he decided to travel, and his features were already set. Nothing could alter his literary physiognomy any more.

Yet, in several ways, this late trip was a passage to more than Europe in search of answers to a number of questions which had troubled him for years. He was torn between his love of solitude and idleness—of the solitude and idleness to which his singleness of purpose had condemned him—and his duty, as an American, to lead an active and useful life among his fellow citizens. He suffered from his isolation, as an artist, in the middle of a new country where all his neighbors were engaged in practical pursuits. He felt like a drone in a beehive. In "The Devil in Manuscript," he described the hero Oberon (and this was the very nickname by which Hawthorne was known to his closest college friends) as drawn "aside from the beaten path of the world, and led . . . into a strange sort of solitude,—a solitude in the midst of men,—where nobody wishes for what [he does], nor thinks nor feels as [he does]."[19] "Like all other men around whom an engrossing purpose wreathes itself, he was insulated from the mass of human kind."[20] Or, to put it differently, like Wakefield, another of his heroes, he had stepped aside for a moment and lost his place among his fellow men forever. He must have craved for lands where no such divorce was imposed on writers and where idleness was not considered so sinful—or so aristocratic and such an anachronism in a democracy. He also felt estranged by his engrossing love of the past in America, a country where all the inhabitants' energies were bent toward the future. He was an expatriate in time. In Europe, he thought, things would be different; there would not be the same tension and the same rush.

Hawthorne's belated pilgrimage was also, to some extent, a search for identity, for his identity as an American. Like all his compatriots, he was still puzzled by St. John Crèvecoeur's query: "What is an American?" He felt intensely American, but in what way did he differ from his English ancestors whose language he still used, whose books he still read? Was there a difference in kind or only in degree between America and Europe? He confusedly wanted to find out what it meant to be an American after half a century of political independence. One of his more or less conscious goals was the discovery of America through Europe—rather than the discovery of Europe for its own sake.

Such were the data of the problem when Hawthorne landed

at Liverpool. But his four years' stay in the land of his forefathers did not provide any solution at all. Though he entitled
his book about his English experiences *Our Old Home,* and
wrote, for instance, "I never stood in an English crowd without
being conscious of hereditary sympathies,"[21] on many other
occasions he did not actually feel at home. He even went
so far as to note once: ". . . In this *foreign land* [italics
added] I can never forget the distinction between English and
American."[22] A rootless dreamer, he craved for roots in England,
but called his craving "this diseased American appetite for
English soil" and "a blind, pathetic tendency."[23] In short,
England acted upon him like a magnet with a pole of attraction
—her past—and a pole of repulsion—her present. He loved her
ivy and her lichens, her wallflowers and her ruins. He loved
her cathedrals and her castles (his own list), but, like a good
democrat, he hated her aristocratic institutions, cursed the class
structure which had made England what she was, and looked
forward to the time when she would be "a minor republic
under the protection of the United States."[24] Thus what he
found in England increased rather than resolved his former
perplexities. There, too, he felt both accepted and rejected,
and his nostalgic love for the past of England conflicted with
his American desire for change and progress; for there were
times when "his delight at finding something permanent"
yielded, as he admitted himself, to "his Western love of
change."[25] In the last resort, he sided with his ancestors and
preferred "his dear native land" for all its "commonplace prosperity"[26] to the "old home" from which his Puritan forefathers
had fled.[27] In spite of all racial and cultural ties, he decided,
there was an unbridgeable gap, "an essential difference between
English and American character"[28]—in other words, a difference
in kind between the two countries—and he decided not to stay
in England after resigning his consulship.

Nevertheless, he did not return immediately to America, but undertook instead to explore France and Italy with his family. This was an entirely different kind of experience. It was impossible for him to feel at home any more. For the next three years, he was an exile in *partibus infidelium,* and the language barrier constantly reminded him of it. He could read French, but the way the natives spoke it baffled him, and he complained of this bitterly and rather amusingly: "If they would speak slowly and distinctly I might understand them well enough, being perfectly familiar with the written language, and knowing the principles of its pronunciation; but, in their customary rapid utterance, it sounds like a string of mere gabble."[29] This discouraged him from the start, and he immediately gave up trying to establish contact with such strange people. The scenery disconcerted him too. In England, he was on familiar ground; ". . . History, poetry, and fiction, books of travel, and the talk of tourists, had given [him] pretty accurate preconceptions of the common objects of English scenery. . . ."[30] On the Continent, on the contrary, everything was new except when he trod in Byron's footsteps, as when, for instance, he visited the Coliseum—and then reality disappointed him: "Byron's celebrated description is better than the reality," he concluded; and he preferred to behold the scene "in his mind's eye, through the witchery of many intervening years, and faintly illuminated . . . as if with starlight. . . ."[31]

Such letdowns were constant. Nothing that Hawthorne saw during this trip fully came up to his expectation and really satisfied him, because everything was different from what he had been accustomed to in America or England. He admired French architecture, but objected to the absence of grass and trees in French cities. He missed the harmonious combination of art and nature which constitutes the charm of English towns.[32] Paris seemed to him a desert of stone and dust. In

Italy, Renaissance architecture left him cold. He preferred English Gothic. Moreover, wherever he went, he found landscapes unsatisfactory. In his opinion, nothing could equal English or American scenery; and he thought Lake Thrasimene, for instance, quite inferior to Windermere, Loch Lomond, and Lake Champlain. So far as the people were concerned, since he could not understand their language, he judged them from the outside without the least sympathy or indulgence. He was repelled by the French. "Truly, I have no sympathies towards the French," he noted, "their eyes do not win me, nor do their glances melt and mingle with mine."[33] He found them superficial, too talkative,[34] and definitely lacking in spirituality. It was the fault of their cooking, he thought, for he wondered "whether English cookery, for the very reason that it is so simple, is not better for men's moral and spiritual nature than French."[35] So he certainly was not one of those "good Americans" who, according to Oscar Wilde, "go to Paris when they die." Instead, he would have approved of Mark Twain's variation on this theme: "Only trivial Americans go to Paris when they die."[36]

The Italians, to Hawthorne's mind, were no better than the French. They were sluggish,[37] lazy, and dirty, he thought. It seemed to him that in Italy "the gait of the people has not the energy of business or decided purpose. Everybody appears to lounge, and to have time for a moment's chat, and a disposition to rest, reason or none."[38] Besides, they were so deficient in practical sense that they allowed their waterpower to play in useless fountains instead of employing it "to turn the machinery of a cotton-mill," for instance.[39] But what shocked him most of all was the Italians' indifference to physical cleanliness and their repugnance to performing ablutions.[40] Their monks positively stank.[41] Universal dirt had similarly roused his indignation at Marseilles: "There is dirt in the hotel, and everywhere else; and it evidently troubles nobody,—no more than if all the people were pigs in a pigsty."[42] There was no escaping "the bad odor of our fallen nature,"[43] and he hated this constant reminder of man's innate corruption. As a Puritan, he instinctively equated hygiene with spiritual purity and was satisfied with nothing short of perfection.[44] In sum, Continental Europe failed to win his heart. He was even repelled by traits whose absence in America he most deplored, since, far from approving of the Italians' sense of leisure, he condemned it as sinful sloth. There was an incompatibility of temper between him and the Latin races. He was exasperated by their liveliness and exuberance, and this blinded him to their more serious qualities. He was further prevented from perceiving anything but surfaces by his linguistic limitations and his inability to come into contact with the people. He traveled as a tourist with his nose in his guidebook. Instead of visiting Europe, he kept reading his Murray and paraphrasing it in his notebooks.[45]

In a letter to Sophia Peabody, he once boasted of being "a most unmalleable man," and, on the whole, this was true. None of the impressions he received during his European journey seems to have appreciably altered him. They were skin-deep experiences. His essence was left unchanged. He remained a staunch New Englander to the end, and in no way was this more evident than in his attitude toward statuary. Unlike Mark Twain, he could never reconcile himself to nude figures under the pretext that "nowadays people [being] as good as born in their clothes . . . an artist . . . cannot sculpture nudity with a pure heart, if only because he is compelled to steal guilty glimpses at hired models."[46] And what is still more ludicrous, Hawthorne was more interested in the works of American sculptors living in exile in Italy than in the statues carved by the greatest Renaissance artists. This was parochialism with a vengeance.

Except for this, in Continental Europe as in New England

and England, he was as usual more attracted by the past than by the present. The problem of Italian unity is never discussed in his notebooks; the presence of French troops in Rome is mentioned, but no reason for it is given. What was this "visionary and impalpable Now" compared to the "threefold antiquity" of Rome, "the city of all times?" To the facts he could ascertain, he preferred the fancies his imagination could conjure up. And he was appalled at the thought of the tremendous accumulation of corruption and evil which made up the history of Rome: ". . . What localities for new crime existed in those guilty sites, where the crime of departed ages used to be at home, and had its long, hereditary haunt! What street in Rome, what ancient ruin, what one place where man had standing-room, what fallen stone was there, unstained with one or another kind of guilt!"[47] This, for him, explained why Roman ruins were haunted by such horrible lizards[48] and the air had become so foul and pestilential.[49] Hawthorne's reaction to all this corruption was ambivalent. There were times when he felt that "all towns should be made capable of purification by fire, or of decay, within each half-century. Otherwise, they become the hereditary haunts of vermin and noisomeness, besides standing apart from the possibility of such improvements as are constantly introduced into the rest of man's contrivances and accommodations."[50] But there were times, too, when he reached the conclusion that "as the sum of all, there are recollections [there] that kindle the soul, and a gloom and languor that depress it beyond any depth of melancholic sentiment that can be elsewhere known."[51] On leaving Rome, Hawthorne even wrote: ". . . We felt the city pulling at our heartstrings far more than London did. . . . It may be because the intellect finds a home there more than in any other spot in the world, and wins the heart to stay with it, in spite of a good many things strewn all about to disgust us."[52]

Now Catholicism may well have been one of the things which puzzled and fascinated Hawthorne's intellect during his stay in Rome. It was a novel experience for him. He had never been exposed to anything like it before. Many of his reactions, of course, were the standard reactions of an American Protestant of his time. The apparent lack of seriousness with which the Italians treated their religion baffled him: ". . . In Italy religion jostles along side by side with business and sport, after a fashion of its own, and people are accustomed to kneel down and pray, or see others praying, between two fits of merriment, or between two sins."[53] He noted with amusement some of their more naïve superstitions: "An inscription," he wrote, for instance, "promises . . . seven years of remission from the pains of purgatory, and earlier enjoyment of heavenly bliss, for each separate kiss imprinted on the black cross. What better use could be made of life, after middle-age, when the accumulated sins are many and the remaining temptations few, than to spend it all in kissing the black cross of the Coliseum!"[54] ". . . Scarlet superstitions,"[55] he called these when he felt in a more militant mood and shared the horror of his ancestors for the Scarlet Woman. But the Catholic church had ceased to be dangerous, he thought. It was dead. It used to be "a true religion," but "now the glory and beauty have departed."[56] The Italian cathedrals were nothing but fossils, empty shells "out of which the life has died long ago."[57] Italy, however, was still "priest-ridden," preyed upon by "sluggish, swinish" monks[58] and led into error by crafty Jesuits who knew how to provide cordials in abundance and "sedatives in inexhaustible variety"; but such a faith, "which so marvellously adapts itself to every human need,"[59] is not the true faith, Hawthorne concluded, and such a church is the work of the devil rather than of God.[60] Yet there were times, too, when he wondered whether, in spite of the indignity of its clergy, the Catholic church did not still

reflect its divine origin after all. "If its ministers were but a
little more than human, . . . pure from all iniquity, what a
religion would it be," he exclaimed.[61] And in his notebooks he
admitted: "It is my opinion that a great deal of devout and
reverential feeling is kept alive in people's hearts by the Catholic
mode of worship."[62]

No wonder, then, that in *The Marble Faun* he made Hilda,
that immaculate, incorruptible, fair-haired New England maiden
go to confession at St. Peter's and unburden her soul and receive
the blessing of her confessor "with as devout a simplicity as any
Catholic of them all."[63] As a matter of fact, the whole book is
pervaded by a spirit which radically differs from that of his
other works. It expresses a new attitude toward evil. True,
Hilda still declares: "If there be any such dreadful mixture of
good and evil . . . which appears to me almost more shocking
than pure evil,—then the good is turned to poison, not the evil
to wholesomeness."[64] But eventually all the characters reconcile
themselves to this "dreadful mixture" instead of being crushed
and plunged into gloom by the discovery of its existence, like
Young Goodman Brown. The passage from innocence to experience is no longer destructive. On the contrary, it enriches.
Man is no longer required to be an angel; and his intermediary
status, halfway between angels and beasts, is invested with new
dignity. Sin—even original sin—is now considered a blessing
in disguise;[65] and Kenyon wonders whether sin which was
deemed "such a dreadful blackness in the universe" is not "like
sorrow, merely an element of human education, through which
we struggle to a higher and purer state than we could otherwise
have attained." Who knows? Perhaps Adam fell "that we might
ultimately rise to a far loftier paradise than his."[66] So Hawthorne discovered in Europe that the Fall was necessary and
prelapsarian purity a rather unenviable form of innocence,
which there was no point in trying to recover. These were most

379

un-Puritan theories, and he probably absorbed them unconsciously in Italy while he was exposed to Catholic influence and was enjoying a more relaxed life than in his native New England.[67] *The Marble Faun* appeared in England as *Transformation*. It was a most appropriate title, for the book depicts the transformation, not only of the Faun, but, in a way, of the author himself.

In the last analysis, therefore, Hawthorne's stay in Europe to some extent modified his Weltanschauung and helped him to solve some of the philosophical problems which obsessed him. But his personal problems remained. He was still torn between the past and the present, between his dreams and reality, between solitude and society; and he felt as solitary as ever—even in the midst of his own family. Shortly after his death in 1864, his wife wrote to a friend: "The sacred veil of his eyelids he scarcely lifted to himself—such an inviolated sanctuary as was his nature, I his inmost wife, never conceived nor knew."[68] He thought sometimes of staying in Europe and settling in England, but he fully realized the dangers of permanent expatriation, which he compared to sitting between two stools.[69] He decided, therefore, to return to America, even at the cost of once more becoming an "isolated stranger" in the "unsympathizing cities of [his] native land," because he did not want to share the fate of those American artists he had observed in Italy whose originality gradually died out or was "polished away as a barbarism."[70] His seven years' exile had in some subtle way unsettled him, however. He was now out of touch with New England and its past, and had been struck with intellectual impotence. Despite all his efforts, he was never able to finish *Dr. Grimshawe's Secret* and *Septimius Felton*. He had gone to Europe too late to renew himself and had "lost his native country without finding another."[71]

HAWTHORNE'S WORKS ABROAD

As a rule, there must be a secret temperamental compatibility, a sort of pre-established harmony, between a writer and his potential public if he is to be accepted by foreign readers in spite of national differences. Thus it was that Poe found in Baudelaire an ideal interpreter and through him became a god in the literary Pantheon of the French symbolists from Mallarmé to Valéry. Hawthorne did not have the same luck.

In France, his reception began under the best auspices. He was introduced to the public through two articles in the *Revue des Deux Mondes* as early as 1852. In the first one, Emile Forgues, after comparing Hawthorne to Charles Nodier and Rodolphe Töpffer, concluded: ". . . There is more philosophical sincerity in Hawthorne's tales."[72] Eight months later, in the same very influential review, Emile Montégut, in his turn, devoted an article to Hawthorne in which he praised him as "the most American writer that America has produced since Emerson," but added: "There is something unhealthy about his writings which one does not notice at first, but which, in the long run, will work upon you like a very weak and very slow poison."[73] Translations soon followed these introductions. *The Scarlet Letter* was translated by Forgues himself as *La Lettre rouge* as early as 1853, but it was an incomplete and amateurish version; and it was only in 1945 that a complete and competent translation by Marie Canavaggia at last appeared.[74] *The House of the Seven Gables* knew a similar fate—though it was very successful in Forgues' translation.[75] The *Tales* were translated by several hands in turn.[76] *The Marble Faun* alone was translated by only one translator, and it had to wait for that until 1949.[77] Hawthorne was never particularly fortunate in his French translators and, unlike Poe, never found an alter ego who identified himself wholly with his works.

His books, as the number of their editions indicate, sold reasonably well, but they never attracted the attention of any major writer or critic. Curiously enough, only Zola seems to have been influenced by Hawthorne. And, even then, though resemblances between *Thérèse Raquin* and *The Scarlet Letter* have been pointed out, no definite influence has been proved.[78] Julien Green, who, as an American by birth and a puritan Catholic, has deep affinities with Hawthorne, has devoted only a brief biographical sketch to him.[79] Only two books of criticism have been written in France on Hawthorne's works, but they are doctoral dissertations and have reached only a very limited public.[80] At an interval of some thirty years, their authors insist both that Hawthorne's books "are unfortunately too little known in France"[81] and have failed "to arouse the same deep interest" as Poe's and Emerson's works.[82]

This relative failure can be explained in several ways. First of all, however impressed most French readers may be by the cleverness of Hawthorne's artistry, they generally object to the slow pace of his narratives and to the tenuity of their contents. This, for example, was André Gide's reaction: "Rather disappointed by a re-reading of *The House of the Seven Gables*," he noted in his diary in 1943, "less sensitive to the poetic halo with which Hawthorne knows how to adorn our external world than to the often exasperating slowness of his narrative. . . . Moreover: he deals only with shadows. And what I like most about modern American literature is the direct contact with life."[83] Francois Mauriac, too, though "fascinated" by *The Scarlet Letter*, has also passed strictures on Hawthorne's art. *The Scarlet Letter*, according to him, is not a great novel. It already shows signs of age because its characters are all of a piece and do not develop freely. But what most repels him is the "puritan Pharisaism," "the falsification of the Gospel" which it depicts, though he finally concludes that the book is "a *tour de force,* a cruel caricature of Christianity which subtly becomes an apology of it and debouches on the problem of evil."[84] In short—and his reaction is representative—he takes exception to the puritanical stiffness and narrowness of Hawthorne and to his naïve, one-sided conception of the human condition. Of all Hawthorne's works, it is held, only *The Marble Faun* contains a mature vision of life, and it was translated too late to be widely known in France. Besides, the psychology of the characters is so childish and the Gothic plot so comically unbelievable that it is almost impossible for a French reader to take the book seriously.

In Italy, as in France, the translations of Hawthorne's major books went through several editions:[85] ten for *The Scarlet Letter,* and seven for the *Tales,* which appeared much later. Except for a few tales, none of his writings was translated into Italian before 1923, when a very free translation of *The Scarlet Letter* by Gino Cornali was published under the title of *La Lettera rossa.* It was only in 1938 that a faithful and reliable version by Augusta Guidetti at last appeared under the more accurate title of *La Lettera scarlatta.* In spite of all these translations, however, Hawthorne does not seem to have been accepted or assimilated by Italian any more than by French readers. And the very fact that so many of these translations were adaptations rather than faithful translations shows the difficulty there was in adopting him in Italy. It is equally symptomatic that his influence never fecundated any Italian writer. The fact that Giovanni Pascoli in *Digitale Purpurea* owes something to "Rappaccini's Daughter" is merely accidental.[86] Hawthorne always remained an extraneous body, the strange product of an alien civilization.

From the beginning, Hawthorne's style was greatly admired in Italy, however. Enrico Nencioni, who was the first Italian critic to write about him, gushed lyrically over it in 1890: "And

what a style! Magnetic, incomparable. A book [he was referring to *The Scarlet Letter*] as sad and as fascinating as sin—
very dark, with here and there brilliant and dazzling colors like
a bird of paradise."[87] Italian critics have always been loud, too,
in their praise of the acuteness of Hawthorne's psychological
analyses. "His method," wrote Federico Olivero in 1913, "consists in revealing little by little with clever reticences the mystery
of a character, until it stands out against a background of darkness."[88] Augusto Guidi later described him as "a writer addicted
to an analytical and introspective method which sometimes reminds the reader of James Joyce. . . ."[89] Other Italian critics
have been interested in Hawthorne because of his description
of the Italian scene in *The Marble Faun,* or because they have,
like Agostino Lombardo, seen in him essentially a very profound
and moving analyst of human solitude.[90]

But for all the subtle and poignant charm of his romances,
Hawthorne has always been regarded in Italy as a foreign
tourist and the queer representative of an outlandish and anti-
quated way of life, a member of, as Cesare Pavese defined it,
that "race of tired and misanthropic searchers for the secrets of
the heart and the dilemmas of moral life."[91]

The history of Hawthorne's reputation in Germany follows
much the same lines as that in France and Italy. Harold Jantz,
in his essay "Amerika in deutschen Dichten und Denken,"[92]
comments on the slight effect that Hawthorne's works have
had in Germany, a situation he attributes to the fact that
German readers probably thought they had enough fantastic
stories and romances in their own literature.

There is only one country in Europe which fully adopted
Hawthorne and took him to its bosom, and that was his "old
home," England. He was a popular writer there from the beginning. In 1851, for instance, there appeared five London
editions of *Twice-Told Tales,* three of *The Scarlet Letter,* and

two of *The House of the Seven Gables;* most of them were cheap editions in the "Railway Series" or "Shilling Libraries."[93] In 1860, an anonymous contributor to the *North British Review* concluded: "The grave sympathy, the homely insight, the classic Puritanism, the rich and meditative intellect, have commended their owner to a multitude of admirers."[94] And this popularity has never declined. In 1929, such an indefatigable champion of all avant garde movements as Herbert Read could still praise the intensity of Hawthorne's art, for "the capacity . . . which he has for putting an emotional emphasis into subjects so dispassionately conceived."[95]

A crucified innocent from the land where men had dreamed of creating a new Garden of Eden but had soon found to their dismay that the old serpent had reappeared by a sort of spontaneous generation, Hawthorne was thus never wholly accepted in Europe, the land of experience, except in the country of his ancestors, where the dream originated. He had turned his back on Europe, and Europe in her turn refused to acknowledge him, to see in his tales and romances anything but beautiful—and rather awkward—illustrations in black and white of the problems, and pseudo-problems, which had tormented his Puritan forefathers. It was a case of imperfect sympathies on both sides—which means that there was communication as well as incomprehension; for, after all, as Roy Harvey Pearce has so happily phrased it, Americans are but "Western Europeans *in extremis,*"[96] and contrary to what Hawthorne himself thought, there is no difference in kind, only in degree, between Europe and America—a discovery which another innocent abroad named Mark Twain made a few decades after Hawthorne when he very wisely reached the conclusion, after several trips to the Old World, that "there is not a single human characteristic which can be safely labeled as 'American.'"

385

Matthew J. Bruccoli

Hawthorne

as a

Collector's Item,

1885-1924*

O NE INDICATION of an author's reputation is the amounts
that collectors are willing to pay for his books. Obviously, there
are many limitations on this method, for literary merit and
collector appeal are not always concomitant qualities. The circumstances under which a major author was published may
make his books too common for the collector, whereas a minor

* For help in preparing this article, I am greatly indebted to: Roger E.
Stoddard, C. E. Frazer Clark, Jr., Peter Keisogloff, John S. Van E. Kohn,
William Runge, Marcus McCorison, Miss Jane Gatliff, the American Anti-
quarian Society, and the Boston Public Library.

author's books may have the combination of characteristics that makes collectors reach deep into their pockets.

Nathaniel Hawthorne is an ideal figure around which to conduct a survey of American book-collecting, for he provides a combination of rarity and literary merit. Until the Melville and James revivals of the 1920's, his position as the great American novelist was not seriously challenged. In so far as such a thing can be determined, Hawthorne was the first American novelist to be collected seriously; and with the exception of sporadic interest in Cooper, the first rank of nineteenth-century American collectors did not bother with other American novelists. In addition to being eminently respectable, Hawthorne's work has great collector appeal. *Fanshawe, The Celestial Rail-Road, Time's Portraiture*, and *The Sister Years* are among the supreme rarities in American literature. Of the two carrier's addresses, there are probably not more than three copies of *Time's Portraiture* and probably not more than six of *The Sister Years*. *The Celestial Rail-Road* is particularly tantalizing to the collector because it exists with two imprints.

On the other hand, the first printings of Hawthorne's four romances are comparatively common—or rather, all but *The Scarlet Letter* seem more common than they really are. The first edition of *The Scarlet Letter* consisted of 2,500 copies, of which a high percentage survived because of the book's immediate success. The second edition of 2,500 copies is also a collector's item because it adds the author's Preface. *The House of The Seven Gables, The Blithedale Romance*, and *The Marble Faun* seem quite common because no attempt was made by the publisher to distinguish between the first printings and the reprints. The first printing of *The House of the Seven Gables* consisted of 1,690 copies, but there were three more printings in 1851 of 1,690, 1,051, and 1,000 copies. The first printing of *The Blithedale Romance* comprised 5,090 copies, and there was a second printing in 1852 of 2,350. The first printing of *The Marble Faun* comprised 8,000 copies, and there were two more printings of 3,000 and 1,500 copies before the conclusion was added, and two separate printings with the conclusion of 1,000 copies each—all in 1860. Only recently has the work of the Centenary Hawthorne differentiated these concealed printings.[1] Although this new information is expected to interest collectors, the obvious fact remains that even the true first printings were too large for real competition to result over them. Of course, collectors have always been eager to acquire association copies of even common books.

In between the great rarities and the romances, there is a group of books which are rare, but not superlatively so—*Twice-Told Tales, Peter Parley's Universal History, Liberty Tree, Grandfather's Chair, Famous Old People, Biographical Stories for Children.* It is clear, then, that collecting Hawthorne appeals to all purses. But this survey will of necessity concentrate on the high-spots because they are more traceable and more meaningful. In general, though, the bottom of the market will be a reflection of the top: that is, when *Fanshawe* or *Twice-Told Tales* bring whopping great prices, *The Scarlet Letter* and *The House of the Seven Gables* will also be selling high.

In Hawthorne's case, at least, collector and dealer activity are significant, for the prices of his books show a steady willingness of men to back their opinions with cash. Apart from its adherence to the laws of supply and demand, there is something lawless about collecting first printings—and this is the source of its attraction. There are sound textual arguments for collecting first printings, but few collectors are textual scholars. There are sentimental excuses for collecting first printings: this is the form in which a masterpiece first appeared in print, and indeed the genius who wrote it may have held this very copy in his hands. But one wonders whether many collectors are really persuaded by this line of thinking. It seems more likely that the serious collector is attracted primarily by the sheer challenge of the game, by the act of pitting his taste, judgment, and acquisitive instincts against those of his competitors. He is also staking his money, and that is what gives collecting its edge. Assuming that a good collector collects authors he has read and appreciates—a fair assumption—the record of Hawthorne collecting is then the record of the men who were willing to bet on their estimations of Hawthorne's enduring position in American literature. Hawthorne has had a loyal rank of brave collectors: Charles B. Foote, William Harris Arnold, George M. Williamson, J. Chester Chamberlain, Frank Maier, Stephen H. Wakeman, Owen Franklin Aldis, and W. T. H. Howe. The best of them did more than assemble libraries—they promoted Hawthorne scholarship, enlarged the canon of his work, and preserved manuscript material. Their catalogues are important reference tools—and monuments to the men.

For the purposes of this survey, 1885 may be taken as the year when the collecting of American first editions first won serious attention; for in 1885, Leon and Brother issued the first bookseller's catalogue devoted to American first editions and Beverly Chew anonymously published the first bibliography of an American author, *The Longfellow Collector's Hand-Book*.[2] Before that time, serious American collectors did not collect American literature; or if they did, they collected Americana or even poetry—but not fiction. The fact that Chew did not put his name on his Longfellow work is almost certainly meaningful. Leon and Chew each appear to have felt diffident enough to preface his volume with an *apologia*. After making a patriotic appeal for American first editions, the Introduction to the Leon catalogue makes a good bibliographical case: "In the first editions the text appears fresh from the author's mind—before those changes which are apt to occur, either from reflection or as the result of unfavorable criticism." If, as has been suggested, Chew wrote the Leon Introduction, his role in the rise of collecting American literature becomes quite important. In the Longfellow bibliography, Chew notes the recent interest in American first editions and "the small amount of bibliographical data obtainable in print."

The Leon catalogue listed thirty-five items for Hawthorne, offering all for sale except *Fanshawe*. The highest price asked was $30.00 for *The Gentle Boy*. *Time's Portraiture, The Sister Years,* and *The Celestial Rail-Road* were not included, although the list claimed to include "all his work published in separate form." Leon supplied Chew with his first American authors, chiefly poets.

In the nineties, the ground was prepared for the great collections that would be formed—and scattered—in the first decade of the twentieth century. Herbert Stuart Stone compiled, in 1893, the first checklist for collectors of American literature—apart from the Leon catalogue—*First Editions of American Authors*.[3] A Harvard undergraduate at the time his book was published, Stone based his lists largely on the collections at Harvard. In the following year occurred the first important auction of a Hawthorne collection at the Foote sale.[4] The Foote catalogue listed fifty-eight Hawthorne items which totaled $648.49, including *Fanshawe* ($155.00), *Peter Parley's Universal History* ($17.50), *Twice-Told Tales* ($22.00), *The Gentle Boy* ($34.00), *Grandfather's Chair* ($25.00), *Famous Old People* ($32.00), *Liberty Tree* ($25.00), *The Celestial Rail-Road* ($58.00), and *The Scarlet Letter* ($27.00). Though not in the same class as the Foote sale, the two auctions of Christian P. Roos' books contributed to the growing interest in Hawthorne collecting.[5] In 1897, thirty-one unexceptional items brought $106.77; and in 1900, a group of thirty-four interesting books brought $333.57, the star being *Peter Parley's Universal History* at $30.00.

The establishment of P. K. Foley's rare-book business in

1896 was an event of signal importance for American collecting. Foley was the greatest dealer in American literature of his time—and, perhaps, of all time—and he took an active role in assembling the collections of Aldis, Wakeman, and Chamberlain. In 1897, he published *American Authors 1795–1895*, which became the standard reference tool in the field.[6] Though it has errors and holes—Foley was not aware of *Time's Portraiture* or of the two imprints of *The Celestial Rail-Road*—Foley's book is a marked improvement over Stone's and includes solid bibliographical information. His first catalogue, September, 1897, included twenty Hawthorne items, of which the best was the *American Magazine of Useful Knowledge* ($10.00). It is curious that in Foley's first sixteen catalogues, up to 1905, there are only two unusual Hawthorne items: an unbound set of what are presumably proof sheets of *The Blithedale Romance* (catalogue 3, March, 1899–$3.00) and *The Sister Years* (catalogue 15, June, 1904–$400.00). Probably, with customers like Wakeman, Aldis, and Chamberlain, Foley found it unnecessary to catalogue his outstanding things.

Between 1903 and 1909, Foley took an active role in building the Aldis American literature collection which was presented to Yale University in 1911.[7] Considerable bibliographical information about Hawthorne was made available during the nineties; and although these checklists were not limited in use to bibliophiles, they almost certainly reflected a growing interest in Hawthorne collecting. In 1890, John P. Anderson appended a bibliography to Moncure D. Conway's *Life of Nathaniel Hawthorne*,[8] and in the same year Louise Manning Hodgkins published her "Guide to the Study of Nathaniel Hawthorne."[9] Gardner Maynard Jones published his "Complete List of Hawthorne's Writings" in 1891;[10] and in 1897, George M. Williamson published "A Bibliography of the Writings of Nathaniel

Hawthorne."[11] Luther S. Livingston, an important influence on the development of American collecting, included Hawthorne in the first of his series "The First Books of Some American Authors" in 1898.[12]

By the beginning of the twentieth century, the elements for a boom in Hawthorne collecting were available, and the centenary of his birth in 1904 brought interest to a peak.

The first important collecting event of the twentieth century was the William Harris Arnold sale in 1901, an event that has not always been recognized as having stimulated interest in American first editions by publicizing these books as investments. Arnold may have collected for the wrong reasons, but just the same he converted many people to the game. He bought his first American first edition on May 16, 1895—it is wholly typical of Arnold to have recorded the event—and, by 1898 he was able to publish his *First Report of a Book-Collector*,[13] in which he displayed an unusual frankness about admitting his concern with profit in collecting books. His boasting about his sleepers must have seemed in terrible taste to the rich and conservative gentlemen collectors of the time. In 1901, Arnold was ready to dispose of his collection, which the catalogue claimed was "by far the fullest collection of First Editions, of the eight authors named, that has ever been sold."[14] The prices, many of them new records, attracted great attention in the collecting world, and Arnold himself was not reluctant to publicize his success. After the sale, he published an elegant catalogue giving both cost and sale prices for each item.[15] It showed that he more than doubled his money: the cost for 709 items was $3,508.16, and the return was $7,363.17. There were sixty-four Hawthorne items in the Arnold sale, for which he had paid $572.45 and received $1,366.72. The Hawthorne high-spots were *Fanshawe* ($200.00 [$410.00), *Peter Parley's Universal*

History ($17.50 [$100.00), and *The Celestial Rail-Road* ($1.00 [$124.00). A copy of *Mosses from and old Manse,* one of two in wrappers then known, appreciated from $18.00 to $62.00. Although these were bargains by today's standards—especially since Arnold was fussy about condition—they were considered remarkable in 1901. *The Literary Collector* was so impressed by the Arnold sale that it distributed to subscribers a list of the prices and purchasers.[16]

Interest in collecting Hawthorne reached a peak during 1904 and 1905. In 1904, the centenary of Hawthorne's birth, there were celebrations in Concord and Salem; Chamberlain organized the Grolier Club exhibition and compiled the informative catalogue;[17] and the New York Public Library had an exhibition which Victor Hugo Paltsits catalogued in the *Bulletin of the New York Public Library.*[18] In the same year *The Literary Collector* published a useful checklist, "First Editions of Hawthorne," which noted the record prices of the books.[19] Appropriately, there were two important auctions in 1904. The French-Chubbuck sale had thirty-seven Hawthorne items which realized $1,099.75[20]—including a *Fanshawe* ($450.00), *Peter Parley's Universal History* ($72.00—the same copy had sold for $17.50 in the Foote sale), the first copy of *The Sister Years* to appear at auction ($290.00), and *Time's Portraiture, 1853* ($60.00).

The Williamson sale in 1904[21] included twelve Hawthorne letters and three exciting manuscripts: "Feathertop," 20 pp. ($750.00); "The Ancestral Footstep," 88 pp. ($650.00); and the only surviving leaf of *The Scarlet Letter,* the title page and Table of Contents ($113.00). In 1908, 170 of Williamson's Hawthorne books brought $1,446.40.[22] This remarkable collection included *Fanshawe* ($300.00) and *The Celestial Rail-Road* ($630.00). But apart from these two items the prices were very modest: the terrifically rare 1851 *Scarlet Letter* in wrappers brought $5.00, and dozens of books went for less than one dollar.

An interesting event of 1904–5 was William K. Bixby's purchase of 165 Hawthorne letters—"the love letters"—from Julian Hawthorne. Bixby permitted the Society of the Dofobs of Chicago to issue these letters in a privately printed edition of sixty-two copies in 1907.[23] In 1916 and 1917, Bixby sold at auction duplicates and selections from his library, including superb Hawthorne material. The 1916 Huntington-Bixby-Church sale, billed as the greatest auction since the Hoe sale, included fifty-three of Bixby's Hawthorne items, which brought $1,651.50, a small total considering that it was nearly all manuscript or association material.[24] The 1917 Huntington-Bixby sale included one lot of thirty-three letters by and to Hawthorne and his family, which went begging at $2,000.00.[25] In 1918, Henry E. Huntington purchased Bixby's manuscript collection, which included 200 of Hawthorne's letters.

Luther S. Livingston's *Auction Prices of Books*[26] shows that by 1904 a great deal of choice Hawthorne material was sold on a rising market. No fewer than ten *Fanshawes* were sold at a range of from $75.00 to $840.00. The list includes seven copies of *The Celestial Rail-Road* ($46.00–$240.00), six copies of *Peter Parley's Universal History* ($35.00–$140.00), ten copies of *Twice-Told Tales* ($10.00–$41.00), thirteen copies of *Famous Old People* ($7.50–$76.00), eleven copies of *The Gentle Boy* ($11.00–$143.00), twenty copies of *Grandfather's Chair* ($11.50–$76.00), nine copies of *Biographical Stories for Children* ($11.00–$36.50), eight copies of *Liberty Tree* ($19.00–$48.00), twenty-one copies of *The Scarlet Letter* ($6.50–$29.00), five copies of *The House of the Seven Gables* ($5.50–$9.00), five copies of *The Blithedale Romance* ($5.00–$60.00 for a presentation copy), and eleven copies of *The Marble Faun* ($7.00–$11.50).

The important Hawthorne events of 1905 were the two book-length bibliographies published by Nina E. Browne[27] and

Wallace Hugh Cathcart.[28] Both volumes are frustrating to work with and are far from definitive, but their existence demonstrates that a high point in collector interest had been reached.

Both Wakeman and Chamberlain began collecting American first editions in 1900, the year before the Arnold sale. Chamberlain purchased Chew's American authors *en bloc* in 1900; and in the five years left to him, he assembled a superb collection of ten authors. When catalogued for auction in 1909,[29] there were 139 Hawthorne items which realized about $4,300, including two copies of *Fanshawe*, seven of *Peter Parley's Universal History*, *Time's Portraiture* (the 1838 and two copies of the 1853 edition), *The Sister Years*, *The Celestial Rail-Road*, and *The Sunday School Society's Gift*. The 1838 *Time's Portraiture*—the first to be sold at auction—brought $550. The *Fanshawes* brought $500 and $350; *The Celestial Rail-Road* brought $380, a new record; *Sister Years* brought $260; and the *Sunday School Society's Gift*, one of three known copies, brought $115. Eight volumes from Hawthorne's own library realized $1,376.

Less information is available on Frank Maier than on Chamberlain or Wakeman. If Maier's Hawthorne collection was not so good as Chamberlain's or Wakeman's, it was nonetheless splendid. His library was auctioned in 1909, nine months after Chamberlain's, and brought $22,324.00 as against $36,484.00 for Chamberlain's.[30] His 121 Hawthorne items brought $1,202.30, a surprisingly low total. Perhaps the Chamberlain sale had temporarily satiated Hawthorne collectors, for many of Maier's rarities went low: *Fanshawe*—$350.00; *Peter Parley's Universal History*—$40.00; *The Sister Years*—$150.00; *Time's Portraiture* (1853)—$50.00; *The Celestial Rail-Road*—$140.00; *Twice-Told Tales*—$10.00. The condition of these books may have been against them, but it is still surprising to see dozens of desirable items going at one or two dollars—first editions of *The House of the Seven Gables* and *The Blithedale Romance,* for example, brought $1.25 each. Aldis was an active buyer at the Chamberlain and Maier sales, as was Walter T. Wallace. When Wallace's books were sold in 1920, some Hawthorne items totaled about $3,200.00: *The Sister Years*—$130.00; *The Sunday School Society's Gift*—$240.00; *Time's Portraiture,* 1838—$450.00 (these three had been bought at the Chamberlain sale); *Time's Portraiture,* 1853—$320.00 (the Maier copy); and two pages of the manuscript of *Time's Portraiture,* $200.00.[31]

Wakeman started collecting in 1900 and found it necessary to retire from business in 1904 to devote all his time to his library. During the centenary year, he had privately printed from the manuscript thirty copies of *Twenty Days with Julian and Little Bunny.* Like the good collector he was, Wakeman had one copy printed on vellum for himself. In 1909, he sold his fabulous collection of manuscripts—including *The Blithedale Romance, Dr. Grimshawe's Secret, The Dolliver Romance, Septimius Felton,* and Hawthorne's journals—through George S. Hellman to J. Pierpont Morgan for $165,000.[32] Of Wakeman's books, which were sold at auction in 1924, John S. Van E. Kohn has written: "This sale dispersed the greatest collection of the nine Wakeman authors ever assembled . . . no comparable collection, take it for all and all, could ever be formed again."[33] The auction catalogue prepared from Wakeman's notes by Arthur Swann has become an indispensable tool for Hawthorne scholars.[34] Wakeman's 179 Hawthorne items brought $9,770, not a high total considering the quantity of inscribed material. Wakeman had *Time's Portraiture, The Sister Years,* and both imprints of *The Celestial Rail-Road*—the only time all four have ever appeared, or will ever appear, in the same sale.

There were bargains in the Wakeman sale. Barton Currie

remarks that many dealers and collectors were unenthusiastic about it—though he doesn't explain why—and that Rosenbach, Wells, and Sessler "hold aloof."[35] W. T. H. Howe was a leading purchaser, and some of his acquisitions were wonderful buys by today's standards. *Fanshawe,* the copy which had brought $410 at the Arnold sale and which Wakeman had paid $450 for, was sold to Howe for $1,025. The copy of *Twice-Told Tales* inscribed by Hawthorne as a betrothal gift to Sophia Peabody had been purchased by Wakeman from Julian Hawthorne for $450;[36] Howe paid $1,000 for it. The copy of *Time's Portraiture* that Howe paid $325 for had been purchased by Wakeman for $75.00. Howe bought four first editions of *The Scarlet Letter,* including Sophia Hawthorne's copy ($400—Wakeman had paid $100) and a presentation copy from Hawthorne to his sister Elizabeth ($350—Wakeman paid $125).[37] *The Sister Years* brought $250. The Fish imprint of *The Celestial Rail-Road* brought $140 and the Wilder $160—well under the $380 brought by Chamberlain's Wilder. For some reason, Hawthorne's copy of the *Laws of Bowdoin College* with eight Hawthorne-Hathorne signatures went for only $27.50. It brought $1,125 five years later in the Kern sale.

The great era of Hawthorne-collecting—and, indeed, of the collecting of nineteenth-century American authors—closed with the Wakeman sale. Many of the treasures owned by Aldis, Williamson, Chamberlain, Maier, and Wakeman have found their way to the Morgan Library, the New York Public Library, the Huntington Library, the Yale Library, and the Alderman Library of the University of Virginia. Which is where they belong, unfortunately.[38]

POSTSCRIPT

After the Wakeman sale, American collecting—and Hawthorne-collecting—changed. It is probably too simple to blame this change on the financial conditions of the 1930's. For one thing, the old breed of collectors typified by Chamberlain and Wakeman died out with these men; for another thing, the younger collectors turned their attention to younger reputations —Melville, James, Twain, and the twentieth-century authors.

No great Hawthorne collections were dispersed during the thirties and forties, although some great items were sold. Two magnificent groups of material from the Hawthorne family appeared in 1931. In April, seventeen lots of letters to and from Hawthorne or his family—"The Property of a Descendant of Hawthorne"—brought $5,437.85 at auction.[39] The star was a letter from Hawthorne to his sister Elizabeth, dated October 1, 1824, which sold for $900.00. A letter from Oliver Wendell Holmes about *The Scarlet Letter* brought $1,450.00. In November, forty-six superb books and manuscripts owned by Miss Rebecca B. Manning brought $10,099.50.[40] The top prices were $2,200 each for inscribed copies of *Peter Parley's Universal History* and *Mosses from an Old Manse* in wrappers. An inscribed copy of *The Scarlet Letter* brought $1,300.00. The books did better than the manuscripts. The highest price brought by a letter was $430.00 for what is apparently the earliest known Hawthorne letter, to Robert Manning, December 9, 1813. Hawthorne's fifteen-page constitution of the Pin Society sold for only $340.00; and the five-page constitution of the Pot-8-O Club, for $375.00.

The 1945 Frank J. Hogan sale had only twelve Hawthorne items, including the December 9, 1813, letter which brought $500.00.[41] The nineteen items in the 1960 Arthur Swann sale did not include any great pieces, but the books were distinguished by their fine condition.[42] The most recent appearance of a major Hawthorne item was in November, 1963, when the manuscript of "A London Suburb"—the largest Hawthorne manuscript to appear at auction since 1904—was sold for $5,500.00.[43]

At least four superb Hawthorne collections have been

Fredson Bowers

Hawthorne's Text

H AWTHORNE's text has been preserved in almost every form possible for a nineteenth-century American author except that no substantive edition was printed without authorial concurrence. An authoritative manuscript lies behind all initial publication, therefore, regardless of the treatment given this document by editorial hand or printing-house styling. The modern textual critic can come as close as possible to the ultimate source of authority whenever such a manuscript is preserved, as in *The*

Marble Faun, for instance; he is further removed when the manuscript is lost and the first-edition printed document (derived from it) must constitute the authority, as in *The Scarlet Letter;* he is furthest removed of all when, as in some of the tales and sketches first published in magazines and gift books, an editor has intervened and (as commonly) the manuscript is not extant to give us the evidence we need to establish the nature and extent of the unauthoritative tinkering, or even indeed the fact of its existence.

In general, only the one document nearest to authority is of primary concern for the establishment of Hawthorne's text. Once a work was set in type, Hawthorne seldom revised it during the course of its textual transmission, and then only in small details, more associated with correcting its obvious errors than improving its form or style by second thoughts. The manuscripts themselves, however, attest to a slow and careful process of revision during composition. The printer's-copy manuscripts of *The House of the Seven Gables,* *The Blithedale Romance,* and *The Marble Faun* manifestly represent authorial fair copies of earlier versions. Original composition could not account for the large number of *currente calamo* repair of eyeskips and small omissions, sometimes only an instant after the slip, sometimes later. A common characteristic of these manuscripts is the inscription of the first few letters of a word and then its alteration to another. True, a change of intention during the act of composition does not preclude many of these, but the habit is so persistent as to lead to the view that some, at least, represent revisions made during the act of copying.

However, the usual correction of error in these manuscripts concerns skips that seem to be due to memorial lapse, or to memorial anticipation, during the process of writing out fair copy. Typical, for instance, is the anticipatory error in *The Blithedale Romance* (Centenary, 12.24-25), which in its corrected form reads, "we professed ourselves almost loth to bid the rude blusterer good-bye." In the manuscript Hawthorne first wrote, ". . . bid the good" before he stopped and, wiping out the still wet letters, superimposed "rud" over "good", and added its "e" before continuing with "blusterer good-bye." The context makes it clear that the tempest could not have been "good" in the original; instead, Hawthorne had anticipated the "good" of "good-bye" as he sped along transcribing another manuscript. Similarly, at 16.18 in the words "there are four of us here, already", Hawthorne first wrote "there are four of h" before he stopped, wiped out the anticipatory "h", and copied "us" before going on to "here".

Evidence of this nature, frequent in all three manuscripts, is cumulatively very strong; but, fortunately, certainty has replaced conjecture for *The Blithedale Romance,* at least, with the recent purchase by the Ohio State University Libraries of a leaf that is definitely part of an earlier manuscript of the book, one probably that is the direct source of the complete final manuscript preserved in the Pierpont Morgan Library. In the forty lines of the text on the recto of this early leaf, ten minor alterations were made during or after inscription. Yet in the corresponding text of the later Morgan manuscript, twenty-three differences between the two exist in corrected or revisory readings, nineteen of these being substantive, that is, concerned with words.

Typical are the changes in the Morgan sentence (46.20-23) "Rumors might fill the social atmosphere, or might once have filled it, there, which would travel but slowly, against the wind, towards our north-eastern metropolis, and perhaps melt into thin air before reaching it" from the version in the Ohio State leaf, "Rumors might exist, or might once have existed, there, which . . . and perhaps melt into thin air before they reached it." Likewise, "The spheres of our companions" was, earlier, "The spheres of other persons"; the freedom of Zenobia's deportment which, in Morgan, "might commend itself as the utmost perfection of manner, in a youthful widow" (47.4-5) had earlier been written as "might seem the consummate perfection of manner, in . . .";[1] Coverdale's speculation that Zenobia had been married is followed in Morgan by, "irresistibly that thought drove out all other conclusions, as often as my mind reverted to the subject" (47.19-21), but in the leaf it had read ". . . as I dwelt upon the subject"; or Zenobia in Morgan protests to Coverdale about his surveillance of her, "I have been exposed to a great deal of eye-shot in the few years of my mixing in the world" (47.25-27), whereas in the earlier version it is ". . . since I have mingled with the world". Moreover, the whole sentence leading up to her protest is a later addition: "Zenobia was conscious of my observation, though not, I presume, of the point to which it led me" (47.22-23).

Whether this leaf was itself a copy of an earlier version is not to be determined from the small amount of available evidence. None of the changes made during its inscription need have resulted from eyeskip or memorial lapse. Although some alterations represent the same sort of revision during writing found in the Morgan manuscript, which we know is a copy, the possibility is ever present that Hawthorne might expand and revise during the process of original composition in the manner that he did while copying out his fair manuscripts. On the other hand, if this leaf be at all representative of the earlier manuscript, it was in as acceptable shape to hand to the printer as was the copy made from it, if cleanness were the only criterion. Thus unless the leaf was actually atypical and Hawthorne felt required to copy out fair a manuscript not legible enough throughout to serve the printer, we are led to the conjecture that the act of copying stimulated him to fresh creativeness (as it does many writers) and hence that he deliberately transcribed the earlier manuscript the more readily to induce in himself the flow leading to really creative revision and thus achieved the final literary form of the work.[2]

To a student of Hawthorne's text, the chief value of this single leaf, so remarkably preserved, is the evidence it provides for the very considerable difference in style and details between the earlier and later versions of *The Blithedale Romance*. When important variation like this occurs, Hawthorne must have formed the new phrasing in his mind after reading what he had before him but before setting pen to paper for the copy. However, to this major revision must be added still another, that more minor variety found in the leaf and also in the Morgan manuscript, which revised material already copied in whole, or in part, in the very act of transcription. The intent of both kinds of revision seems to be the same. It is a notable fact that in his second and third thoughts Hawthorne almost always expands, and seldom condenses. The added detail, then, occupied his mind, on the testimony of the manuscripts, and not the problem of recasting for sharper (in the sense of more concise) expression, although it is true that one-for-one substitutions of words may appear that offer greater precision. The main point is, Hawthorne did not boil down his work in revision, but instead amplified it.

On the evidence of the Ohio State leaf of *The Blithedale Romance*, the major part of the expansion was accomplished between the earlier version and the fair copy for the printer. Under these conditions, the vast amount of Hawthorne's revision of his works will forever remain hidden. Yet even while he was in process of inscribing the fair copy, or was reviewing it, self-contained additions do take place. Whole sentences may be added, as that prefacing Zenobia's narrative of "The Silvery Veil": "From beginning to end it was undeniable nonsense, but not necessarily the worse for that" (108.1-2); or, as Coverdale leads Foster and Hollingsworth to the pool, the interlineation, "A nameless presentiment had again drawn me thither, after leaving Eliot's pulpit" (231.17-18). The longest insertion during inscription is the three paragraphs of conversation between Zenobia, Hollingsworth, and Coverdale represented by Centenary 68.6-20 in the chapter "A Modern Arcadia."

More common are such additions as in *The House of the Seven Gables*, 29.23-24, where "It appeared to be his doom to spend eternity" is deleted, and followed by "From the look of unutterable woe upon his face, it appeared to be his doom to spend eternity". A constant drumfire of such expansive second thoughts appear in the revisions within the final manuscripts. In *The Blithedale Romance*, for instance, "Her writings", while being copied, became "Her poor little stories and tracts" (44.2-3). Many additions are interlined above carets, just possibly a sign that they were made at some later time. Typical is the added description of Zenobia's jewels "like lamps that burn before some fair temple" (191.32), or the specification added to Coverdale's account of voices and laughter that they were "proceeding from the interior of the wood" (209.9). That, among the masqueraders, Moll Pitcher held a "broomstick in hand" (210.5), and Silas Foster "leaned against a tree" (210.8) we know only from additions.

The substitutions, usually of individual words, show Hawthorne striving for precision of language and of idiom, as well as exactness of physical description. A "city-residence" becomes a "town-residence" while being inscribed (40.6); Hollingsworth's proposed building is distinguished not as "the material type, in which his philanthropic dream had embodied itself" but as the one in which it "strove to embody itself" (56.17); Priscilla claps her hands as is the "custom", not the "habit", of young girls (60.19); the colonists' working clothes were an "epitome", not a "presentment", of defunct fashions (64.3); cold skepticism "smothers", not "murders", our spiritual aspirations (101.34); in brooding over recollections we "subtilize", not "convert", them into something akin to imaginary stuff (105.1); the Veiled Lady has "sybilline", not "oracular", responses (111.9); Moodie is an "elderly", and not an "old", man (5.4); Hollingsworth is "three or four" years older than Coverdale, not "two or three" (7.25); Foster remarks, with superior idiom, that Zenobia's shoe "never was made on a Yankee last" (231.27), not "never made in Yankee land"; and so on.

Something may be told, occasionally, either about the particular difficulty Hawthorne had in writing certain passages, or else that there may be more invention and less copying, when there is a marked rise in the number of alterations, as throughout Zenobia's narrative, "The Silvery Veil."

In *The House of the Seven Gables*, Hepzibah had almost invariably been denominated the "Old Maid" in the narrative; but at some later time, Hawthorne went back over the whole manuscript and substituted a variety of paraphrases, like "elderly maiden", "maiden lady", "elderly person", "recluse", "old Hepzibah", "old gentlewoman", "mistress of the house", or simple "Hepzibah". In *The Marble Faun*, Kenyon was originally named "Grayson" for about half the manuscript.

The notable care expended on revision in the manuscripts is wanting in the history of the transmission of the printed text once it had been set in type. Despite the fact that Griswold, of *International Magazine*, made ten verbal alterations in printing "The Snow Image," Hawthorne did not change a one of these back to his original when he collected the tales; and in the collected editions, he even let stand in "The Wedding Knell" the editor Goodrich's sentimentalized "embrace" for his own "touch" in the remarkable query to the decrepit couple who after forty years are about to be married, "But why had she returned to him, when their cold hearts shrank from each other's touch?"[3]

No changes were ever ordered by Hawthorne in the plates of *The House of the Seven Gables* or *The Blithedale Romance*; and he followed Fields's advice to leave the text of *The Scarlet Letter* alone in an exact reprint when a second edition was called for.[4] In a letter to E. P. Whipple, of May 2, 1852, accompanying the just finished manuscript of *The Blithedale Romance* sent for his criticism, Hawthorne warned, "should you spy ever so many defects, I cannot promise to amend them; the metal hardens very soon after I pour it out of my melting-pot into the mould."[5] Whether the late addition of the final chapter to this romance preceded the dispatch of the manuscript to Whipple, or resulted from his criticism, is undemonstrable. However, the paragraph added in proof almost at the end of this chapter suggests continuing care. Nonetheless, by and large it would seem that Hawthorne divested himself of responsibility for his text, like most authors, once a book had been published.

A small exception may just possibly be found in *The Marble Faun*, first published in England in 1860 under the title *Transformation*, although the case is doubtful. In what appears to be the third American printing, fourteen changes were made in the plates, all but one of which bring the respective readings into conformity with the joint readings of the manuscript and English edition.[6] Several of these correct real errors in substantives, like "art" for the error "heart", and "dead" for "dread"; a few correct obvious misprints like "Etrucean" and "dirtly". But others alter small matters of punctuation that would be odd even for the author to notice. Thus, wanting evidence in letters or other such material, we cannot tell whether it was Hawthorne who sent this list to Ticknor in order to correct errors he had observed in the American edition. The time element is probably too short, and perhaps the conjecture is best that the American publishers were responsible for these alterations on the authority of the English text or of a late stage of its proofs. If so, the substitution of "on" for "for" in I.225.22 (first-edition reference) of the Boston 1860 edition is inexplicable since it is found nowhere else.

The first American printing of *The Marble Faun* is full of problems not yet solved. Despite the presumption that it was set from English sheets, as planned, certain errors in the Boston typesetting can have derived only from misreading of the manuscript itself, such as "kind" (English "kindly") at II.56.16 when the "ly" of the manuscript has been so worked over as to resemble a deletion. The errors "would" at II.29.5, II.31.25, and II.260.29 derive from Hawthorne's handwriting in which "co" is easily misread as "wo". Again, when in II.250.20 the American edition misprints "lost", in the English, as "last", the manuscript "o" has been traced over in a way that might have caused confusion. At II.61.25, American "sorrier" repeats the manuscript, whereas the English print has "sadder"; at II.201.3 the same situation holds for American edition and manuscript "avails" (as a noun) versus the English edition "proceeds". These latter two readings must either be sophistications by the English publisher overlooked (or accepted) by Hawthorne, or proof-corrections in the English edition.

It is interesting and very likely significant that all of the variants occur in Volume II of the American edition, a fact that seems to indicate a difference in printer's copy between the two Boston volumes. (The alternative would be proof read back against the manuscript, a hypothesis one would scarcely wish to entertain.) This oddity requires, and will receive, further investigation. So far as is known, the manuscript never left England, and it is difficult to see why it should have been sent to Ticknor in America and then returned to England. One excellent possibility remains, that Volume I was set from corrected English proof-sheets but Volume II, because of a recorded delay in getting sheets to America,[7] from uncorrected English proofs. If so, the Boston 1860 errors would have been faithful reproductions of corresponding errors in the earliest English proofs that Hawthorne detected and altered. If uncorrected common errors can be found in the English and American editions, like "with foot" (London II.9.7; Boston I.198.9) in Volume I for manuscript "with her foot" (protested by Hawthorne to his English publishers on March 7, 1860, but left unchanged), then the case can be demonstrated.

The importance of rigorous bibliographical examination of copies is illustrated by the 1860 printings of *The Marble Faun* in the Boston edition. In what seems to be the fourth impression, the first American printing to contain the revised conclusion, sixteen further changes were made in the plates. Five of these are misprint errors created by an unproofread resetting and replating of a page (I.98); the others concern spelling and punctuation. Since most of these latter go contrary to the forms of the manuscript and to Hawthorne's generally observed characteristics, it is clear that this round of plate-alteration was made by the publisher and is without authority.

However, if the third printing, with its authoritative plate-changes, had not been firmly distinguished by collation on the Hinman Machine from the first and second impressions, an editor collating the fourth printing with the added conclusion back against an earlier one might by chance have picked a first or second impression. If so, he would have observed all of the third- and fourth-impression variants mixed in together without differentiation, and their quite opposing indications of authority would have proved puzzling in the extreme. Only when extensive machine collation isolates the first and the second impressions from the third—all without the conclusion—

can the unique variants either of the third or of the fourth printings be properly assessed for what they are and their textual authority determined.[8]

Hawthorne's manuscripts differ from the books printed from them in certain verbal readings (substantives), and extensively indeed in the system of punctuation, capitalization, word-division, and spelling (i.e. the accidentals). A conservative estimate would put these latter differences at about two thousand in *The Blithedale Romance* and at not less than three thousand in *The House of the Seven Gables*. The obvious question arises to what extent, if at all, was Hawthorne responsible for these numerous variants in the accidentals between manuscript and print.

That he was not responsible for several large classes seems demonstrable. The general forms of the accidentals are similar in *Seven Gables* and in *Blithedale*, set in the same shop within a year of each other and partly by the same two compositors. For instance, both prints regularly use syntactical commas plus dashes in a sentence like the following, quoted from its first-edition form in *Blithedale*: "Nobody else in the world, I am bold to affirm,—nobody, at least, in our bleak little world of New England,—had dreamed of Paradise that day, except as the pole suggests the tropic" (9.22-10.2). Yet, in neither manuscript do commas ever supplement dashes in such a construction. One would scarcely wish to argue that Hawthorne made hundreds and hundreds of such proof-corrections in the *Seven Gables* sheets and then ignored the new system and reverted to his former ways in the manuscript of *Blithedale*.

But Hawthorne does supplement parentheses with commas, as in the following from the same manuscript: "The snow-fall, too, looked inexpressibly dreary, (I had almost called it dingy,) coming down through an atmosphere of city-smoke . . . "

(11.19-23). The prints of both romances reverse the usage in the manner of the first edition here: "inexpressibly dreary (I had almost called it dingy), coming down. . . . "

House style, of course, has been imposed rigorously on both prints. In word-division, for example, it is impossible to believe that Hawthorne forsook his invariable forms like "tomorrow" and altered them in proof to uncharactertistic "to-morrow". In spelling one would hesitate to argue that he revised in proof his invariable "Oh" to first-edition "O", "Aye" to "Ay", or "faulter" to "falter". Or in capitalization that, as in 53.25-26, he would find cause to reduce to lower-case from manuscript capitals such semi-personifications as "Unpardonable Sin" and "Devil".

That Hawthorne "approved" of the form his manuscripts took in print can scarcely be maintained; but, like other authors, he was helpless to prevent the imposition of house style on his work. Hence if one wants what Hawthorne wrote presented in the way that he wrote it (not the way the printer thought it should be), the manuscript must serve as the copy-text for a definitive edition, and not the first edition. In so doing, an editor preserves Hawthorne's intentions to the maximum. That this preservation is not an academic matter can be illustrated by many small differences in meaning that develop between manuscript and print owing to the compositor's lack of understanding of the nuances of what he is setting. A typical example is *Blithedale* manuscript "they perpetrated so hideous a clamor, that methought it might have reached, at least a little way, into the eternal sphere." This represents a different sense from the compositor's version in the first edition, "that methought it might have reached, at least, a little way into the eternal sphere" wherein "at least" modifies "reach" instead of "a little way" as in the manuscript (202.7-9).

However, the case for the retention of the author's instead

of the printer's forms of the accidentals does not rest only on such evident distortions of meaning, serious as is their cumulative effect. Instead, an author's accidentals are a part of his total style by which he conveys meaning. I quote with pleasure from a letter to me by Professor William Charvat after he had compared the manuscript and the first-edition punctuation of *The House of the Seven Gables*:

> It comes to me now, for the first time, that Hawthorne's style is essentially parenthetical, and that this characteristic reflects the basically essayistic, generalizing, and speculative quality of his fiction. His parentheses give him latitude and flexibility that this quality requires. He modulates the degree of isolation of a unit by selecting (usually) just the right pair of separators: parentheses, or dashes, or commas. I don't think he did this selecting consciously, and probably the restoration of his own punctuation after the compositors mangled it, looked like too much drudgery. Certainly, the compositors show very little sensitivity about his modulations.

To this most perceptive statement only two small exceptions can be taken. The rather frequent alterations of commas to dashes about parenthetical statements during the inscription of the manuscripts might seem to indicate some degree of consciousness on Hawthorne's part about the effects of his modulation. Second, he could scarcely interfere in proof with the all-pervasive house-styling. He would have bankrupted himself in extra charges for alteration, and his publishers might well have been so annoyed as to order his corrections to be ignored.

When, as in *Fanshawe* or *The Scarlet Letter*, the first edition must be the authority in the absence of a preserved manuscript, the house-styled accidentals in considerable part must be thought of as authoritative, in the sense that they are characteristic of the only documentary authority there is for this particular work. Hence, when the print is consistent, as with the supplementary syntactical commas in parenthetical dash constructions in *The Scarlet Letter*, the knowledge that the lost manuscript would not have agreed cannot permit editorial emendation that would remove them. A student of Hawthorne manuscripts could in many respects restyle various of such first editions to enforce agreement with what it is clear must have been the different manuscript usage. But no consistency is possible in a process like this, for only a bare majority, perhaps, of the features of the accidentals are susceptible of alteration with such certainty. Thus all internally consistent features of a first-edition copy-text must be retained in default of the evidence of its lost manuscript.

The case is altered, however, when the first-edition copy-text is not in itself consistent, either because of compositorial slips or because of variable usages on the part of the different compositors who set the book. Although in *The Scarlet Letter* different compositors rigidly followed house style in what words were to be set with final *-or* and what with final *-our*, for instance, *Fanshawe* is by no means consistent in this and in dozens of other matters affecting the accidentals and their forms. By matching the different compositorial habits in dealing with nine selected variables, a critic can discover that five different compositors set *Fanshawe*, and with tolerable accuracy for a considerable part he can determine the exact pages that they set. Once the book is divided in this manner, we can readily see that each workman followed in a different way what we may suppose to have been the consistent characteristics of the manuscript. Some of the five, perhaps even four of them, will agree in one respect in dealing with some Hawthorne usage after their own style, whereas only one may reproduce what the manuscript form almost certainly was. Or the proportion may be reversed, in bewildering variety.

It suffices that only a pedant would be able to defend the proposition that every such variable in *Fanshawe* has other than technical authority. As a result, an editor can have a field day noting every difference in treatment of the accidentals, relating it to the five compositors, and then choosing the form that represents Hawthorne's known characteristic. By matching "authorities" in this manner, an editor can indeed go a tolerable way (in a manner impossible for the more uniform *Scarlet Letter*) toward reconstructing a number of surely authentic features of the lost manuscript of *Fanshawe* without ever forsaking the documentary authority contained in the typesetting of some one or more compositors of the first edition. The edited text, in this manner, can in truth be more authoritative in its details than the first edition, but never without reference to some authoritative reading within that edition.

When manuscripts are preserved, only a small amount of such cleaning-up is called for. Instead, the central problem of authority comes to rest on the reconstruction of the proofreading. That is, when variation appears between manuscript and print, it can have only two sources: it can come from the unauthoritative compositor, or it can come from Hawthorne authoritatively altering the typesetting in proof to another reading. The problem is to distinguish the two.

In the thousands of accidentals variants, a textual critic can quite definitely decide for some categories that the compositorial house style is so opposed to Hawthorne's own normal characteristics that no hypothesis can hold that in the print these could have come from Hawthorne's proof-correction. On the other hand, a very large number of the changes in the accidentals between manuscript and print are so relatively indifferent as to be incapable of adjudication. In such cases, the odds favor retaining the manuscript reading. Even if Hawthorne indeed had changed a few of these and the editor is unwittingly rejecting his final preference, the number of such occurrences will be very small compared to the large number of compositorial variants that he can avoid foisting on Hawthorne if he will cling, generally, to manuscript authority. Ordinarily, the critical methods that may succeed with many verbal variants have no chance of success in dealing with accidentals.

However, two categories of accidentals might seem to offer some hope for a distinction. These are the alteration of parenthetical commas to dashes, and the splitting apart of a long sentence, its parts joined by a semicolon, into two separate sentences. The reason that these might be significant is that they represent distinct trends within the manuscript revisions themselves; and it would be only reasonable to conjecture that this tendency could carry over into the proof stage.

Analysis of the first, the frequent change of manuscript parenthetical commas to dashes in the print, yields only negative results. When one selects a group of such examples at random and then examines the typography of the lines in question, it frequently becomes evident that the line with the dashes is so loosely set that no compositor would have spaced it so wide if the considerably narrower commas had first been set and the dashes added only in proof. When lines with dashes are correctly justified, no argument can be made that the dashes are proof-alterations, since these would often have upset the normal spacing and caused a noticeable crowding. Hence, though no critic can deny the possibility that some few of these changes might have been made in proof by the author, it is possible to demonstrate that many could not possibly have been proof-corrections. In these circumstances, no criteria obtain consistently to identify authoritative changes, and any attempt to select examples from the first edition to emend the manuscript readings must be abandoned.

Unfortunately, no greater success attends an effort to establish as Hawthorne proof-alterations the breaking-up of lengthy semicolon sentences into two separate sentences, as happens during the inscription of the manuscript. Since only eleven examples occur between manuscript and first edition, this number is not out of line with probability and could well represent changes in proof. But discouraging evidence accumulates. For instance, in the work of all four major compositors, many more examples occur of short manuscript sentences made into long sentences by semicolons than the reverse. Frequently the compositors seemed to have joined these sentences because they objected to the common Hawthorne practice of starting a sentence with a conjunction. It would seem, then, to be significant that, contrary to compositorial preference, not one of the possible Hawthorne proof-changes in splitting up sentences starts with a conjunction.

More to the point, the stints of the compositors are marked in the manuscript; and thus one can easily discover that of the eleven examples seven appear in pages set by one compositor, Fox, two in the work of Munn, and only one apiece in Henderson's and Emery's stints. This imbalance points very suspiciously toward the hypothesis that the changes are printer's styling, particularly Fox's. However, there is always an outside possibility that chance has operated and that bibliographical reasoning has been misled. And a few of the changes, like the two within a few lines of each other at the turn of the page between Fox and Henderson (Centenary 44.3, 44.10), are tempting to attribute to the author. But bibliographical reasoning has not been misled. Fox and Henderson are among the compositors who, the year before, had set *The House of the Seven Gables*. Among these various workmen, only Fox splits manuscript sentences in two, this occurring five times in his stint, but nowhere else in the whole book. The repetition of this discrepancy in the typesetting of Fox and Henderson in two manuscripts cannot be ignored. If Hawthorne did indeed change a sentence or two in proof in this manner, no evidence to identify any such alteration can be adduced.

Since these two categories of accidentals furnished the best test of the possibility that some of Hawthorne's changes of punctuation or other accidentals in proof (if any) might be ascertained, the case appears to be hopeless without special evidence. Hence any editorial emendations in these respects from the first edition must be made sparingly, and then chiefly to correct slips in the manuscript. It is unlikely that very many will be authoritative.

The question of the substantives, or wording, is of more immediate critical importance, and certainly these verbals represent a field where criticism can properly operate in decisions concerning authority. A typical book is *The Blithedale Romance*, in which one may count a total of forty-nine substantive variants between manuscript and print, omitting the correct setting of the various dittographic errors in the manuscript. Normal expectation would divide these into authorial proof-alterations and compositorial variants not noticed by the author. The question is, which is which.

The view that Hawthorne was a careless and comparatively uninterested proofreader rests on his willingness to proofread non-creative work, like his biography of Pierce, without the copy; or his disinclination to bother with proofreading himself the collections of his tales and sketches that had already appeared earlier in print. The latter, especially, supports the view (indicated in some references in letters) that Hawthorne distrusted the ability of the printer to read his handwriting and wanted to see proof, not at all for the opportunity it offered to improve his work, but only to assure himself that his manuscript words had been correctly transferred to print.[9] But this attitude implies some scrupulousness and accompanying care. The

record ordinarily is very good indeed that his proofreading overlooked only a small number of printer's corruptions in his
romances.

What the errors were that he found and corrected, we shall
never know in the absence of any preserved proof-sheets, for
these readings in the print would have been altered to agree
with the manuscript. Some variants may be those of the professional proofreader who would normally have read over and
marked proof before it was sent to the author. An exasperated
remark in a letter to Mansfield of February 10, 1850, concerns
The Scarlet Letter and "a certain proofreader whom I am, just
now, afflicted with" (MS, Berg Collection, New York Public
Library). Such corrections Hawthorne could agree with or
excise; but we have no means of knowing whether this publisher's reader may not have returned sometimes for a final
reading after the author had finished and at that time made
changes that could not have been seen by the author. Possibly
this happened with a reading or two in *The Blithedale Romance*
(see below). The only authorial variants, of course, that we
have the opportunity of recognizing are those that are revisory
in their nature and thus depart from a satisfactory manuscript
reading.

Of the forty-nine substantive variants in *The Blithedale
Romance,* the Centenary editors believe that at least twenty-eight
represent Hawthorne's literary revisions in the proof-sheets; ten
represent his correction in proof of unsatisfactory manuscript
readings, although some of these may already have been changed
by the compositor; and eleven represent printer's errors that
he overlooked and that an editor must reject.

The editorial process by which these are separated into their
categories is largely a critical one. Widely variant readings, like
first-edition "recognize her as his" for manuscript "consider her
his" (74.32), present no particular difficulty in assigning to the

author, just like "influence" for manuscript "agency" (7.30), "creditable" for "to his credit" (30.2), or "autumn to autumn" for "season to season" (211.33). On the contrary, any editor acquainted with Hawthorne's vocabulary would reject as a vulgarization the first edition's "inspired" for manuscript "inspirited" (180.4); and, on the face of it, "winter" for manuscript "wintry" (85.11) is corrupt, for the month is April and the cold weather has three times elsewhere been referred to as "wintry".

As illustrating the real scrupulousness of Hawthorne's occasional changes, the example of first-edition "roof" versus manuscript "roofs" (148.34) is salutary. Coverdale is looking out of his hotel window at the back of a range of houses which, we are told, is connected by a single roof. The backs, or offices, of these houses have "roofs" along which a cat wanders. A button-wood tree aspires to overtop what in the manuscript is the "roofs" but in print is the "roof" of the residences. The singular must be right, since the plural has been used only for the ground-floor offices. Moreover, in the Notebook entry from which this description is copied almost verbatim, the singular is used for the same circumstance. A small point, indeed, but indicative of Hawthorne's care.

The prime textual difficulty comes in the indifferent variants not susceptible of critical assessment, and in their nature most readily associated with compositors' memorial lapses: readings like first-edition "I am" for manuscript "I'm" (232.13), or "hanging up by" for "hanging by" (144.18). In such cases, when insufficient grounds exist for a sound critical judgment, the evidence suggests, in the romances, that more authentic Hawthorne proof-corrections exist in the first edition than printer's errors that were overlooked. Hence the odds favor the working hypothesis that any variant between print and manuscript not identifiable almost certainly as a printer's error is more likely than not to represent a proof-alteration.

In some very small part, unexpected confirmation of this view comes from the first English edition of *The Blithedale Romance*. We know that Chapman and Hall published this edition more than a week before the American, and that their text was set up using as copy the proofs of the American typesetting rushed across the Atlantic in batches. We know that Fields, then in England, had ordered these proof-sheets to be sent as the plates were returned from the stereotyper.

The interesting question then arises whether, in these circumstances, the English typesetting preserves any readings that at a later state of proof-correction were altered in the American sheets before printing and publication. The evidence is fragmentary, but in a few examples no doubt can exist that when the English first edition agrees with the manuscript against the American first edition, the reading of the American print must represent such a proof-alteration. The most prominent example is the agreement at 74.32 in "consider her his" as against the first-edition "recognize her as his", a variant in the print that one would not wish to assign to compositor or to publisher's reader. Another, although the variant itself is largely indifferent, is the agreement in "I'm" versus the first-edition "I am".

On the other hand, the fact that the English edition follows the majority of what appear to be the authoritative Hawthorne proof-alterations in the American sheets (thirty-six of the thirty-eight substantive variants selected as authoritative, in fact, without consideration of the more difficult punctuation agreements) appears to confirm the hypothesis that normally Fields' instructions were followed and that the copy sent to England consisted of proofs pulled from stereotype plates made from the typesetting in its finally corrected form. It is certain, for instance, that the passage a few lines before the conclusion (247.26-32) added in proof could not have been sent abroad from the original state of the proof-sheet for gathering 18.

If one takes into account the evidence for other proof-changes in the sheets containing the suspected readings, only two possibilities suggest themselves. With the possible exception of one or two sheets, the proofs in question sent abroad could not have been in their original uncorrected state. Hence the readings in the American sheets that alter the forms in which the English edition agrees with the manuscript must represent either (1) alterations made in the stereotype plates before printing, or (2) alterations ordered at a later stage than the original proofs either by Hawthorne or a publisher's reader but before stereotyping.

Careful examination on the Hinman Machine of the suspected readings in later printings of the American edition where alteration of the plates would be likely to expose itself in spread or battered letters and in somewhat out-of-line typesetting fails to produce any evidence that the plates were altered. Hence the second hypothesis appears to be the one that must be held. In this connection, it is simpler to assume that the printers sometimes found it difficult without undue delay to follow Fields's instructions about sending proofs from plated type pages, and on at least some occasions caught the mail with packets of proof from corrected but unplated type pages. Then, before plating, final instructions were received that resulted in the subsequent alterations revealed in the English edition. Certainly the sheets containing these variants appear to support this hypothesis by tending to run in sequences: sheets 5, 6, 7, then sheet 10 alone, and finally sheets 16 and 17.

The occasional usefulness of English editions to a study of the generally more authoritative American print is well illustrated by this example, and so, in reverse, the usefulness of the Boston 1860 typesetting to the generally more authoritative English edition of *The Marble Faun*.

Excisions in a manuscript without substitution often present a problem to a textual critic, but not to an editor of Hawthorne. Since his whole revisory bent was towards amplification instead of condensation, very few such excisions appear other than of casual words here and there. An interesting example occurs in *The Blithedale Romance* when Coverdale induces Hollingsworth to explain to Silas Foster their dread that Zenobia has committed suicide. In the manuscript Hawthorne first wrote, on folio 187:

> "And so you think she's drowned herself!" he cried, with his eyes half out of his head, from mere surprise. "What on earth should the young woman do that for? Why, she has more means than she can use or waste, and lacks nothing to make her comfortable, but a husband—and that she could have, any day! There's some mistake about this I tell you!"
> "Come," said I, shuddering. "Let us go and ascertain the truth."

Perhaps because he wanted to reduce the number of times that he utilized Foster's crude reactions for shock effect, Hawthorne at some point deleted the passage ", with his eyes . . . " to " . . . I tell you" so that Coverdale's answer "Come," followed immediately on Foster's original exclamation. But, then, he decided to restore the passage, and on the verso of folio 188, with some rearrangement, he wrote the following:

> I turned away my face.
> "What on earth should the young woman do that for?" exclaimed Silas, his eyes half out of his head with mere surprise. "Why, she has more means . . . some mistake about this, I tell you!" (230.31-231.2)

In *The Blithedale Romance*, however, there are three other passages that were deleted but not restored. Two of these were excisions only of a sentence or a clause (10.23-24; 17.15-16), but the third consisted of twenty-one lines in the manuscript (175.5-27). It is interesting to observe that one of these concerns sexuality, and two liquor. The one truncates a mental image Coverdale has of Zenobia in the garb of Eden, following a joking exchange between the two on his arrival at Blithedale. The other allows Coverdale to regret that in forsaking his snug town quarters to drive to Blithedale in a wintry storm, he had left behind a bottle or two of champagne and a "residuum of claret in a box"; but then Hawthorne removes the mention of strong liquor by deleting the phrase "and somewhat of proof in the concavity of a big demijohn".

The long excision, on the other hand, contains a satiric if not bitter attack on temperance workers who attempt to take away strong drink from the poor without an idea that liquor must be replaced with something else of good if the effort is to succeed. The general tone is indicated by such a quotation as, "The temperance-men may preach till doom's day; and still this cold and barren world will look warmer, kindlier, mellower, through the medium of a toper's glass; nor can they, with all their efforts, really spill his draught upon the floor, until some hitherto unthought-of discovery shall supply him with a true element of joy."

These three passages stand out as unique excisions presumably made for other than literary purposes. Although the faint possibility exists that E. P. Whipple suggested them when he read over the manuscript before it was sent to the printer, the natural candidate is Sophia Peabody Hawthorne, who was the closest at hand and certainly the most influential. Before her marriage, she had urged on Bronson Alcott censorship of the published version of notes made on "unpleasant subjects." Hawthorne's American Notebooks exhibit her deletions of his references to smoking, drinking, and "low company," as well as her firm attitude toward his occasional levity about drunkenness. Especially, the forthright satire on temperance men could not have pleased her.

It seems likely that Hawthorne withdrew the three passages in deference to the sensibilities of his wife. If so, it may not be the first evidence that an author's text has been affected by the influence of the marital bed, perhaps, but it will do in default of a better.

Afterword

Lionel Trilling

Our Hawthorne

H ENRY JAMES's monograph on Hawthorne must always
have a special place in American letters, if only because, as
Edmund Wilson observed, it is the first extended study ever to
be made of an American writer. But of course it is kept in the
forefront of our interest by more things than its priority. We
respond to its lively sense of the American cultural existence
and the American cultural destiny, to James's happy certitude
that, in describing the career of the first fully-developed

American artist, he celebrates the founder of a line in which he himself is to stand pre-eminent. And we can scarcely fail to be captivated by the tone of James's critical discourse, of a mind informed and enlightened, delighting in itself and in all comely and civilized things; it is the tone of the center, far removed from the parochialism which (together with strength) James imputes to Poe as a critic. For the student of American literature in general, the little book is indispensable.

But the student of American literature for whom Hawthorne is a particular concern must experience some degree of discomfort as he reads James on his author. He will be aware that through James's high and gracious praise there runs a vein of reserve, even of condescension. In an attempt to account for this, the student will perhaps reflect that Hawthorne made himself susceptible to condescension, for he was often at pains to avow the harmlessness of his temperament, to dissociate himself from the fierce aggressions and self-assertions of the literary life; he seems to ask from his readers a tender and cherishing affection rather than the stern regard which we give to the more violent or demonic personalities—or, simply, to the personalities more overtly masculine—whose assault upon us we learn to forgive. Then too, it is not hard to understand that James, in the full pride of his still youthful powers, might have been tempted to slight a predecessor, no matter how truly admired—a predecessor who, although he did indeed show how much could be accomplished in the way of art, did not achieve a body of work which, in bulk and fierce affronting power, equals that which his successor planned for himself in sublime confidence.

But when our student of Hawthorne has canvassed the reasons to be found in the personal circumstances of either man, he is bound to see that something beyond the personal is at work to produce James's reserve or condescension. He will understand that his explanation must ultimately refer to a cultural assumption to which James has given expression. And this assumption, when he examines it, will force upon him the awareness that, in the degree that he feels close to Hawthorne, the breach between his own contemporary culture and that of Henry James is very great. James's little book appeared (in the "English Men of Letters Series") in 1879, and in the time between then and now there has taken place a revision of critical sensibility the extent of which can scarcely be overestimated.

In his third chapter, which deals with *Mosses from an Old Manse* and *Twice-Told Tales*, James sets forth his view of the nature of Hawthorne's artistic enterprise by taking issue with the opinion of Emile Montégut, an able French critic, notable to us for his special and informed interest in American literature. In 1860, in an essay called "Un Romancier Pessimiste," Montégut had dealt extensively with Hawthorne, representing him as a writer of dark and, indeed, misanthropic mind. He spoke at length of Hawthorne's concern with conscience, sin, and hell, and "the tortures of a heart closed before man and open to God,"[1] subjects for which the descendant of a long line of Puritans would naturally show a predilection. Montégut has but little sympathy to give to the Puritan mentality, and he speaks in harsh terms of what he takes to be Hawthorne's exemplification of it; yet it is clear that he understands Hawthorne's dark preoccupation to constitute his chief interest, the very substance of his seriousness. To this view James responds with extreme and satiric impatience. He denies the darkness of Hawthorne's mind and in the course of doing so actually seems to deny that it is a serious mind. For he tells us that we must understand Hawthorne's concern with conscience to be largely "ironical." He does not use the adjective in the sense which will occur most naturally to the reader of today, the sense which is cognate with "ambiguous" and suggests a source of emotional power. He intends a meaning of the word which is close to whimsical playfulness. "He is to a considerable extent ironical—this is part of his charm—part even, one may say, of his brightness; but he is neither bitter nor cynical—he is rarely even what I should call tragical."[2] And James goes on: "There have certainly been story-tellers of a gayer and lighter spirit; there have been observers more humorous, more hilarious—though on the whole Hawthorne's observation has a smile in it oftener than may at first appear; but there has rarely been an observer more serene, less agitated by what he sees and less disposed to call things deeply into question."[3]

To the religious elements of the stories, James gives no credence beyond an aesthetic one. Hawthorne, he says, used religion for his own artistic purposes; from the moral life of Puritanism his imagination "borrowed" a "color" and "reflected" a "hue,"[4] but he experienced no conviction whatever.[5] James certainly abates nothing in his description of the terrors of Puritanism, of how the "shadow of the sense of sin" could darken the individual life and lead it either to despair or to a catastrophic rebellion. But he is quite certain that Hawthorne was not adversely affected by his Puritan heritage—he did not "groan and sweat and suffer" under it, nor did he throw it off in anger. " . . . He contrived, by an exquisite process, best known to himself, to transmute this heavy moral burden into the very substance of the imagination, to make it evaporate in the light and charming fumes of artistic production."[6]

James is unequivocal and emphatic in his belief that Hawthorne's interest in Puritanism was nothing but artistic. He tells us that our author gave his imagination license to "amuse" itself with the faith of his ancestors, to make their morality its "playground"; what for his forebears was the principle of existence, he made into one of his "toys."[7] "The old Puritan moral sense, the consciousness of sin and hell, of the fearful nature of our

responsibilities and the savage character of our Taskmaster—
these things had been lodged in the mind of a man of Fancy,
whose fancy had straightway begun to take liberties and play
tricks with them—to judge them (Heaven forgive him!) from
the poetic and aesthetic point of view, the point of view of
entertainment and irony."[8] James has no quarrel with fancy,
but he adheres to the Coleridgean doctrine that it is a lesser
faculty than the imagination; and although he does not doubt
that it is within Hawthorne's capacity to command the imagination, he understands the tales to be chiefly under the control of
fancy. " . . . As a general thing," he says, "I should characterize the more metaphysical of our author's short stories as
graceful and felicitous conceits."[9]

What are we to do with a judgment of this sort—how are we
to escape its embarrassments? It is one of our great masters who
speaks, and we hold him to be great not only in the practice
of his art but also in its theory. From him many of us learned
how high, even sacred, is the mission of the artist, and from him
we derived many of the tenets by which we judge success in
art. Yet it is he who makes this estimate of another of our
masters, the one who, of all Americans, was the master of Henry
James himself.

I need scarcely detail the ways in which, by our modern
judgment, James goes wrong. Yet it will be well to have the
prevailing present view explicitly before us, and it could not
be more exactly defined than by the existence of the useful
volume called *A Casebook on the Hawthorne Question*. The
editor of the *Casebook*, Professor Agnes Donohue, has gathered
together ten of Hawthorne's best known stories; to each of six
of these she has appended two interpretative essays of more or
less recent date; following this is a selection of famous critical
estimates of our author; and in a series of appendices which

includes lists of critical topics for student papers, there is a bibliography which, although it is intended to be minimal, runs to thirty-two books and the same number of articles. Why it is that Hawthorne makes a "question" for us and how our literary community has gone about answering what has been posed to us is very clearly explained by the editor in her Preface.

> The ten stories and sketches in the Casebook disclose a signal ambiguity in Hawthorne—his attitude toward man's moral nature. Sometimes he seems to assert the depravity of man while at the same time he dreams of an Adamic hero guileless in his prelapsarian Eden. He vacillates between trusting the human heart's intuitions as good and advancing his conviction that the heart is a "foul cavern" which must be destroyed to be purified.
>
> Hawthorne's ambivalence about guilt and innocence can be seen as a lodestone that draws into its magnetic field other problems of human life. He writes of innocents initiated into shrewdness; secret sin and isolation; compulsive rituals of atonement and sacrifices; self-righteousness becoming fanaticism; science confronting original sin; witch-craft and devil worship; carnal knowledge and guiltless love; the search for a home, a father, a self—in short, man's dark odyssey in an alien world.
>
> The ambiguity in Hawthorne's stories is at once his triumph and, for some literalistic critics, his failure. The tension it creates is a dramatic asset. Many of the tales, or romances as he thought of them, are multi-leveled, ironic explorations of the human psyche—capable of endless extensions of meaning and of stimulating repeated analysis and interpretation.[10]

Comparing the two views of Hawthorne, that of James and the established modern view which Professor Donohue summarizes, we must, in all humility, feel that ours is the right one. It recommends itself on its face. No doubt James's ironical entertainer makes a graceful and charming figure as he amuses himself with the toys strewn over the playground of a disused morality. But how can any member of the literary community fail to conclude that there is an intrinsic superiority in the grave, complex, and difficult Hawthorne we have learned to possess, the Hawthorne who represents "man's dark odyssey in an alien world?"

It is, of course, fair to remember that Hawthorne's view of himself was ostensibly more in accord with James's view of him than with ours. "The sketches are not, it is hardly necessary to say, profound; it is rather more remarkable that they so seldom, if ever, show any design on the writer's part to make them so. They have none of the abstruseness of idea, or obscurity of expression, which mark the written communications of a solitary mind with itself. They never need translation. . . . Every sentence, so far as it embodies thought and sensibility, may be understood and felt by anybody who will give himself the trouble to read it, and will take up the book in a proper mood."[11]

To which the modern student of Hawthorne will say that his author is a foxy fellow indeed, and go on to explain what "read" really means, what is the extent of the necessary "trouble" that the reader will have to give himself, and what constitutes the "proper mood" in which the book is to be taken up. It is no secret how we achieved our modern Hawthorne, our dark poet, charged with chthonic knowledge, whose utterances are as ambiguous as those of any ancient riddling oracle, multi-leveled and hidden and "capable of endless extensions of meaning and of stimulating repeated analysis and interpretation"—it is plain that the Hawthorne of our day came into being at the behest of of the famous movement of criticism that began some forty years ago, that movement of criticism which James could know nothing of, although he was to be one of its pre-eminent subjects.

If we undertake to say how the critical movement put us in possession of our Hawthorne, we will probably not be content

435

to describe the process only in terms of the good effects of "close reading." The techniques of investigation and pedagogy which were employed by the critical movement are of manifest importance, but an understanding of modern criticism in its historical actuality requires that we be aware of an intention which is anterior to every technique. That intention was to give literature a new force and authority. Or perhaps we should say that the intention was to support the new degree of force and authority that literature was claiming for itself. The technical methods of modern criticism are summed up for us in the famous footnote in which Mr. Eliot told us that the spirit killeth but the letter giveth life. But by this statement Mr. Eliot said something more than that it is necessary to pay strict attention to the minute details of literary art, or that criticism is not to be thought of as the adventures of a soul among masterpieces. He was making a statement about the nature of literature. We may understand him to have been saying that literature is of a *primitive* nature. For although the allegiance to "the letter" which he urged upon us will at first glance suggest intellectuality, and an intellectuality of a rather haughty sort, and something like a scientistic glorification of precision, qualities which the critical movement in general does indeed often seem to claim for itself, it is actually an expression of belief in the magical force and authority of words and their arrangement, as in a charm or spell, an expression of belief that literature characteristically makes its appeal to archaic human faculties which have been overlaid by civilization and deeply hidden.

My reference to its belief in the "primitive" nature of literature will tell us only a little about the very large and very complex intention of modern criticism. But it may serve to remind us that the critical movement, in its diverse groups and parties, set itself up in opposition to what a social psychologist has called the "respect revolution" of our time. The phrase refers to the culture of democratic-capitalist industrialism and to that culture's devaluation of certain traditional ideas, modes of life, personnels, qualities of art, etc. The conception of art as "primitive," as taking its rise in an older mode of life, may be thought of as a way of challenging those aspects of the respect revolution which were rationalistic, positivistic, vulgar, and concerned with superficial and transitory rather than with deep and permanent things.

The phrase I have borrowed, awkward and jargonistic as it is, may serve to propose the thought that cultural impulses stand in the closest proximity to social impulses and are often scarcely to be distinguished from them—to speak of the respect revolution may remind us that a strong cultural preference has much in common with social antagonism. Thus, to take an example which is relevant to our occasion, Parrington represents Hawthorne as being virtually an enemy of the common people because of the delicacy of his art, his concern with the inner life and the problem of evil, and his coldness to the enthusiasms of transcendentalism, which Parrington calls "the revolutionary criticism that was eager to pull down the old temples to make room for nobler."[12] This translation of modes of thought and of artistic imagination into social modes, or the other way around, is natural and inevitable in our day; and, of course, it was practiced by the members of the critical movement itself. Everyone is aware of how important in his thought about poetry Mr. Eliot's social and political ideas were; in America many practitioners of the New Criticism took positions more or less like Mr. Eliot's. The instance of Dr. Leavis reminds us that even within the movement itself there were sharp antagonisms of social preference, although at this distance in time the differences between one party and another are perhaps already of less importance than the antagonism which all parties showed to the social values that had been established by the respect revolution.*

The social emotions which were involved in the critical movement do not in themselves immediately concern us, but I mention them in order to suggest how charged with will, how deeply implicated in the bitter moralities of choosing among social styles, was the intellectual tendency that gave us the Hawthorne we know.

But if we do indeed owe our Hawthorne to the movement of criticism, it may be that our new possession is a little compromised by the somewhat fatigued reputation of criticism in recent years. In 1956, in his University of Minnesota lecture, Mr. Eliot expressed what he was not alone in feeling—a degree of disenchantment with the enormous critical activity of our age.† He was ready to affirm that our criticism was very brilliant, but he felt it necessary to say that "it may even come to seem, in retrospect, too brilliant."[13] By which he meant, I think, too busy, too eager to identify ironies, to point to ambiguities, and to make repeated analyses and interpretations.

Expectably enough, one objection that Mr. Eliot made to the hyperactivity of criticism is that it interferes with our private and personal relation to the literary work, that it prevents our freedom to respond to it in our own way. I should go further

* In the social-psychological view, Dr. Leavis is presumably no less "aristocratic" than Mr. Eliot. At any rate, I am—I picked up the phrase "respect revolution" from an essay in which it is said that my volume *The Opposing Self* "defends an aristocratic attitude toward the respect revolution in terms of an implicit romantic notion of inner direction" (Albert J. Brodbeck, "Values in *The Lonely Crowd*: Ascent or Descent of Man?" in *Culture and Character,* ed. Seymour Martin Lipset and Leo Lowenthal [1962], p. 59). The author may be right, but I sometimes think that my book might just as accurately be said to defend an inner-directed attitude toward the respect revolution in terms of an implicit aristocratic notion of romanticism.

† I should here take note of Mr. Eliot's statement that the critical movement ought not to be thought of as deriving from him.

than this and say that the brilliant busyness of criticism has not only changed our relation to literature, to art in general, but has even changed our conception of the nature of art, and in a way that, when we stop to think of it, we cannot be entirely happy about.

The situation that I would describe is by way of being a paradox. Of this paradox the first term is our belief that the vulgar art-product, the art-product characteristic of the respect revolution, stands in a relation to the public that is radically different from the relation to the public which is maintained by the work that commands our best attention and admiration. The former, the "popular" or middlebrow work, consciously refers itself to the public and is shaped by its response to public prejudices and desires. The latter, the work of genius or disinterested talent, refers itself only to the inner life of its creator and is to be judged only by the truth of its representation of that innerness. Our commitment to this criterion constitutes, as M. H. Abrams tells us, the basis of our modern aesthetic. In his admirable *The Mirror and the Lamp,* after describing the "mimetic" theories of art of classical antiquity and the "pragmatic" theories of the Renaissance and the eighteenth century, Professor Abrams goes on to speak of the "expressive" theories of our own time: "The first test any poem must pass is no longer, 'Is it true to nature?' or 'Is it appropriate to the requirements either of the best judges or the generality of mankind?', but a criterion looking in a different direction; namely, 'Is it sincere? Is it genuine? Does it match the intention, the feeling, and the actual state of mind of the poet while composing?' The work ceases then to be regarded as primarily a reflection of nature . . . , the mirror held up to nature becomes transparent and yields the recorded insights into the mind and heart of the poet himself."[14] This is surely true, yet an accurate account of the first criterion of modern judgment must not lead us to believe that our response stops with our testing the congruity between the created work and its maker's inner life at the time of its creation. We must be aware that, once we have made our way into the artist's inner life in order to decide whether or not the created work is congruent with it, the artist's inner life ceases in some degree to be inner. It is on public view, available to general scrutiny.

The artist, of course, makes no objection to his innerness being thus publicized. If we consider the situation of the arts in general in Paris between 1885 and 1914, which is the definitive period of the modern epoch, we can say that it was characterized by the passionate devotion of the artists to their inner lives, to their personal and peculiar visions. But in all the history of art was there ever a movement which was so conscious of a public, even though in its deficiencies rather than in its legitimate expectations, and so determined to impose itself upon the public? The artist himself often led the enterprise of making his work prevail, but this was not necessary—when once its sincerity and genuineness were agreed upon by a faithful few, there gathered around the work a band of fighting men to carry it on to the field in force, like the Ark of the Covenant, each member of the band deriving strength from the sacred object, becoming ever more confirmed in his own sincerity and genuineness while bringing into ultimate question the authenticity of the heathen public.

Hence our paradox. Never, in a secular culture, has the inner life seemed of such moment as it does in our culture. And never has the inner life been lived so publicly, so much in terms of significant associations and allegiances, of admirations and rejections that make plain how things stand within.

As a result, it becomes ever more difficult for a work of art to be thought of as existing in itself or in our private and personal experience of it—its existence becomes the elaborate respect systems that grow up around it, that huge penumbra of the public effort to understand it and to be in a right relation to it, and to make known to the world the completeness of the understanding and the rightness of the relation that has been achieved. The work exists less in itself than in the purview of one or another of the public agencies we have set up for the service of the inner life; of these one of the most notable is surely literary criticism, which, as it has established itself in the universities, constitutes a great new profession, ever growing in its personnel and in its influence.*

The extent of our author's public existence will not seem irrelevant to the Hawthorne Question (since there is such a thing), for Hawthorne's relation to the public of his own day was a matter of great moment in his thought about himself. Hawthorne seems never to have been sure whether to be ashamed or proud of his lack of success with the mass of his countrymen. And, of course, this was not merely a question of his career but of his moral life, feeling as he did that to be removed from one's fellow-beings was to commit a mortal sin. His ambivalence is expressed in the Preface to *Twice-Told Tales*. He tells us—it is touching to hear him say it—that the stories are written in "the style of a man of society," that they are "his attempt to open an intercourse with the world."[15] Yet Hawthorne's impulse to privacy is definitive of his genius. We think so and he thought so. The delicate, the fragile, the

* For an interesting account of the part played by public agencies—"museums, university art departments, professional publications"—in the establishment of new painting, see Harold Rosenberg's column in *The New Yorker*, September 7, 1963, pp. 136-46. Mr. Rosenberg's estimate of the power—one might say the fury—of criticism is worth noting: "The future does not come about of itself; it is the result of choices and actions in the present. Criticism, including art criticism, is a form of conflict about what shall be. If history can make into art what is now not art, it can also unmake what is now art. It is conceivable that Michelangelo, Vermeer, Goya, Cezanne will someday cease to be art; it is only necessary that, as in the past, an extreme ideology shall seize power and cast out existing masterpieces as creatures of darkness."

evanescent, all that could not survive the public touch or gaze, made his conception of success in art. Of his tales, he says that "they have the blue tint of flowers that blossomed in too retired a shade,—the coolness of meditative habit which diffuses itself through the feeling and observation of every sketch."[16] The flower was for him the perfect symbol of the created work: he was at pains to revise his ancient family name so that it would be more precisely that of a beautiful flower-bearing tree, its blossoms delicate and brief, its integrity and isolation enforced by its thorns or spines.

It is all too possible that in having made Hawthorne public, in having busied ourselves to discover that he is a Question, which then we must bestir ourselves to answer, we have lost much of the charm and fragrance which may well be his essence. James was much engaged by the beauty of Hawthorne's work, by its textures and hues, of which he speaks not so much with critical admiration as with personal delight. Of this surface aesthetic, the modern critics of Professor Donohue's volume say little. Their concern is with an aesthetic of depth, an aesthetic of the arrangement of quasi-doctrinal significances. One cannot have everything, but whoever has first read Hawthorne in child-hood—James makes a point of his having done so—will be inclined to feel that something he once knew is missing, something that spoke to him, and very movingly, before ever ambiguity was a word, some magic that had its abode in the forests and haunted The Notch and played around the Great Stone Face, and that bound together the dark forest and the dark recesses of the moral life and the dark backward and abysm of the national past.

It is a loss, but no doubt we must teach ourselves to sustain it cheerfully. For how else are we to deal with Hawthorne than in the public way we do deal with him? He belongs in the canon of our spiritual heritage, and how else is one to impart that heritage, how else is one to be a serious critic or a university teacher, if he is not as *active* as he may be in response to his subject? And if one perhaps goes on to think of his profession as having a more than pedagogic function, as being charged to make some contribution to the effort of spiritual discovery of our time, one may not surrender one's right to press each work as hard as one can in order to make it yield the full of its possible meaning.

Henry James's Hawthorne will not suit the purposes of the teacher or critic, neither his strictly professional nor his larger cultural and spiritual purposes. What can we do with a Hawthorne who, in dealing with the heavy moral burden which was his ancestral heritage, not only refused to accept it as his own but contrived to make it "evaporate in the light and charming fumes of artistic production," a sort of ethical prestidigitator?

I confess to being of the opinion that in establishing our Hawthorne as against Henry James's Hawthorne we have lost something of considerable value. But I am constrained to heed the contention that we have gained more than we have lost. I must even be aware that we have even acquired an augmented canon. For us today, none of Hawthorne's stories surpasses in interest "My Kinsman, Major Molineux." James does not mention this great story. And, indeed, it is only in relatively recent years that it presents itself as demanding inclusion in any selection of Hawthorne's work—when Austen Warren in 1938 and Newton Arvin in 1946 prepared selected editions of the tales, neither of the two editors, whose literary intelligence is of a very high order, included the story we have come especially to prize. Its Dionysian darkness, its brilliant, bitter, ambivalent humor, were not yet available to them, not yet available to us.

Let us, then, stay confirmed in our belief that the Hawthorne we now have is the right one. But it may be worth asking why it is that James's Hawthorne is so different from ours. I said earlier that James's view was not merely personal, that it was controlled by a cultural assumption. Remembering the year of the monograph, 1879, at the apogee of Victorianism, we are tempted to say that this assumption is part of the ideology of Philistinism which always hovered over even the best thought of the Victorian era. What we mean by Philistinism surely accomodates James's almost angry insistence that our author is not dark or bitter or pessimistic, is not to be called "tragical," virtually not serious, that he is childlike in the indulgence of his fancy, that his only concern is to amuse himself and entertain us; and this is not to mention James's dislike of "symbols and correspondences," of "seeing a story told as if it were another and a very different story."[17] James, of course, figures in our minds exactly as an avowed enemy of Philistinism, yet an ideology works in mysterious ways, no one can be sure of being immune from all its effects, and it may be that we have to admit that James was in accord with some of the questionable aspects of his epoch.

This possibility might be sustained by the recollection of a famous passage from *The Ambassadors*, the speech that Lambert Strether makes to Little Bilham. "Live all you can," Strether says to his young friend, "it's a mistake not to. It doesn't so much matter what you do in particular, so long as you have your life. If you haven't had that, what have you had? . . . "[18] When, in the 1940's, James was in the full tide of the great revival of interest in him, this speech was frequently quoted. Twenty years ago the little homily seemed to touch the American consciousness in a very intimate way. *Live all you can; it's a mistake not to.* How much that seemed to say about America— our nation gave us much, but it was ever reluctant to grant us the right to have our lives. No one thought that the implied doctrine was the whole of James, yet it seemed very much at

444

the center of his work, and it validated him for many readers who might otherwise have been put off by him, just as now, in a different cultural moment, it accounts, as I think, for much of that diminution of interest in James which is to be observed.

What did James mean by having one's life? He meant something really quite simple and actual and tangible. He meant Paris—surely he meant that first. He meant all that was possible to do and enjoy in Paris and not in Woollett, Massachusetts—he meant having intense erotic relationships; and breaking the code of respectability without pain of conscience; and Gloriani's garden; and sunny days on the river; and Mme de Vionnet's beauty and charm, and her manners and place in society. "To live" meant to know and to have the pleasures of the world.

James gave perfect credence to the pleasures of the world. He believed them to be real even at those moments when he was most intensely aware that they might be involved with vulgarity and even cruelty. He gave an equal credence to the sanctions which control and limit the ways in which the pleasures of the world may be seized, and to the moral sensibilities which propose the circumstances in which the pleasures of the world—perhaps the world itself—must be surrendered. The credence he gave to pleasure and the credence he gave to moral sanction together define James's certitude that the world is *there*: the unquestionable, inescapable world; the world so beautifully and so disastrously solid, physical, material, "natural."

And I think that it is because the world is so very much there for James that our interest in his work has receded from the high point it reached two decades ago. It does not move us now as it once did to hear him say, "Live as much as you can; it's a mistake not to." Whatever Paris and Gloriani's garden and a free and happy sexuality may mean to our practical con-

445

sciousness (perhaps everything!), to our literary or spiritual consciousness they now mean but little. If we can imagine a novelist of our own moment who matched James in genius, we cannot easily suppose that he would give anything like James's credence to the good "thereness" of the world, to the necessity of having one's life. By the same token, we cannot easily suppose that he would give anything like James's credence to the moral sanctions which control and limit the ways in which the pleasures of the world may be grasped. These two credences, as I say, are the ground of James's art, constituting as they do his acceptance of the world's reality. They make the element of his work that tends to alienate it from the contemporary consciousness, that allows us to wonder whether we must not judge James to have been touched with the Philistinism of his epoch and therefore misled in his judgment of Hawthorne.

Our contemporary feeling about the world, alien from that of James, is much in accord with that of Franz Kafka. Everything about Kafka is still in dispute, perhaps even more than it formerly was, now that our response to him has become more precise and discriminating. But almost everyone will agree that Kafka's work gives very little recognition, if any at all, to the world in its ordinary actuality, as it is the object of our desires and wills, as we know it socially, politically, erotically, domestically; or, if it recognizes the world at all, it does so only through what it perceives of the radical incompatibility of world and mankind. Of all studies of Kafka, that by Günther Anders seems to me most satisfying, if only because it responds so fully to Kafka as a *force,* speaking of him as a "dangerous" writer and questioning whether it is "wise" to admire him. Anders tells us that Kafka "provided exactly the mixture of sensation a certain class and generation of readers . . . most desired, pandering to their self-conscious sense of having reached the last phase of individualist sensibility. For here indeed were stories about the individual in his purest, most isolated role—yet told in a tone which showed how pointless was his position in the world. The hero was still the center, but the center of complete indifference."[19] In another passage, Anders speaks of Kafka's tone as transforming "men and things into a kind of *nature morte*."[20] The "class and generation of readers" which was given what it wanted by Kafka is said by Anders to be that which flourished in 1925. If this dating is accurate for Europe, it is not accurate for America, where Kafka, like James, made his strongest impression upon our literary culture in the forties and continues to stand well to the fore of our interest while James recedes into the background.

The name of Kafka had to turn up sooner or later in any discussion of Hawthorne, for our awareness of Kafka has done much to license our way of reading our author. Everyone perceives certain likenesses between Hawthorne and Kafka. They were similarly, although not equally, remote from the public; and to the public view, they presented temperaments of which a defining element was a quality of personal gentleness at variance with the subversive nature of their work. There is a very considerable degree of similarity in their preoccupations— "man's dark odyssey in an alien world" may serve to describe Kafka's as well as Hawthorne's. They stood in equivalent relations to religion: unbelievers both, their imaginations were captivated by the faiths with which they were connected by family tradition, and from these unavowed faiths they derived the license for the mythic genre which constitutes so much of their appeal, for the representation of agencies of human destiny which are not of the actual world. Then, too, having in mind Kafka's negation of the world of actuality, I think it can fairly be said that there is something comparable in the way that Hawthorne deals with the world. He encourages the comparison when he tells us that he does not write novels but "romances," by which he means that his fiction does not make a very determined reference to the concrete substantialities of life, the observation and imitation of which is the definitive business of novels. We may surmise that his "simple" and "thinly-composed" society, as James called it,[21] was congenial to his creative disposition, for it facilitated the enterprise that is characteristic of him, the representation of the world as being susceptible to penetration and suffusion by agencies not material and mundane. And it was exactly Hawthorne's happy acceptance of a thinly composed society that James jibed at. He himself craved thickness; that famous list he drew up of the solid interesting actualities that were not at the disposal of Hawthorne's art, or the art of any American—"no Epsom nor Ascot!"—tells us, of course, what he was claiming for his own use when he transplanted himself to England, finding there, in its unassailable Britannic citadel, the Philistine solidity of world that he needed. And needed, one is inclined to say, not only as an artist but as a person—one has the sense that Hawthorne's art, because it represents a world which is only thinly composed, made James *nervous*.

What most troubled James in Hawthorne's work is not likely to trouble the reader who exercises the characteristic highly developed literary sensibility of our time. Indeed, as I have suggested, that modern reader is likely to find a measure of security in the very circumstance that made James anxious: in the degree that the world can be thought of as thinly composed, the autonomy of spirit is the more easily imagined.

But it is just here that we are likely to go astray in our perception of Hawthorne. For if it is true that Hawthorne's world is thinly composed, whatever its composition lacks in thickness is supplied by an iron hardness. Among the similarities to be observed between Kafka and Hawthorne, there is—after all, and despite first appearances—this decisive difference between them,

448

that for Hawthorne the world is always and ineluctably *there* and in a very stubborn and uncompromising way. A passage in *The Marble Faun* tells us how perdurably Hawthorne understood it to be there. Kenyon, Hilda, and Miriam have been talking at length and fancifully about Count Donatello's resemblance to the antique statue of the dancing faun. "The foregoing conversation," we are told in that shameless explicit way that was once possible, "had been carried on in a mood in which all imaginative people, whether artists or poets, love to indulge. In this frame of mind, they sometimes find their profoundest truths side by side with the idlest jest, and utter one or the other, apparently without distinguishing which is the most valuable, or assigning any considerable value to either. The resemblance between the marble Faun and their living companion had made a deep, half-serious, half-mirthful impression on these three friends, and had taken them into a certain airy region, lifting up, as it is so pleasant to feel them lifted, their heavy earthly feet from the actual soil of life. The world had been set afloat, as it were, for a moment, and relieved them for just so long of all customary responsibility for what they thought and said."[22] It is merely the conversation of "creative" persons that Hawthorne says he is describing, but we surmise that he would wish us to have in mind as well the works of art which they create, that he means to define the relation in which the artist stands to the world. If that is so, we will not fail to observe that what Hawthorne emphasizes in his account of this relation is not the power of the artistic imagination but the intractable weight and actuality of the world. For a brief moment the artist takes flight, and sometimes he can even set the world afloat; but only for so long as his words are being uttered; when again he falls silent, the world is no longer a balloon and his feet walk again on earth, on "the actual soil of life."

449

Of possible conceptions of the artist's relation to the world, this is indeed a very modest one. And if at any time in our judgment of Hawthorne we become aware, as indeed we must, of moments when his power as an artist seems insufficient to the occasion, we might reasonably attribute what weakness we discern to a conception of the artist's manner of dealing with the world which is less bold and intransigent than it might be.

When it comes to power—to, as we say, sheer power—Hawthorne is manifestly inferior to Kafka. Of Kafka's power an impressive index is the fact that his version of man's dark odyssey proceeds without touching upon cases of conscience. What an intransigence of imagination is needed to conceive man's spiritual life as having no discernible connection with morality! In such relations between man and man as are represented in Kafka's work, it is never a possibility that one man can help or injure another. The idea "I did him wrong" is foreign to Kafka's mind. The idea "I did wrong" is, of course, omnipresent, but this means only "I did not do the required thing, that which the Law demands; and therefore I shall be punished." Many readers of Kafka cannot endure the necessity of supposing that a punishment does not refer to an act that is bad in a moral sense; they are made acutely uncomfortable by the conception of an ordained suffering that is not to be understood in moral terms, or at least, and almost as good, in characterological terms. They feel it necessary (like Job's friends) to adduce moral explanations; and when they can discover no actual transgressions to sustain their argument, they fall back upon traits of temperament—Gregor Samsa becomes a cockroach because he is an insufficiently developed or positive person, really a cockroach at heart; Joseph K. is accused and condemned by the Court because he did not have a rich and "related" emotional life. Those who are appeased by such explanations can only with difficulty be made aware that, for what they take to be the cruel injustice which Kafka describes, they substitute an injustice still more cruel. Such readers are scarcely to be praised for their literary competence, but more than the readers who respond more appropriately, they, by their resistance to Kafka's imagination, best suggest its power.

And not only its power is to be attributed to the intransigence of his imagination but also the extraordinary aesthetic success which Kafka consistently achieves. Aesthetically, it seems, it is impossible for him to fail. There is never a fault of conception or execution, never an error of taste, or logic, or emphasis. As why should there be? An imagination so boldly autonomous, once it has brought itself into being, conceives of nothing that can throw it off its stride. Like the dream, it confronts subjective fact only, and there are no aesthetically unsuccessful dreams, no failed nightmares.

The dream, it need scarcely be said, plays its part in the imagination of Hawthorne too, and most markedly in those of his works which touch us most deeply. But it is obvious that the "spontaneous, peremptory, and obligatory nature of dreaming"* manifests itself far less in Hawthorne than in Kafka. Over Hawthorne's imagination, the literal actuality of the world always maintains its dominion. This must always be kept to the forefront of our understanding of Hawthorne even though we go on to say that he made it his characteristic enterprise to represent the moral life as existing beyond mere practicality, to show it to us as a mystery, as being hidden, dark, and dangerous, and as having some part of its existence in a world which is not that of ordinary knowledge. This other world, in which the presence of divinity is to be dimly apprehended, interpene-

---

*I take the phrase from the remarkable "Studies on the Psychopathology of Sleep and Dreams," by Charles Fisher, M.D., and William C. Dement, M.D., in the *American Journal of Psychiatry*, CXIX, No. 12 (June, 1963), 1163.

trates the world of material circumstance, and, in doing so, provides the quotidian world with its most intense significances.

When Hawthorne is successful in suggesting the interpenetration of the two worlds, he affects us profoundly. But we cannot fail to be aware of how readily his belief in the other unseen world can be checked by his sense of this world's actuality, how often it falls short of being spontaneous, peremptory, and obligatory. James's extreme dislike of allegory and the use of emblematic devices make him unduly harsh in condemnation of the flaming celestial A in The Scarlet Letter; he judges the scene to be "not moral tragedy, but physical comedy."[23] But we all agree to the principle of his objection and recall how much too often Hawthorne gave occasion for its being made. "Roger Malvin's Burial" may serve as our example of the characteristic weakness. The informing idea of this story is superb, and its execution is adequate to its conception up to the moment when we are asked to consider "whose guilt had blasted" the topmost bough of the oak, that withered bough which is to fall at the moment when Reuben Bourne has expiated his sin. Perhaps no other work of literature proposes so forcibly the idea that morality is not bounded by the practical, that it creates a habitation for itself which is not only of this world, that it moves, by some process of transcendence, from practicality into absoluteness, or at least to unreasoning piety. The morality that Hawthorne has been conceiving has, as it were, the power of the dream, for it is indeed spontaneous, peremptory, and obligatory; but the incident of the falling bough, which is intended to enforce upon us the belief that the moral law has just these qualities as its defining attributes, is itself merely gratuitous; it seems scarcely the work of the imagination at all, rather of the author's will; so far from strengthening the credence we give to the preternatural world, it leads us to think that the author's own belief is seeking support.

Eventually Hawthorne lost all power of belief in the other world, and with it all power of creation. The last years of his life are terrible to contemplate. His labor seems to have been as devoted as it ever was, but he confronted white paper with the knowledge that nothing he now might put on it could have value. We have Kafka at hand to suggest the dreadfulness of the doom: it was as if Hawthorne's gift had been confiscated in punishment for some indiscernible sin. "By 1860 he had worked himself dry," Edward H. Davidson tells us in the introduction to his edition of that one of the several gray chaotic efforts to which has been given the name of *Dr. Grimshawe's Secret*. "The 'present, the actual,' he confessed, was too pressing, and in *Grimshawe* he tried to write a sermon for his time without any of the moral insights which had been his special distinction in the years before he had gone to England."[24]

Yet if we set aside the misery of the decline—that fate which must sometimes seem all too peculiarly American!—and set aside, too, the instances of aesthetic failure in the great period, we have to say that Hawthorne, even when he was not intimidated by the "present, the actual," must be judged to lack the power of imagination which we expect him to have when we respond to the degree of power he actually does have. Despite the best efforts of the critics, the contemporary reader must always, I think, be disappointed by Hawthorne. With so much readiness to apprehend the dark, the unregenerate, and evil itself, why must he be so quick to modulate what he sees? He is capable of conceiving the terrible black veil which Mr. Hooper wears over his face, and of pointing to the guilt that we each incur and hide and long to reveal—why, having triumphed in the creation of the dread emblem, must he raise the question of whether the veil is not an egotism, an object of irony? His most famous single utterance loses its great potential force in its rhetoric of qualification: "Be true! Be true! Be true! Show

453

freely to the world, if not your worst, yet some trait whereby the worst may be inferred!" Why not, we ask, actually your worst? If it is correct to say with Professor Davidson that the "special distinction" of Hawthorne lies in his "moral insights," we are in effect saying that he was concerned to look into something that is there to be looked into, and when we say this, we knew that an investigation of objective reality cannot have the same imaginative freedom and force as an affirmation or a negation, which has only a subjective obligation. Hawthorne's vision of the moral life, although it does indeed reach in one direction to the transcendental or spiritual, reaches in the other direction to the psychological, leading the reader to ask, "Is this true to the fact as I know it?" To the readers of Hawthorne's own time, the psychological observation of the novelist, especially when it discovered the dark and subversive elements of the mind, served as a liberation; but we have become inured to psychology—to the typical highly developed reader of our time, it does not bring the old liberation of surprise, and one may even detect in our literary opinion the belief that, insofar as it is a knowledge derived from observation and susceptible of being systematized, made into a science, it constricts rather than enlarges our imagination of man. Hawthorne was, F. O. Matthiessen has said, primarily concerned with questions of moral cause and effect—"not sin but its consequences for human lives is Hawthorne's major theme."[25] I would demur a little from this judgment, for I think that sin itself held a fascination for Hawthorne. But there can be no doubt that his awareness of consequences was never far distant from his concern with sin itself. In short, he always consented to the power of his imagination being controlled by the power of the world.

But the modern consciousness requires that an artist have an imagination which is more intransigent than this, more spontaneous, peremptory, and obligatory, which shall impose itself upon us with such unquestionable authority that "the actual" can have no power over us but shall seem the creation of some inferior imagination, that of mere convention and habit. Our modern piety—I use the word in its good sense—is of the autonomous self, or at least of the self as it approaches autonomy in its tortured dream of metaphysical freedom. Hawthorne could indeed conceive of our longed-for autonomy. But his own piety was committed elsewhere.

There is an episode in Daniel Cory's recent book about Santayana which suggests the nature of Hawthorne's piety as I understand it. Mr. Cory tells us how, as a young man, he could not understand why Santayana should have described *The Realm of Matter,* the first of the four volumes of *The Realms of Being,* as "essentially the work of a moralist," and, with a touch of impatience, Santayana said to him, "Don't you understand by now that the real object of piety is matter—or Nature, if you prefer. It is the idea of Might—the ineluctable Yahveh of the Hebrews, when this primitive notion has been freed of its local and superstitious accretions." And Mr. Corey goes on to say that "all his life Santayana had been convinced that the religious attitude of *respect for God* is at bottom the same thing as our sense of dependence on an efficacious but largely unfathomed 'background' of human experience. . . . When our naive ideas of God or Nature have been stripped of their pictorial and emotional accretions, what we are left with is the defiant core of both these ideas: the ineradicable conviction of primordial Might that impinges upon and ought to control the ambition of the distressed mind."[26]

Whose is the shout we hear, the bitter cry of protest at these words? Whose else could it be but the outraged spirit of William Blake, in whose existence we all participate? The great offended voice is raised to assert the power of the artist's imagination to deny the reality of the primordial Might, or to challenge and overcome it, or to interpose between it and us a dream, which, perhaps in the degree that it terrifies, commands our assent and holds out the promise of freedom.

If that is indeed what ideally we expect the imagination of the artist to do, Hawthorne does not satisfy our expectation. Again and again, in what we judge to be his too limited faith in the imagination, he admits, even insists, that the world is there, that we are dependent upon it. His quick response to the non-rational, his lively awareness of the primitive and chthonic, of the dark roots of life, does not deflect the naturalistic and humanistic tendency of his mind. At his very most powerful, he does not interpose his imagination between us and the world; however successfully he may project illusion, he must point beyond it to the irrefrangible solidity.

He feared "the ambition of the distressed mind" and before the primordial Might he maintained an attitude of almost studied modesty, we might say of childlikeness when we remember what irony and malice he was capable of attributing to a child. Like a child, he takes liberties and plays tricks; he amuses himself and entertains us; he takes somber moral principles and makes them into toys—we have but to give to the idea of play the consideration it deserves to see that Henry James's description of his activity is not so deficient in justice as at first it seems. Of his playfulness, the ambivalence and ambiguity which are so often noted of him are essential aspects. They do not, I think, bring him close to Kafka's mute, riddling power—through them, rather, he approaches to "Que sçais-je?", the ironic childlike question, the question which conscious or calculated modesty asks, out of which all the questions come.

It is questions that Hawthorne leaves us with. It is, really, not at all clear why Young Goodman Brown must live out his life in sullenness because he refuses to sign the Devil's pact;

nor is it clear why Robin must join the violent mob in laughter at his kinsman before he is his own master, and indeed it is not clear why being his own master is a wholly admirable condition. To consult ourselves for answers is to become aware of our dependence upon that part of the "efficacious but largely un-fathomed background of human experience" which lies very close at hand, within our very selves, and which reminds us of our dependence upon its further reaches.

And in the degree that he does not dominate us, Hawthorne cannot wholly gratify us, moderns that we are. Exquisite artist though he be, he yet suggests to us the limitations of art, and thus points to the stubborn core of actuality that is not to be overcome and seems to say that the transaction between it and us is, after all, an unmediated one; and by his ambiguities and ambivalences he seems to imply that we—each one of us alone—must make our investigations and our terms as best we may. He has no great tyrant-dream in which we can take refuge, he leaves us face to face with the ultimately unmodifiable world, of which our undifferentiated human nature is a part. He does not even permit us what seems a complete view of the desperateness of our situation—nothing complete, nothing ultimate.

No, it is not gratifying. Yet if we tell the truth about our experience of Hawthorne, some of us will say that as we read him—or at moments as we read him—we have a sensation of having been set at liberty. It is not an entirely comfortable con-dition. We find ourselves at a loss and uncertain in the charge of an artist so little concerned to impose upon us the structure of his imagination. We look for a more coercive will, and are insecure in its lack. Yet perhaps we feel, too, an impulse of exhilaration charged through our art-saturated minds, a new pleasure in being led carelessly or playfully to one or another dangerous place and being left alone to look at the danger in our own way. The pleasure cannot last long—probably more is needed in the life around us before such independent confrontations of our dependence will seem natural to us, and a kind of joy. Our judgment of Hawthorne may have to be that he is not for today, or perhaps not even tomorrow. He is, in Nietzsche's phrase, one of the spirits of yesterday—and the day after tomorrow.

Notes

Notes

Marcus Cunliffe

1. Austin Warren, *Rage for Order* (Chicago, 1948), p. 88.

2. Daniel Hoffman, *Form and Fable in American Fiction* (New York, 1961), p. 193. Hawthorne's source, to which Hoffman refers, was Joseph B. Felt, *The Annals of Salem from Its First Settlement* (Salem, Mass., 1827).

3. Arlin Turner, *Nathaniel Hawthorne: An Introduction and Interpretation* (New York, 1961), pp. 2-3.

4. Hubert H. Hoeltje, *Inward Sky: The Mind and Heart of Nathaniel Hawthorne* (Durham, N.C., 1962), pp. 343-45.

5. Hoeltje, p. 348; Hoffman, p. 201, quoting passages from *The American Notebooks*, ed. Randall Stewart (New Haven, 1932), p. 27. The work by Skidmore, a member of the New York Workingmen's Party, was entitled *The Rights of Man to Property! being a Proposition to make it equal among the adults of the present generation: and to provide for its equal transmission to every individual of each succeeding generation, on arriving at the age of maturity* (New York, 1829). An excerpt is reprinted in Joseph L. Blau (ed.), *Social Theories of Jacksonian Democracy* (New York, 1947), pp. 355-64.

6. See, for example, Maurice Beebe, "The Fall of the House of Pyncheon," *Nineteenth-Century Fiction*, XI (June, 1956), 1-18, which maintains Hawthorne's novel has the organic shape of an ascending spiral curve.

7. Quoted in Rudolph Von Abele, *The Death of the Artist: A Study of Hawthorne's Disintegration* (The Hague, 1955), p. 58.

8. Henry James, *Hawthorne* (London, 1879), p. 49.

9. Yvor Winters, *In Defense of Reason* (New York, 1947; reprinted from *Maule's Curse*, 1938), p. 170.

10. February 7, 1843. See Bliss Perry (ed.), *The Heart of Emerson's Journals* (London, 1927), p. 194.

461

11. Hoffman, pp. 193-94.

12. Hoffman, p. 191.

13. The novels by Holmes are *Elsie Venner* (1861), *The Guardian Angel* (1867), and *A Mortal Antipathy* (1885). The mother of the heroine of *Elsie Venner* is bitten by a snake, and Elsie becomes a sort of serpent-woman. Holmes's suggestion is that her venomous traits are medical rather than moral in origin, and require treatment not punishment.

As for mesmerism as a literary device, it was still in vogue in 1888; the hero of Edward Bellamy's *Looking Backward: 2000-1887* is mesmerized so completely that he sleeps for a hundred and thirteen years.

14. See Henry Christman, *Tin Horns and Calico: An Episode in the Emergence of American Democracy* (New York, 1945), for a good account of this confusing yet highly instructive "war." It is worth noting, as one element in the confusion, that the Democrats—Hawthorne's party, and the party of the common man, according to their own statements—took the side of the landlords, while the supposedly aristocratic Whigs supported the Anti-Renters.

ROBERT C. ELLIOTT

1. Review article in *Westminster Review*, LVIII (1852), 596-97. For identification of authorship, see James D. Rust, "George Eliot on *The Blithedale Romance*," *Boston Public Library Quarterly*, VII (1955), 207-15.

2. The alternative is to conclude with Frederick C. Crews, "A New Reading of *The Blithedale Romance*," *American Literature*, XXIX (May, 1957), 147-70, that the book is constructed with the fiendish ingenuity of a Nabokov novel. The interpretation is interesting but will not hold up under sustained scrutiny.

3. *The Blithedale Romance* is a mine of rich themes that Hawthorne opens but does not work out. The relationship of Zenobia to Priscilla is, as Marius Bewley says, ultimately incoherent, but implies everything James was to develop so fully in the Chancellor-Tarrant relation in *The Bostonians* (*The Complex Fate* [London, 1952], p. 19).

4. "Hawthorne—Pastoral and Politics," *New Republic* (September 5, 1955), p. 19; the essay is included in Howe's *Politics and the Novel* (New York, 1957).

HARRY LEVIN

1. Van Wyck Brooks, *The Dream of Arcadia: American Writers and Artists in Italy, 1760-1915* (New York, 1958), p. 105; see also Anthony Winner, "Adjustment, Tragic Humanism and Italy," *Studi Americani*, VII (Rome, 1961), 311-61.

2. Nathaniel Hawthorne, *The Marble Faun, or The Romance of Monte Beni* (Boston and New York, 1883), p. 422.

3. *Ibid.*, p. 15.

4. Nathaniel Hawthorne, *Passages from the French and Italian Note-Books* (Boston and New York, 1883), pp. 260-61.

5. Henry James, *Hawthorne* (New York, 1879), p. 160.

6. Henry James, *William Wetmore Story and His Friends* (Boston, 1903), II, 225.

7. *French and Italian Note-Books,* p. 120.

8. *Ibid.,* p. 221.

9. *The Marble Faun,* p. 348.

10. *French and Italian Note-Books,* p. 331.

11. *Ibid.,* p. 283.

12. *Ibid.,* p. 172.

13. *Ibid.,* p. 167.

14. *The Marble Faun,* p. 98.

15. *Ibid.,* p. 25.

16. *Ibid.,* p. 172.

17. *Ibid.,* p. 167.

18. Herman Melville, *Pierre: or, The Ambiguities,* ed. Henry A. Murray (New York, 1949), p. 503.

19. Charles Dickens, *Pictures from Italy* (London, 1882), p. 419.

20. *William Wetmore Story,* I, 126.

21. *French and Italian Note-Books,* p. 89.

22. *The Marble Faun,* pp. 84-85.

23. *Ibid.,* p. 34.

24. *Ibid.,* p. 35.

25. *Ibid.,* p. 191.

26. *Ibid.,* p. 247.

27. *Ibid.,* p. 378.

28. *Ibid.,* p. 403.

29. *Ibid.,* p. 392.

30. *Ibid.,* p. 437.

31. *French and Italian Note-Books,* p. 291.

32. *Ibid.,* p. 293.

33. Merton M. Sealts, *Melville as Lecturer* (Cambridge, 1957), pp. 138-39.

34. *The Marble Faun,* p. 31.

35. *Ibid.*, p. 237.

36. *Ibid.*, p. 331.

37. *Ibid.*, p. 19.

38. *Ibid.*, p. 519.

39. D. H. Lawrence, *Studies in Classic American Literature* (New York, 1930), p. 123.

40. *The Marble Faun*, p. 519.

41. *Ibid.*, p. 498.

42. *Ibid.*, p. 522.

43. *Ibid.*, p. 128.

44. *Ibid.*, p. 390.

45. *Ibid.*, p. 499.

46. *Ibid.*, p. 158.

47. *Ibid.*, p. 306-7.

48. *William Wetmore Story*, I, 296, 329.

EDWARD H. DAVIDSON

1. *Hawthorne's Doctor Grimshawe's Secret*, ed. E. H. Davidson (Cambridge, Mass., 1954), p. 194.

2. *The Complete Works of Nathaniel Hawthorne*, ed. G. P. Lathrop (Boston, 1883), XI, 491.

3. *Grimshawe*, p. 56.

4. Second MS draft of "Septimius Felton," Pierpont Morgan Library, p. [40].

5. *Works*, XI, 515.

6. *Grimshawe*, p. 54.

7. *Ibid.*, p. 151.

8. *Ibid.*, pp. 151, 152.

9. *Ibid.*, p. 147.

10. *Ibid.*, p. 173.

11. *Ibid.*, pp. 149-51.

HYATT H. WAGGONER

1. I do not mean to imply here that Emerson's thought is wholly contained within the pat label "philosophic Idealism." Emerson had his experiential side, his pragmatic and even existential emphasis, as the way in

which some of his religious thinking anticipates Tillich should remind us. I do not find it easy to decide which is the "essential" Emerson, partly because he modified the early idealism as the years went by, partly because, as I see it, so many of the insights and feelings of the private man failed to get expressed in the public philosophy. In any case, the contrast between the two men that I am here developing is by no means absolute. It is intended to throw into relief certain aspects of Hawthorne's position, not to clarify Emerson's. As I have suggested above in discussing Hawthorne's relation to transcendentalism, Hawthorne was something of an idealist too, as his opposition to materialism suggests.

Nevertheless, after whatever qualifications may be necessary on both sides of the comparison, the two men seem to me quite different, not only in temperament, but in the emotional colorations of their thinking, and so in the final meanings for us of their visions of life. I cannot imagine Hawthorne's ever having written, as Emerson did in the 1836 essay on nature, "Therefore is Nature ever the ally of Religion. . . . The advantage of the ideal theory over the popular faith is this, that it presents the world in precisely that view which is most desirable to the mind."

Daniel Hoffman

1. In an appendix to *Mythology and the Romantic Tradition in English Poetry* (Cambridge, 1937), Douglas Bush has listed American poems on mythical subjects. In the sixty years between 1786 and 1845, there were published but fifteen, while thirty appeared in the next two decades (pp. 577-79). In 1855 appeared both Bulfinch's *Age of Fable* and Longfellow's *The Song of Hiawatha*.

2. Bush, *op. cit.*, pp. 526-27.

3. Hawthorne's letter to James T. Fields, quoted by G. P. Lathrop in his Introductory Note to Hawthorne's *Works* (Boston, 1883), IV, 10.

4. See Hugo McPherson, "Hawthorne's Major Source for His Mythological Tales," *American Literature*, XXX (November, 1958), 364-65.

5. Charles Kingsley, *The Heroes; Or, Greek Fairy Tales for My Children* [1855], (New York, 1882), p. 20.

6. *The Eccentric Design* (New York, 1963), pp. 116, 136.

7. *Democracy in America*, trans. Reeve, Part II, Book I, chap. xvii.

8. *Anatomy of Criticism* (Princeton, 1957), pp. 304-5.

9. *The Piccolomini*, II, iv, 123-34. Although this work is a translation of Schiller's play, the speech quoted is Coleridge's own interpolation; see Coleridge's note in *Complete Poetical Works*, ed. E. H. Coleridge (Oxford, 1912), II, 647.

10. Hutchinson, *History* . . ., ed. L. S. Mayo (Cambridge, 1936), I,

187. See G. H. Orians, "The Angel of Hadley in Fiction," *American Literature*, IV (November, 1932), 257-69.

11. Motif A580 (Culture hero's [divinity's] expected return); see Stith Thompson, *Motif-Index of Folk Literature* (Bloomington, 1955). Citations include references to legends of Holger, Balder, and King Arthur.

12. I have discussed the traditions of providences and wonders in Puritan writings known to Hawthorne in *Form and Fable in American Fiction* (New York, 1961), pp. 23-32.

13. This paragraph synopsizes the discussion of "My Kinsman, Major Molineux" in *Form and Fable in American Fiction*, chap. vi. See chapters vii-xi for a fuller discussion than appears in the present essay of "The May-Pole of Merry Mount," "Young Goodman Brown," and the three American romances.

14. "Hawthorne and the Tradition of Gothic Romance" is explored by Jane Lundblad in *Nathaniel Hawthorne and European Literary Tradition* (Upsala and Cambridge, Mass., 1947).

15. That the Devil's Compact is Hawthorne's principal theme is argued by William Bysshe Stein in *Hawthorne's Faust* (Gainesville, Fla., 1953).

16. *The American Adam* (Chicago, 1955), pp. 13-14.

17. Peter B. Murray, "Mythopoesis in *The Blithedale Romance*," *PMLA*, LXXV (December, 1960), 591-96.

18. *Anatomy of Criticism*, pp. 136-37.

Roy Harvey Pearce

1. In this and what follows, I make use of my *Savages of America* (Baltimore, 1953), particularly pp. 112-14 and 160-68.

2. I have studied in detail "My Kinsman, Major Molineux" and the other stories I put in this group in "Hawthorne and the Sense of the Past; or, The Immortality of Major Molineux," *ELH*, XXI (1954), 319-27.

Larzer Ziff

1. Arthur Miller, "Introduction," *Collected Plays* (New York, 1957), p. 44.

R. W. B. Lewis

1. Perry Miller and Thomas H. Johnson, *The Puritans* (New York, 1938), p. 60.

2. In his fine introduction to the Modern Library edition of *The Bostonians* (New York, 1956), Irving Howe makes a similar point within a somewhat different context.

EDWIN FUSSELL

1. Materials for the present essay are drawn from my forthcoming book, *Frontier,* and used with permission of its publishers, the Princeton University Press.

2. Quoted in Manning Hawthorne, "Nathaniel Hawthorne Prepares for College," *New England Quarterly,* XI (1938), 72.

3. Quoted in Samuel T. Pickard, *Hawthorne's First Diary* (Cambridge, 1897), pp. 4-5; further remarks along the same lines in *The American Notebooks,* ed. Randall Stewart (New Haven, 1932), p. 169.

4. The known facts about the Western tour are given in Randall Stewart, *Nathaniel Hawthorne: A Biography* (New Haven, 1948), pp. 42-43.

5. "In the settlement of America we have to observe how European life entered the continent, and how America modified and developed that life and reacted on Europe. . . . The frontier is the line of most rapid and effective Americanization."—"The Significance of the Frontier in American History," *Annual Report of the American Historical Association for the Year 1893,* p. 201. This is precisely the passionate progress of Hester Prynne: "It was as if a new birth, with stronger assimilations than the first, had converted the forest-land, still so uncongenial to every other pilgrim and wanderer, into Hester Prynne's wild and dreary, but life-long home" (chap. v).

6. "The Missionaries," in *Legends of the West* (Philadelphia, 1832), p. 96.

7. *Margaret, A Tale of the Real and Ideal* (Boston, 1845), p. 11.

8. See *The American Notebooks,* p. 31 (forest), p. 56 (forest, brook, and cavern), and p. 159 (Hawthorne lost in a Concord forest, trying to walk from his own house to Emerson's).

9. The correct reading of this Notebook passage was kindly supplied me by Norman Holmes Pearson.

10. Randall Stewart, "Hawthorne's Contributions to *The Salem Advertiser,*" *American Literature,* V (1934), 336.

11. The source of Hawthorne's description—but with no implications of the poetic imagination—is in *The American Notebooks,* pp. 124-25. The Notebook passage is dominated by Hawthorne's feeling of compositional frustration, and in that context the frontier metaphor was useless. Probably it came to mind when he had successfully completed *The Scarlet Letter* and was casting about for a figure to express problems solved.

12. "It was there I first got my cursed habits of solitude."—Quoted in James T. Fields, *Yesterdays with Authors* (Boston, 1871), p. 113.

EDWIN H. CADY

1. *The Letters of Emily Dickinson*, ed. Thomas H. Johnson and Theodora Ward (Cambridge, Mass., 1958), II, 649.

2. *The Poetical Works of Henry Wadsworth Longfellow* (Boston, 1866), III, 130-32.

3. In E. C. Stedman (ed.), *An American Anthology, 1787-1900* (Boston, 1900), p. 78.

4. "At the Saturday Club," *The Poetical Works of Oliver Wendell Holmes* (Boston, 1892), II, 271.

5. E. C. Stedman, *Hawthorne and Other Poems* (Boston, 1877), p. 12.

6. This seems from the whole record clear in spite of the well-known spat between Sophia Hawthorne and her family and James T. Fields over book royalties. Cf. esp. James C. Austin, *Fields of the Atlantic Monthly* (San Marino, 1953), pp. 240-43. According to Frank Luther Mott's estimates, *Twice-Told Tales, The Scarlet Letter,* and *The House of the Seven Gables,* became "Overall Best Sellers in the United States" and *Mosses from an Old Manse* one of the "Better Sellers" (*Golden Multitudes* [New York, 1947], esp. pp. 130-31).

7. *The Scarlet Letter* (Columbus, O., 1962), p. lxiii.

8. That sort of folksy celebrity was attested by such pieces as "A Day in Hawthorne's Haunts," by "A Westerner," *Overland Monthly*, IV (June, 1870); A. B. Harris, "The Old Manse at Concord," *Appleton's*, VIII (September 14, 1872); G. H. Holden, "Hawthorne Among His Friends," *Harper's*, LXIII (July, 1881); Julian Hawthorne, "The Salem of Hawthorne," and "Scenes of Hawthorne's Romances," *Century*, XXVIII (May, July, 1884); M. D. Conway, "Hawthorne's Villa at Florence," *Nation*, L (June 19, 1890); and, at last, W. S. Nevins, "Homes and Haunts of Hawthorne," *New-England Magazine*, N.S. IX (November, 1893).

9. Austin Warren, *Nathaniel Hawthorne* (New York, 1934), p. lxxxix.

10. Alexander Japp.

11. In addition to Stedman's poem, *loc. cit.*, see Laura Stedman and George M. Gould, *Life and Letters of Edmund Clarence Stedman* (New York, 1910), esp. II, 283-94.

12. Richard H. Fogle, "Organic Form in American Criticism, 1840-1870," in *The Development of American Literary Criticism*, ed. Floyd Stovall (Chapel Hill, 1955), p. 106.

13. "The First Century of the Republic in Letters," *Harper's*, LII (February, 1876), 527.

14. *A Study of Hawthorne* (Boston, 1876), pp. 328-30.

15. *The Memoirs of Julian Hawthorne,* ed. Edith Garrigues Hawthorne (New York, 1938), p. 127.

16. *Hawthorne* (Garden City, n.d.), pp. 56-58.

17. *Ibid.,* p. 106.

18. *Ibid.,* p. 115.

19. *Ibid.,* p. 154.

20. Review, *Atlantic* (February, 1880). See Kirk and Kirk (eds.), *Criticism and Fiction and Other Essays* (New York, 1959), pp. 229-36; cf. Louis J. Budd, "W. D. Howells' Defense of the Romance," *PMLA,* LXVII (*March,* 1952), 32-42.

21. No definitive study of this aspect of American literary history has been made. Cf. Virginia Harlow, *Thomas Sergeant Perry* (Durham, N.C., 1950); Helen McMahon, *Criticism of Fiction: A Study of Trends in the Atlantic Monthly, 1857-1898* (New York, 1952); E. H. Cady, *The Road to Realism* . . . (Syracuse, 1956), pp. 218-21, 240-43, and *The Realist at War* . . . (Syracuse, 1958), esp. pp. 1-55; E. H. Cady and David L. Frazier (eds.), *The War of the Critics over W. D. Howells* (Evanston, Ill., 1962); Eugene Current-García and Walton R. Patrick (eds.), *Realism and Romanticism in Fiction* (Chicago, 1962).

22. *The Century,* XXV (November, 1882), 25-29.

23. *Letters of Charles Eliot Norton,* ed. Sara Norton and Mark Antony De Wolfe Howe (Boston, 1913), II, 225.

24. "The New Battle of the Books," *Forum,* V (July, 1888), 570.

25. "The New Story-Tellers and the Doom of Realism," *Forum,* XVIII (December, 1894), 480.

26. Henry C. Vedder, *American Writers of To-Day* (New York, 1894), p. 270.

27. *My Literary Passions* (New York, 1895), p. 140.

28. For representative examples, many of them of substantial importance as essays, see G. P. Lathrop, "The Novel and Its Future," *Atlantic,* XXXIV (September, 1874); Julian Hawthorne, "Agnosticism in American Fiction," *Princeton Review,* N.S. XIII (January, 1884) ["Novels and Agnosticism," in *Confessions and Criticism* (Boston, 1887)], and "Hawthorne's Philosophy," *Century,* XXXII (May, 1886); H. W. Mabie, "A Typical Novel," *Andover Review,* IV (November, 1885); Anon., "Novel-Writing as a Science," *Catholic World,* XLII (November, 1885); Maurice Thompson, "The Analysts Analyzed," *Critic,* VI (July 10, 1886); W. L. Courtney, "Hawthorne's Romances," *Fortnightly Review,* XLVI (1886); C. C. Starbuck, "Nathaniel Hawthorne," *Andover Review,* VII (January, 1887); Andrew Lang, "America's Classic Author," *Critic* XVI, (May 10, 1890); K. Hillard, "Hawthorne as an Interpreter of New England," *New England Magazine,* N.S. XII (August, 1895); W. C. Lawton, *The New England Poets: A Study of*

Emerson, Hawthorne, Longfellow, Whittier, Lowell, Holmes (New York, 1898); L. E. Gates, "Hawthorne," *Studies and Appreciations* (New York, 1900).

29. *Literary Friends and Acquaintance* (New York, 1900), pp. 56-57.

30. *Mark Twain's Notebook,* ed. A. B. Paine (New York, 1935), p. 157.

31. In Ralph Barton Perry, *The Thought and Character of William James* (Boston, 1935), I, 316.

32. *Mark Twain–Howells Letters,* ed. Henry Nash Smith and William M. Gibson (Cambridge, 1960), II, 534.

33. *Heroines of Fiction* (New York, 1901), I, 162, first printed in *Harper's Bazar* (May-December, 1900).

34. "Nathaniel Hawthorne," *Library of the World's Best Literature,* ed. C. D. Warner and others (New York, 1897), XVIII, 7061.

35. "Hawthorne," *Studies and Appreciations* (New York, 1900), pp. 96, 108-9.

36. Some sense of the mere scope of Hawthorne commentary, 1864-1900, may be had from the facts that there are, not counting reviews, miscellanea (mere reminiscence, evidences of the personality cult, poems, plays, opera, etc.) or passing mention (illuminating as such asides may be), at least twenty-seven substantial and significant magazine articles, ten books, and distinct parts of perhaps twenty more volumes devoted to Hawthorne during the period. The whole body of materials is being studied by Everett Hatch, to whom, for bibliographical assistance and for the benefit of his judgment regarding some of the ideas here presented, I am cordially grateful.

ROGER ASSELINEAU

1. Marion L. Kesselring, *Hawthorne's Reading, 1828-1850 (A Transcription . . . of Titles Recorded in the Charge-Books of the Salem Athenaeum),* (New York, 1949).

2. See Arlin Turner, "Hawthorne's Literary Borrowings," *PMLA,* LI (June, 1936), 545.

3. F. O. Matthiessen, *American Renaissance* (New York, 1941), p. 210.

4. *Ibid.,* p. 211.

5. *Passages from the French and Italian Note-Books* (Boston, 1872), I, 232.

6. Henry James, *Hawthorne* (London, 1879), p. 45.

7. See above, note 2.

8. Jane Lundblad, *Nathaniel Hawthorne and European Literary Tradition* (Upsala and Cambridge, Mass., 1947), p. 46. The author quotes in particular the testimony of Julian Hawthorne and that of G. P. Lathrop, Hawthorne's son-in-law, in *A Study of Hawthorne* (1876), p. 164.

9. A note preserved in the Huntington Library, quoted by Jane Lundblad, p. 35.

10. *French and Italian Note-Books*, II, 276. Mme de Staël, on the contrary, altogether failed to interest him. When he saw Coppet, he noted: ". . . Coppet, where Madame de Staël or her father, or both, were either born or resided or died, I know not which, and care very little."—*Ibid.*, p. 274.

11. See Jane Lundblad, *op. cit.*, pp. 57–58.

12. "Hawthorne: Looking Before and After," *Shelburne Essays*, Second Series (Boston and New York, 1905), p. 174.

13. Norman Holmes Pearson, "The French and Italian Notebooks by Nathaniel Hawthorne" (Unpublished dissertation, Yale University, 1941), Introduction, pp. iii–iv.

14. *The Marble Faun* (Boston and New York, 1883), p. 191.

15. Henry James, *op cit.*, p. 162.

16. "The Journal of a Solitary Man," an uncollected piece attributed to Hawthorne, published anonymously in the *American Monthly Magazine*, N.S. IV (July, 1837), 47.

17. *Letters of Hawthorne to William D. Ticknor* (Newark, 1910), I, 99–100.

18. *The English Notebooks by Nathaniel Hawthorne*, ed. Randall Stewart (New York, 1941), p. 92.

19. *The Snow-Image, and Other Twice-Told Tales* (Boston, 1852), p. 205.

20. "The Prophetic Pictures," *Twice-Told Tales* (Boston, 1837), p. 253.

21. See also this passage: "When our forefathers left the old home, they pulled up many of their roots, but trailed along with them others, which were never snapt asunder by the tug of such a lengthening distance, nor have been torn out of the original soil by the violence of subsequent struggles, nor severed by the edge of the sword."—*Our Old Home* (Boston, 1863), p. 23.

22. *English Notebooks*, p. 270.

23. *Our Old Home*, pp. 23, 22.

24. When about to leave England for Italy, Hawthorne entrusted his young English friend, Henry Bright, with the keeping of his manuscript notebooks and told him that, if not claimed sooner, they should be published by the end of the century. "By that time, probably," he wrote Bright, "England will be a minor republic, under the protection of the United States" (Julian Hawthorne, *Nathaniel Hawthorne and His Wife* [Boston, 1884], II, 168).

25. *Our Old Home*, p. 70. In the same passage Hawthorne even exclaimed with an enthusiasm and optimism quite unusual with him, but nonetheless typically American: ". . . Let us welcome whatever change may come,—change of place, social customs, political institutions, modes of worship,—trust-

ing that, if all present things shall vanish, they will but make room for better systems, and for a higher type of man to clothe his life in them, and to fling them off in turn."

26. Preface to *The Marble Faun*, p. 15.

27. "An American seldom feels quite as if he were at home among the English people. If he do so, he has ceased to be an American."—*Our Old Home*, p. 75.

28. *Hawthorne's Doctor Grimshawe's Secret*, ed. Edward H. Davidson (Cambridge, Mass., 1954), p. 21.

29. *French and Italian Note-Books*, I, 4-5. For her part, Miss Shepard, the American governess of his children, noted: "Mr. Hawthorne pretends that he can't speak French, although I am sure he knows it very well; and he follows me around, when we stop at the stations or custom-house, to make me talk for him. He says he shall be dumb all the time that he is on the continent."—Norman Holmes Pearson, *op. cit.*, p. 748.

30. *Our Old Home*, p. 74.

31. *The Marble Faun*, chap. xvii, p. 182.

32. *French and Italian Note-Books*, I, 19, 33.

33. *Ibid.*, p. 12.

34. *Ibid.*, p. 45.

35. *Ibid.*, p. 9.

36. In a notebook kept in the Library of the University of California at Berkeley.

37. *French and Italian Note-Books*, II, 250.

38. *Ibid.*, p. 180.

39. *The Marble Faun*, chap. xvi, p. 174.

40. *Ibid.*, p. 227. See also the following passage: "The Italians appear to possess none of that emulative pride which we see in our New England villages, where every householder, according to his taste and means, endeavors to make his homestead an ornament to the grassy and elm-shadowed wayside" (p. 340).

41. *Ibid.*, p. 227.

42. *French and Italian Note-Books*, pp. 42–43.

43. *Ibid.*, p. 134.

44. Mrs. Hawthorne noted: ". . . A native idiosyncrasy, which always made me feel that 'the New Jerusalem' . . . 'where shall in no wise enter anything that defileth . . .' would alone satisfy him, or rather alone not give him actual pain."—*Ibid.*, p. 123.

45. Norman Holmes Pearson even points out that Hawthorne quotes Byron in his notebooks only when Murray does so and provides him with the text of the quotations (*op. cit.*, p. 825).

46. *The Marble Faun,* chap. xiv, p. 149. See also chap. xv, p. 162; and *French and Italian Note-Books,* I, 179.

47. *The Marble Faun,* chap. xlv, p. 468.

48. "A brown lizard with two tails—a monster often engendered by the Rome sunshine—ran across his foot and made him start."—*Ibid.,* chap. xxii, pp. 230-31. ". . . He saw no living thing, save a brown lizard (it was of the tarantula species) [sic] rustling away through the sunshine."—*Ibid.,* chap. xxvii, p. 287.

49. "The spell being broken, it was now only that old tract of pleasure-ground, close by the people's gate of Rome—a tract where the crimes and calamities of ages, the many battles, blood recklessly poured out, and deaths of myriads, have corrupted all the soil, creating an influence that makes the air deadly to human lungs."—*Ibid.,* chap. x, pp. 111-12.
Hawthorne's daughter, Una, nearly died of a fever while in Rome.

50. *Ibid.,* chap. xxxiii, pp. 346-47.

51. *Ibid.,* chap. xii, p. 135.

52. *French and Italian Note-Books,* I, 234.

53. *The Marble Faun,* chap. xvii, p. 184.

54. *Ibid.,* p. 183.

55. *The Marble Faun,* chap. xlv, p. 473.

56. *French and Italian Note-Books,* I, 258.

57. *Ibid.,* II, 184.

58. *The Marble Faun,* chap. xxix, pp. 307-8.

59. *Ibid.,* chap. xxxviii, pp. 392-93. See also the passage at the end of chap. xlv (p. 473) where Jesuits are described as "eager propagandists who prowl about for souls, as cats to catch a mouse."

60. See, for instance, the beginning of chap. xxviii entitled "Altars and Incense" in *The Marble Faun* and also: " . . . The exceeding ingenuity of the system stamps it as the contrivance of man, or some worse author. . . ." —Chap. xl, p. 419.

61. *The Marble Faun,* chap. xl, p. 418.

62. *French and Italian Note-Books,* I, 95-96.

63. Concluding words of chap. xxxix entitled "The World's Cathedral."

64. *The Marble Faun,* chap. xlii, p. 438.

65. *Ibid.,* chap. xlvii, p. 491.

66. *Ibid.,* chap. l, p. 519. See also the last two pages of chap. xlvii, pp. 491-92.

67. In a way Hawthorne's stay in Europe was a Puritan's holiday. Contrary to what one might have expected, he was extremely fond of French wines; and at one point in his *English Notebooks,* he discusses the comparative merits of Clos Vougeot and Chambertin with the authority of a true connoisseur (p. 316; see also *French and Italian Note-Books,* I, 25). Wine

has always been the best antidote to Puritanism. In this respect, it is to be noted that England became Puritan only after she lost her hold on the Continent, and wine ceased to be drunk in the British Isles. Chaucer was a drinker of claret and composed the *Canterbury Tales* under its influence. The tone of English literature changed completely after England was cut off from Bordeaux. A new era began with Lord Methuen's treaty with Portugal in 1703. It placed English literature under the direct influence of port wine for over a century.

Hawthorne also made the discovery that on the Continent people ignored the Sabbath and enjoyed themselves very nicely and without rowdiness. He seems to have approved of this custom, for he wrote in his notebook: "Sunday with these people [the Italians] is like any other feast-day, and consecrated to cheerful enjoyment . . . they have no need to intensify the Sabbath except by making it gladden the other days."—*French and Italian Note-Books*, II, 186. What a difference from Sunday in New England, or even England, in those days. In England, Hawthorne had bought a copy of *Renshaw's Diary and Almanac for 1858* (see James D. Hart, "Hawthorne's Italian Diary," *American Literature*, XXXIV [January, 1963], 562). Each pair of facing pages was divided into six days only. Nothing was supposed to happen on Sunday.

In Rome, during the Carnival, Hawthorne admired the natural restraint of the people: ". . . He would admire a people who can so freely let loose their mirthful propensities, while muzzling those fiercer ones that tend to mischief. Everybody seemed lawless; nobody was rude. If any reveller overstepped the mark, it was sure to be no Roman, but an Englishman or an American."—*The Marble Faun*, chap. xlviii, p. 499.

68. Letter of Mrs. Hawthorne to Mrs. Fields, May 30, 1864, quoted by N. H. Pearson, *op. cit.*, p. lxi. The manuscript is in the Boston Public Library.

69. *French and Italian Note-Books*, II, 162.

70. *The Marble Faun*, chap. xv, pp. 159-60.

71. *French and Italian Note-Books*, I, 292-93.

72. ". . . Il y a plus de sincérité philosophique chez Hawthorne."—E. D. Forgues, "Nathaniel Hawthorne," *Revue des Deux Mondes*, XIV (April 15, 1852), 365.

73. ". . . C'est l'écrivain le plus américain que l'Amérique ait produit depuis Emerson." "Il y a dans ces écrits quelque chose de malsain qu'on ne distingue pas d'abord, mais qui, à la longue, finit par agir sur vous comme un poison très faible et très lent."—Emile Montégut, "Un roman socialiste en Amérique," *Revue des Deux Mondes*, XVI (December 1, 1852), 811, 816.

74. Nathaniel Hawthorne, *La Lettre écarlate*, trans. Marie Canavaggia (Paris, 1945), with an Introduction by Julien Green, "Un puritain homme de lettres: Nathaniel Hawthorne," pp. 7-19. This translation was followed by a third one ten years later: *La Lettre écarlate*, translated, with an Introduction, by Charles Cestre (Paris, 1955).

75. The first translation by Emile Forgues, under the title of *La Maison aux sept pignons*, had six editions with Hachette from 1865 to 1886. The second translation by Marie Canavaggia appeared for the first time in 1945.

76. In 1858, Hachette published *Le Livre des merveilles*, a translation of *A Wonder-Book* by Léonce Rabillon, to which Hawthorne alluded in his *French and Italian Note-Books*, 11, 251. In 1866, there appeared a translation of some of the *Twice-Told Tales* by E. A. Spoll. The best and most complete French translation of Hawthorne's tales is that of Charles Cestre, *Contes* (Paris, 1934), with a long critical introduction of eighty-one pages by the translator.

77. *Le Faune de marbre*, trans. F. Villaret.

78. See R. J. Niess, "Hawthorne and Zola," *Revue de littérature comparée*, XXVII (October-December, 1953), 446-52. There may also have been an influence of "The Great Stone Face" on *La Réponse du seigneur*, by Alphonse de Chateaubriant; see Fernand Baldensperger, "A propos de Nathaniel Hawthorne en France," *Modern Language Notes*, LVI (April, 1941), 343-45.

79. See note 74.

80. L. Dhaleine, *Nathaniel Hawthorne—Sa vie et son oeuvre* (Paris, 1905); L. E. Chrétien, *La Pensée morale de Nathaniel Hawthorne* (Paris, 1932). There also appeared more recently a very searching essay: Jean-Jacques Mayoux, "Hawthorne et ses miroirs," in *Vivants Piliers* (Paris, 1960), pp. 43-60; and an important doctoral dissertation by Jean Normand on "Hawthorne: l'univers de la création intérieure" is now in the press.

81. Dhaleine, *op. cit.*, p. 459.

82. Chrétien, *op. cit.*, p. 3.

83. "Assez déçu par la relecture du *House of the Seven Gables*. . . . Moins sensible au halo poétique dont Hawthorne sait envelopper notre monde extérieur, qu'à la lenteur souvent exaspérante du cheminement de son récit. . . . De plus: littérature de reflet. Et ce que je goûte le plus, dans la littérature américaine d'aujourd'hui, c'est le contact avec la vie."—André Gide, *Journal 1939-1949* (Paris, 1955), pp. 224-25.

84. François Mauriac, "La Vérité devenue folle," *Figaro Littéraire*, September 10, 1955, pp. 1, 2.

85. For the history of the reception of Hawthorne's works in Italy, see Camillia Zauli-Naldi, "La Fortuna di Hawthorne in Italia," *Studi americani* (1960), pp. 183-201 (a critical bibliography).

86. See Agostino Lombardo, *La Ricerca del vero* (Rome, 1961), p. 27.

87. "E che stile! Magnetico, incomparabile. Libro tristo a attraente come il peccato—Densamente fosco, con qua e là dei vivaci colori smaglianti di uccello del paradiso."—Quoted by Camillia Zauli-Naldi, *op. cit.*, p. 189.

88. "Il suo metodo consiste appunto nel rivelarci a poco a poco, con accorte reticenze, il mistero del carattere, finchè esso spicca sullo sfondo della

tenebra."—Federico Olivero, "Nathaniel Hawthorne," *Nuova antologia*, July 1, 1913, p. 43.

89. ". . . Un scrittore legato a un metodo analitico e introspettivo che in qualche momento si direbbe joyciano. . . ."—Quoted by Camillia Zauli-Naldi, *op. cit.*, p. 193.

90. "Tutta l'opera hawthorniana si può invero considerare anche come uno studio, che più profondo e commosso e efficace non potrebbe essere, dell'umana solitudine."—Agostino Lombardo, *op. cit.*, p. 164.

91. "La stirpe degli Hawthorne e dei Melville, infaticati e misantropici scrutatori dei segreti del cuore e dei dilemmi della vita morale."—Cesare Pavese, *La Letteratura americana e altri saggi* (Turin, 1951), p. 60.

92. In *Deutsche Philologie im Aufriss*, ed. Wolfgang Stammler, III (Berlin, 1957), 146-205. Horst Oppel is of the same opinion: "On the whole, Nathaniel Hawthorne seems to have exercised no influence on any poet or writer, though he represents classical American fiction and two of his masterpieces, *The Scarlet Letter* and *The House of the Seven Gables*, were translated remarkably early (1851)." ("Überhaupt keinen Einfluss auf Dichter und Schriftsteller scheint Nathaniel Hawthorne ausgeübt zu haben, obwohl er zur klassischen amerikanischen Erzählkunst gehört and zwei seiner Meisterwerke, *The Scarlet Letter* und *The House of the Seven Gables*, erstaunlich früh [1851] übersetzt wurden.")—Paul Merker and Wolfgang Stammler (eds.), *Reallexikon der deutschen Literaturgeschichte*, I, 55-56.

I am indebted for my information concerning the impact of Hawthorne in Germany to Professor Hans-Joachim Lang, of the University of Tübingen, and to Professor Hans Galinsky, of the University of Mainz, and his two assistants, Dr. Klaus Lubbers and Dr. Walter Rahn. The subject has never been thoroughly explored.

93. See Bertha Faust, *Hawthorne's Contemporaneous Reputation: A Study of Literary Opinion in America and England, 1828-1864* (Philadelphia, 1939), p. 110.

94. *Ibid.*, p. 112. See also Clarence Gohdes, "The Reception of Some Nineteenth-Century American Authors in Europe," *The American Writer and the European Tradition*, ed. Margaret Denny and William H. Gilman (Minneapolis, Minn., 1950), p. 109.

95. Herbert Read, *The Sense of Glory* (Cambridge, 1929), p. 176.

96. Roy Harvey Pearce, "Literature, History and Humanism—An Americanist's Dilemma," *College English*, XXIV (February, 1963), 364.

MATTHEW J. BRUCCOLI

1. Matthew J. Bruccoli, "Concealed Printings in Hawthorne," *Publications of the Bibliographic Society of America*, LVII (First Quarter, 1963), 42-49.

2. *Catalogue of First Editions of American Authors . . . by Leon &
Brother* (New York, 1885), and *The Longfellow Collector's Hand-Book*
(New York, 1885). It is possible to move the date of the inception of
American first-edition collecting back to 1875, the year when the *Index to
American Poetry and Plays in the Collection of C. Fiske Harris* (Providence,
1875) was published—see Roger E. Stoddard's "C. Fiske Harris, Collector
of American Poetry and Plays," *PBSA,* LVII (First Quarter, 1963), 14-32.

3. Cambridge, 1893.

4. November 23, 1894; Bangs.

5. April 13, 1897; Libbie. March 12, 1900; Bangs.

6. Boston, 1897. See also C. F. H. [Charles F. Heartman], *Patrick
Kevin Foley* (The Book Farm, 1937).

7. See Donald C. Gallup's "Aldis, Foley, and the Collection of American
Literature at Yale," *PBSA,* XLII (First Quarter, 1948), 1-9.

8. New York, 1890, appendix pp. 1-13.

9. *Guide to the Study of Nineteenth Century Authors,* Part 2 (1890),
pp. 15-20—not seen.

10. *Salem Public Library Bulletin,* I (October, 1891), 46-48—not seen.

11. *The Book Buyer,* XV (October and November, 1897), 218-220,
326-27.

12. *The Bookman,* VIII (September, 1898), 38-43.

13. New York, 1898.

14. January 30, 1901; Bangs. The catalogue appears to have also been
published as a book. Arnold's eight authors were Hawthorne, Bryant,
Emerson, Holmes, Longfellow, Lowell, Thoreau, and Whittier.

15. *A Record of First Editions . . . Collected by William Harris Arnold*
(New York, 1901).

16. Not seen.

17. *First Editions of the Works of Nathaniel Hawthorne* (New York,
1904).

18. "List of Books, etc. by and relating to Nathaniel Hawthorne," VIII
(July, 1904), 312-22.

19. VIII (August, 1904), 109-16.

20. February, 1904; Libbie.

21. March 1, 1904; Anderson 274.

22. January 30, 1908; Anderson 626.

23. *Love Letters of Nathaniel Hawthorne* (2 vols.; Chicago, 1907).

24. March 29, 1916; Anderson.

25. February 26, 1917; Anderson 1280.

26. New York, 1905, Vol. II.

27. *A Bibliography of Nathaniel Hawthorne* (Boston, 1905).

28. *Bibliography of the Works of Nathaniel Hawthorne* (Cleveland, 1905).

29. February 16, 1909; Anderson 725; and November 4, 1909; Anderson 777. Chamberlain's other authors were Bryant, Emerson, Holmes, Irving, Longfellow, Poe, Thoreau, and Whittier.

30. November 16, 1909; Anderson 782; and November 22, 1909; Anderson 784. Maier's other authors were Bryant, Emerson, Holmes, Irving, Aldrich, Field, and Howells.

31. March 22, 1920, American Art.

32. George S. Hellman, *Lanes of Memory* (New York, 1927), pp. 42-47.

33. *Grolier 75* (New York, 1959), p. 98. This volume is essential for any study of American book-collecting.

34. April 28, 1924; American Art. The priced catalogue was published as a bound book by the American Art Association in 1924. Wakeman's other authors were Bryant, Emerson, Holmes, Longfellow, Lowell, Poe, Thoreau, and Whittier.

35. *Fishers of Books* (New York, 1931), p. 277.

36. A considerable quantity of great Hawthorne material—inscribed copies, letters, and manuscripts—was peddled by Julian Hawthorne during his various financial crises.

37. Howe's library was purchased for the New York Public Library by Albert A. Berg in 1940. Some of Howe's books were exhibited in 1937 at the Lockwood Memorial Library of the University of Buffalo—*A Catalogue of an Exhibition of . . . Nathaniel Hawthorne* (Buffalo, 1937).

38. Something must be said about the Hawthorne activities of America's greatest bookseller. Dr. A. S. W. Rosenbach does not seem to have handled a great deal of Hawthorne, but he did sell some superb things. Hearst bought the manuscript of "A London Suburb" and a Dickens manuscript for $400. Owen D. Young got a bargain when he bought 146 letters from Hawthorne to Ticknor for $3,600, even though the letters had been published (*Letters of Hawthorne to William D. Ticknor* [2 vols.; Newark, 1910]). The manuscript of *Tanglewood Tales*—the only substantial manuscript still in private hands—was sold to Adrian Van Sinderen for $28,750.

39. April 29, 1931; American Art–Anderson 3911.

40. November 19, 1931; American Art–Anderson 3927.

41. January 23, 1945; Parke–Bernet 627.

42. March 22, 1960; Parke–Bernet 1961.

43. November 6, 1963; Parke–Bernet 2222. On January 28, 1964—after this article had been set in type—nineteen important Hawthorne items were sold at the Ribal sale (Parke–Bernet 2250) for a total of $5,860. The twenty-page manuscript of "Lichfield and Uttoxeter" brought $4,250. A